World History in Brief

Major Patterns of Change and Continuity

VOLUME TWO SINCE 1450

Third Edition

PETER N. STEARNS

Carnegie Mellon University

LONGMAN

An imprint of Addison Wesley Longman, Inc.

New York • Reading, Massachusetts • Menlo Park, California • Harlow, England
Don Mills, Ontario • Sydney • Mexico City • Madrid • Amsterdam

Publishing Partner: Pam Gordon
Executive Marketing Manager: Sue Westmoreland
Supplements Editor: Jen McCaffery
Project Coordination and Text Design: Ruttle, Shaw & Wetherill, Inc.
Cover Designer/Manager: Nancy Danahy
Cover Illustration: Map of the Arctic by Mercator, 1595
Art Studio: Mapping Specialists Limited
Full Service Production Manager: Joseph Vella
Photo Researcher: Photosearch, Inc.
Electronic Page Makeup: Ruttle, Shaw & Wetherill, Inc.
Senior Print Buyer: Hugh Crawford
Printer and Binder: The Maple-Vail Book Manufacturing Group
Cover Printer: Coral Graphic Services, Inc.

For permission to use copyrighted material, grateful acknowledgment is made to the copyright holders on p. 681, which is hereby made part of this copyright page.

Library of Congress has cataloged the single-volume edition.

Please visit our website at http: //longman.awl.com

ISBN 0-321-00223-7

12345678910—MA—01009998

Brief Contents

Detailed Contents

v

Preface

World history courses are becoming increasingly fundamental at the college level for several reasons. Most obviously, as global issues fill our television screens and newspapers, Americans must gain perspective on the dynamics of events and patterns and must understand the diverse societies around the globe that help shape our future. History—often, even history rather remote in time—explains how the world became what it now is, including why global influences loom larger than before. The United States itself is peopled by groups with different heritages, again from around the world. Finally, world history raises some classic issues of historical interpretation, allowing its students to sharpen their understanding of how to interpret change and historical causation and providing a rich field for comparative analysis. Some educators, to be sure, still prefer to concentrate on Western civilization, arguing that it lies at our origins and, sometimes, that it is measurably superior, but while the Western heritage must be included in a world history approach, it is increasingly clear that a purely Western overlay cannot describe the world as we need to know it.

World history demands a commitment to a global rather than a West-centered approach. This book seeks to show how different civilizations have encountered the various forces of contemporary life—for example, population growth, industrialization, and international currents in diplomacy and art. Western civilization is included as one of the great world societies, but the text also studies East Asian, Indian, Middle Eastern, East European, African, and Latin American civilizations in order to achieve a genuine world-wide perspective.

This is a relatively short text, designed to allow additional readings and analytical exercises. World history teaching must follow the precedent of other survey history courses in reducing the emphasis on coverage and sheer memorization in favor of materials that provide facts that can be used to build larger understandings. Overwhelming detail, therefore, is not the chief goal of this book, but rather the presentation of enough data to facilitate comparison and assessment of change and to highlight the major developments in the world's history. Students can readily refer to larger reference works if they wish to follow up on themes of special interest with greater factual detail. For their convenience, a list of suggested readings follows each chapter.

World history also demands a balance between the examination of individual societies, within which the lives of most people are played out, and attention to the larger interactions across regional boundaries. These global interactions include trade, cultural contact, migrations, and disease. This text presents the major civilizations through a narrative overview combined with emphasis on leading political, cultural, social, and economic characteristics. Grasp of these characteristics, in turn, facilitates comparisons and assessments of change. Chronological divisions—the basic periods of world history—reflect successive stages of international contact, from relative isolation to regional integration to the formation of global systems. This periodization is not conveniently tidy for the whole of world history, but it captures the leading dynamics of change at the global level.

Using the civilization focus plus the international periodization, students can follow the themes of change and continuity across time. For example, we can track and compare the juxtaposition of the traditions and novel forces that have shaped the modern world; the response of China or Latin America to the issues of the modern state; or the conditions of women in developing and in industrial economies. How different societies respond to common issues and contacts, and how these issues and contacts change over time: this is the framework for grappling with world history. By focusing on these problems of comparison and assessment of change, the text uses the leading patterns of world history to provide experience in analysis that will apply to other historical studies beyond the survey.

Several changes mark this third edition, in addition to corrections and improvements throughout the text. Attention to periodization and interregional contacts has increased, providing a clearer basis for discussions of global change; there is also more explicit comparison. New biographical highlights have been included, adding additional emphasis on the human components of world history. "Focal Points" at the beginning of each chapter frame the chapter contents by raising key questions and thereby setting learning goals. "History Debates" sections highlight some crucial but contested issues of interpretation. Of course, the text has been updated to include the developments and shifts since the mid-1990s.

I must add a personal note. World history has been a late love for me. I was trained in Western history, with an education that encouraged, though it did not require (the fault was mine), a largely Western focus. I increasingly chafed against my ignorance not of current world events but of the perspective, the historical understanding, that would give such events meaning. Belatedly schooled in world history, I have found continued reading and teaching in the field an endless source of fascination, a perpetual window for contemplating the varieties and unities of the human condition. I can only wish the same pleasure for many others, colleagues and students alike.

SUPPLEMENTS

The following supplements are available for use in conjunction with *World History in Brief*.

FOR THE STUDENT

World History Map Workbook in two volumes. Volume I (to 1600) and Volume II (from 1600) prepared by Glee Wilson of Kent State University. Each volume includes over 40 maps accompanied by over 120 pages of exercises. Each volume is designed to teach the location of various countries and their relationship to one another. Also included are numerous exercises aimed at enhancing students' critical thinking abilities.

Longman World History Atlas. This four-color atlas contains a wide variety of historical maps. It is available shrink-wrapped with *World History in Brief* at low cost

Mapping World Civilizations: Student Activities. A free student workbook by Gerald Danzer, University of Illinois, Chicago. Features numerous map skill exercises written to enhance students' basic geographical literacy. The exercises provide ample opportunities for interpreting maps and analyzing cartographic materials as historical documents

FOR QUALIFIED ADOPTERS

Instructor's Manual/Test Bank. Written by Peter Stearns, this useful tool provides a guide to using the text book, suggestions for structuring a syllabus for the world history course complete with assignment ideas, chapter summaries, multiple choice, short answer and essay questions, and map exercises.

TestGen EQ program. Written by Peter Stearns, this computerized test bank available for Windows includes multiple choice, short answer, and essay questions. The package includes the Quizmaster EQ program for networked testing.

Guide to Advanced Media and Internet Resources for World History by Richard M. Rothaus of St. Cloud University. This pamphlet provides a comprehensive review of CD-ROM, software and Internet resources for world civilization including a list of the primary sources, syllabi and article, and discussion groups available on-line.

Discovering World History Through Maps and Views, Second Edition, by Gerald Danzer, University of Illinois, Chicago, winner of the AHA's James Harvey Robinson Award for his work in the development of map transparencies. The second edition of this set of 100 four-color transparencies is completely updated and revised to include the newest reference maps and the most useful source materials. These transparencies are bound with introductory materials in a three-ring binder with an introduction on teaching history with maps and detailed commentary on each transparency. The collection includes source and reference maps, views and photos, urban plans, building diagrams, and works of art.

Longman-Penguin USA Value Packages in World History. Twenty classic titles from Penguin USA are available at a significant discount when bundled with any Longman world history textbooks.

ACKNOWLEDGMENTS

Many people helped shape this book. I am grateful to Barry Beyer, Donald Schwartz, William McNeill, Andrew Barnes, Donald Sutton, Erick Langer, Jayashiri Rangan, Paul Adams, Merry Wiesner-Hanks, and Michael Adas, who aided my understanding of world history in various ways. Comments by Steven Gosch and Donald Sutton, and editorial assistance by Clio Stearns, greatly aided in the preparation of this revised edition. Other colleagues who have furthered my education in world history include Ross Dunn, Judith Zinsser, Richard Bulliet, Jerry Bentley, and Stuart Schwartz. I also thank the various readers of earlier drafts of this manuscript, whose comments and encouragement improved the end result: Jay P. Anglin; Richard D. Lewis; Kirk Willis; Arden Bucholz; Richard Gere; Robert Roeder; Stephen Englehart; Marc Gilbert; John Voll; Erwin Grieshaber; Yong-ho Choe; V. Dixon Morris; Elton L. Daniel; Thomas Knapp; Edward Homze; Albert Mann; J. Malcom Thompson; Peter Freeman; Patrick Smith; David Mc-Comb; Charles Evans; Jerry Bentley; John Powell; B. B. Wellmon; Penelope Ann Adair; Linda Alkana; Samuel Brunk; Alexander S. Dawson; Lydia Garner; Surendra Gupta; Craig Hendricks; Susan Hult; Christina Michelmore; Lynn Moore; Joseph Norton; Elsa Nystrom; Diane Pearson; Louis Roper; and Robert H. Welborn.

My gratitude extends also to Pam Gordon, Jessica Bayne, and Daniel Cooper, whose editorial assistance has been vital. Sincere thanks to Karen Callas and Cordelia Stearns for help with the manuscript. I have been taught and stimulated as well by my students in world history courses at Carnegie Mellon University. And thanks, finally, to my family, who have put up with my excited babble about distant places for some time now.

Peter N. Stearns

The World in 1450

World history in 1450 stood on the brink of major change—not for the first time—but it also embraced powerful forces of continuity and tradition. One well-established component involved distinct civilizations, with particular definitions of political and social institutions and well-articulated cultures.

China had long been a dominant force in East Asia, emphasizing a strong state and Confucian beliefs in hierarchy and order, along with several religions including Daoism. India, the dominant society in Southern Asia, was politically unified less often than China. It derived coherence from majority adherence to Hinduism (though there was a strong Muslim minority) and from the caste system, which organized social inequality through traditional laws and rituals governing contact. Both India and China were active merchant societies, but Chinese merchants suffered, somewhat ironically given their importance, from low cultural prestige in the Confucian tradition.

The Islamic Middle East (including North Africa) formed the final major Asian center. It had for centuries been unified under the Arab caliphate, but this Arab government had collapsed in the 13th century as part of a regional decline. Islam remained a vigorous, unifying force, and in the 15th century a new Muslim group, the Ottoman Turks, were beginning to conquer large sections of the Middle East and Southeast Europe. Muslim trade routes continued to play an important role in the Indian Ocean and the Eastern Mediterranean.

Strong civilization traditions existed elsewhere. Major kingdoms in sub-Saharan Africa benefited from extensive trade and cultural contact with Islam, which was an important minority religion in West Africa and in the Swahili trading cities of the East African coast. Societies in Southeast and East Asia utilized cultural influences from India and China, while creating their own amalgams. Parts of Southeast Asia were Buddhist, though Islamic traders and missionaries were gaining ground in Indonesia, Malaysia, and the southern Philippines. Chinese influence predominated in Vietnam, Korea, and Japan—although local factors intermixed. Japan, for example, remained a feudal society, often wracked by internal warfare, despite its admiration for Chinese example.

European civilizations were Christian. This included an Orthodox Christian strand, long anchored in the Byzantine Empire but spreading to Russia and other areas, and Roman Catholicism that stressed the authority of the pope, the faith of Western and Central Europe. Much of Western Europe was also a feudal society, although with the power of rival monarchies gaining ground along with increasing merchant activity. Civilization centers in the Americas, finally, included major Indian empires in Mexico/Central America plus the Inca domain that stretched down the Andes.

Along with particular civilizations and their characteristics, world history in 1450 embraced a host of international contacts. The Americas stood apart: They had no biological, cultural, or technological contacts with other world societies since the migration of Asians to these lands thousands of years before. But Africa, Asia, and Europe were joined by increasingly important trade routes, the cultural contacts brought by merchants and religious missionaries, and gradually shared technologies and not so gradually shared diseases. Shortly before 1450, in the 13th and 14th centuries, Mongol conquests in much of Asia and Eastern Europe had accelerated technological exchange, bringing knowledge of explosive powder and printing westward from the advanced technological areas of Asia. Intensifying exchange had also brought a major epidemic disease, Bubonic Plague, from initial centers in China to other parts of Asia, the Muslim world, and Europe. Cultural contacts persisted as well. Major world religions had carved out their regional holds earlier, which led among other things to vivid mutual hostility between Christian Europe and the Muslim Middle East—a hostility that had not prevented Europe from borrowing extensively from Islam. But there were still religious boundary changes on the margins, particularly with the continued advance of Islam in Southeast Asia. The rapid decline of the Byzantine Empire, in southeastern Europe and the northern Middle East, and the advance of the Turks were readjusting Christian and Muslim territories during the 15th century itself.

Both the framework of individual civilizations and the effect of international contacts affected ordinary people. In 1450, most people, in the world were peasants who depended on agriculture for their livelihood. But all major agricultural societies produced a surplus, which allowed for a minority of urban populations including merchants and craft producers. Other social groups in some regions included slaves, used in a variety of occupations including service in the government and army. Important regions were not primarily agricultural; Central Asia, for example, continued to host groups of nomadic herders, whose travels and invasions had frequently brought new contacts among bordering civilizations. Most societies were patriarchal and emphasized the primary domestic obligations and inferiority of women. But particular forms of patriarchy varied. The three major world religions—Islam, Christianity, and Buddhism—all emphasized women's spiritual potential but did not overturn patriarchal arrangements. India's gender traditions, firmly patriarchal, involved some cultural appreciation for women's cleverness as well as their roles as mothers, which differed from those of Confucian societies where deference and hierarchy were stressed—along with particular practices of subordination, such as footbinding.

International balances had shifted significantly in the century before 1450. Mongol dominance had come and gone, though a Mongol group still held on in Russia, which had experienced serious decline. Changes in Arab culture and politics, and the fading of the Byzantine Empire, opened the Middle East to new forces. Western Europe suffered from the effects of Bubonic Plague and the validity of the particular Christian culture that had flourished earlier was being questioned. The region also worried about its international position, eager for trade with Asia but without many sophisticated goods to offer in exchange, and anxious about the traditional power of Islam to its south. Yet growing political sophistication and wider merchant activity expressed important strengths. China, briefly dominated by the Mongols, was in a period of renewed vigor. The Chinese had even ventured some massive trading expeditions in the Indian Ocean, until more traditional internal interests prompted a halt to this policy in 1433.

World history for the centuries before 1450 had been heavily shaped by growing international contacts; the spread of world religions; the particular importance of Arab Islam; and the extension of the forms of civilizations, such as organized states and more elaborate systems of social inequality, to new parts of Europe, Japan, Southeast Asia, sub-Saharan Africa, and the Americas. These themes had taken shape after the collapse or readjustment of great classical empires—hence the designation of the 450–1450 period as "postclassical." Postclassical themes did not end in 1450. Indeed, world contacts were about to be recast and intensified once again. But spreading religion became a less important force than before; Arab civilization no longer played its previously dominant role, despite its still important strength; and the spread of civilization receded in significance in part because so many regions of the world were already involved. At the time, people had some awareness of momentous changes, like the fall of Christian Byzantium to the Turks or the lingering effects of the Bubonic Plague. With the benefit of hindsight, we can see even more adjustments: world history in 1450 was on the verge of a set of sweeping redefinitions in basic themes and framework. Basic new periods in world history open rarely, but the mid-15th century ushered in one of those moments.

PART IV

A New World Economy, 1450–1750

INTRODUCTION: THE NEW THEMES IN WORLD HISTORY

The defining features of the period in world history that began in the later 15th century involved a manifold transformation of the world network that had developed during the postclassical period. It should be no surprise that the leading society in the new international economy was Western Europe, rather than the Middle East or China. The rise of the West rested on several factors, but new naval technology ranked high among them. A second change involved the incorporation of the Americas in international exchange. This had immense impact on the Americas but also, particularly through the spread of American foodstuffs like corn and potatoes, on the rest of the world. A third change involved, quite simply, the growing importance of international commerce and the intensification of internal commercial exchange. Several societies saw their basic political and social structures altered by their place in world trade, while commercial relationships affected life in an even broader range of civilizations.

This new global age saw many other changes besides the redefinitions of the world economy. A host of new empires formed, not just the ones begun from Western Europe's new colonial outreach. Individual civilizations experienced significant innovations, like the new cultural influences in India or the expansion of Confucianism in Japan. Changes of this sort, including different patterns of dynamism during the period itself, left their mark even later on, defining varied opportunities in the 19th and 20th centuries.

The new period in world history is sometimes called "early modern" because of the importance of many of the new features, including the world economy, in setting a framework for developments in the past 200 years. The early modern period began with the rise of the West, the opening of the Americas to international contact, and the surge of several new Asian empires along with Russia—all taking shape soon after 1450. It ended around 1750, when the West began to experience a further transformation—known as the Industrial Revolution—that would alter world relationships yet again.

251

The Postclassical World in Transition, About A.D. 1400

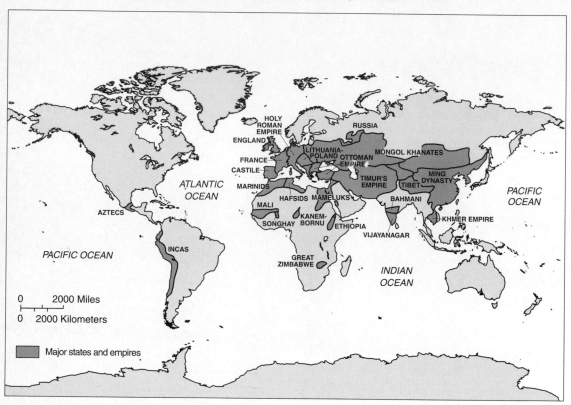

THE RISE OF THE WEST

Between 1450 and 1750, the West, headed initially by Spain and Portugal, then by Britain, France, and Holland, gained control of the key international trade routes. It established colonies in the Americas and, on a much more limited basis, in Africa and parts of Asia.

At the same time, partly because of its new international position and the growing impact of commerce, the West itself changed rapidly, becoming an increasingly unusual kind of agricultural civilization. Commerce began to alter the social structure and also affected basic attitudes toward family life and the natural environment. A host of new ideas, some of them springing from religious reformers, created a novel cultural climate in which scientific principles increasingly held pride of place; the scientific revolution gradually reshaped Western culture as a whole. More effective political structures emerged by the 17th century, as Western monarchs began to introduce bureaucratic principles similar to those pioneered long before in China.

A vital facet of the early modern period, then, consisted of the West's expansion as an international force and its simultaneous internal transformation. Like the previous world-class civilization, Arab Islam, the West developed a diverse and dynamic culture and society, which were both the results and causes of its ascending international position.

THE WORLD ECONOMY AND GLOBAL CONTACTS

It was as a result of initiatives mainly from the West that the world network set up in the previous period intensified and took on new dimensions. The change involved more than the fact that the Europeans, not the Muslims, dominated international trade. It involved an expansion of the world network to literally global proportions, well beyond the geographical scope of previous linkages. Far more of Africa, and above all the Americas, were brought into contact with other cultures and included in international exchanges for the first time. At the end of the period, in the 18th century, Polynesian and Australian societies began to undergo the same painful integrating experience.

Effectively, by 1750 there were no more fully isolated societies of any great size. The new globalism of human contacts had a host of vital consequences that ran through early modern centuries. The human disease pool became fully international for the first time, and peoples who had previously been isolated from most of the rest of the world suffered immensely from their exposure to diseases for which they had developed no immunities. The global network also permitted a massive exchange of plants and animals. Cows and horses were introduced to the Americas, prompting substantial changes in American Indian habits in economy and warfare alike. American food crops were spread around the world, bringing sweet potatoes, corn, and manioc (a plant grown for its root) to China, corn to Africa, potatoes and tobacco to Europe—innovations that in many places prompted great changes in agricultural production.

One result of this food exchange, through most of the world including Asia and Western Europe, was a rapid population expansion. World population had declined in the late classical period, then bounced back as people gained new resistance to contagious disease. Population gains in the postclassical period, in places like Europe, were significant. But rates of increase in the early modern centuries, except in Latin America and Africa, reached unprecedented levels.

Even globalization, though its impact was vast, did not exhaust the changes wrought in the world network during the three centuries after 1450. Far more than in the postclassical era, the period between 1450 and 1750 saw a set of definite and highly unequal relationships established among a number of civilizations. During the postclassical millennium, 450 to 1450 c.e., a few areas had contributed relatively inexpensive raw materials (including labor power in the form of slaves) to more advanced societies, notably China and the Islamic world; this was true for the West and parts of Africa and Southeast Asia. Though economic relationships in these instances were unequal, they did not constrain the "raw-materials-producing" societies too severely, because international trade was simply not of overriding importance yet. After 1450 or 1500, as Western commerce expanded internationally, the West began to set up relationships with a number of areas that produced pronounced dependence and subordination in the international economy. Areas such as Latin America depended heavily on sales to export merchants, on imports of processed goods, and on Western ships and merchants to handle international trade. Dependence of this sort might have political ramifications in creating weak governments

open to foreign intervention; it certainly affected labor relations by encouraging commercial exploitation of slaves and serfs; and it even tied in with cultural impositions from the West on some of the dependent areas. It is vital to stress that much of the world, particularly in the great Asian civilizations, remained outside this set of relationships, but there was a growing tendency to draw closer toward it, as occurred in India and much of Indonesia by the 18th century when the level of Western overseas expansion increased further.

THE GUNPOWDER EMPIRES

The centuries after 1450 could also be designated "the age of the gunpowder empires." The development of cannons and muskets in the 15th and 16th centuries, through the combination of Western technology with previous Chinese invention, obviously spurred the West's expansion. Ship-based artillery was fundamental to the West's mastery of international sea lanes and many ports and islands. But gunnery was picked up by other societies as well. The Ottoman Turks used Hungarian-built cannons in their successful siege of Constantinople in 1453. The subsequent Ottoman Empire relied heavily on land-based guns to supplement trained cavalry. The rise of a new Russian Empire after 1480 also built on the growing use of guns, and the Russian economy was subsequently reshaped to provide the manufacturing basis for the new military hardware. Three other key empires—the Mughal in India, the Safavid in Persia, and the 17th-century Manchu dynasty in China—relied on the strength of the new gun-supported land armies. Guns also played a role in Japanese and African history during the period.

Clearly, guns supported important military changes that in turn supported new political organization—colonial empires in the case of the West, where naval strength played a particularly important role, and new land agglomerations through much of Asia and Eastern Europe and, to an extent, in Africa. Here were developments largely independent of Western influence, which in fact counterbalanced the growth of Western power to a considerable degree. The rise of the Russian Empire ran through the whole period, and while not as important as the rise of the West, it was certainly a vital theme, involving among other things the progressive elimination of an independent central Asia. For the first time since the development of agriculture, nomadic herding peoples ceased to be a major force in world history. The rise of the Ottomans and Mughals was a bit shorter-lived, but echoed through the first two centuries of the period and, in the case of the Ottomans, created one of the most durable empires known in world history. The new land-based empires affected a massive number of people and long overshadowed, at least in the eyes of most Asian leaders, the Western surge.

COMMERCE AND ITS OUTREACH

This was also an age of world commercialization. Market exchange played an increasing role in shaping economic activity. The world remained predominantly agricultural, but agriculture was now modified more than ever by specializations that depended on market transactions, as well as by the activities of merchants and the lure of money. Heightened commercial activity was one of the means by which rising populations could be sustained in advance of major technological change in the means of production. Commerce not only spread knowledge of new foodstuffs but also allowed increased specialization in production that could heighten output, as some regions concentrated on goods they were best suited to grow or manufacture, relying on trade for other materials.

The intensification of international trade, under the sponsorship of Western traders but also involving merchants in other societies, played an important part in the general expansion of commerce. Not only did many Latin Americans produce precious metals and agricultural products for sale to the West; many other Latin Americans produced foods and clothes to sell to workers in the export sectors. Internal trade increased within Latin America, particularly by the 18th century. Similar patterns emerged in West Africa. Earlier international trade routes, oriented toward North Africa, were diverted to a new Atlantic commerce organized by European merchants. African kings and merchants organized goods to sell in this trade, particularly slaves, and received manufactured products, including guns, in exchange. Again the West was encouraged in its own commercial expansion, as considerable profits could be realized in the slave trade; the Americas were transformed through the introduction of new African populations and a new kind of slavery; and Africa itself was diversely affected by the new exchange.

The spread of commerce went beyond these Western-dominated transactions, however. Both China and Japan witnessed the rapid growth of market exchanges within their own boundaries, as production and sale of foodstuffs, beverages, and the like expanded. A general trend—the Western-dominated international economy and its growth—was thus supplemented by some parallelisms in some other parts of the world, where internal trade far outweighed international exchange. And this meant not only a surprisingly widespread commercial and urban surge, but also some broader effects in terms of culture and society. In most cases without toppling the land-based aristocracy, merchants in a number of societies, not just the West, gained new influence. Growing trade also played a role in some societies (in the West but also, for instance, in Japan) in encouraging some groups to reduce their commitment to religion and other worldly goals in favor of a focus on secular pursuits. The expansion of commerce, in other words, though not producing a uniform new version of an agricultural economy or society, had some wider reverberations in many parts of the world.

MAJOR CIVILIZATIONS

The redefining of the world economy—the intensification of commerce, the inclusion of the Americas, and the rise of the West with its new naval technology—affected each major civilization to some degree. Even more than during the postclassical period, it becomes important to ask: How was each civilization affected by the new global developments? How were relationships with the West defined? How were new foodstuffs utilized? How was commerce handled? These questions follow the new framework of world history in the early modern period, but the answers still vary. Because of prior traditions and new, separate developments, each civilization related to the global framework in distinctive

East Asia	Middle East (Ottoman Empire)	India and Southeast Asia	Latin America
1336–1573 Return of Japan to feudalism.			
1368–1644 Ming dynasty.			
1405–1433 Great Chinese fleets.			
	1453 Capture of Contantinople.	**1498** Vasco da Gama (Portugal) to India.	
	1520–1566 Suleiman the Magnificent.	**16th century** Portugal's acquisition of trading rights, some trading stations in Siam, Burma, Indonesia.	**1501** Introduction of African slaves.
	1526 Capture of Hungary.	**16th century and later** Formation of Sikh religion.	**1500–1519** Spanish conquest of West Indies, including Puerto Rico, Cuba.
		1510 Portuguese acquisition of Goa.	**16th century** Church organization of Spanish colonies established; Jesuit and other missions.
		1526–1529 Babur invasion from Afghanistan.	**1519 ff.** Cortés expedition to Mexico.
		1526–1761 (officially 1857) Mughal empire.	**1521** Capture and destruction of Tenochtitlán; building of Mexico City.
			1531 Pizarro conquest of Inca empire.
			1527–1542 Viceroyalties established for Central and South America.
			1532ff. Spanish explorations of California and Pacific coast of North America.
1542 Portuguese traders to Japan.			**1536** Spanish settlement in Buenos Aires.
1557 Macao taken by Portugal.			**1542** Enactment of new laws forbidding Indian slavery.
1577–1598 Hideyoshi general in Japan; centralization.			**1549** First Portuguese government in Brazil.
1597 Ban on foreign missions.			

Western Civilization	Russia and Eastern Europe	Sub-Saharan Africa

1300 ff.
Italian Renaissance: i.e. Giotto
(1276–1337);
Petrarch (1304–1374);
Leonardo da Vinci (1452–1519);
Machiavelli (1469–1527);
Michelangelo (1475–1514).

1450 ff.
Northern Renaissance. Erasmus
(1466–1536).

1455
First European printing press,
Mainz, Germany.

1494 ff.
French and Spanish expeditions
in Italy.

1517
Luther's 95 theses; beginning of
Protestant Reformation.

1534
Beginning of Church of England.

1541–1564
Calvin in Geneva.

1519–1521
Magellan expedition around
world.

1462
Much of Russia freed by Ivan III
(Ivan the Great) from Tatars.

1480
Moscow region free.

1533–1584
Ivan the Terrible, first to be
called tsar; boyar power reduced.

1552–1556
Russian expansion in central
Asia, western Siberia.

16th century
Spanish, Portuguese, and Dutch
ports on West African Coast.

1550–1649
Religious wars in France,
Germany, Britain.

1588
Defeat of Spanish Armada by
English.

1618–1648
Thirty Years' War.

1642–1649
English Civil War.

1562
Beginning of British slave trade.

1591
Fall of Songhai empire.

The Early Modern World (continued)

East Asia	Middle East (Ottoman Empire)	India and Southeast Asia	Latin America
			1565 Rio de Janeiro founded by Portuguese. **1569** Catholic Inquisition set up for Spanish America; limitation of intellectual freedom.
	1571 Loss of Lepanto navel battle.		
1600–1868 Tokugawa shogunate. **1635** Japanese travel abroad forbidden; policy of isolation. **1644** Suicide of Ming emperor. **1644—1912** Qing dynasty. **1662–1722** Emperor Kang Hsi.	**1683** Failure of assault on Vienna.	**1608** First trade concessions from regional princes granted to England. **1627–1668** Jehan emperor; tolerance for Hindus reduced. **1632–1653** Taj Mahal built. **1641** Capture by Dutch of major spice trade center in Indonesia; beginning of control of island of Java. **17th century** British and French forts on east coast of India. **1658–1707** Aurangzeb emperor; high taxes, intolerance against Hindus; rise of Hindu resistance.	**1612** Wider colonization of Brazil begun by Portugal.
1727 Chinese-Russian frontier treaty.	**1710–1711, 1736–1739, 1768–1774** Wars with Russia and Austria; loss of Balkan and central Asian territory. **1729** First Muslim Arabic printing press.	**18th century** Mughal decline; rise of Sikh state (1708 ff) and states of southern India. **1744, 1756–1763** French-British wars in India.	**1717 ff.** Spanish colonies established new provincial capitals. **1720** Occupation of Texas by Spain. **18th century** Several popular rebellions in Spanish colonies and by creoles.
1774 ff. White Lotus society risings. **1784** Chinese persecution of Jesuits.	**1798** Brief capture of Egypt by Napoleon.	**1756** "Black hole" of Calcutta. **1764 ff.** British control of Bengal.	**1794** Haitian uprising against France led by Toussaint L'Ouverture; independence and end of slavery there.

Western Civilization	Russia and Eastern Europe	Sub-Saharan Africa

17th century
Scientific revolution. Galileo (1564–1642); Newton (1642–1727).

1643–1715
Louis XIV in France; absolute monarchy; wars (1667–1668; 1672–1678; 1688–1697; 1701–1713).

1688–1690
Glorious Revolution in Britain; parliamentary regime; some religious toleration; political writing of John Locke.

1604–1613
Time of Troubles.

1613–1917
Romanov dynasty.

1637
Russian pioneers to Pacific.

1649
Law enacted making serfdom hereditary.

1689–1725
Peter the Great.

1700–1721
Wars with Sweden.

1703
Founding of St. Petersburg.

1626 ff.
French coastal settlements.

1650 ff.
Intensification of slave trade.

1652
Dutch colony on Cape of Good Hope.

18th century
Enlightenment. Voltaire (1694–1778).

1712–1786
Frederick the Great of Prussia; "enlightened despotism."

1756–1763
Seven Years' War: France, Britain, Prussia, Austria.

1775–1783
American Revolution.

1762–1786
Catherine the Great.

1773–1775
Pugachev revolt.

1772, 1793, 1795
Partition of Poland.

1785
Laws enacted tightening landlord power over serfs.

1713
Right granted to Britain to import slaves to Spanish colonies.

18th century
Regulation of regional slave trade by West African kingdom of Fon.

1760 ff.
Fanning out of Dutch in South Africa.

1770 ff.
Encounter with Bantu farmers; conflict for land.

Late 18th century
Increase in Muslim conversions in Sudan region.

1754–1818
Founding of Islamic kingdom (in present-day Nigeria) by Usman dan Fodio.

ways. Above all, Western Europe by no means exercised uniform authority around the world; in many places its explicit influence, during the early modern period, remained negligible.

Furthermore, developments within each civilization, independent of the global framework, also caused important changes. On the one hand, some societies displayed great dynamism during the 15th and 16th centuries, only to trail off later; their new problems affected their regions' history during this period and subsequently as well. Yet other societies developed important new political and cultural resources during the period, which would have an impact later.

The global framework intensified within the early modern period as well. By 1700 the West's activities were looming larger not just in key areas such as the Americas, the Asian island groups, and the coast of West Africa, but in Asia and Eastern Europe as well. A new Russian urge selectively to copy aspects of the West and the establishment of growing British control in parts of India expressed two facets of this shift. Even Japan, which had responded to the new world economy by effective isolation, began to show modest new openness, rescinding a ban on translating Western books.

By 1750 it is fair, with all the advantages historians have of knowing how their stories turn out, to note that civilizations that were not in a position to react effectively to the West's new world role were verging on decline—whereas a mere century before, this would have been a considerable distortion of a more complex international balance. After 1750, in large part because of another major transformation within the West—the emergence of a revolutionary industrial economy—the theme of Western predominance took on new meaning, which is why the periodization of world history changes at this point once again.

Western Civilization Changes Shape, 1450–1750

Focal Points

Western Europe changed in many ways during the early modern period: compare a status summary for the year 1750 with that for 1450. Europe's world position, its political structures, its social structures, and its culture had all shifted profoundly. "Big changes" in this period include the replacement of feudalism with national monarchies; greatly increased commercialization and the shift away from serfdom to wage labor; and a decline of traditional popular beliefs plus the rise of science. These themes must be charted through a variety of internal movements like the Protestant Reformation or the 18th-century Enlightenment. Why did Europe change so rapidly? What continuities from the postclassical period can still be traced?

BASIC CHANGES

Between 1450 and 1750, Western European society went through a series of profound transformations. Each century produced at least one major new current. The 15th century featured the Renaissance, which began indeed a bit earlier in Italy and then spread to northern Europe. In the 16th century, the Protestant Reformation upstaged the continuing impact of the Renaissance, breaking the unity of Western Christendom; and the Catholic Reformation responded. Political turmoil dominated the first half of the 17th century, but a still more profound alteration resulted from the scientific revolution, one of the most basic reorientations of intellectual life in the history of any civilization. Finally, during the first half of the 18th century, the Enlightenment extended the principles of the scientific revolution to generate new views of politics and society, indeed new views of human nature itself.

Thinkers in the Enlightenment professed embarrassment at the very existence of the medieval period, which seemed to them so remote and backward in contrast to their own proud sophistication. This view was in fact too strong, as well as unfairly demeaning to the achievements of medieval society: the heritage of the Middle Ages was still visible in political, intellectual, and economic life. But there was no question that Western civilization, to an extent unusual among major civilizations since the classical period, showed a marked ability to change its focus.

So much seemed to be changing, in fact, that it sometimes proves difficult to find coherent directions in the period as a whole. Transformation was not neat: different movements overlapped, like the Renaissance and the Reformation. Some events represented a resurgence of earlier values. The Reformation, for example, stemmed in part from a very medieval piety, though it had quite nonmedieval results. Yet while it is important to gain a sense of the flavor of specific developments, it is also possible to observe general trends. The various movements tended to strengthen the central state in the European monarchies, though for different reasons. Historical processes added up, even more clearly, to a substantial transformation of Western intellectual and artistic life, with the ultimate result a decline in the religious approach to understanding the world and the eventual substitution of a rational, scientific framework. Trends of this sort were gradual, often messy, usually incomplete. But they gave shape to a vibrant period in Western history.

This was also a time of fundamental change in Western economic and social life. Developments in these areas were just as important, in fact, as the overall revolution in intellectual outlook, and more important than political change. The Western economy became unprecedentedly commercialized, and technologically—for the first time—the most advanced in the world. The European family took on unusual contours, and its importance in certain aspects of Western life grew.

Between 1450 and 1750, political, cultural, and economic shifts involved Western civilization increasingly in the larger world. Traders and explorers in overseas colonies brought back new techniques and new cultural values. Even more obvious, from 1500 onward, Western society drew increasing wealth from its global contacts. In turn, based on its new internal dynamism, Western Europe began to influence other civilizations in a variety of ways.

PATTERNS OF EARLY MODERN WESTERN HISTORY

THE RENAISSANCE

The spotlight in Western history, around 1400, was on Italy. This region had never fully embraced medieval customs, especially feudalism. The peninsula was largely organized in terms of city-states, some ruled by kings, others by aristocratic or merchant councils, still others by military tyrants. Many city-states had extensive trade and cultural contacts with other parts of the Mediterranean. From these exchanges, especially with Byzantium, Italian scholars gained new appreciation of Greek and Latin literature. At the same time, growing commercial wealth encouraged cities like Florence and Venice to create new artistic styles to celebrate their exciting achievements.

From Italy's mixture of trade and scholarly and artistic endeavor came the movement known as the Renaissance, which took shape in the 1300s. It started most clearly as a literary and artistic movement. Writers such as Dante, Petrarch, and Boccacio—all three writing in Italian as well as the traditional Latin—began to deal with more strictly secular subjects than had been popular in the Middle Ages. Petrarch wrote love sonnets to his Laura; other poems praised his own valor in climbing mountains—a new sign of individualism and pride in human achievement. Boccacio wrote earthy stories of love and lust, and though he later recanted, professing his devotion to religious faith, his earlier interests won a wide audience. In art, Giotto developed a new sense of perspective, allowing three-dimensional portrayals of nature. Both writers and artists began to copy classical styles, writing of and painting gods and goddesses and human scenes, rather than strictly Christian motifs; and their work reflected increasing realism.

Seldom has an age produced as many cultural "greats" as did the Renaissance in Italy. A host of architects designed churches and public buildings in classical styles, renouncing the Gothic. Leonardo da Vinci advanced the realistic portrayal of the human body in art, even painting pictures of medical dissections. Michelangelo's statues offered graphic displays of human musculature. Overall, Italian Renaissance art, developed from the 14th through the early 16th centuries, stressed themes of humanism—a focus on humankind as the center of intellectual and artistic endeavor. The humanistic concerns spread also to music, where elegant choruses sang of love, drink, and the beauties of nature. A new interest in human history also emerged, and several Renaissance historians, using a newly critical approach to past documents, challenged traditional church claims in such areas as the origins of the papacy.

Maria Portinari (b. 1456) was the wife of a Florentine banker (Tommaso, c. 1432–1501) who made a fortune as a representative in Medici banking interest in Bruges, Flanders (now Belgium). This portait, by the Flemish master Hans Memling, shows her richly but somberly dressed. Her slightly melancholy expression may have seemed appropriate in terms of religious piety, for the Renaissance in northern Europe maintained a strong spiritual tone for laypeople. Historians have also realized that the Renaissance, striking as it was in terms of cultural innovation, may have led to deterioration in the position of upper-class women, treated increasingly as ornaments and kept away from most of the new sources of learning. What personal results would a woman like Maria Portinari perceive from the changes sweeping through Western Europe in the 15th century? (The Metropolitan Museum of Art, Bequest of Benjamin Altman, 1913, 14.40.627)

The new spirit extended also to political theory. Writing around 1500, the Florentine Niccolò Machiavelli described as realistically as possible what a ruler had to do to gain and maintain power: how to use cruelty, how to sway public opinion. Machiavelli combined detailed knowledge of Italian politics of his time with use of Greek and Roman example—a characteristic Renaissance mixture.

The Italian Renaissance had flourished in part because Italy was so free from the medieval political forms that continued to influence much of the rest of Europe. During a good deal of the Italian Renaissance, France and England were locked in their Hundred Years' War. Then late in the 15th century the larger monarchies started to gain strength. France and Spain looked greedily upon the weak Italian city-states and embarked on wars of conquest in the 1490s. Italian trade also began to decline as interest shifted away from the Mediterranean, to the Atlantic trade routes that France, Spain, and England soon dominated.

But as Renaissance creativity faded in its Italian birthplace, it passed northward. Northern artists directly copied the new themes and styles of the Italians. Palaces in the classical style became the rage among northern rulers like Francis I of France, who increasingly fancied themselves patrons of the arts. Northern humanists gained growing knowledge of Latin and Greek literary and philosophical sources; soon they turned to writing in their own languages. Typical northern humanists, like Erasmus in the Netherlands, were more religious than some of their Italian counterparts, but shared their interest in human affairs and a pure style. The Renaissance spirit also continued in such 16th-century writers as England's Shakespeare and France's Rabelais; they dealt with a wide variety of earthly subjects with emphasis on human passions and drama. Their works, and those of Spain's Cervantes, developed new literary traditions in their respective nations.

Classical themes and styles in the Italian Renaissance: *Birth of Venus* by Botticelli.

The northern Renaissance had political implications as well. Renaissance kings increased their pomp and ceremony and tried to increase their power. Francis I claimed new authority over the operations of the Catholic church in France. Leading monarchs from the Tudor dynasty in England, particularly Henry VIII and Queen Elizabeth I, ruled with strong hands. They encouraged trading companies and colonial enterprises, and even passed laws on how to deal with the poor. During the Renaissance, monarchs also cultivated a more open interest in wars of conquest than their medieval predecessors had done. England pursued a lengthy effort to conquer Ireland; France invaded Italy and tried to construct alliance systems to counter the power of Spain and the Holy Roman Empire, both ruled for a time by a single royal house, the Habsburgs. Francis I even allied briefly with the sultan of the Ottoman Empire; the alliance meant little in practical terms, but showed that political interests had gained ascendancy over the traditional Christian hostility to Islam.

The Northern Renaissance emphasized greater introspection and spirituality: *Melancholia* by the German painter Albrecht Dürer. (The Metropolitan Museum of Art, Fletcher Fund, 19.73.85)

THE RELIGIOUS UPHEAVAL

Political and economic patterns in Renaissance Europe, however, were soon embroiled in the currents of the next major change—the Reformation. In 1517, a German monk named Martin Luther nailed a document containing 95 theses to the door of a church in Wittenberg. He was specifically protesting claims made by a papal representative that the buying of indulgences for money would advance salvation. For Luther, the idea of indulgences became an utter perversity; according to his reading of the Bible, salvation could come only through faith, not through works and certainly not through the money that the Renaissance popes were seeking for the upkeep of their own expensive court. Luther's protest, rebuffed by the papacy, soon led him to challenge most of the traditional Catholic sacraments and the authority of the pope himself.

The stand taken by the German monk gained wide support. Many Christians believed that the Catholic church had become too corrupt, that many of its practices were hollow. Some Renaissance intellectuals welcomed Luther's use of original documents, like the Bible, and also his nationalistic defiance, as a German, against religious rule from Rome. A number of individual rulers liked Lutheranism because it broadened their authority; they could direct Lutheran churches without the interference of still-powerful popes. Some ordinary people, finally, saw in Lutheranism a religious inspiration to speak out against their poverty and against the landlords who dominated their lives, though Luther renounced the idea of popular protest. As Luther firmly rejected Catholic attempts to bring him to heel, Lutheranism spread widely in Germany and also in Scandinavia.

Once Christian unity was breached, other Protestant groups sprang forward. In England, Henry VIII set up an Anglican church, initially to challenge papal attempts to enforce his first marriage, which had failed to produce a male heir. (Henry would ultimately have six wives in sequence; he had two of them executed.) Henry was also attracted to some Lutheran doctrines. His son and his daughter, later Queen Elizabeth, were Protestants outright, so the Anglican church became increasingly Protestant in doctrine as well as a separate form of church government. Still more important were the churches inspired by Jean Calvin, a Frenchman who set his base in the city of Geneva. Calvinism insisted on God's predestination, or prior determination, of those who would be saved; nothing humans could do, and certainly no sacraments, could win God's favor. At the same time, those elected to God's grace had the obligation to encourage others to behave morally and to gain knowledge of the Bible. Calvinist ministers became moral guardians and preachers of God's word, not special sacramental representatives of the deity. Like other Protestant ministers, they could marry. Calvinism sought the participation of other believers in local church government; it also promoted wider popular education, so that more people could have direct access to the Bible (which various Protestant groups now translated into the vernacular languages). Calvinism was accepted not only in parts of Switzerland but also in Germany and France, where it produced strong minority groups, and in the Netherlands, England, and Scotland.

Beginning about 1550, the Catholic church, though unable to restore religious unity, reacted to Protestantism. Church councils not only condemned Protestant doctrine; they also returned to the papacy a greater sense of religious concern. A new order of monks, the Jesuits, became active in politics, education, and missionary work, helping to retain the faith of most Catholics in Italy and Spain and to win back some terri-

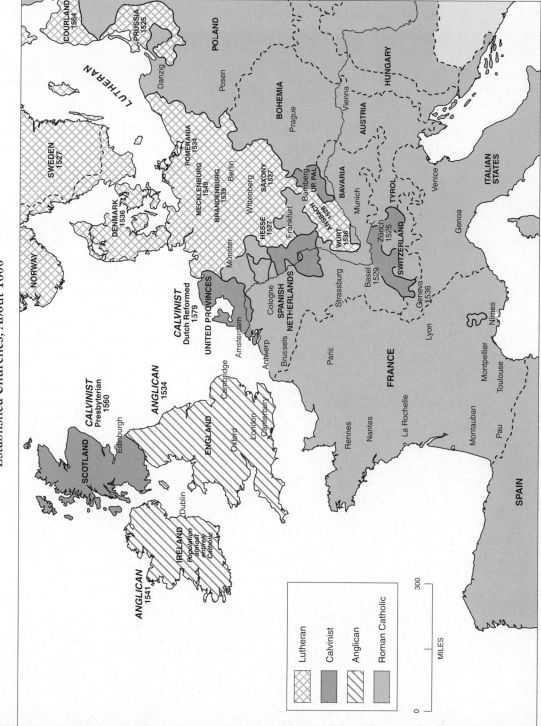

Established Churches, About 1600

COURLAND 1564

PRUSSIA 1525

LUTHERAN

POLAND

Danzig

Posen

SWEDEN 1527

POMERANIA 1534

MECKLENBURG 1549

BRANDENBURG 1539

Berlin

BOHEMIA

Prague

HUNGARY

Vienna

NORWAY

DENMARK 1536

Münster

Wittenberg

SAXONY 1527

Frankfurt

Bamberg

UP. PAL 1528

BAVARIA

AUSTRIA

Munich

TYROL

Venice

ITALIAN STATES

HESSE 1527

ANSBACH 1528

WURT 1536

Zürich 1525

SWITZERLAND

Genoa

CALVINIST Dutch Reformed 1579

UNITED PROVINCES

Cologne

SPANISH NETHERLANDS

Amsterdam

Antwerp

Brussels

Basel 1529

Geneva 1536

Strassburg

Lyon

Nîmes

CALVINIST Presbyterian 1560

ANGLICAN 1534

Paris

FRANCE

Montpellier

Toulouse

SCOTLAND

Edinburgh

Cambridge

ENGLAND

Oxford

London

Canterbury

Rennes

Nantes

La Rochelle

Montauban

Pau

SPAIN

ANGLICAN 1541

Dublin

IRELAND Population almost entirely Catholic

Lutheran

Calvinist

Anglican

Roman Catholic

0   300

MILES

267

tories initially open to Protestantism, such as Hungary. The result was a revivified Catholic church.

The rise of the Protestant churches triggered a long period of religious war in Europe. During the second half of the 16th century, France was the scene of major battles between Protestant and Catholic groups. The conflict ended only with the granting of tolerance to Protestants in 1598. Catholics and Protestants waged war recurrently in Germany, though several negotiations were held in the hope of dividing Germany among Catholic and Protestant states. In 1618 the Thirty Years' War broke out, in which foreign powers as well as Germans fought out their religious passions. The Spanish monarchy, self-appointed chief defender of the Catholic faith, tried to aid its co-religionists, while Swedish armies assisted the Protestant cause in a war so bloody that it reduced Germany's economic activity and its population level for many decades. The war ended with Spain's power reduced and with a reluctant agreement to religious division among the German states. Religious passions helped fuel a war between the Netherlands and Spain, in which the former ultimately won its independence. Religious strife simmered in England during parts of the 16th century, until Queen Elizabeth imposed a peace under a rather tolerant Anglican church; strife erupted again in the 1640s, contributing to a civil war in which Calvinists fought Catholic sympathizers. Eventually the Anglican church was restored, but with tolerance for other Protestant groups. The English Civil War ended formally in 1660, but the full settlement, including limited religious toleration, was reached only in 1688–1689.

For the most part, the Reformation, which had dominated Western political as well as religious history during the greater part of the 16th century, was assimilated in Europe by the first half of the 17th century. Even the Thirty Years' War in Germany was as much a battle among national monarchies as it was a religious dispute. Thus France, during that war, sided with Protestant forces in order to weaken its enemy Spain. Although Protestantism and revived Catholicism had a lasting impact not only on the religious map but on social and economic life as well, the battles among Christian groups no longer set the agenda for events in Europe itself. By 1650 it was becoming clear that Western Christianity was permanently divided, and unintended effects of the Reformation began showing up in business and family life.

In this context, during most of the 1600s, attention shifted to culture and politics. In culture, the leading development was the spate of new scientific discoveries, culminating in the great physical laws set down by Isaac Newton. Scientists learned how gravity works; they determined that the earth was not the center of the universe, but rather rotated around the sun; they discovered how blood circulates in the human body. Perhaps most important, they developed a coherent statement of how the scientific method functions, through a combination of rational hypothesis, empirical testing through observation or experiment, and final generalization in theory or law. Far more than the Renaissance, the scientific revolution of the 17th century produced a fundamental reorientation of Western intellectual life.

THE RISE OF THE MONARCHIES

During the same period, leading Western monarchies gained new organizational power. With Spain in growing eclipse, after a century of glory in defense of the church and as Europe's major colonizer in the New World, France emerged as the bellwether nation. The

French monarchy decisively defeated the remnants of feudal political forces during the 17th century. After 1614, the kings stopped summoning the national parliament. The greatest French monarch of this period, Louis XIV, also rescinded the toleration of the Protestants. No group was allowed officially to limit the monarch's power. This political system, perfected under Louis XIV, was called, appropriately enough, "absolute monarchy." Louis, dubbing himself the Sun King, extended his patronage of the arts. He built sumptuous palaces, where the nobles competed for royal favor instead of cultivating their independent power base in the provinces. Military administration improved, as Louis' advisors built better forts and established ways to supply provisions to troops in the field. Louis set up military hospitals and even a military pension plan. Absolute monarchy also meant increasing attention to economic controls, mainly in the interest of securing greater tax revenue. The state tried to encourage exports and regulated manufacturing within France.

Absolutism was copied in a number of other countries. Particularly noteworthy was the rise of monarchies in central Europe along absolutist lines. Prussia, long a backward regional state in eastern Germany, began to strengthen its administration and expand its armies, gaining new power among the various German states. The Habsburg monarchs, though still titling themselves Holy Roman Emperors, worked to develop a solid monarchy in Austria. After Habsburg forces managed to repel the armies of the Ottoman Empire, by 1700 their rule extended to Hungary as well.

One of the clear purposes of the new absolute monarchs was to wage war. Louis XIV conducted several major wars, extending France's boundaries in the north and east. It took a coalition of other powers, including England, Holland, and some of the German states, to keep his ambitions in check. In the 18th century, France and England fought several times, though mainly in their colonies in North America and India. Prussia and Austria also fought, with Prussia winning important new territory. The idea of recurrent battle among the national monarchies and alliance systems designed to prevent any one European power from becoming dominant gained increasing ground.

The pattern of absolute monarchy continued into the 18th century. The French monarchy, exhausted by the wars and ruinous taxation of Louis XIV, was weaker than before, but despite numerous reform movements no new political system emerged. Prussian administration became more efficient. The Prussian kings, led by the able Frederick the Great, tried to improve agricultural production and extend education, while maintaining absolute political power and emphasizing military strength. Rulers like Frederick, because of their reform interests and their fascination with new political ideas, enjoyed calling themselves enlightened despots rather than absolute monarchs, but the difference was not substantial.

Absolutism, enlightened or otherwise, was not the only political form to surface in Europe during the 17th and 18th centuries. In Britain and the Netherlands, parliamentary monarchies developed that built more clearly on older postclassical traditions through which kings would be checked by some kind of assembly. In England, the power of Parliament had been curbed during the reign of the strong Tudor kings of the 16th century, but the institution had not disappeared. Then, when less able monarchs in the 17th century tried to introduce taxes without parliamentary consent, supporters of Parliament joined religious dissidents in attacking royal power. One king, Charles I, was executed during the English Civil Wars of the 1640s, and for a time England was ruled by a military dictatorship. The monarchy, restored in 1660, again tried to defy Parliament while flirting with Catholicism. It was this combination that brought a final settlement, in the so-called Glorious Revolution of 1688–1689. A new king was called in, under parliamentary authority, establishing the principle that Parliament, not the king, had supreme power in the realm, though royal power remained considerable through the 18th century. The crown could not suspend laws, levy taxes without parliamentary consent, or maintain a standing army in time of peace. The assembly was to meet regularly rather than depending on the king's summons. Parliament itself remained a largely medieval body, with a hereditary House of Lords and a House of Commons, whose members were elected by small numbers of voters. Campaigns for parliamentary office after the Glorious Revolution involved few questions of principle and a great deal of bribery. But Parliament had unquestioned power, and no English king could pretend to absolutism, though royal power remained extensive through the century.

Thus Western civilization, now divided by religion, was for a time divided by political systems as well. Absolute monarchs not only ruled without parliaments; they also created governments with larger bureaucracies and greater functions than the government of England (united with Scotland in 1700 to form Great Britain). At the same time, absolute monarchies were in some ways less flexible than the parliamentary states. They depended on efficient rulers, not always produced by the accidents of heredity, and they tended to provoke discontent if their wars were unsuccessful or their taxes too high. Popular dissatisfaction mounted particularly in France during the 18th century and would result in massive revolution in 1789. Ultimately, through this revolutionary current, a greater degree of political unity would return to Western society. Until then, the absolutist and parliamentary impulses were largely separate, and both were important in expressing significant aspects of the evolving Western political tradition.

After the turmoil of the religious wars, it was the development of the new political systems and the recurrent military conflicts that gave the clearest superficial shape to Western history from the early 1600s until the 1750s. Ironically, the new divisions within Europe only spurred Western influence in other parts of the world. Catholics and Protestants, not content with their internal rivalry, spilled over into rival missionary efforts in Asia and the Americas. National monarchies battled overseas as well. Prussia and the Habsburg monarchy fought in Europe alone, but, by the 18th century, Britain and France were prepared to wage war on virtually a worldwide basis. Thus the last of the strictly monarchical wars in Western history, called the Seven Years' War in Europe for the good reason that it lasted from 1756 to 1763, saw Prussia beat back an effort by Austria to restrict its growing power, while Britain and France battled on three continents. Even earlier, English-Dutch, English-Spanish, and French-Spanish conflicts over territory and control of the seas had encouraged the formation of new European colonies in various parts of the world. Seemingly endemic tensions in Western society were now affecting the wider course of world history.

POLITICAL INSTITUTIONS AND IDEAS

The growth of the power and efficiency of the national state was the key political trend in early modern Europe. The Renaissance encouraged the greater splendor and ceremony, including artistic patronage, of the ruler's court. Renaissance interests also tended to weaken religious restraints on political power; even the Renaissance papacy acted more like a secular government, concerned with amassing wealth and acquiring art objects, than like a religious institution. Except in the Italian city-states, new government structures were not developed during the Renaissance, but there was a change in tone and motivation.

The Reformation enhanced the power of the state quite simply by weakening that of the church. Even Catholic monarchies, like those of France or Spain, gained because the Catholic Reformation papacy depended on them for support. Jesuit advisors, though devoted to the Catholic cause, also helped secular rulers increase their power. In the Protestant camp, Lutheran kings and princes and the English monarch as head of the Anglican church took over control of church government directly.

Still, before 1600, important medieval patterns persisted in politics. In particular, the aristocracy retained considerable power. Many church disputes, like the religious wars in France, found some aristocrats using the Protestant cause to support their claims against the monarchy. Revolts by nobles occurred again in France in the 1660s, when Louis XIV was a child, but this was a last gasp. The English Civil Wars featured landowning gentry backing the parliamentary cause against the king—whose main defenders were also landowning aristocrats. But the political power of the nobility finally declined. Many landowners could not keep pace with economic change, and they depended for their livelihood on securing government jobs. Improvements in the quality of guns and cannons weakened aristocratic military power, though in the main the leading army commanders were appointed from the ranks of the nobles. The aristocracy was by no means dead as a political force, even aside from the parliamentary system in England, which gave landowners great power. But in most monarchies, the balance had shifted decisively to the kings.

As stronger monarchies emerged, culminating in absolutism and enlightened despotism, bureaucracies became more sophisticated. French kings began to appoint regular administrators of provincial districts, who could manage the court system, supervise roads and other public works, and oversee the collection of taxes. Many bureaucrats were drawn from middle-class ranks, which helped check aristocratic power. The steady improvement in military organization gave kings larger and more reliable armies than ever before in Western history. These forces were used not only to fight wars but also to repress popular protest at home. New measures like the provision of regular uniforms for troops, introduced widely by 17th-century kings, symbolized the increasing professionalism of the military forces.

New state functions developed. During most of the 17th and 18th centuries, the reigning economic theory, called mercantilism, held that states should provide the basic framework for the economy, to promote tax revenue and make sure that other nations did not gain an advantage. England and Holland, as well as the absolute monarchies, practiced a mercantilist system. They levied tariffs on imported goods, tried to encourage the growth and activity of their merchant fleets, and sought colonies to provide raw materials and a guaranteed market for manufactured goods. Some governments even built factories to foster national industry and discourage imports from foreign producers. In the 18th century, enlightened kings like Frederick the Great also tried to introduce new crops and farming methods and to stimulate population growth, held to be a vital source of military strength. Many governments broke down local internal barriers to trade, again for the

Louis XIV's palace at Versailles. Built as a lavish celebration of absolute monarchy, Versailles demonstrates the regular, classical style predominant in 17th and 18th century Western Europe.

sake of the national economy. State-sponsored road building increased. Here were important extensions of Western ideas of what the state should be responsible for. While economic activities were valued mainly for their impact on military capability and international competition, some rulers were approaching the belief that one of the duties of government was the promotion of national prosperity.

During the early modern period, the growth of state powers and functions propelled the leading West European governments toward the front rank of all governments in the world, in terms of the resources they could command and the ways they could control relatively large territories. Some of the Western measures, of course, duplicated earlier advances in administration introduced in places like China. It was also true that Western governments could not rival the territorial size of the great empires of the day, but they did have more effective contact with their national units than many of the Asian empires maintained with their more diverse holdings. Some popular loyalty to the kings, some hints indeed of a sense of national identity visible where national churches formed, supplemented the institutions of the monarchy. This period was, in sum, an important stage of state-building and organizational efficiency in a number of Western nations. Regular contacts with ordinary people still did not exist, but even popular protests began to suggest an expectation that the government should help in times of need.

The practical limits on the power of the expanding states of early modern Europe were buttressed by increasing ideological attacks, for political theory grew in importance as an expression of Western culture. A few theorists, to be sure, supported the absolute monarchs. In addition to Machiavelli's frank appraisal of how to use raw power, there emerged a "divine right" school of thought that held that kings derived their power directly from God and were accountable only to Him. Even this theory differed from traditions in some other civilizations, which claimed that the king or emperor was himself divine, but the distinction may not have meant much in practice.

Yet divine right theory was not the dominant approach in Western political theory of this time. Machiavelli himself, in his longer works, wrote of the importance of councils to balance the ruler's power. From the Renaissance onward, classical examples were cited, from Athens and republican Rome, to show the importance of representative institutions to express some popular sentiment and curb the excesses of kings. Calvinist writers, building on the experience of self-government in local churches and eager to protect their "true" faith against hostile governments, also developed theories about the limited powers of kings and states. The most substantial theoretical statements arose in England in the aftermath of the Civil Wars. John Locke believed that basic political power lay with the people, who could withdraw it, even through revolution, if a ruler behaved arbitrarily. Peoples' rights to life, liberty, and property should be protected against the state. These ideas were taken up, during the 18th century, by Enlightenment writers in France and elsewhere, many of whom advocated the founding of parliaments on the English model and even the drafting of formal constitutions to ensure individual rights and provide additional constraints on royal power.

In other words, as some of the traditional limits on kings declined, and as royal power expanded notably in many countries, some new restraints were being suggested. The fact that England provided an alternative model of government structure was vital in this ideological movement. But the theories themselves were important, as many people in France came to believe that absolute monarchy was an inappropriate political form. Some ideas, not just of upper-class parliaments but of genuine popular political rights, were sketched, and some ordinary people began to share similar beliefs. During the English Civil Wars, and again in the 1760s, popular movements arose in Britain to demand direct political representation for the common folk.

Along with growing government power, then, came a new statement of ideas that governments should be controlled and limited—a significant restatement, in other words, of a recognizable Western political tradition.

THE FERMENT IN WESTERN CULTURE

Renaissance humanism added important new elements to Western culture, in part, of course, by reviving classical styles and values in literature and art. The aesthetic value of the arts, rather than their service to religious goals, gained new attention. The Reformation and Catholic response represented a distraction, to some extent, from this movement. Protestant churches were characteristically spare, lest artistic images detract from the focus on God's great power. Church music assumed a vital role, and Luther himself wrote some powerful hymns. In fact, Renaissance-inspired artistic themes continued even as religious conflict spread. Shakespeare's plays, for example, showed little interest in religious subjects in their evocation of political drama and human comedy and tragedy. Then, in the 17th century, classically inspired art and literature gained a new lease on life. In France a series of powerful dramatic writers, led by the playwright Racine, used classical themes directly to express human emotions. Architecture and painting similarly borrowed classical motifs and scenes—though with some new decorative embellishments, in what is called the Baroque style.

More fundamentally, the Renaissance and Reformation, although very different in specific focus, promoted important new cultural values. Individualism was one such value. Renaissance writers vaunted the power of the individual. The concept of the "Renaissance man" expressed the conviction that talented human beings could excel in many fields and take legitimate pride in their own accomplishments. Reformation theology, to be sure, carefully placed God's power above human capability. But Reformation writers also talked of the importance of a direct relationship between the individual and God, without the mediation of priests and sacraments. Although Protestant churches in fact exercised substantial controls over the moral and religious behavior of their flocks, individuals were encouraged to think on their own about their relationship to God.

Writers of both the Renaissance and the Reformation spoke of the importance of the past, the source of stylistic inspiration or religious guidance. Scholars from both periods turned to a critical examination of historical documents as a key source of truth. But, particularly in the Renaissance, the idea of human progress also began to surface. Renaissance writers believed in their superiority over medieval authors, and some wondered whether a more general advance in human knowledge and aesthetic sensibility was not underway.

Finally, secular interests gained ground. Renaissance writers incorporated humanistic themes in their works, though most continued to accept the importance of religious values as well. Reformation theologians were adamant in their hostility to purely secular concerns. But by breaking up Christian unity and producing the series of religious wars, the Reformation led many people to question whether the church was quite so important as medieval thinkers, or Reformation leaders themselves, had claimed. Even by the late 16th century, some writers, like Michel de Montaigne in France, emphasized that tolerance and peace were far more vital than any effort to establish a single religious truth. Western Christianity had long depended on the idea of religious uniformity. This is not an essential belief in a religious society; most Asian civilizations had long generated more religious diversity or effective tolerance. In the West, however, Christianity since the Roman Empire had produced a passionate commitment to a single truth, with alternatives seen not just as wrong but as dangerous. Early Protestant leaders maintained this view; Calvin even had heretics executed. But the fact was that religious unity no longer existed, and given this challenge to the particular Western religious tradition, it was probably inevitable that secular values would become prominent.

The Renaissance and Reformation also drew more people than ever before into contact with formal ideas. Renaissance intellectuals were very interested in promoting education, though primarily for the elites. They wanted the upper classes to gain new appreciation of classical literary styles and philosophies, and they set standards for upper-class education that have lasted, in Western society, into our own century. It was also during the Renaissance that Western society developed the printing press, a technique well advanced in Asia but new to the West and now improved by the use of movable block type. (Paper also became common in the West at this point, though the first factory, copied from the Arabs, had been established in the 13th century.) Printing was first used by its German inventer Gutenberg to produce Bibles, but by the end of the 15th century, printing presses were spewing out hosts of Renaissance materials. Then, with the Reformation, printing presses spread to the literate public the theological disputes that convulsed Western religious leaders. Most people still could not read, but the rate of literacy began to rise, particularly in Protestant areas, and those who could read had a variety of styles and viewpoints to engage them.

It was during the 17th century, however, that the real break in Western culture occurred, thanks in large part to the scientific revolution. Important artistic work continued. So did significant endeavors in theology, both Protestant and Catholic. The most widely published works were sermons and other religious tracts. Western culture, in other words, remained vigorously diverse, even contradictory. But it was the rise of science that provided the most significant single theme.

The scientific revolution consisted of new knowledge, particularly about physics and astronomy but also about biology and chemistry. It consisted of new instrumentation to measure the heavens and examine microscopically the creatures of the earth. The movement represented increasing defiance of past wisdom. Scientists who proved that old ideas about an earth-centered universe were wrong were also showing that the ancients could

This shop in Italy shows the early printing press in the West, and Renaissance technology at work.

be dramatically improved on. Many found these claims shocking, precisely because the belief in ancient wisdom was so deeply ingrained. Galileo, who insisted on the heliocentric universe, was forced to recant by the Catholic church. But steadily the idea of progress in knowledge through experiment and critical thinking gained ground. In France, René Descartes boldly set out to re-examine all past wisdom, his theory being that nothing should be assumed correct simply because of tradition. Skepticism was the order of the day among vanguard intellectuals; by the 1680s this approach was being directly applied to religion, as writers sought to disprove beliefs in miracles and other Christian claims.

The European scientific revolution built on the current of direct observation and experiment that had begun in the later Middle Ages, with work on optics and other subjects. In the 16th century, this current began to swell. It was then that a Polish monk, Copernicus, used astronomical observation and mathematical calculation to prove that the Hellenistic belief that the earth was the center of the universe was wrong; rather, the earth moved around the sun. His finding was taken up shortly before 1600, when a great surge of astronomical observation began, from Italy to Scandinavia. Scientists discovered new planets and also developed new understanding of the principles of planetary motion. Again using a combination of observation and experiment, Galileo and others began to

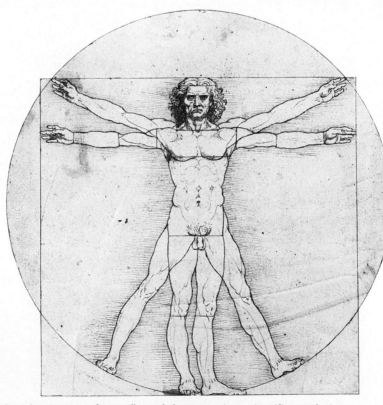

Renaissance art often reflected the emerging scientific revolution: anatomical sketches by Leonardo da Vinci.

generate theories about the impact of gravity, proving experimentally that Aristotle had committed a basic error in claiming that, in a vacuum, heavy bodies would fall faster than light bodies.

While work of this sort greatly advanced the knowledge of physics, biology too gained ground. Better instrumentation and observation led to more accurate understanding of the human anatomy. The Englishman William Harvey showed how the blood circulates. Other scientists studied the behavior of gasses. Thus, by the mid–17th century, the Western world was producing a veritable explosion of knowledge about the physical universe; as part of this process many intellectuals came to challenge the idea that learning was best approached through reverence for tradition, for experiment was seen as an alternative, and more accurate, path to truth.

The scientific revolution also applied to science much of the rationalism that had informed Greek and then medieval scholastic thinking. Here was a crucial link in Western intellectual life, even amid great change. Most scientists believed that they could do more than disprove old theories and discover new data. They believed that they could formulate general laws of natural behavior—that there was a correspondence between human reason and the orderliness of the universe. Here, the physics of Isaac Newton late in the 17th century seemed to culminate a long quest. In three basic laws Newton established how physical motion operated, on earth and throughout the universe: a physical body preserves its momentum in a straight line unless forced by outside pressure to deviate; change of motion is proportional to the impressed force and takes place in the direction to which the force is applied; and to every action there is always an equal reaction. Additional work on the law of gravity showed why planets stay in orbit and explained why objects fall at the same speed. Laws of this sort could be mathematically expressed, and Newton and others added not only to scientific theory but also to mathematical knowledge, particularly in the area of calculus.

What had occurred, by 1700, was a real intellectual revolution in the West, and the establishment of a central position for the scientific approach that no civilization had ever before ventured. The importance of the scientific outlook in Western history after the late 16th century therefore raises the obvious comparative question: why the West? Several other civilizations had produced significant scientific achievement. Byzantium preserved Hellenistic science, though it did not advance it and did not encourage scientific work elsewhere in Eastern Europe. Important science in India and the Middle East was ultimately limited by the rise of narrower religious concerns and, at key points, by political instability. China poses a more interesting case still, for the Chinese preserved a long tradition of elaborate empirical work. Unlike the West, of course, China had little contact with scientific discoveries outside its borders; it lacked the exciting spur of mastering Greek and Arab learning. Chinese thought also tended to stress ethical knowledge over elaborate inquiry. Chu Hsi's emphasis on knowledge might have encouraged scientific inquiry, but it was modified by traditional Confucian stress on the values that individuals carried within themselves. Chinese science itself differed from the Western approach in its more complete empiricism—its lack of large, rationalistic attempts to fathom general laws of nature. Thus, despite extensive biological and physical data, the Chinese did not generate an overall sense that science was a key to basic understanding. Finally, we will see that at the time Western science began to surge, Chinese intellectual life was becoming more conservative, a fact that would, ironically, encourage Chinese scholars to ignore Western scientific achievements for some time.

Western science involved popularization as well as basic discoveries. Information about the new science spread widely among the educated public. Scientific societies were founded to promote research. Many business and professional people began to dabble in science, finding new species of plants and animals and participating, however humbly, in this exciting expansion of knowledge. Popularized tracts explained scientific laws and advanced the idea that knowledge was progressing and that reason, not faith, was the key to understanding how the world works.

Through scientific ferment, which simply extended as time went on, religion declined in importance in providing a basic intellectual framework. Rationalistic science became more vital in shaping habits of thought than ever before, in any civilization. Without destroying art, it clearly superseded creative expression as well; as one result, the late 17th and 18th centuries were not particularly significant in terms of stylistic developments, except in music. The way to think was to think scientifically. Rationalism would generate steady progress in knowledge, as intellectual leaders gradually turned away from a belief that classical learning was the basic channel to truth. Rationalism might have other beneficial effects as well. Scientific writers like Francis Bacon, in England, argued that further discoveries would lead to technological improvements, making life easier and more rewarding.

These ideas gained ground during the 18th century. Scientific work continued. Chemists discovered the functions of oxygen. Biologists acquired increasing knowledge of the variety of animal and plant species. A science of psychology began to take shape, as scholars studied the workings of the human mind.

More important still was the effort to adapt the principles of the scientific revolution to discussions of human nature and human affairs. Enlightenment thinkers, centered in France but operating in many countries, continued to popularize science and to attack errors of faith and superstition. They also developed a number of social sciences by writing of political and economic systems. The basic idea was that rational laws could be applied to social behavior as well as to physical behavior, producing an understanding of how this human aspect of the world works. The Scottish philosopher Adam Smith, in his *Wealth of Nations*, thus posited a number of clear principles of economic behavior, based on the idea that people act according to their self-interest and, through competition, will work to promote economic advancement if they are not distracted by government interference. This was a compelling statement of the doctrine of laissez-faire, that private initiative rather than state intervention promotes economic progress. Smith's work was also a founding effort in economics as a social science that is based on the belief that general models of human behavior can be rationally derived.

Enlightenment thinkers advocated a powerful view of the goodness and rationality of human beings themselves. Progress in knowledge convinced them that more general human progress was also possible. Children can improve through education; older methods of discipline were attacked. Criminals can become useful members of society if treated humanely; traditional methods of punishment were attacked. Political life can improve if people are left free, if states do not try to force religious conformity, and if governments pay some attention to popular demands. The Enlightenment did not in fact produce a single political theory. Many writers were attracted to the idea of enlightened despotism, believing that a reform-minded ruler could produce social progress. Others talked of the importance of constitutions and parliaments. But they all agreed that political life, like other aspects of life, could be reformed, through rational calculations and belief in the essential goodness of human nature. Late in the Enlightenment, during the 1780s and 1790s, this kind of thinking even produced statements of socialism, framed as arguments that property relations should be reformed in the name of equality; and of feminism, in the form of assertions that women as well as men should participate in political life and benefit from legal reforms.

The Enlightenment, then, served as the intellectual origin of a host of modern impulses in Western society. It developed modern political movements, from liberalism through socialism. In emphasizing secular rather than religious thinking, it outlined a rationalistic social science approach that continues to describe this part of the Western intellectual arsenal even today. It promoted a host of humanitarian reform movements. Most basically, by extending and translating the results of the scientific revolution, it established the framework for modern Western intellectual life. There were changes to come, to be sure. Most Westerners no longer think in precisely the terms of the Enlightenment. But many of the issues and the fundamental approaches of the Enlightenment remain current. Simply put, the modern way of thinking, in Western society, took shape between about 1680 and 1750.

The Enlightenment hardly won everyone over to its camp. Broader dissemination of some of the basic ideas was still to come. Numerous Christian writers objected vigorously to Enlightenment thinking, and they had many followers. But the Enlightenment was a popularizing movement. Leading writers, like the Frenchman Voltaire, who argued for human freedom and against church domination, became wealthy through sales of their works. From the aristocracy to the urban artisanry, many people were aware of at least some of the Enlightenment claims. Huge publishing ventures, like the *Encyclopédie* in France and later the *Encyclopaedia Britannica* in England, tried to sum up all relevant human knowledge in Enlightenment terms, with emphasis on science and social science and a pronounced interest in technological improvements. Furthermore, the Enlightenment was essentially a Western-wide movement, striking sparks not only in France and Britain but also in Italy, Germany, Scandinavia, and the British colonies of North America. In this sense it rivaled the earlier spread of Christianity in providing a common cultural framework for Western civilization.

TRANSFORMATIONS IN ECONOMIC AND SOCIAL LIFE

THE ROLE OF COMMERCE

During the early modern period, a steady expansion of commerce, along with the substantial changes in culture, helped transform Western life. Renaissance leaders were proud of the commercial bustle of their cities. Reformation thinkers also tended to favor trade. Luther and Calvin reduced the traditional sense that merchants might be pursuing false values. Since ordinary people could have direct links with God, the duties and tasks of everyday life were not seen as contradicting religious purposes. Of course, God came first; but commercial success might demonstrate that God's favor had been won. Not all Protestants became fervent entrepreneurs, however, and Catholic business activities grew as well. But there was some relationship between the spread of Protestantism and the increasing interest in commerce. Finally, the expanding monarchies encouraged merchants to form powerful trading alliances. State backing helped organize great merchant companies to trade with Russia, India and Southeast Asia, and the Americas.

Commerce was also stimulated by the new supplies of gold and silver brought back from the New World, particularly from Spain's American colonies. During the 16th century these precious metals produced a price revolution in Europe. As the supply of money rose on its traditional gold-and-silver base, production of foods and manufactured goods could not keep pace, and the result was rapid inflation. Rising prices encouraged merchants to take greater risk, because they could borrow money with the understanding that it would be worth less when they had to pay it back. Capitalists also saw the profits to be made in trade with far-flung parts of the world. Asian spices commanded handsome prices. From the late 16th century onward, grain from Poland and Russia and furs, sugar, and tobacco from the Americas were imported at increasingly rapid rates, through trade organized by the European merchants.

Commercial expansion began to focus greater attention on Europe's manufacturing base. Growing wealth at home produced new markets for goods, and there was also a need to produce goods to sell on the foreign markets. While most production remained in artisan hands, a significant expansion of domestic manufacturing took place under capitalist auspices. Merchants in this system provided raw materials, particularly textile fibers, to workers scattered in rural cottages, who spun and wove the fibers into cloth on simple machines; their products were then collected and paid for, and put up for sale by the merchants on a wide market. Even in the artisan system, commercial expansion created a growing gap between guild masters and their journeymen; as masters pushed their workers to produce more, many journeymen became a permanent paid labor force manufacturing items like books, guns, and metal tools for wide market sales.

European technology steadily improved in this climate of economic expansion. Better mining techniques allowed increased production of iron and coal. Better mill wheels facilitated the processing of grains. Textile equipment, though still manually guided, was also becoming more sophisticated. By the 17th century, European technology had no peer in the world in most branches of production, and the pace of change continued high. Early in the 18th century the first steam engine was devised in England to pump water out of deep mine shafts. And in 1733 the Englishman James Kay invented the flying shuttle, which automatically interwove fibers to make cloth; with this new system, one weaver could now do the work of two, though the looms were still powered by hand.

Improvements in agriculture were somewhat slower in coming, though the expansion of commerce and the growth of cities encouraged increasing numbers of farmers to produce for the market. Late in the 17th century, Dutch farmers began to experiment with new crops that would replenish the fertility of the soil without necessitating periods of fallow, in which nothing could be grown. The Dutch, hard-pressed to support a large population in a small land, also developed new methods of draining swamps and providing dikes to keep out ocean tides. Interest in agricultural improvement spread further in the 18th century, and many societies were organized to disseminate knowledge of new crops and fertilizers and new machines to sow seeds.

The tide of economic change must not be exaggerated, however. Most people continued to use rather traditional methods, both in agriculture and in manufacturing. Most people still did not depend heavily on market sales for their livelihood. The merchant class expanded, but it did not yet command the highest social levels. Many, indeed, still aspired to become aristocrats in their own right, for money-making alone did not provide adequate prestige. Still, Western Europe became more substantially commercialized than ever before. Enlightenment thinkers, generally hostile to the aristocracy, which they saw as an idle class, praised hard work and profit-making, a sign that social values were changing even before the social structure had been revolutionized.

One clear effect of commercial expansion was that Europe's wealth increased. An Englishman, writing in the late 1580s about village life, "noted three things to be marvelously altered in England within his own sound remembrance." First: farmers' cottages had more chimneys, which meant they were bigger and better heated. Second, beds and pillows had replaced straw mats for sleeping. And third, pewterware, instead of wooden utensils, was used for eating. With time, the list of standard-of-living gains continued to expand. By the early 1600s French peasants began to consume wine fairly regularly with their meals. This was a sign of greater wealth, and also of the growing market production of wines, which could not be effected in every area of France. By 1700, ordinary people in Western Europe were consuming coffee, tea, and sugar—all imported goods that they had to buy on the market and that they therefore had to have enough money to afford. By this time, European farmers and artisans had far more objects in their possession—tools, furnishings, and the like—than any other people in the world.

Yet new wealth was by no means evenly distributed. Some parts of the Western world were richer than others. Material standards lagged in Germany, in part because of the devastation of the Thirty Years' War. They also lagged in Spain, where merchant activity remained rather low despite the influx of wealth from the colonies; most Spanish gold passed to the vigorous merchants and banks of northern Europe. Social disparities also intensified. As a core group of farmers or substantial peasants increased—the people who could sell a bit to urban markets and whose living standards rose—the poverty of those without property also grew. Western Europe by the 17th century faced significant problems of poor relief. Almshouses and other institutions designed to aid the poor, but also to isolate them, were one common result. The existence of growing pockets of poverty amid rising wealth represented another important theme for European society; it is a contradiction with which Westerners are still grappling today.

Social and economic change also produced recurrent unrest. Many journeymen resented the growing power of guild masters and formed journeymen's associations to promote their own interests. The first strikes in Western history occurred during the Renaissance. Riots were even more common, continuing a theme from the later Middle Ages. Peasants periodically rose against ever-steeper exactions from landlords. Both rural and urban riots surfaced when grain and bread were in short supply. Considerable popular unrest accompanied the tensions of the Reformation. French peasants rose in many regions during the 1590s, in the aftermath of the religious wars. They attacked their landlords, who "had reduced them to starvation, violated their wives and daughters, stolen their cattle and wasted their land," while urban merchants with whom they had to trade sought "only the ruin of the poor people, for our ruin is their wealth." Popular unrest also surfaced during the English Civil Wars, with farmers and urban workers organizing to demand political rights and economic reforms. The uprisings produced an amazing series of revolts around 1648, not only in England but also in southern Italy and elsewhere. Protest declined somewhat during the next decades, partly because population growth, which had been substantial during the 16th century, leveled off. But the early modern period was not a peaceful time in Western society, even aside from the recurrent wars.

THE ROLE OF THE FAMILY

Social change also involved the Western family. During the 15th and 16th centuries the characteristic structure of the family began to shift, producing a "European-style" family that was quite different from the patterns of most other agricultural societies. The ingredients were simple. First, common people began to marry at a rather late age—about 27 or 28 (members of the aristocracy, in contrast, married much earlier). And a substantial minority of ordinary people never married at all. The reason for these developments was a desire to protect family property against the demands of too many children. Late marriages led to reduced birth rates, so that a given family would not have more than three or four children living to adulthood. But, while understandable, such a system required considerable self-control and family supervision, for it meant that young people passed many years between puberty and the point at which heterosexual activity was generally permissible—in marriage. Tensions increased between young adults and older parents, for economic independence and marriage normally depended on the death or retirement of the elderly. Generational suspicion forced most older people to prepare careful contracts to spell out what support they would get from their children if they turned over their land. The new family pattern also promoted greater interaction between men and women. Men remained officially and legally the heads of their families. But with the emphasis now on rather small units, featuring husband and wife and their children, economic cooperation between men and women probably increased. Generally, the new family structure shielded the Europeans from the population density that had long been a fact of life in East Asian and Indian society.

During the 17th century and beyond, changes in the quality of family life were added to the earlier structural shifts. Europeans began to spend more leisure time in the family environment. Meals at home became more elaborate than before. This was partly the result of growing wealth, but it also involved some explicit choices. Women became the family agents who regulated its social life, preparing more intricate dishes and presiding over mealtime ceremonies and conversation. Here was a new aspect of Western family life that continued to gain in importance until very recently.

Family affection was also increasingly encouraged. Seventeenth-century Protestant writers stressed the importance of love as an ingredient of family life. As one English minister put it, "Keep up your Conjugal Love in a constant heat and vigor." This growing emphasis on the family as a pleasurable emotional center, which spread to Catholic areas by the 18th century, was a substantial transformation. Fostered by religious developments, it may also have been a reaction to rapid social and economic change in the wider environment; families were seen as a comfortable and reliable refuge. Here, too, themes were set in motion that have carried on to recent times. There were implications, finally, for the treatment of children in this new family environment. By the late 17th century, many writers were advocating love, rather than harsh physical discipline, as the means of dealing with children; they developed the revolutionary idea that parents owed children certain rights and protections, rather than, as tradition held, that children were obliged to accept whatever their parents might impose. Implications of change for women were ambivalent. Their nonproduction role in the family improved, but opportunities narrowed; in Protestant areas, the abolition of religious orders made marriage more vital for women.

Changes in family life, along with the shifts in broader economic and social structure, reveal a society that was beginning to alter some very basic patterns. Fundamental features of daily existence, even human emotion or at least its recommended expression, were taking new forms. Here was a potential source of further change as well. For if, as an example, parents began to change the way they treated children, spanking them less often, trying to draw them more actively into an orbit of parental affection, these children might grow up to be somewhat different kinds of adults. During the 18th century, child-rearing practices changed still further. Widespread Western practices of swaddling young children—wrapping them tightly so that parents could work without worrying about children's coming to harm—began to disappear. Children were left freer, given more active adult care in place of physical restraints. These changes, widely urged by Enlightenment writers, who believed that children could improve through better treatment, had substantial implications for the formation of Western adults. For if child rearing became more free, might adults not also seek greater liberty?

CONCLUSION: HOW EARLY MODERN TRENDS IN THE WEST INTERRELATED

The various trends of early modern Western society did not neatly mesh. There was overlap, to be sure. Commercial development and economic expansion were encouraged by some of the ideas of the Renaissance and Reformation, though not always intentionally; economic change also underlay some of the key values of the Enlightenment. Increased interest in carefully planned organization showed in business ventures, publishing, and statecraft. Even more amorphous values, such as greater individualism, related cultural and religious movements to capitalism and possibly to family organization—the family was seen less as an economic institution, more as an emotional bond among individuals.

On the other hand, different currents had varied results, and many key shifts were slow and uneven. Changes in beliefs and the economy, however, added up to a major strain on people at various levels. One key symptom was a wave of witchcraft trials that occured in many parts of Western Europe, and ultimately New England, from the late 15th century until the middle of the 17th century. Europeans had long believed in witches and magical powers, but they had never considered these forces to be such ominous threats as they did during these decades, when witchcraft trials sent hundreds of accused people to death and involved many thousands in mounting hysteria. Many factors were behind this sweeping fear. New anxieties about the poor were one cause, since many of the accused were among those bypassed by the growing prosperity. Protestant–Catholic divisions, shaking convictions about where religious truth lay, contributed to the fear. So did uncertainties about the changing roles of women and the elderly in the family (most accused witches were female, said to be "used by the devil," and a disproportionate number were elderly), and also new confusions about how to deal with sickness (whether through doctors or by superstitious remedies). A new belief system was taking shape in Western society, but its early stages left many people insecure and fearful.

Just as the witchcraft hysteria stemmed from a variety of intense concerns generated by change, so the end of the witchcraft trials signified the continuing spread of new ideas about how to understand the world. Growing numbers of officials and ordinary people simply stopped believing that witchcraft was a real phenomenon, capable of disrupting the laws of nature. While witchcraft beliefs persisted, and a few trials continued into the 18th century, the craze ended in most places by the 1680s. The spread of Enlightenment ideas in later decades, while again not universal in a society in which most people still could not read, was a further sign that Western outlook was shifting in some common directions.

For all its tensions and confusions, the fact remained that by the 18th century, Western Europe had created a distinctive kind of agricultural society, compared to the traditions of the other great civilizations of the world. Its unusual qualities stemmed primarily from the changes that had been occurring since the late 15th century at almost all levels of social activity. The West was unusually commercial, unusually scientific, and shaped by family structures that encouraged property control and considerable individualism. And, not accidentally, Western society was simultaneously extending its influence to the rest of the world, despite political organizations that were in many ways inferior to the world's great empires of the time.

SUGGESTED READINGS

For an overview of developments in Western society during this period, including extensive bibliographies, see Sheldon Watt, *A Social History of Western Europe, 1450–1720* (1984), and John Merriman, *History of Modern European Civilization*, v.I (1996). Charles Tilly, *Big Structures, Large Processes, Huge Comparisons* (1985), offers an analytical framework based on major change; see also Tilly's edited volume, *The Formation of National States in Western Europe* (1975), and Fernand Braudel, *Civilization and Capitalization*, 3 vols. (1952). Coverage of the Renaissance and the religious transformations can be found in: J. F. New, *The Renaissance and Reformation: A Short History* (1977); K. H. Kannenfeldt, ed., *The Renaissance: Medieval or Modern* (1959); J. Atkinson, *Martin Luther and the Birth of Protestantism* (1981); D. Knowles, *Bare Ruined Choirs* (1976); J. H. Plumb, *The Italian Renaissance* (1986); O. Chadwick, *The Reformation* (1983); Steven Ozment, *The Age of Reform, 1520–1550* (1980); and Hubert Jedin and John Dolan, eds., *Reformation and Counter Reformation* (1980). On the vital changes in science, consult H. Butterfield, *Origins of Modern Science* (1965), and A. R. Hall, *From Galileo to Newton, 1630–1720* (1982). Crucial political changes are dealt with in G. Clark, *Early Modern Europe from about 1450 to about 1750* (1960). Europe's economic development is treated in R. L. Reynolds, *Europe Emerges: Transition Toward an Industrial World Wide Society 1600–1750* (1972) and R. Ehrenberg, *Capital and Finance in the Age of the Renaissance* (1948). On vital transformations in popular life and behavior in the period, see: Peter Burke, *Popular Culture in Early Modern Europe* (1978); P. Ariès, *Centuries of Childhood: A Social History of Family Life* (1965); P. Stearns, ed., *The Other Side of Western Civilization*, vol. 2, 6th ed. (1999); and Merry Wiesner-Hanks, *Women and Gender in Early Modern Europe* (1993).

CHAPTER 15

The West and the World: Discovery, Colonization, and Trade

Focal Points

Western Europe's growing role in the world brought new influences and new constraints to a number of areas. These developments can be studied in sequence. What were the sources of Europe's new strength? What areas came under particular European influence, and why were other areas—such as most of Asia—less affected? How did Europe reshape aspects of sub-Saharan African society, and what aspects were relatively untouched? Why was Europe's influence in the Americas so much greater than in Africa? What were the characteristics of the new civilization that began to emerge in Latin America? To what extent was it different from European settlements in North America?

THE BASE OF NEW EUROPEAN POWER

Why does a civilization begin to move up in the ranks of the various cultures of the world, gaining new power and importance? The question is hardly less complex than the issue of why civilizations decline. In the case of the West, in its explosion to world prominence after 1450, the problem is enhanced by some of the civilization's overall drawbacks: here was a society still politically divided, often locked in internal wars and intense social unrest, with a relatively small total population. How could it, in the space of a few centuries, win control of the world's oceans and some of its richest lands?

The answer to this question can be divided into two kinds of factors: those that are measurable and material, and those deriving from culture and outlook. On the material side, the West, even as it launched its systematic explorations in the Atlantic in the 15th century, was gaining in technological sophistication. It was not yet the world's most advanced society in overall technology, but it was moving in that direction. It certainly had superiority over sub-Saharan African and American Indian cultures in manufacturing and agricultural know-how. More specifically, Western skills in shipbuilding and navigation, aided by refinements in the compass and other directional devices, were at a high level and would improve steadily to the point that, by the 16th century, they would surpass the attainment of East Asia. Even more specifically, West Europeans had been quickest to develop high-quality gunnery, using the knowledge they gained of Chinese gunpowder to forge a weaponry that was awesome by the standards of the time (and more than a bit terrifying to many Europeans themselves, who had reason to fear the new destructive power of their own armies and navies). The West would maintain its weapons advantage over all other civilizations in the world into the 20th century, and even today its arms technology is among the most highly developed. A crude but possibly accurate explanation of the West's rise, then, would focus simply on its technological edge in the art of killing and intimidating.

But sophisticated weaponry and other technological superiority may not have been the whole story. Europe's problems, including an unfavorable balance of trade with Asia and the fear of Muslim power, created some special motives for Western leaders. East Asia had some comparable technological leads, surpassing the West not in weaponry but in navigation during the 15th century; but it chose not to exploit these advantages in a quest for new roles in the wider world. Outlook, as well as material means, had to be conducive. Earlier civilizations that had influenced wide sectors of the world beyond their borders, notably classical India and then Islam, had usually possessed an active merchant spirit, and certainly the West had this in abundance from its medieval and Renaissance–Reformation heritage. In Christianity, the West also had a religion eager to spread the truth to heathens, even by force. Trade and Christianity would typically go hand in hand in the West's new surge. The specific culture of the Renaissance may have contributed as well. Certainly it was no accident that the first discoveries in the Atlantic occurred during the Renaissance, when some Europeans were feeling a new thirst for achievement and knowledge. The zeal of a Henry the Navigator to penetrate the unknown and the sheer adventurism of a Christopher Columbus related closely to other Renaissance enthusiasms. Finally, even the divisions within Europe pushed toward a new world role. National monarchies soon competed for discoveries and colonies, as part of their overall rivalry.

The period of discovery and early colonization was an exciting demonstration of Western power and daring. It also changed some key patterns of world history, which means that it must be assessed not only from the standpoint of European efforts, but also in terms of impact on the cultures it affected. Here, several zones developed, ranging from the Americas—where the European arrival began quickly to change basic cultural patterns toward creation of new civilizations or outright assimilation with the West—to East Asia, where European activities made little difference to the historical patterns of the next several centuries. Between these two extremes were several societies: Africa, where European contact caused important alterations in some regions but had little impact on others; India and the Middle East, where Western pressure grew but without unseating earlier traditions; and Russia, whose own new quest for power was colored by knowledge that the West had forged ahead.

HISTORY DEBATE

The West as World Leader

The view of the West's new role in the world has undergone some striking transformations in recent decades. Old history textbooks—in the West, of course—used to picture Columbus as a clear hero, opening the New World to progress. But in an age of anticolonialism, new views of Western ascendancy have shifted the picture. Columbus brought disease and dominance to the Americas, and European exploitation would gradually worsen the environment as well. What is the most accurate historical evaluation?

Historians have also compared Westerners with the previous essentially world power, the Arabs. Both world powers seized slaves and interfered with local cultures; both could look down on other peoples; both encouraged economic imbalances in world trade to their own profit. But other comparative verdicts are unflattering. Christians were often less tolerant than Muslims had been. The West seized more territory by force and was more likely to seek complete surrender in war than the Arabs had been. In some quarters, West-bashing has become a popular intellectual pastime. Even aside from some editorial views, questions about Western motives and culture remain important. At the same time, of course, new technology gave the West greater powers than the Arabs had enjoyed, and some results may reflect this new imbalance more than distinctive greed. Finally, at various points and in some areas, growing Western influence (even when resented) may have had some beneficial effects, aside from the growing profits in Western coffers.

PATTERNS OF EXPLORATION AND TRADE

When West Europeans began to push out into the wider world, their knowledge of where they were going was surprisingly scanty. To be sure, Viking adventurers from Scandinavia had crossed the Atlantic in the 10th century, reaching Greenland and then North America, which they named "Vinland." But they quickly lost interest, in part because they encountered Indian warriors whose weaponry was good enough to beat back the intruders.

As we have seen, scattered expeditions from Spain and Italy into the Atlantic dotted the later Middle Ages, but they had no results. It took new technical knowledge, particularly the navigational devices learned from Asia, and growing problems, in the form of new needs to reach Asia directly and to seek gold to pay for the desired Asian products, to permit a more systematic effort in the 15th century.

The initiative came from the small kingdom of Portugal. The rulers of this country had just finished driving out the Muslims, who still threatened from North Africa. This threat, and the surge of energy that sometimes accompanies expulsion of an occupation force, prompted the Portuguese during the 15th century to look for conquests in Africa. Portugal's rulers were drawn by the excitement of discovery, the harm they might cause to the Muslim world, and a thirst for wealth—for European legends of gold in Africa and elsewhere were abundant spurs to ambition. This was not mere greed; Europe's lack of gold to pay for its trade with Asia was becoming a serious problem. A Portuguese prince, Henry the Navigator, directed a series of expeditions down the African coast and outward to islands such as the Azores. Beginning in 1434 the Portuguese began to press down the African coast, each expedition going a little farther than its predecessor. They brought back some slaves and many stories of gold hordes that they had not yet been able to find.

Later in the 15th century, Portuguese sailors ventured around the Cape of Good Hope, planning to find India and also the African east coast, which was held to be the source of gold. They rounded the Cape in 1488, but weary sailors forced the expedition back before it could seek India. Then, after news of Columbus's discovery of America for Spain in 1492, Portugal redoubled its efforts, hoping to stave off the new Spanish competition. Vasco da Gama's fleet of four ships reached India, with the aid of a Muslim Indian pilot picked up in East Africa in 1497. The Portuguese mistakenly believed that the Indians were Christians, for they thought the Hindu temples they saw were churches. And they faced the hostility of Muslim merchants, who had long dominated trade in this part of the world. But they managed to return with a small load of spices.

This success set in motion an annual series of Portuguese voyages to the Indian Ocean. One expedition, blown off course, reached Brazil, where it proclaimed Portuguese sovereignty. With growing experience, both Portuguese and Spanish expeditions became increasingly comfortable with voyages in the South Atlantic and the Indian Ocean. Portugal began to set up forts on the African coast and also in India—the forerunners of such Portuguese colonies as Mozambique, in East Africa, and Goa, in India. By 1514 the Portuguese had reached the islands of Indonesia, the center of spice production, and also China. By 1542 a Portuguese expedition arrived in Japan, where a missionary effort was launched that met with some success for several decades.

Meanwhile, only a short time after the Portuguese quest began, the Spanish reached out with even greater force. Here too was a country only recently freed from Muslim rule, full of missionary zeal and a desire for riches. The Spanish had traveled into the Atlantic during the 14th century. Then in 1492, in the same year that the final Muslim fortress was captured in Spain, the Italian navigator Christopher Columbus, sailing in the name of the new Spanish monarchy and its rulers, Ferdinand and Isabella, set off for a westward route to India, convinced that the round earth would make his quest possible. As is well known, he failed, reaching the Americas instead and mistakenly naming their inhabitants "Indians." Although Columbus believed to his death that he had sailed to India, later Spanish expeditions brought a firm realization that they had voyaged to a region that Europeans and Asians had not traveled to before. One expedition, headed again by an Italian initially in Spanish service, Amerigo Vespucci (see p. 292), gave the New World its name. Spain, eager to claim this American land, won papal approval for Spanish dominion over most of what is now Latin America, though a later treaty awarded Brazil to Portugal.

Finally, a Spanish expedition under Ferdinand Magellan set sail westward in 1519, passing the southern tip of South America and sailing across the Pacific, reaching the In-

Discoveries in the 15th and 16th Centuries

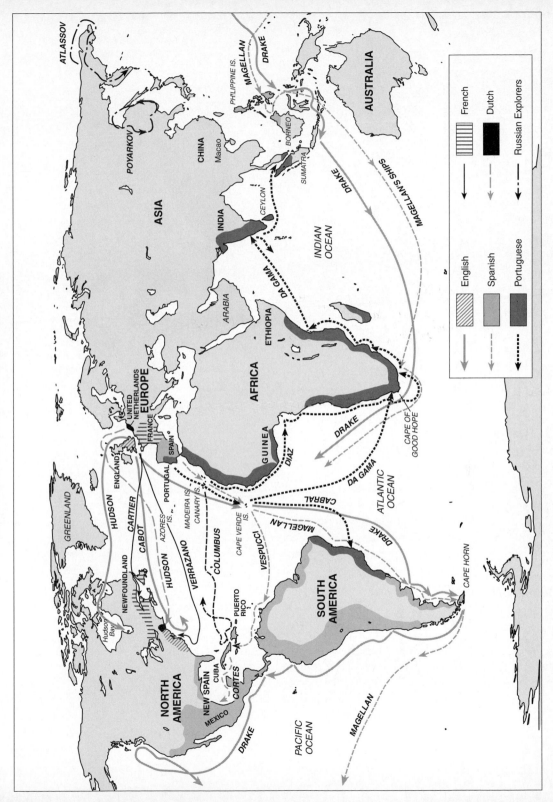

Ship technology in the expanding West. This is the *Vittoria,* the only one of Magellan's five ships that completed the first circumnavigation of the globe in 1522. (The Granger Collection)

donesian islands in 1521 after incredible hardships. It was on the basis of this voyage, ultimately the first trip around the world, that Spain claimed the Philippines, which were to be Spanish territory until 1898.

Portugal emerged from this first round of exploration with coastal holdings in various parts of Africa and the Indian port of Goa; a lease on a Chinese port, Macao; short-lived interests in trade with Japan; and, finally, the claim on Brazil. Spain asserted its hold on the Philippines and various Pacific islands, and on the bulk of the Americas. During the 16th century the Spanish moved to back up these claims by military expeditions to Mexico and South America. The Spanish also held Florida in North America, and ultimately sent expeditions northward from Mexico into California and other parts of what later became the southwestern United States.

Later in the 16th century, the lead in further exploration passed to northern Europe. In part this was because Spain and Portugal were now busy digesting the gains they had already made; in part it was because northern Europeans, particularly the Dutch and the British, improved the design of oceanic vessels, producing lighter, faster ships than those of their Catholic adversaries. Britain won a historic sea battle with Spain in 1588, in which the British navy and adverse weather routed a massive Spanish Armada. From this point onward, the British and Dutch, and to an extent the French, vied for dominance on the seas.

French explorers crossed the Atlantic first in 1534, reaching Canada, which was claimed in France's name. French voyages increased in the 17th century, as various expeditions pressed down from Canada into the Great Lakes region and the Mississippi valley.

The British also turned their attention particularly to North America, starting with a brief expedition as early as 1497. The English hoped, in vain, to discover a northwest passage to India, but in fact accomplished little beyond exploration of the Hudson's Bay area of Canada during the 16th century. England's serious work began in the 17th century, with the colonization of the east coast of North America.

The Dutch entered the picture after winning independence from Spain and quickly became a major competitor with Portugal in Southeast Asia. The Dutch sent substantial numbers of sailors and ships to the region, ousting the Portuguese from the Indonesian islands by the early 17th century. Voyagers from the Netherlands explored the coast of Australia, though without much immediate result. Finally, toward the middle of the 17th century, Holland established a settlement on the southern tip of Africa, mainly to provide a relay station for its ships bound for the East Indies.

Dutch and British exploration and trade were government-sponsored, but unlike the Spanish and Portuguese expeditions, and to some extent the French, they owed much to the private initiative of merchant groups. The Netherlands, Britain, and France all chartered great trading companies, like the Dutch East India Company or the British firm of similar name. These companies were given government monopolies of trade in the regions designated, but they were not rigorously supervised by their own states. Thus semiprivate companies, formed by pooling merchant capital and amassing great fortunes in commerce, long acted almost like independent governments in the regions they claimed. For some time a Dutch trading company virtually ruled the island of Taiwan, off the coast of China; and the British East India Company played a similar role in parts of India during much of the 18th century.

TOWARD A WORLD ECONOMY

By the 16th century, then, West Europeans had gained control of most of the world's seas. They were moving freely across the Atlantic Ocean and with some regularity across the vast Pacific as well—the first time in world history that this kind of endeavor had ever occurred. The Europeans did not displace all Asian shipping from the coastal waters of China and Japan, nor did they completely monopolize the Indian Ocean; and in East Africa, Muslim merchants remained active. But Muslim and Hindu traders were now confined to regional specialties; they did not command the chief routes. In the Mediterranean, finally, where European power had been growing even earlier, the Spaniards inflicted a decisive defeat on the navy of the Ottoman Empire, in the battle of Lepanto in 1571; with this setback, any hope of a new Muslim rivalry to European naval power ended. By this time, the greatest competitors for the Europeans were other European states, and their battles would pepper world history from this point until the mid–20th century. By the 16th century European traders even carried products from one part of Asia to another, earning money by dealing with goods where Europe had no direct involvement at all. World trade and its expansion lay largely in Western hands.

Amerigo Vespucci (1451–1512) is the only person in world history to give his name not to just one whole continent, but two. Vespucci was a talented Italian navigator in Spanish, then Portuguese service who, on the heels of Christopher Columbus, crossed the Atlantic to the new world and charted some of the coast of North America. Like Columbus, he was a tireless self-publicist, who reached out to Europe's educated readership with information about the New World and about his country's accomplishments. Vespucci's first name was applied to the continents of the Western hemisphere, because his charts showed that whole continents, and not just strings of islands, were involved. In this illustration *Vespucci Studying the Stars,* by Stradanus, Vespucci is portrayed in association with the new scientific and technical devices beginning to capture European imagination, vital in the voyages of discovery. He holds an astrolabe which, by measuring altitudes of stars, allowed calculations of latitudes and times. What other symbols helped promote the new European surge, and Vespucci's own exaggerated reputation?

Into the 18th century, however, the Europeans' power, though astonishing by their own or anyone else's previous standards, was a sea power, and sea power had limits. Only in special circumstances were the Europeans able to penetrate inland, far from the protection of their ever-improving ship's cannon. The major exception, of course, was in the Americas, where the Spanish gained continental control and the English and Portuguese important regional centers. Elsewhere, the European grasp extended mainly to islands—with the control of major parts of the Indonesian islands the most substantial achievement—and scattered port cities. Even in Africa, where the Europeans had greater influence than they did in most parts of Asia, European control was mainly coastal until after 1800. In the Middle East and Eastern Europe, Westerners seized no territory at all, though their trading influence was actively felt; in East Asia, even their commercial efforts were kept to a minimum after a brief initial flurry.

Hence, outside the Americas, the Europeans affected but did not dominate major civilizations. We will see their influence and its limitations in subsequent chapters. Even in India, until the 18th century, European entry and the seizure of a few coastal cities were fairly minor incidents, hardly rivaling the ongoing presence of Muslim government in a largely Hindu population.

It is important, then, not to exaggerate the significance for world history of what the Europeans liked to call their age of exploration. There was no question of their new strength, but until about 1800, when the situation changed, they were not yet directing the world stage.

Yet Western Europe was beginning to shape new global economic contracts, which brought them great advantage and affected economic activity in many other parts of the world. Europe's wealth went up rapidly because of profits drawn from the Americas, Africa, and even Asia. The Europeans never found the golden treasures they had hoped for, but they did gain access to vast supplies of gold and particularly silver in the New World. Spain was the chief initial beneficiary of this wealth, but bankers and merchants in northern Europe soon profited even more substantially. With the new supply of precious metals and concomitant control of shipping the Europeans were able to turn the balance of world trade in their favor for the first time. Spice and tea plantations in southern Asia began to produce for the growing European market on terms of trade set no longer by the rarity of their products but by the buying power of the West.

Then, as Europeans used some of their wealth to improve their own manufacturing base, they increasingly offered manufactured products to the world market—guns, cloth, and metal wares—instead of precious metals alone. The division was deliberately fostered by the policies of the Europeans themselves, whether as governments or as giant trading companies. The reigning theories of mercantilism urged 17th- and 18th-century Europe to monopolize as much manufacturing as possible, leaving other parts of the world to specialize in agricultural production or mining. By the 18th century, several parts of the world were producing raw materials or foodstuffs for a Western market and receiving more sophisticated and expensive manufactured goods in return. Russia and Poland sold grain; Africa, slaves; the Americas, sugar, silver, and tobacco. These goods, because they involved less processing, tended to command lower prices than did Europe's own products. And so a global economy was being shaped in which much of the world sold goods (generated by cheap labor) to the West, which sold more expensive items and in whose ships the goods were exchanged. Here was the beginning of a division in the world economy between haves and have-nots, which echoes to the present day.

The impact of the division could run deep. Basic labor systems increasingly responded to economic position. Western Europe required labor flexible enough to participate in growing manufacturing; hence it increasingly developed a wage-labor force, often ill-paid. Areas dependent on producing raw materials, particularly where workers were in short supply because of disease, relied on compulsory labor systems, like slavery or extensive serfdom, that could keep costs down for unskilled work. Gender was affected. In many areas, men were responsible for an increasing amount of production for sale, relegating women to more household tasks. New slave traders preferred men: two thirds of all African slaves sent to the Americas were male, and this extended systems of polygamy in Africa itself as a means of dealing with excess females.

But this was only the beginning of an international economy dominated by the West. Most people were not deeply affected by the new patterns of trade. The Chinese were far more heavily influenced by new foodstuffs brought by European traders, by the seeds and tubers they introduced from the Americas, than by Europe's world economic position. Most Asians, Russians, Africans, and even many American Indians were not drawn into production for the world market as yet, though it is true that Europe's financial influence reached farther than their ships did. Here is another factor, along with outright European contacts, to be weighed in dealing with the development of major civilizations between 1450 and 1800.

In three major cases, however, European influence did go farther, even in the early modern centuries, so that major alterations in historical patterns resulted. Developments in sub-Saharan Africa, Spanish or Latin America, and North America revealed the power of Western penetration and an emerging new world economy to reshape politics, culture, and individual lives.

AFRICA

It was long assumed, by prideful Westerners, that African history did not really begin until the coming of the Europeans. This of course is nonsense; African culture had evolved significantly before the Europeans poked down the Atlantic and, more to the point, it continued into the 19th century to develop apart from European influence. Yet the Europeans did have profound effects on a number of regions, and this new ingredient must be intertwined with other trends to describe African diversity after about 1500.

European penetration of Africa was limited by several factors. Transportation barriers were as great for them as for the Africans; it was hard to move inland from the coast, particularly in the thickly forested areas; moreover, the main rivers were not navigable for any distance. Disease hit the Europeans hard, for they lacked the extent of immunity to tropical diseases that Africans, themselves bothered by disease, had developed. Most important, the political powers of most African kingdoms were sufficient to block European entry until the 19th century. To be sure, the great African empires ended with the fall of Songhai late in the 16th century; and in the south there was nothing to match the earlier Zimbabwe. But regional kingdoms flourished, some old, some rising for the first time. This meant that in most instances Europeans had to negotiate carefully with African leaders, offering real value in exchange for value received; and, with a few exceptions, they could not seize territory.

Here, for example, is how a Dutch representative described the king of the West African kingdom of Benin (where the Dutch traded actively during the 17th century, replacing the Portuguese as principal European contacts):

> I saw and spoke to the king of Benin, in the presence of his great counsellors. He was seated on an ivory throne under a canopy of Indian silk. He was about forty years old and of lively expression. According to custom I stood about thirty feet away from him. So as to see him better I asked permission to draw closer. He laughingly agreed.

The representative was also awed by the splendor of the palace, as big as the stock exchange in Amsterdam, supported by "wooden pillars encased in copper, where the victories of the kingdom are recorded."

European activity, however, did make a difference. The Portuguese and then other Europeans, particularly the French, set up forts and urban settlements along the western coast, usually paying rent or by other arrangement with local rulers. With this base, the Europeans altered West African trading patterns. They encountered many valuable goods in Africa—cloth and iron items—but their main interests lay in gold, ivory, and slaves. They found African merchants as well as political rulers to be demanding negotiators, but they did have goods to offer in return: cloth, iron tools, and above all muskets. European imports reduced African craft production, which disrupted the economy severely. Dependence on weapons imports also brought change. Not infrequently, Europeans participated as allies in wars among African kingdoms, where their firepower could spell the difference in outcome. These trading activities brought new contacts to West Africa, drawing the region into a European-dominated world economic network and away from traditional trade routes across the Sahara to North Africa. The presence of Western trading stations on the coast also had an effect on some urban Africans, leading to a limited number of conversions to Christianity.

West Africa was more specifically and deeply affected by the growing Atlantic slave trade, which began in the 16th century but intensified greatly after about 1650. West African slaves were purchased by sea captains from Holland, Britain, and particularly France, to be sold in the North and South American colonies and the West Indies. Slavery was not new to this region of Africa, as many states had held troops captured in battle as slaves. But the European demand transformed a traditional practice beyond recognition. Between 1500 and the end of the slave trade in the 19th century, as many as 12 million Africans may have been taken away as slaves. This exodus, one of the greatest and most terrible forced movements of peoples in human history, devastated some regions of West Africa, which lost population rapidly and found it difficult, in the absence of sufficient younger workers, to maintain traditional economic levels. But some West African states profited from the slave trade, at least in the short run. The actual capture and sale of slaves to European merchant sailors was almost always handled by African agents, who traded slaves for guns, gold, and other goods. One new, unusually centralized state, the Fon kingdom of the 18th century, organized all its dealings with Europeans in a single spot, to minimize contact between Europeans and inland Africans. The state carefully regulated and taxed the slave trade, controlling the import of firearms and ammunition.

Thus the impact of the massive slave trade on West Africa was mixed, and not simply the result of unchallenged European profiteering. (Though there were huge profits to be made from the exchange, even after paying the African agents; this was one source of rising merchant wealth in Western Europe.) Many parts of West Africa came to depend on the slave trade for their own economies. But damage was done. African birth rates grew

Origins of 18th-Century Slave Trade

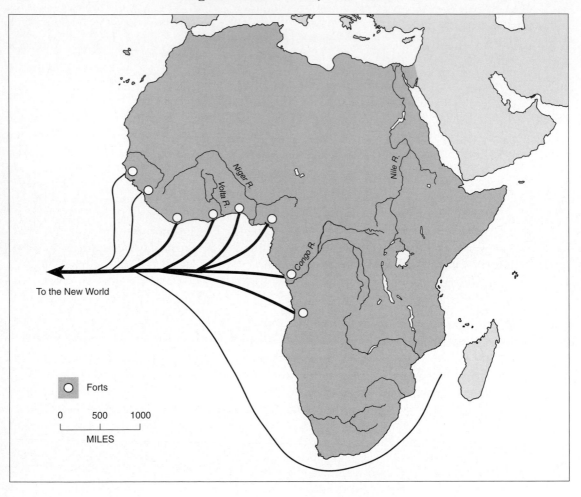

more slowly than those of most other societies through the 19th century, in part as a result of sheer population loss. Economic development was surely retarded, though it is hard to say exactly how much change would have come had the slave trade not interfered. In addition, relations among West African kingdoms grew more warlike and chaotic, as various states armed to gain slaves, others to try to prevent raids. Destabilization was not complete, and again there was variety, depending on how a given kingdom handled negotiations; indeed, some West African kingdoms deliberately stayed out of the trade altogether. But there is no question about the serious impact on West African history for more than two centuries.

And there was no question about the results to the slaves themselves:

As the slaves come down . . . from the inland country, they are put into a booth or prison, built for that purpose near the beach, all of them together; and when the Europeans are to re-

BIOGRAPHY

OLANDAH EQUIANO

Olandah Equiano was one of the rare Africans taken in slavery and able, later, to write about his experiences. He was born in a Nigerian village, Isseke, in 1745, to a wealthy, slave-owning family. He was kidnapped and in 1756 taken to Barbados and then to Virginia. Finally able to buy his freedom from a Quaker master, he went to England in 1767. By this point he was both literate and well read. He became active in the antislavery movement, publishing his memoirs in 1788 as a protest against the whole institution of slavery. He poignantly described his desperate feelings when he and his sister were tied up and put in sacks, and then separated from each other. He detailed the greater brutality of European slave shippers, compared to his initial African captors, and the massive disorientation of being mixed with strangers and sent to an unknown land with no chance of return. This account was one of the first entries in a wave of literature by former slaves and a growing movement against the system on both sides of the Atlantic.

ceive them, they are brought out into a large plain, where the ships' surgeons examine every part of every one of them. . . . Such as are allowed good and sound are set on one side, and the others by themselves; these rejected slaves are called Makrons, being above 35 years of age, or defective in their lips, eyes or teeth, or grown grey. . . . Each of the others passed as good is marked on the breast with a red-hot iron, imprinting the mark of the French, English, or Dutch companies so that each nation may distinguish their own property. . . .

And then, after a week or so, the voyage across the Atlantic began, a terrifying, foul experience in which as many as half the slaves would die. For the survivors, a life of servitude in a strange land was the reward.

Slave trading also disrupted another part of the western coast, in the territory of Angola, which came under increasing Portuguese control. The Portuguese, initially interested in precious metals, soon concentrated on slaves for Brazil. Ruling Angola outright, through the agency of corrupt local officials, they produced growing chaos in this region for centuries. Here, in contrast to the picture farther north in present-day countries like Nigeria, there was no question of some compensatory benefits from the European quest for slaves; Angola simply suffered.

Finally, the southern end of Africa was affected strongly by European penetration. Holland planted a small colony on the Cape of Good Hope in 1652, to help supply its ships bound for Asia. This community of *Boers* (the Dutch word for farmers) soon escaped Dutch control, fanning out on large farms in a region still lightly populated by Africans.

The Boers clashed with local hunting groups, enslaving some of them. Later, after 1770, they came into increasing contact with Bantu farmers, opening a long battle for control of the region that still affects the nation of South Africa today.

European influence on African history between 1450 and 1800 was thus intense but, in the main, regional. It set new forces in motion in southern Africa and Angola, and strongly affected the economic and political life of West Africa without, however, overturning all previous patterns.

Other parts of Africa were scarcely affected by the West during these centuries. Ethiopia, though Christian and in some contact with Portuguese missionaries, remained aloof. East Africa had little to do with Europeans; here, trading patterns were still oriented toward the Middle East, and both Africans and Arab traders pushed into the interior in search of agricultural products and slaves. The slave trade to the Middle East and North Africa also expanded in the early modern period; totalling perhaps three million people, it remained more modest than its Atlantic counterpart.

Overall, the patterns of African culture remained much as before. Politically, most of the continent was organized in regional kingdoms, with rulers who allied with local leaders and operated in the style of divine kingship. Most Africans remained polytheistic, though Islam was a potent force in the Sudan region. Late in the 18th century, conversions to Islam began to increase in this area, as the religion became a popular force and not simply an elite badge. Scholars like Usuman dan Fodio (1754–1818) argued against the traditional policy of living tolerantly alongside nonbelievers. Usuman and his followers, active in Muslim scholarship and law, conducted several holy wars in the western Sudan, winning over many ordinary people and producing a number of well-organized new states.

In another continuing trend, Bantu migration southward persisted. This movement, as noted, would bring Bantus into conflict with Dutch settlers. The severe crowding it produced in Bantu lands by around 1800 prompted Bantus to begin to organize into more coherent political units.

Finally, while African economic life was deeply affected by European trade at least in some key regions, there was no massive change in economic forms or technologies on the continent overall. Europeans did bring in corn seeds from the New World, which were adopted by many African farmers and thereafter used as a staple food. But, perhaps because of the slave trade, the crop did not produce significant population increase at this point; indeed, relative to world population growth, the African share actually fell.

In sum, major changes occurred in Africa between 1450 and 1800. Some of these changes were of European origin or represented African reaction to European contacts, but others were quite distinct, resulting from Islam or Bantu migration. No single force mobilized more than individual regions of the continent; and, beneath the surface, important traditional patterns of politics, art, belief, and social organization largely persisted.

COLONIZATION IN LATIN AMERICA: THE BIRTH OF A NEW CIVILIZATION

European impact on the Americas was far more massive than that in Africa: here, the Europeans began to alter basic patterns as early as the 16th and 17th centuries, creating a new civilization in Latin America and extending Western civilization to the eastern seaboard colonies of North America. The natives' lack of iron weapons and their devastating vulnerability to disease created a context far different from Africa. African independence long contrasted with the spreading European colonies in the Americas. The colonization process, of course, also brought the Americas into the mainstream world history and linked the two continents to the emerging world economy on conditions set mainly by the Europeans themselves.

In Central and South America and the West Indies, Spanish efforts to follow up exploration with outright conquests began early in the 16th century. The chief goals were God and gold: the Spanish hoped to tap what they believed was the vast wealth of the new lands—their appetites whetted by the rich ornaments they encountered among groups like the Aztecs and by a taste for myth; and, as the most powerful Catholic state, soon heavily influenced by the active Jesuit order, they planned to win new converts to Christianity. Expeditions occupied leading West Indian islands, including Cuba, starting in 1519. Soon after this, a small army under Hernán Cortés conquered Mexico from the Aztecs. While pockets of American Indian resistance remained in parts of Central America until the later 17th century, Spanish control was essentially complete by 1550. By this point the empire extended loosely into parts of what are now the southern and southwestern United States.

From their colony in Panama, the Spanish moved into South America. They took over the northern part of the continent fairly easily, against loosely organized American Indian cultures. In 1531 an expedition attacked the Inca empire, having heard of the treasures to be won there. Hard fighting was necessary to seize Peru, but the Spanish commander, Pizarro, ultimately prevailed. From this base, other missions extended along the Andes mountain chain, finding the Amazon River and seeking the silver mines of Bolivia. Spanish expeditions also moved into Argentina, founding a settlement in Buenos Aires in 1536. Only at the end of the 16th century, however, did the Spanish really begin to colonize Argentina, introducing cattle raising and other forms of agriculture once the thirst for quick riches had somewhat abated. Finally, early in the 17th century the Portuguese began to move in from small coastal settlements in Brazil, to take effective hold of much of the vast interior territory.

The conquest of Latin America, complete in outline during the 17th century, was amazingly swift. This was no well-coordinated, carefully planned venture. Many expeditions, such as Pizarro's against Peru, were essentially mounted by groups of adventurers or private merchants. And all the campaigns, even those sponsored by Spanish government representatives, were small. How did they win such a vast territory so easily?

Superior technology was of course a key. The Indians lacked not only guns and cannons but also horses and metal weapons of any sort. The Europeans also profited from civil wars and dissent within Indian ranks. Hostility to the Aztecs provided Cortés with many Indian allies at first. The Inca empire was weakened by internal warfare shortly before Pizarro's arrival. Trickery played a role: many Spanish commanders initially negotiated treaties with Inca, Aztec, and other leaders, only to violate the agreements at the earliest opportunity, often putting their erstwhile allies to death. And the hold of the Europeans was not at first thorough. Many Indian villages were left untouched by Spanish or Portuguese presence for decades; many local Indian leaders were given considerable autonomy so long as they pledged loyalty to the new colonial government.

Yet, in scarcely more than a century, the Spanish had decapitated the leading American Indian civilizations, destroying their political structures and trampling their formal cultures. Their task was aided not only by their desire to impose "civilization" on non-Christian peoples, but also by the diseases, particularly smallpox, that they brought with them. Indians, so long isolated, had no resistance to these scourges. The result resembled plague impacts at the end of the classical and postclassical periods in Eurasia, but it was even worse. Within less than a century 90 percent of the Mexican population had been wiped out; entire populations on the West Indian islands vanished. Overall, as has been noted, 80 percent of the previous Indian population of North and South America would die off as a result of disease. Here was a great vacuum, which the Europeans increasingly tried to fill.

LATIN AMERICAN CIVILIZATION

After the conquest period, the Spanish and Portuguese settled down to the construction of new political and religious institutions and a new economic framework for their vast colonies. The result, during the 17th and 18th centuries, was essentially a formative period for a new, Latin American civilization, closely tied to Europe but also distinct in significant ways.

Politically, this new civilization was characterized by the rule imposed from the outside by the monarchies of Spain and Portugal. European-born men held virtually all of the administrative positions, in what became substantial bureaucracies. Two main provinces were created, called "viceroyalties"—one administered from Mexico, the other from Peru; later, the huge South American holding was further divided, with new centers in Argentina and Colombia. In theory, this governmental system was highly centralized. In fact, the territories were much too vast for effective central control, which meant that church leaders, estate owners, and villagers had considerable latitude. Latin America would long be characterized by a gap between seemingly strong political authority and the actual weakness of the state in relation to local regions and to institutions like village and hacienda.

One result of the gap between government claims and the reality of very loose state control was a sense that government power ought to be increased, that this was the chief problem in Latin American society. Even in the 18th century, Spanish colonial administration tried to expand its authority, and the quest would continue in the 19th and 20th centuries as well. A second result was that the centralized system, however superficial in reality, prevented much participation in the new society, as most colonials were firmly barred from governmental activity. Spain further tightened the monopoly of Spanish-born appointees in the later 18th century, producing new grievances among the native-born creoles.

Culturally, the leading feature of the new society was a fervent and pervasive Catholicism. Far more than the Spanish and Portuguese governments, the Jesuits and other missionaries moved actively among the common people, working hard to extirpate earlier Indian religions and replace them with Christianity. Many Indian groups long remained isolated from this effort, but there was steady change. Mission schools, an exten-

Latin America by the 18th Century

sive network of local churches, and destruction of American Indian culture soon produced measurable results. The power and success of the new conquerors helped make the missionaries persuasive. But they also offered a gentler religion with greater sympathy for ordinary people than any of the religions the Indian civilizations of South and Central

America had developed. While American Indians resented the abolition of many ceremonies, and even maintained some in secret, the elimination of human sacrifice and the power of the earlier priestly castes may have been welcomed by many. And there were many opportunities for syncretism. Many Indians blended some earlier gods or goddesses with Catholic saints, thus helping to cushion change while producing a lively and distinctive religious art.

The Europeans also sought to introduce some features of their wider culture. Major cathedrals were built in Spanish Baroque style, and public buildings also followed European architectural models. Cities were established as islands of European order, picking up on the traditional belief in urban life the Spanish inherited from the Romans and Arabs. Gridlike streets radiated out from a central plaza, which was graced by a major church and a government building and jail. But Westernized artistic culture was not yet advanced. Spanish-style religious paintings were attempted, but they could not match the vigor of Christianized Indian or mestizo designs. Literature was virtually nonexistent, as

Franciscan mission cloister in Brazil.

the Spanish authorities discouraged printing save in a few centers. Furthermore, American Indian artistic forms continued to survive, in pottery and textile design. This was not high art, but it maintained an important diversity in Latin American culture that would have fuller effects in the future. Outside of the extension of Catholicism, then, Latin American culture was clearly in a formative stage but showed signs of some differentiation from purely European models.

Two kinds of economic activity coexisted in this early period of Latin American history. First, many Indians and *mestizos*—people of mixed Spanish and Indian ancestry—operated in a village or small-town economy, producing corn and other foods for largely local needs. The economic life of many Indian villages, with their communal ownership of the land, was virtually undisturbed—for while the Spanish eliminated the leading institutions of American Indian society, they did not cut off the feet.

Along with this local village structure was an economy geared for export, and specifically for the profit of the Spanish and Portuguese. This economy involved mining operations, particularly in the Andes region, where 16,000 tons of silver were pumped out for Europe by the year 1650.

The market economy also promoted large landed estates set up by the Spaniards or by creoles—Europeans born in the new land. The Spanish did not attempt to enslave many Indians, partly because of fierce resistance and partly because Catholic leaders, eager to protect their new converts, opposed such policy. But they did set up a network of large estates. As Indians died of European diseases, land was left vacant and was often seized by mestizos or Spaniards, who gained government authorization of ownership. At first it seemed that the original Spanish conquerors might become a feudal nobility, but the Spanish government, aware of the importance of more central control, resisted this pattern save in a few areas. Nevertheless, many large estates resulted from land grants and seizures, particularly when a brief effort at direct governmental distribution of Indian labor failed. Estate owners worked hard to command labor resources, increasingly scarce as the Indian population shrank. An early form of labor control, not necessarily attached to a single estate, was the *encomienda*, where the Spanish or creole grantee was given rights over a certain percentage of Indian labor. This was one source of the labor used in silver and mercury mines in the Andes region; at its height labor drafts generated 13,000 workers a year for the leading mine. More common still was the *hacienda*, a large estate on which a number of Indian villages were granted to a Spaniard, often one of the initial conquerors. Village inhabitants on the hacienda were required to pay tribute in goods (food and textiles) plus providing labor service. This system, which after a generation or two turned into effective ownership of the village lands, closely resembled the harsher forms of earlier European serfdom; the landlord provided some protection and a court system for his villagers, in return for payments in kind and almost absolute control over the farmers. Finally, in a few cases estate owners hired low-paid Indian or mestizo laborers, who were encouraged to go into debt and officially forbidden to leave until often impossible sums were paid off—again, a means of attempting to reduce rural freedom to deal with the twin realities of labor shortage and market opportunity.

Haciendas and the other estate forms did not, for the most part, produce for the export trade directly. But they did yield grains and meats that were sold to mining centers and the growing populations of port cities and administrative capitals like Mexico City.

The Portuguese Baroque style of architecture was used frequently in South America: San Francisco church in Salvador de Bahia, Brazil.

Thus a vigorous Latin American market agriculture developed, but on the basis of low-paid or servile labor under effective landlord control.

A somewhat different version of estate agriculture arose in the West Indies and some parts of the South American continent, particularly Brazil. Here the crops produced—tobacco and especially sugar—were intended for sale in Europe. These estates used hundreds of thousands of black slaves imported from Africa, initially in part because local labor was so scarce as a result of disease. Three times as many Africans were brought to Latin America and the Caribbean as to North America. Not only Spanish and Portuguese holdings, but also British, French, and Dutch West Indian islands developed this slave-holding system. This was a slave-based economy on a scale never before known, the result of the commercial opportunities and appetites of the new global economy.

Latin America thus quickly developed an economy dependent on a world market, for which it produced agricultural and mining products; additional specialized commercial farming supplied the mining and governmental centers. Relatively little manufacturing was undertaken, save for local needs; most elaborate manufactured products and craft items were imported from Europe. Here was the rawest case in which European intrusion produced a dependent economy. Latin American landowners could reap tidy profits from their sales on the market, but they relied for their success on a low-paid, fully or partially unfree, labor force.

Strong social gradations followed from this economic pattern, and they were enhanced by racial divisions. Spanish and Portuguese settlers were much less firmly racist

Indians in South America work gold and silver for the Spaniards: 16th century woodcuts.

than their English counterparts to the north. But Latin American society was rather firmly split between a minority of political officials, mine owners, and landlords, and the majority of impoverished workers. The owning classes were European-born or creole; the masses were Indian, black, and—the largest group overall—mestizo. There were of course some local merchants and shopkeepers, but the size of this middling group was small. Almost all the European trade was handled by the Europeans themselves.

Colonization and economic change inevitably affected gender relations. Though European officials tried to discourage intermarriage, the fact that most colonists and imported slaves were male inevitably encouraged sexual unions with American Indian women. Indian family arrangements were often disrupted, and the growth of the mestizo population accelerated. Marriage among African slaves was often forbidden — for example, in Brazil — which led to an additional set of sexual patterns.

As agriculture spread, based on local crops and also crops and animals introduced from Europe (cattle, sheep, rice, wheat), the Latin American population began to grow, despite the shock effects of disease among the Indians. Prosperity increased also, during the 18th century, and many creole owners became wealthy. But resentment grew as well. Spanish and Portuguese policies were designed to keep Latin America subservient, and in the 18th century would-be enlightened despots in both countries tightened controls over the colonies. The colonial administrations imposed heavy taxes on Latin American trade and limited this trade to a few ports and a handful of privileged companies. Contact with the more advanced economies of northern Europe was banned, though in fact some illegal trade developed, particularly with Britain, which was in fact allowed to import slaves. Latin Americans grew increasingly restive under these limitations and also because of their exclusion from political rule. Many creoles traveled in Europe and learned of the new political theories of the Enlightenment. In Colombia and other centers, some new kinds of intellectual activity arose, as scientific discoveries and reform ideas were discussed. This intellectual ferment was modest, confined mainly to cities and to creoles; but, added to the other, more widespread grievances, it set the base for a series of wars of independence that produced the first massive slave revolt in Haiti, in 1798, and then swept across virtually the entire society between 1808 and 1820.

By the 18th century, a Latin American civilization was taking shape on the basis of ongoing popular traditions among many Indian peoples, new political, cultural, and technological influences from Europe, and the special conditions of the colonial economy and government. The civilization depended heavily on European models but it was not identical to Europe. Racial diversity, slavery and the estate systems, the nature of the export economy, and popular cultural mixture with Catholicism set it apart; so did the combination of wide governmental claims with limited actual authority over local conditions. Latin American civilization, still new, was also capable of important change. New cultural products, a more vigorous internal economy, and creole contacts with the European Enlightenment all displayed the power of innovation during the 18th century itself. So, in a different way, did a new series of Indian risings in the Andes region, toward the end of the century, with leaders combining novel political demands with references to the Inca heritage.

WESTERN CIVILIZATION IN NORTH AMERICA

French colonial holdings in Canada and along the Mississippi River, though vast on paper, were only lightly administered. Important French settlements were set up only in parts of Canada. The French were far more interested in their West Indian islands, which produced so profitably for the European market. From North America they gained only some fur trade and some leverage against Britain's growing empire.

The British colonies along the eastern seaboard, however, were another matter. By the 18th century, three million European settlers had established themselves in these colonies, and a large number of African slaves had been imported as well. In the southern colonies a slave-holding estate system developed—producing rice, sugar, tobacco, and dyes—that in many ways resembled the system of the West Indies and of Brazil. Britain imposed some of the same limitations on all the colonies that Spain established for its Latin American holdings. Governors were appointed from Britain; taxes were high; manufacturing was discouraged as the British sought to protect their markets in the colonies and gain cheap raw materials and foodstuffs.

Yet the society that developed in the British colonies was far closer to Western European forms than was that of Latin America. The colonies operated their own assemblies, which provided considerable political experience; local town governments were also ac-

Sor Inès de la Cruz (1651–1695) was one of the unusual women in premodern world history who broke through to public prominence on the basis of her personal intellectual qualities and piety. Author, poet, musician, and social thinker, she was welcome at the viceroy's court in Mexico City. She represented the growing attempt to produce a European-style and heavily Catholic culture in the new Latin American civilization. Like many Christian thinkers before her, she ultimately gave up her wider interests, at the urging of her religious superiors, to concentrate on purely spiritual matters. Why did religion give some women a chance to rise in early modern world history? Were colonial conditions in the Americas more or less favorable to women in public life than to those in most settled societies?

tive. Despite British regulations, a substantial manufacturing economy developed, and the North Americans ran extensive trading companies and merchant shipping. North American products were less interesting to Western Europe than were those of Latin America and the West Indies. The southern colonies, to be sure, produced tobacco and later cotton, using unfree labor, which served as leading exports. And southern planters imported expensive craft products from Europe. Here was a dependent economy quite similar to that of Latin America. But in New England and the Middle Atlantic colonies, aside from some furs and woods, there were no natural resources of great interest in the early modern world economy. So these colonies were left free to develop their own localized agriculture and also their own trading patterns, including merchant shipping and local manufactures based on family businesses and wage labor. Britain did try to impose more characteristic dependency with new regulations and taxes in the 1760s, but by this point it was too late; the colonial economy was not as advanced as that of Western Europe, but it had a somewhat similar range of activities, including growing merchant zeal.

The North American colonists' intellectual contacts with Europe were also vigorous. North America was closer to Europe than Latin America was. The tie with Britain gave North Americans access to one of the most dynamic centers of political theory and scientific inquiry in the Western world. Hundreds of North Americans during the 18th century contributed scientific findings to the British Royal Society, and discussion groups among American intellectuals were active as well. North American literacy rates were quite high, which encouraged participation in European-derived intellectual life. In contrast, Latin America's ties to Spain, where Enlightenment activity was more modest, limited its access to the new intellectual currents of Western civilization.

British, and to an extent French, North America thus grew up less as a separate culture than as part of Western civilization. There were vital differences, of course. The North American colonies did not produce a full aristocracy, of the sort that still dominated West European society; this fact gave freer rein to the values of merchant groups and free farmers. Colonial governments were also weak, by European standards, with few functions beyond defense and a rudimentary system of law courts. North American family patterns were somewhat distinctive. Blessed with more abundant land, North Americans had higher birth rates than their European counterparts during the 17th and 18th centuries. They treated children with greater care; thus the practice of swaddling children was less common in British North America. Americans placed somewhat greater emotional reliance on the family, because of the strangeness of their surroundings. Most important of all, the North American colonies did have a slave-holding system that, though concentrated particularly in the South, would strongly affect the history of the whole region—even after slavery was finally abolished.

North Americans were conscious of their distinctiveness. They lacked Europe's elaborate art and great cities, though by the 18th century imitation of European artistic forms was well under way. They felt somewhat inferior to Europe, but rejoiced in what they saw as a greater freedom (slavery aside) and a more youthful vigor. But the habit of copying Europe remained strong as well. In fact, the British colonies were sufficiently similar to Europe that the course of their history would closely resemble that of the rest of the expanded Western world. Even when the colonies rebelled, in 1776, they did so in the name of Western political ideals and proceeded to establish a government that, though it maintained some distinctive features, remained clearly within the range of Western political values.

NORTH AND SOUTH AMERICA: REASONS FOR THE DIFFERENCES

Western penetration of the Americas from 1450 to 1800 thus had two leading results. It created an important though distinctive version of Western civilization in North America. It created an essentially new civilization, though one with unusually close ties to Western patterns, in South and Central America and in Mexico. Because of its size and economic role, Latin American civilization was by far the more important in world history during the early modern period.

How and why did these two outcomes differ? Part of the distinction rests with differences between Spain and Portugal, on the one hand, and Britain and northern Europe, on the other. Spain was an intensely Catholic country, with a fervent missionary impulse, but it was somewhat removed, particularly after 1600, from the mainstream of European intellectual life. Spain lacked a substantial merchant class of its own, which contributed to the Latin American emphasis on landed estates rather than elaborate commerce. Spain's impulse toward claiming centralized control discouraged extensive political life in

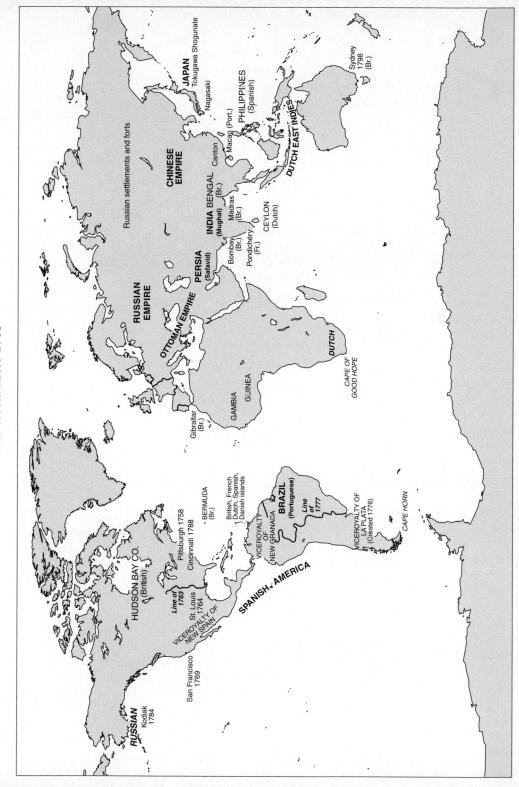

The World After 1763

RUSSIAN EMPIRE

CHINESE EMPIRE

JAPAN
Tokugawa Shogunate
Nagasaki

Russian settlements and forts

OTTOMAN EMPIRE

PERSIA
(Safavid)

INDIA BENGAL
(Mughal) (Br.)

Bombay
(Br.)

Madras
(Br.)

Pondichéry
(Fr.)

Canton

Macao (Port.)

PHILIPPINES
(Spanish)

CEYLON
(Dutch)

DUTCH EAST INDIES

Sydney
1798
(Br.)

Gibraltar
(Br.)

GAMBIA

GUINEA

DUTCH

CAPE OF
GOOD HOPE

HUDSON BAY CO.
(British)

Line of
1763

St. Louis
1764

Pittsburgh 1758

Cincinnati 1788

BERMUDA
(Br.)

British, French,
Dutch, Spanish,
Danish Islands

VICEROYALTY OF
NEW SPAIN

San Francisco
1769

RUSSIAN
Kodiak
1784

SPANISH AMERICA

VICEROYALTY
OF
NEW GRANADA

BRAZIL
(Portuguese)

Line
of
1777

VICEROYALTY OF
LA PLATA
(Created 1776)

CAPE HORN

the new colonies. Latin American civilization, though still not fully formed, thus emerged with a political tradition, an economy, and a social structure quite different from what was to become its northern neighbor.

Latin America also developed a different racial balance from that of the English colonies. Disease decimated the American Indian population everywhere, but because of their prior size substantial concentrations persisted in Latin America. North American Indians were also less fully organized into agricultural societies and they were more easily forced to move. The Indian role in the ultimate culture and social structure of North America was not great. In Latin America, in contrast, though particularly in Central America and the Andes region, the values and labor contributions of a sizable Indian group played an ongoing role. The rise of a large mestizo population, virtually unknown in the more racially conscious English colonies, added to the differentiation. Latin American civilization resulted in part from a fusion of Western and Indian peoples and social forms; it also had a much larger African slave contingent. North America saw a much more straightforward extension of Western values over small, often badly treated and segregated Indian and African minorities.

From these early differentiations, Latin America and what became the United States and Canada were to follow largely different historical rhythms. To be sure, struggles for independence occurred almost simultaneously. The North American colonies (apart from Canada) rose first, and most of Latin America, inspired in part by this very example, soon followed. But from these wars came quite different results, in the political features of the new nations and in their economic base, as the new United States quickly joined Western Europe in industrialization, while Latin America remained in its more dependent position in the world economy.

CONCLUSION: THE WORLD ECONOMY REVISITED

Like all major developments in human history, the rise of the Western-dominated world economy brought gains and losses. It tended to increase economic inequalities among civilizations. Latin America and major parts of Africa, drawn into the world economy as producers of largely unprocessed goods that depended on cheap or slave labor, had scant reason for rejoicing, though individuals in each society profited along with the Europeans. Furthermore, the inequalities of the world economy tended to be self-perpetuating. In some basic respects, Africa and Latin America remain dependent economies to this day, unable to control their own economic destinies; and in many respects the West continues to benefit from this relationship. Only the English colonies of North America, on the fringe of dependency into the 18th century, managed fully to break away and become part of the dominant economy of the West.

The world economy also, however, unleashed a new profit motive, through the spread of commercial capitalism. This motive, though capable of great exploitation, also supported technological innovation as another means of increasing production at low cost. Before long this thirst, backed by the capital already earned in world trade, would produce vast changes in methods of manufacture, which in turn brought some measurable benefits even beyond Western society.

Before this occurred, however, other civilizations in the world, not fully caught up in the world economy but touched by it, had to define their own relationship to the West and to the new patterns of trade. Some, like China and the Middle East, were no strangers to commercial capitalism, though they had not before encountered it on such a scale. Because of previous economic and technological strength, because of strong political structures and a sense of distinctive values, most of Asian and Eastern Europe remained partly external to the world economy into the 18th century, participating in it to a degree but not engulfed by it. But they, too, faced the prospect of change, even if they resolved to remain stable.

SUGGESTED READINGS

Excellent discussions of Western exploration and expansion are C. M. Cippolla, *Guns, Sails and Empires* (1985), and J. H. Parry, *The Discovery of South America* (1979). Important recent work includes Alan K. Smith, *Creating a World Economy: Merchant Capital Colonization and World Trade, 1400–1825* (1991); Michael Pearson, *Port Cities and Intruders: The Swahili Coast, India, and Portugal in the Early Modern Era* (1998); and James Tracy, ed., *The Rise of Merchant Empires* (1990), and *The Political Economy of Merchant Empires* (1991). See also C. R. Boxer, *Four Centuries of Portuguese Expansion* (1969); W. Dorn, *The Competition for Empire* (1963); Alfred Crosby, *The Columbian Exchange: Biological and Cultural Consequences of 1492* (1972); C. A. Bayh, *Indian Society and The Making of the British Empire* (1988) ; and D. K. Fieldhouse, *The Colonial Empires* (1971). See also J. H. Elliott, *The Old World and the New, 1492–1650* (1970), and J. K. Thornton, *Africa and the Africans in the Making of the Atlantic World, 1400–1800* (1997).

On Latin America, consult: James Lockhart and Stuart B. Schwartz, *Early Latin America* (1982); Lyle N. Macalister, *Spain and Portugal in the New World* (1984); Eric Williams, *Capitalism and Slavery* (1964); J. Fagg, *Latin America* (1969); S. J. Stein and B. H. Stein, *The Colonial Heritage of Latin America* (1970); and A. Lavin, ed., *Sexuality and Marriage in Colonial Latin America* (1989).

On the slave system, O. Patterson, *Slavery and Social Death: A Comparative Study* (1982), and D. B. Davis, *Slavery and Human Progress* (1984), are both useful. On other key topics, consult: Nancy Farriss, *Maya Society under Colonial Rule* (1984); Louisa Schell Hoberman and Susan Migden Socolow, eds., *Cities and Society in Colonial Latin America* (1986); and Stuart Schwartz, *Sugar Plantations and the Formation of Brazilian Society* (1985). On the slave trade, see: James Rawley, *The Transatlantic Slave Trade* (1981); Roger Anstey, *The Atlantic Slave Trade and British Abolition* (1975); Paul Lovejoy, *Transformations in Slavery: A History of Slavery in Africa* (1983); Patrick Manning, *Slavery and African Life* (1990); and Joseph Miller, *Way of Death* (1989).

Readable texts on the West and Asia and Africa include: Paul Bohannan and Philip Curtin, *Africa and Africans,* 3d ed., (1988); Martin Hall, *The Changing Past: Farmers, Kings, and Traders in Southern Africa* (1987); Leonard Thompson, *A History of South Africa* (1990); A. Hyma, *The Dutch in the Far East: A History of the Dutch Commercial and Colo-*

nial Empire (1942); and S. D. Pen, *The French in India* (1958). See also K. N. N. Chaudori, *Trade and Civilization in the Indian Ocean* (1985). A provocative though controversial overview of the development of a new global economy is Immanuel Wallerstein's *The Modern World System*, 2 vols. (1980). For source reading, see P. Curtin, ed., *Africa Remembered: Narratives by West Africans from the Era of the Slave Trade* (1967). On colonial North America, see Jack Greene and J. R. Pole, eds., *Colonial British America: Essays on the New History of the Early Modern Era* (1984).

The Rise of Eastern Europe

Focal Points

Russia both expanded territorially and changed greatly during the early modern centuries. What were the main directions of change? How was Russia's position different in 1750 from its position in 1450? Russia developed new contacts with the rest of Europe during this period, but only some of its changes moved in directions similar to those of the West. What aspects of Russian society remained distinctive, and why? Russia should be compared to other societies also. Like the Ottoman and Mughal empires, discussed in Chapter 17, Russia developed a new multinational state in this modern period. Why was it relatively more successful than its counterparts in creating a more durable land-based empire?

FACTORS IN RUSSIA'S EARLY MODERN SURGE

Along with Africa and the Americas, Russia and Eastern Europe were dramatically affected by the rise of the West during the early modern period. By the 18th century, some smaller regions, such as Poland, produced cheap grains for export to the West on the basis of serf labor in a fashion not unlike the economy of Latin America. The Russian story was different, however. In contrast to the Americas, where local populations had little choice, Russian leaders deliberately chose to imitate certain Western ways. This pattern began haltingly in the 16th century and then accelerated in the 18th. Explicit choice did not preclude important tensions as the Russian economy encountered more Western influence and as cultural reactions followed efforts to imitate. But Russia's relation to the West was distinctive.

One reason for the distinctiveness lay in a new expansionary trend, launched in the 15th century, that initially had nothing to do with the West. Russia's dynamism increased long before it had significant contacts with the West. The West was later courted, though very selectively, to help maintain the expansionary thrust—again, a combination different from the forced Western impact on the Americas or, as we will see, from the more hesitant responses in most of Asia.

What causes a civilization to rise? The question, now a familiar one, remains complex. Western civilization expanded on the base of a diverse but distinctive culture, which produced an aggressive, conquering spirit and a rapidly improving technology. Russia's case, coincident in time, was different. Shaking off Mongol domination, the Russians embarked on a policy of conquest without a major technological spur. The twin themes of Western ascendancy and Russian growth describe important patterns in world history between 1480 and 1800; these currents would become even more important in the 19th and 20th centuries. They contrasted with the more traditional framework of most other civilizations, including the great societies of eastern and southern Asia, during the early modern period.

Russia shared some expansionist ingredients with the West. Both might look back to the precedent of the Roman Empire as an example of what societies could do when they are truly great. Both were Christian, and though the Russian missionary spirit was less active than that of the West, Christianity may help explain a common desire to reach out for new victories. But Russia long lagged behind the West technologically; it remained backward by Western standards into the 20th century. It lacked the merchant tradition or commercial expertise of the West; indeed, Russia during the early modern period depended considerably on Western-directed trade patterns. In these respects, Russian differences from the West increased in the early modern period.

Russia did have a large and gradually growing population. It occupied a strategic geographical location, hovering between Europe and Asia, surrounded, save on the north, by few natural barriers. This position made it vulnerable to invasion, as the Mongols had proved, but it also facilitated expansion when the Russians decided to follow the Mongol example. Russia also embraced some excellent natural resources though climate placed some limits on agriculture. Russia's iron ore spurred manufacturing and weaponry. Furs and timber could be traded not only with the West but also with Asia, which helped feed expansion.

The early modern period saw an elaboration of characteristic Russian social and political institutions. Earlier, Russian civilization had been barely sketched. Now, building on many precedents, it became more fully formed. And it became much more important, as the Russians constructed one of the world's great empires.

PATTERNS OF EARLY MODERN RUSSIAN HISTORY

Russia's emergence as a new power, first in Eastern Europe and western Asia and ultimately on a still larger scale, depended initially on gaining freedom from Mongol (Tatar) control. Mongol influence had not reshaped Russian institutions substantially, though many Russians had adopted Mongol styles of dress and social habits. Most Russians remained Orthodox Christians; and most of them readily recalled a separate identity from the Mongols. Moreover, local Russian princes had continued to rule, though paying tribute to the Mongol military overlords. It was the duchy of Moscow that served as the center for the Russian liberation effort, beginning in the 14th century. Under Ivan III, or Ivan the Great, who claimed succession from the Rurik dynasty, a large part of Russia was finally freed after 1462. Ivan organized a strong army—giving the new government a military emphasis it would long retain. He also used Russian and Orthodox loyalties—that is, a kind of nationalism along with religion—to win support for his campaigns. By 1480,

Moscow had been freed from payment to the Mongols and had gained a vast territory running from the borders of Poland, in the west, to the Ural mountains.

It was under Ivan that Russian beliefs in an imperial mission took on new shape. Ivan's marriage to the niece of the last Byzantine emperor gave him the chance to claim himself the protector over all Orthodox churches and also to insist that Russia had succeeded Byzantium as the "third Rome." Ivan accordingly entitled himself tsar, or Caesar—the "autocrat of all the Russians." The next important tsar Ivan IV, or Ivan the Terrible, attacked the Russian nobles whom he suspected of conspiracy; many were killed. But Russian expansion continued nevertheless. Ivan III and Ivan IV encouraged some peasants to migrate to the lands seized from the Mongols and other groups, particularly in the south, along the Caspian Sea, and in the Urals. These peasant-adventurers, called Cossacks, were true Russian pioneers, combining agriculture with daring military feats on horseback. During the 16th century the Cossacks not only completed the conquest of the Caspian Sea area but also, early in the century, moved across the Ural Mountains into Siberia, beginning the gradual takeover and settlement of these vast plains.

Russian expansion occurred despite the setbacks the Russian economy and culture had suffered under Mongol rule. Russia had become almost entirely agricultural, its earlier urban and merchant past largely forgotten. There was little trade and only localized manufacturing; though some commerce developed with Central Asia, creating regional economic ties, subsistence agriculture predominated. Not only peasants but also many landlords lived in poor material conditions. Rates of illiteracy were unusually high for an agricultural society, and artistic and literary production had almost ceased. In this situation, Russia was open to some new influences from Western Europe, with its expanding commercial apparatus. Ivan III had been eager to launch diplomatic missions to leading Western states as an emblem of Russia's renewed independence and a sign that it wanted contact with the Western network of international relations. During the reign of Ivan IV, British merchants established trading relations with Russia, selling manufactured products in exchange for furs and raw materials. Soon, outposts of Western merchants were established in Moscow and other centers.

Ivan IV's death without an heir set off the Time of Troubles, early in the 17th century, in which Russian nobles, the boyars, attacked tsarist power; several neighboring states, including Sweden and Poland, captured Russian territory. But in 1613 a noble assembly chose a member of the Romanov family as tsar; this family would rule Russia until the great revolution of 1917. Michael Romanov drove out the foreign invaders and restored order, though the power of the nobles limited the tsarist government until late in the 17th century. Even amid some confusion, however, Russian military efforts continued; successful wars against Poland won Russia part of the Ukraine, including Kiev, and stretched the Russian boundaries in southeastern Europe to the Ottoman Empire.

A second Romanov, Alexis, restored the tsarist autocracy by abolishing the assemblies of nobles and gaining new powers over the Russian church. Alexis was eager not only to gain power but also to purify the Orthodox church of many of the superstitions that had crept in during Mongol times. His reform movement, however, antagonized some Russians, who were known as "Old Believers"; their resistance to the church reforms caused thousands of them to be exiled to Siberia or southern Russia, where they extended

Russia's colonizing activities. Alexis also developed cultural as well as economic contacts with Western nations.

Alexis's son, Peter I, or Peter the Great (1689–1725), greatly expanded his father's work. He was an energetic leader of exceptional intelligence. A giant himself, standing 6 feet 8 inches, he was eager to reform his giant nation still further. He traveled widely in the West, incognito, seeking Western allies for a crusade against Turkish power in Europe. He even worked as a ship carpenter in Holland, gaining an interest in Western science and technology and bringing scores of Western artisans back with him to Russia. Politically Peter defended the tsarist autocracy firmly, putting down revolts with great cruelty. In foreign policy, Peter attacked the Ottoman Empire without substantial result, and then warred with Sweden, winning extensive Russian territory on the eastern coast of the Baltic Sea and reducing Sweden to the status of a second-rate power. Russia now had a "window on the Baltic," including an ice-free port, and from this time onward became a major factor in European diplomatic and military conflict. Peter the Great, in accordance with his desire to reform Russia in some Western directions, commemorated Russia's entry into the European diplomatic orbit as a major player by moving his capital from Moscow to the new Baltic city that he named St. Petersburg.

Internally, Peter's reforms concentrated mainly on streamlining Russia's bureaucratic and military apparatus and increasing central control under the tsar. He improved the organization and weaponry of the army and with aid from Western advisors, created the first Russian navy. New munitions factories and shipyards facilitated this effort, and a substantial iron industry developed: Russia would not depend on the West for weapons production. Peter completed the elimination of old noble councils, creating a set of advisors under his control and a specialized set of ministries in their stead. The central government appointed provincial governors, and while town councils were elected, here too a tsar-appointed magistrate served as final authority. The church was placed still more firmly under state control, with the tsar as head of the church and a committee of bishops, under his direction, responsible for running religious affairs. Peter's regime rationalized law codes and extended them through the whole empire. The tax system was reformed, and taxes on ordinary Russian peasants steadily increased. Finally, the bureaucrats who ran this whole apparatus were given special training, and Peter relied on non-nobles as well as nobles in a search for the best possible talents.

Peter the Great thus sought a state and military force organized well enough to compete with what he now saw as his rivals and peers in Western Europe. He also introduced some additional reforms designed to make Russian manners—particularly those of the aristocracy—more Westernized. Edicts were issued requiring nobles to shave off their beards and wear Western dress; in symbolic ceremonies Peter cut off the long, Mongol-type sleeves that were a feature of nobles' garments. Women in the upper classes were encouraged to become less isolated. These reforms were more than cosmetic, designed to enhance Russia in Western eyes and to jolt the noble class out of established routine.

This was, however, a very selective Westernization process. While the education and culture of the aristocracy were profoundly altered (enhancing the tsar's control along with Westernizing much of the ruling class), the conditions of the masses were not significantly changed. Peter had no desire to imitate the growth of wage labor, as opposed to serfdom, in Western Europe. Nor was he interested in the parliamentary monarchies of the West.

Nor, finally, did he undertake a full imitation of the Western economy. His technological borrowing focused on heavy industry and munitions. He did not encourage a massive merchant class or a major role in the world economy. Westernization increased Russia's economic contacts with the West, as not only technology but artistic items had to be imported, paid for by growing raw materials and grain exports. Russia was an unequal partner in this trade, which was handled by Western trading companies. But the bulk of the Russian economy remained outside this orbit, focusing on agriculture and on limited trade with central Asia; and it remained far different from its counterpart in the West.

Peter's death in 1724 was followed by several decades of weak rule, dominated in part by power plays among army officers who guided the selection of several ineffective emperors and empresses. Peter III, the nephew of Peter the Great's youngest daughter, reached the throne in 1762. He himself was retarded, but his wife, a German-born princess (see p. 318) who changed her name to Catherine, soon took matters in hand and continued to rule as empress after Peter III's death. Catherine—later, Catherine the Great—flirted with the ideas of the French Enlightenment, summoning various reform commissions that did very little. In fact, her goals continued to be those of her illustrious predecessors: to centralize power under the crown and enlarge Russia's territory. She put down a vigorous peasant uprising, led by Emelian Pugachev, butchering Pugachev himself. She used the Pugachev rebellion as an excuse to extend the powers of the central government in regional affairs, while confirming the nobles' control over most of the land. Catherine resumed Peter the Great's campaigns against the Ottoman Empire, with much greater success; she won new territories, including the Crimea, bordering the Black Sea. Catherine also stepped up Russian interference in Polish affairs, finally agreeing with Austria and Prussia to divide, or partition, this once-vigorous state. Three partitions of Poland, in 1772, 1793, and 1795, finally eliminated Poland as an independent state, giving Russia the lion's share of the spoils. Finally, Catherine speeded the colonization of Russia's holdings in Siberia and encouraged further exploration, claiming the territory of Alaska. Russian explorers even moved down the Pacific coast of North America into what is now northern California, while tens of thousands of pioneers spread over Siberia.

By the time of Catherine's death, in 1796, Russia had passed through slightly over three centuries of extraordinary development. It had freed itself from all traces of foreign rule; had constructed a strong central state; and, perhaps most important, had extended its control over the largest land empire in the world at that point.

Russia's expansion had followed three basic directions. First, it had moved eastward, into the vast stretches of Siberia, most of which had previously been inhabited by hunting-and-gathering peoples. This expansion had brought Russia to China's borders, which were regulated by the 18th-century Amur River agreement. Russia's thrust into East Asia was bolstered by vigorous, sometimes forced, colonization; being "sent to Siberia" was no 20th-century invention, as thousands of Old Believers and other dissidents could attest. But Siberia also offered new lands for agriculture; and colonization not only added to Russian resources but also benefited some of the colonizers.

Russia's second direction was toward the south, into central Asia. This expansion brought Russia to the borders of the Ottoman Empire, and Russia's increasingly successful rivalry with this empire was a key factor in the Ottoman decline. Russia's central Asian holdings brought Russian control over a number of diverse ethnic groups, mostly Muslim.

Catherine the Great (1762–1796) was one of the great rulers in Russian history and the only woman in their number. A German-born princess, she married Peter III, who was mentally impaired, and soon took over effective control of government. She continued to rule as tsarina after Peter III's death. True to her own origins and to the legacy of Peter the Great, Catherine continued a Westernization program, and in her 1762 portrait is shown fully dressed in Western fashion—though with a military emphasis that was no accident. Catherine also maintained more distinctive Russian traditions, and was not willing to allow Western influences to weaken her autocratic power. Many of her reform moves, as a result, were mere facades. Catherine was also responsible for laws that gave nobles more power over their serfs, and, at the end of her life, for banning Western contacts and Western-inspired writings during the French revolution. In addition to her impact on Russian history, which included successful expansionist moves, Catherine is one of the lively personalities of world history, surrounded by hosts of stories and myths of great and varied sexual appetites. Even with the advantages of noble birth and marriage, what qualities would a woman need to make this kind of mark in history?

This control was again enhanced by vigorous colonization by the Cossacks, bringing not only Russian rule but a strong ethnic Russian presence in this region. Russian occupation of central Asia eliminated once and for all this region's long role as a center of periodic invasions directed at other parts of Europe and Asia.

Finally, Russia moved westward along the Baltic and into Poland. By 1796, Russian borders bumped against those of Prussia and Habsburg Austria; most of the smaller nations of Eastern Europe had been eliminated. Here, too, Russia took over the government of many minority peoples, including various other Slavic groups, some Germans, and many Jews. And the Russian empire propelled itself into the mainstream of European diplomacy, winning alliances at various points with a number of Scandinavian and central European nations and opening both naval and overland access to further incursions into Europe in the future.

For Russian expansion was by no means complete by 1800. Further efforts to extend were mapped out in all three directions. The Russian government had established a clear and successful tradition of careful military aggrandizement. Segments of the Russian people had demonstrated a vigorous pioneering spirit, which took them into new, sometimes hostile lands, quite like the settlers of North America during much the same period. Not too long after 1800, a French aristocrat, Alexis de Tocqueville, commenting on the dynamism of the new United States, compared American growth to that of the world's "sleeping giant"—Russia. He predicted that these two pioneering nations would someday emerge even more strongly in world affairs, and that they resembled each other, in their exuberant growth, more than anyone yet realized. His foresight was acute.

RUSSIAN POLITICAL INSTITUTIONS

Russia's political structure was firmly autocratic, a centralized apparatus under the tsar. This structure had been suggested in earlier Russian history, through the Byzantine example and the Orthodox tradition of church-state linkage; it was enhanced by the military government's need to drive out the Mongols and by the example of the Khans. Russia's steady territorial expansion was furthered by the strong central government and, in turn, served to bolster the regime.

Russian tsars did not, to be sure, develop extensive direct contacts with ordinary Russian subjects, though they pretended to be "fathers" to their people. Newly acquired

Tsar Peter the Great cutting off the beard of an Orthodox Old Believer. This 18th-century cartoon shows the westernization of hair styles.

HISTORY DEBATE

A Russian Civilization?

Historians continue to wonder how best to fit Russia into the larger patterns of world history. A traditional impulse among Western historians was to include Russia as part of overall European history from the 15th century onward. But Russia has never been Western (though of course it may become so in the future, as many Russians currently hope and as others fear). In the 15th and 16th centuries, even as Italian artists and technical advisors were brought in, Moscow's high culture remained Byzantine; libraries, though still small, were filled with Byzantine books, mainly religious. Russia was also heavily influenced by Central Asia. The tsar called himself the khan of the north, to impress Central Asian peoples, and took oaths of loyalty from this region on the Koran. Central Asian models long guided the bureaucracy. Clearly, Russia emerged as a civilization under mixed influences, which it would continue to try to blend even when more extensive, though selective, Westernization began.

territories were often run for a time rather separately from tsarist control, by freedom-minded Cossacks. Only gradually did the tsarist government regularize all their holdings. Most peasants were ruled by noble landlords, particularly during the 17th and 18th centuries. They had scant access to tsarist courts, but rather were confined to a judicial system directed by their own landlords. Peasants on a given estate regulated their own mutual relations through village governments, which tried to settle land disputes and other matters on the basis of communal tradition. Because of the power of landlords and the importance of village, or *mir*, governments, Russia was in some ways quite decentralized, as Latin America was becoming though without the colonial overlay. At this point, the Russian empire could not compare to the Chinese in the size or varied functions of its bureaucracy.

Yet the tsars did wield great power, and by the 18th century there was no formal institution to check their power. Like China, for example, but unlike the Western monarchies, the tsars established a secret police to prevent dissent and to supervise the bureaucracy itself. The Chancery of Secret Police was initially established by Peter the Great and survived, though under different names and with changing functions, until the late 20th century.

One key to the tsars' great power rested in their special relationship with the nobility—the Russian boyars. At the end of the period of Mongol rule, the boyars possessed extensive land holdings and hereditary titles. There was potential here for substantial aristocratic defiance of the tsar's wishes. Periodically, as during the Time of Troubles, this kind of opposition did develop; it had some institutional base, for a time, in the councils of nobles called to determine tsarist succession. But Russians had no tradition of feudalism to

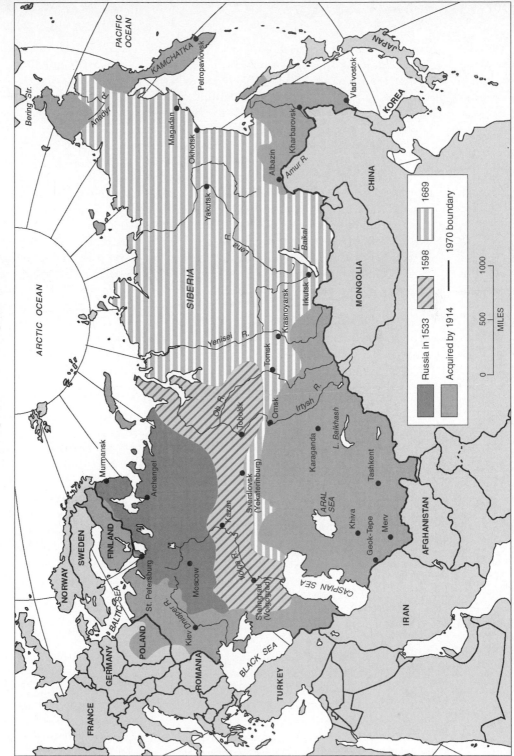

Russian Expansion in Europe and Asia

compare with that of the West. Furthermore, Russia's rapid expansion allowed tsars to grant additional lands to new nobles, whose loyalties were more firmly tied to the crown. Here was a key way in which military expansion strengthened tsarist rule and encouraged the tsars to continue to seek more territory. From Ivan III onward, tsars steadily pressed both new and old nobles to serve the state as military commanders and bureaucrats; they were not allowed to develop separate political loyalties. Thus Russia's aristocracy differed crucially from its counterpart in the West, since it viewed itself as an extension of the state rather than as a partial opposition force. Later tsars, such as Peter the Great, in promoting new bureaucrats to aristocratic ranks, confirmed this state-service orientation.

In many ways the expansion of the tsarist state resembled the rise of absolute monarchy in Western Europe. Indeed, Peter the Great deliberately copied some of the organizational and military structures of states like Prussia. In the West, as in Russia, aristocratic power declined in relation to that of the central state. The collapse of the nobles' councils in Russia was reminiscent of the long period in which the French Parliament was not called. The seeming resemblance between their government and that of much of the West encouraged rulers like Catherine the Great to dabble in the Western theories of enlightened despotism. But similarity was not identity. Russia lacked the church-state division and the feudal and parliamentary traditions that still surged in the West. It did not generate the constitutional political theories that flourished in the West during this period, and indeed Russian rulers were at pains to censor literature incorporating this kind of Western thought. It was not astonishing then that when political revolution rekindled the idea of limiting monarchical power in the West, from 1789 onward, Russia stayed resolutely apart.

Russia's efforts at partial Westernization, not surprisingly, confirmed the empire's autocratic tradition. Under Peter the Great and Catherine the Great, change came from the top down. It increased the hold of the tsar over the nobles, while genuinely seeking to retrain them. No Western monarch attempted such abrupt treatment of the aristocracy as Peter did in patronizingly slicing the traditional costumes of his boyars. None tried to impose education on them, as Peter did in requiring that all nobles and other bureaucrats learn mathematics. Russian bureaucratic procedures and culture may indeed have benefited by this forced dose of Westernization, in the form of better schools, increased literacy, and more science; but it was clear that this kind of reform movement reflected and enhanced the special place of an autocratic central government in Russian political life.

RUSSIAN CULTURE

For most Russian people, culture during the early modern period meant the Orthodox religion and traditional oral expressions—the heroic epics, the rich musical life, the often witty proverbs designed to explain life's vagaries. The carefully structured rituals of the Orthodox church and the worship of many saints allowed ordinary Russians to pray for victories or for protection from disease and famine. They represented the focal point of an elaborate system of festivals, more numerous in Russia than in the West, in which feasting and celebration contrasted with the ordinary work routine.

Russian religious art: icon of the Annunciation, Moscow school.

Russian cultural traditions revived in many ways after the Mongol period. From the 15th to the 17th centuries, icon painting became increasingly distinctive as a Russian art form. From individual heads of saints and the Holy Family, Russian painters moved to more abstract and complex religious scenes. In literature, the tradition of narrative histories and chronicles written by monks resumed.

During the early modern period as a whole, however, Russian culture was marked by important tensions—between popular tradition and elite tastes, and between Westernizing tendencies and a desire to define special Russian characteristics.

Under Ivan the Great and Ivan the Terrible, Italian architects were imported to design church buildings and the magnificent tsarist palace in the Kremlin in Moscow. These architects did not introduce Western styles without modification, however. They generated some fusion between Renaissance classicism and Russian building traditions, producing the ornate, onion-shaped domes that became characteristic of Russian (and other East European) churches.

With Peter the Great and Catherine the Great, the Westernizing impulse went further. The leading aristocrats converted almost entirely to Western cultural influences. Many nobles during the 18th century spoke only French, and some did not know Russian at all. European artistic styles began to displace the icon-painting tradition; cultural forms such as the ballet were taken over so fervently that they became part of Russia's own heritage. Western-type schools encouraged new interest in science and secular philosophy. The public buildings of St. Petersburg were carefully constructed in Western classical styles. Russia was at this juncture still absorbing the Western cultural impulse; later, in the

Miracle of St. George and the Dragon, early 16th century.

19th century, Russians would contribute powerfully to the Western pool of literature, science, and music. At this point, before 1800, elite culture was largely imitative.

Furthermore, Western influence was by no means uniformly welcomed. Ordinary Russian peasants, even the provincial nobility, were largely untouched. A growing cultural gap between the upper class and the masses developed that would be resolved only through revolution in the 20th century. And some literate priests and nobles protested the Westernizing impulse in the name of an often vaguely defined Russian soul. One wrote to the tsar Alexis: "You feed the foreigners too well, instead of bidding your folk to cling to the old customs." A number of cultural leaders tried to articulate traditional or "patriotic" forms opposed to the new influences.

Russian culture during the early modern period thus saw important improvements represented by revitalized art forms and some fruitful mergers with Western styles. Literacy and schooling advanced, though only a minority of Russians were affected; few Russians entered an essentially Western intellectual orbit. But this was not yet an integrated culture. While revived interest in science and new forms of painting and architecture were significant influences in Russian intellectual life, the most enduring single legacy was a heritage of ambivalence about Russia's relationship to the West. Collectively, after a period of stagnation in their own nation's artistic development, Russia's cultural representatives were torn between a desire to imitate the West and a desire to define Russian val-

Steeple of the Preobrazhenskaya church, with wooden carving on the characteristic Russian domes. (The Granger Collection)

ues as different from and superior to those of the West. In one form or another, this ambivalence continues to characterize Russian cultural development.

ECONOMY AND SOCIETY IN RUSSIA

As Russia moved partially into a Western diplomatic orbit and appropriated a number of Western cultural forms, the empire's economy and society pushed in rather different directions. Here was one of the key signs that Russia remained a separate civilization, though one with some special ties to the West.

As the Western economy became increasingly commercial, Russia continued to be resolutely agricultural, save for the iron-manufacturing sector and the continuation of active trade in Central Asia. Its economic growth, while considerable, rested on the extension of its agricultural lands as the empire itself expanded, as well as on the increasingly effective use of vast mineral resources. Russia developed only a small merchant class. Indeed, aristocrats deliberately discouraged local merchants, who were seen as potential rivals. Growing trade with the West was handled by the communities of British, Dutch, and other Western traders from their enclaves in Moscow and St. Petersburg, though Russian merchants were more active in the overland commerce with Asia. Russian cities, as a result, were small, embracing less than five percent of the total population.

Most Russian agriculture was designed for local consumption; few peasants were engaged in a market economy, and few even handled much money. Village artisans supplied most of the manufactured goods that the masses of the population required and could not make themselves. Luxury items and more complex equipment were largely imported from the West. Village-level technology did not change rapidly.

Russia did, however, enter the world economy, and on somewhat better terms than areas like Latin America or even sub-Saharan Africa, despite the empire's backward economic condition after the period of Mongol rule. In exchange for Western goods and commercial services, including merchant shipping, Russia initially offered furs, along with timber supplies from its vast northern forests. Then, in the 18th century, the empire began to sell grain to the West, from the rich lands of the Ukraine and, later, from Poland. Furthermore, Peter the Great used government officials to help organize a growing mining industry, so that Russia sold considerable quantities of iron ore to the West as well. Government-sponsored improvements in Russia's network of rivers and the development of St. Petersburg as a major Baltic port facilitated this process.

The government in Russia essentially took the place of merchant capitalists in organizing mining exports, just as it took the lead in sponsoring munitions factories and related iron-processing works. Here was an important extension of government functions under the tsars, from Peter the Great onward, that helped Russia maintain some balance with the more commercially developed West. Russia used government regulation and unusually rich natural resources to avoid falling hopelessly behind in the world economy.

But the key to Russia's economic advance lay in the reliance on unfree labor. Some slave workers were used, into the 18th century, as war brought many captives. More important, however, was the pervasive and rigorous system of serfdom. As serfdom increasingly loosened in the West, it tightened in Russia and other parts of Eastern Europe. For by using cheap servile labor, Eastern Europe sought to participate in the world market, taking advantage of the West's growing demand for grains and minerals. Serfs worked most of the land, and the government also assigned serfs to the iron mines and metallurgical factories.

Ironically, prior to the Mongol conquest, Russian peasants had been mainly free farmers, their legal position superior to that of their Western counterparts. But after the expulsion of the Tatars, increasing numbers of Russian peasants fell into debt and had to accept servile status to the noble landowners when they could not repay. From the 16th century onward, the Russian government actively encouraged this process. Essentially the government offered support of serfdom to the aristocracy, in exchange for loyalty. As new territories were added to the empire, the system of serfdom was extended where it had not been known before. By 1800 half of Russia's peasantry was enserfed to the landlords, and much of the other half owed comparable obligations to the state. Various laws passed during the 17th century tied the serfs to the land; a 1649 act fixed the hereditary status of the serfs, so that people born to that station could not legally escape it.

Serfs on the landlords' estates were taxed and policed through their landlords and were even bought and sold like ordinary property. While peasants varied somewhat in wealth and used village governments for community regulation, most remained impoverished and ill-educated. And the legal servitude of most peasants only tightened with time. While Catherine the Great sponsored a few model villages to display her enlightenment, in fact she turned over the government of the serfs to the landlords more completely than ever before. A law of 1785 allowed landlords even to administer harsh penalties to any of their serfs convicted of major crimes or rebellion. Serfdom spread to new regions, with nobles granted other new rights. Here was proof positive of the vital political basis of serfdom, as Catherine bought the loyalty of the nobles by giving them, in effect, rule over half of the Russian masses.

In Russian serfdom, not only on the landed estates but also in the mines, the key obligation was not money payment or payment in kind, though taxes were high and rising as the government needs for revenue increased. Labor service, the *obrok*, was the obligation that made economic sense of this system. Peasants owed up to a tenth of their yearly labor to their landlords or to the state. This was the labor that produced the grain available for export and that serviced the mines and factories.

Russia's distinctive social and economic system worked well in many respects. It produced enough revenue to support an expanding state and empire. It underwrote a wealthy upper aristocracy and its glittering, Westernized culture. It supported a far larger number of more modest gentry, who did not live well and who often resented the Western ways of the imperial court but who were secure in their position and in their loyalty to the tsar. The system also promoted considerable population growth. Population nearly doubled in the 18th century, to 36 million people, and while some of this growth came as a result of territorial expansion, most was due to natural increase. For an empire that contained few regions of great fertility, and where the climate was harsh, this was no small achievement, though periodic famines and epidemics continued to bedevil Russia into the 20th century, for this was a poor land in many ways. But there could be no question that the economy had advanced.

Yet the Russian system suffered from important limitations. There was little incentive for agricultural improvements; most methods remained rather primitive. Peasants certainly lacked the motivation, for whatever surplus they produced was not theirs. Landlords, copying Western interests in the 18th century, did form associations to exchange information on new crops and methods, but little was done. Given the secure base in servile labor, there seemed scant need for change. Indeed, pressure from landlords caused the government to enact measures against a growing system of peasant-run domestic manufacturing and trade in the 18th century, for the aristocracy feared that growing peasant wealth might challenge its rule. So Russia did not experience a significant increase in internal commerce or consumer-directed production comparable to that occurring in the West.

Most important, the system generated recurring peasant unrest. Russian peasants, though mainly loyal to the tsar, harbored bitter resentments against their landlords, who were seen as having taken lands that rightfully belonged to the peasants. Periodic rebellions attacked manorial records, seized land directly, and sometimes killed landlords and their officials. The Pugachev uprising was the leading 18th-century example of this kind of outburst. But there were others, and the series would continue and swell in the 19th century. Peasants had more than a sense of grievance; they also had tight links to each other through village government and traditions of communal support. They maintained strong family ties, extending among collateral relatives; the Russian family network was thus larger than that of the West, with less stress on the purely nuclear unit. Community and family bonds provided a political basis for action, and while the peasants were never successful against the power of the landlords or the military strength of the state, they could not be permanently repressed.

Not surprisingly, by the early 1800s it was clear that Russia had a major "peasant problem." Not only by Western standards, but also in terms of an interest in economic advance and political order, it seemed increasingly clear that something had to be done about Russia's unfree masses. Also not surprisingly, it was very difficult to decide what to do.

CONCLUSION: THE WORLD'S FIRST WESTERNIZATION EFFORT

Russia, particularly during Peter the Great's rule and onward, was the first non-Western civilization to attempt a partial "Westernization." It was close to the West and shared some of the same religious traditions. It had emerged from the Mongol period aware of its backwardness and eager to use Western models as a partial remedy. What Russian leaders had attempted, in Westernization from the top down, would be tried to some extent in other societies, and is being tried still in our own day. The Russians sought to select key Western forms, not to make their society entirely Western but to change it enough that it could compete with the West militarily. Thus the emphasis was on bureaucratic training and military organization and armament. But there was some sense that still more should be done, that cultural styles and even personal manners should change in Western directions; hence the movement, among the upper classes, in styles of dress as well as in art.

Yet this was a limited effort. Westernization was used to enhance the distinctive Russian autocracy, not to import the full, complex political culture of the contemporary West and certainly not to change the beliefs of the masses. Russia's leaders—like many later Westernizers elsewhere—did not want to reproduce Western civilization. Small wonder that by the late 18th century some intellectual dissidents, attracted by the West, pressed for further change—though other writers continued to urge the sanctity of Russian traditions.

Rather, the Westernization current fed into the more general growth of the Russian state and empire. Limited changes were sufficient, in combination with Russia's vast size, population, and resources, to maintain the country's growing role in world diplomacy, challenging smaller nations in eastern and central Europe and challenging China and the Ottoman Empire in Asia. In strictly economic terms, Russia's relationship to the Western-dominated world economy was not vastly superior to that of Latin America; in both cases, the trems of trade were disadvantageous and in both cases the success that was won depended on unfree labor. But in the military and political sphere, the story was quite different. Russia carved out one of the great landed empires in world history.

Suggested Readings

Two important source collections for this period of Russian history are T. Riha, ed., *Readings in Russian Civilization*, vol. II: *Imperial Russia 1700–1917* (1969), and Basil Dmytryshyn, *Imperial Russia: A Sourcebook 1700–1917* (1967). Excellent general coverage is provided in N. Riasanovsky, *A History of Russia*, 4th ed. (1993); see also Otto Hoetzsch, *The Evolution of Russia* (1966). On more specialized topics, consult: H. Kohn, *The Mind of Modern Russia* (1955); M. Raeff, *Peter the Great, Reformer or Revolutionary?* (1963); H. Rogger, *National Consciousness in Eighteenth Century Russia* (1963); and A. Kahan, *The Knout and the Plowshare: Economic History of Russia in the 18th Century* (1985). Peter Kolchin, *Unfree Labor: American Slavery and Russian Serfdom* (1987), is an important comparative study.

CHAPTER 17

The Ottoman and Mughal Empires

Focal Points

Two great Muslim states were created during the early modern period, one covering much of the Middle East and the Balkans, the other much of India. Both the Ottomans and the Mughals brought new influences to their regions, including great political and military strength. What were their major contributions? Both empires also, however, began to decline during the 17th century. What were the symptoms of decline? Why did these empires begin to fade relatively soon after their peak success? Why did the Mughal empire decline much more rapidly than its Ottoman counterpart? One result of Mughal decline was growing European penetration of India by the 18th century, an intrusion that had not yet occurred in the Middle East.

THE MUSLIM EMPIRES

The Ottoman and Mughal empires resembled Russia in establishing large landed holdings with new boundaries during the early modern period. They also, like Russia, embraced a host of different linguistic, ethnic, and religious groups. Neither empire, however, attempted Westernization in this period, even selectively. Early Mughal emperors had a tolerant interest in Western culture, including religion, but there were scant results; the Western intrusion into India later was a matter of conquest and economic exploitation. Ottoman rulers, with minor exceptions, explicitly avoided borrowing from the West.

While not rigorously isolated—unlike East Asia—both Muslim empires followed their own paths during most of the early modern period, introducing important changes that had little to do with the West or the world economy. Contacts with the West did increase with time, so that in contrast to East Asia a more substantial Western presence began to affect internal developments, particularly in India, by the late 17th to early 18th centuries. Here again are distinctive cases, unlike either East Asian isolation or Russia's partial Westernization, in which trends during the early modern period created important new patterns, ultimately shaping the relationship to the larger global framework.

The evolution of the Middle East and India after 1450 revolved around the rise of two great Muslim empires, one brought by the Turks to the Middle East, the other by Turkish-Mongol conquerors who ruled over the Hindu majority in India. (A third Muslim empire, the Safavids, developed for a time in Persia.) The Muslim empires provided new political and military solidity to their Asian territories. Under the Ottomans, the previous political decline of the Arab caliphs was reversed. Under the early Mughals, India achieved a degree of political unity rarely before attained. The existence of these empires, along with China's expanded territory and the rise of Russia, divided most of Asia, North Africa, and Eastern Europe into four great agglomerations by 1700; only Southeast Asia, Japan, Korea, Persia, and some regional Arab principalities in the desert areas of the Middle East were omitted, along with the westernmost North African kingdom of Morocco.

The Ottoman and particularly the Mughal empires were not, however, as solidly based as those of China and Russia. The Mughals represented a minority religion as well as a foreign political force. The Ottomans, though sharing religion with the Arab majority of their empire, were also outsiders, who looked down on the Arab population for their political and military weakness. Perhaps, as a result, neither of these new empires created an integrated culture. Important cultural developments occurred, but earlier religious and artistic traditions remained. Nor did either empire generate lasting economic strength. The earlier commercial glories of India and the Arabs were not recaptured, and economic conditions tended to stagnate. Both empires were partially drawn into the European-dominated world economy at disadvantageous terms. Finally, both empires began to decline well before 1800. In India, this resulted in direct European penetration during the 18th century. The Ottoman Empire remained intact, but by 1800 it was on the way toward becoming what the Europeans called a "sick man" in world affairs.

While the decline of the two empires ultimately facilitated the West's rise to world influence, as southern and western Asia could not generate a durable competitor to its surge, it is important to realize that these developments embrace only the last century or so of the early modern period. For at least 200 years, and longer in the case of the Ottomans, it was the power and splendor of the great emperors that counted, dazzling European observers even as they gradually won new trading rights in the two regions.

THE OTTOMAN EMPIRE

THE EXPANDING FORCE OF THE NEW MIDDLE EASTERN STATE

The Ottoman Empire had taken shape during the several centuries before the early modern period, though its full blossoming followed the Turkish conquest of Constantinople in 1453. Turkish groups had been moving into the Middle East, from their original lands in central Asia, for some time. They served in the armies of the caliphs and as advisors. This interaction spread Islamic belief and knowledge of urban cultural styles and government even to those Turks still in central Asia.

The Osmanli group of Turks, or Ottomans as they became known by Europeans, were not one of the original Turkish peoples involved in Middle Eastern affairs. Their movement into the region came later, stimulated in part by the rise of the Mongol empire in

Asia during the 13th and 14th centuries. Large numbers of migrants took over lands at the northern rim of the Middle East, in the country that is now Turkey—the only part of the Middle East that was heavily populated by Turks—where they became an agricultural people. Regional Osmanli leaders, emphasizing their military abilities, began to press against both the Arabs and the Byzantines. The Ottomans were fervent warriors, spurred by intense Islamic beliefs and tight military brotherhoods. By the 14th century their leaders began to call themselves sultans, as they settled in the plains of Anatolia, the heartland of present-day Turkey. The first sultan, Orkhan, set up a new army, called "Janissaries," in order to fight the remnant of the Byzantine Empire in southeastern Europe. He had already won some European territory by 1400. The Ottomans viewed this conquest of Christian lands as a virtual crusade, and during the 1390s they captured Serbia, Bulgaria, and Greece. Already the Ottoman Empire was the strongest state in the Middle East in the wake of the collapse of the Abbasid caliphate.

But the chief prize was Constantinople itself, the capital city of eastern Christendom. Several Turkish sieges failed before Sultan Mehmet II, known as "the Conqueror," finally won through in 1453, aided by the use of a huge cannon and by the strict discipline he imposed on his troops. The Turks set up their imperial capital in what was now a Muslim city. Soon after this, the Turks conquered Arab Syria and also took over the Greek islands and the last Byzantine settlements around the Black Sea. By 1517, Egypt was conquered, the last of the regional Arab kingdoms that had survived the fall of the caliphate. The Ottoman Empire was thus heir to both Arab and Byzantine lands, setting up one of the largest empires the Middle East had ever known and one that proved to be the last great unification movement in the region that has occurred to our own day.

During the 16th century, Ottoman conquests continued. The sultans took over part of Persia and much of the southern Arabian peninsula. They pursued their fighting in Europe, attacking several Italian cities and conquering Hungary after a victory in 1526. In 1529 they besieged the Habsburg capital city of Vienna, in Austria, though this effort failed. The Ottomans were deep into European territory. They also captured islands in the Mediterranean. The conquest of the island of Cyprus in 1571 led to the establishment of a Turkish settlement that coexisted uneasily with the Greek majority in a tension that persists to this day. Minor conquests continued until 1715, though in most respects the highwater mark of the empire as a subjugating force was reached in the late 16th and early 17th centuries.

By this point the Ottoman Empire embraced the whole of southeastern Europe to the Danube River. It included Tatar provinces in the Crimea as the Ottoman Empire stretched around virtually the entire circumference of the Black Sea. It encompassed most of the Middle East, with some desert Arab regions and the smaller Safavid empire in Persia alone escaping its grasp; and it controlled most of North Africa. Ottoman rule over the holy cities of Mecca and Medina gave the empire new religious force, and the sultans took over the title of Caliph of Islam, implying some direct leadership in the Muslim faith; as Caliphs, the sultans required that their names be used in prayers in the mosques of the faithful.

The Ottoman Empire, though of greatest importance in the Muslim world, played a vital role in European history as well. By its hold over the Balkan lands of southeastern

Europe, the Ottomans preserved this region from direct Western control; a minority of Balkan people converted to Islam.

The Ottoman Empire itself rested on two leading principles. The first, visible from the early Osmanlis onward, involved strong military organization and conquest. The Ottomans, like many other imperial conquerors, depended heavily on a fairly steady diet of expansion, which gave military leaders rewards in the form of new territories, plus slaves to serve as troops; when conquests largely ceased, the empire became increasingly troubled.

The second Ottoman principle, like that of Arab conquerors before them, was one of considerable tolerance for the various peoples in their vast realms. Mehmet II did not attack the Greek Orthodox church, indeed appointing a new patriarch to provide separate religious government for this people. Christians were taxed more heavily than Muslims, and in the provinces of southeastern Europe they were forced to perform labor duties and contribute boys as soldiers. In the main, Christianity remained strong in southeastern Europe and, as a minority religion, in parts of the Middle East, and individual Christians rose high in the Ottoman government. Jews too were widely tolerated, as the Turks again demonstrated their willingness to accept a multiracial and multireligious society. The Turks did harbor some disdain for their fellow Arab Muslims and decidedly favored Sunni beliefs over the Shi'ite minority; but for the most part, Arab Muslims, from ulema scholars to the ordinary faithful, were not disturbed in their religious practices. Many Ottoman sultans were personally pious, interested in religion and culture as well as military affairs.

The greatest of the Ottoman sultans, near the height of the empire's power, was Suleiman, who ruled from 1520 to 1566. Known as "the Magnificent" to European traders, who marveled at the wealth of his court, he was called "the Legislator" by the Turks themselves because of his interest in just and disciplined rule. Though not a joyful warrior—indeed, portraits reveal a rather gloomy man burdened by the cares of state—Suleiman did pursue the policy of conquest. It was under his rule that the kingdom of Hungary was conquered and new portions of the Middle East, particularly present-day Iraq, were won from the Persians. Suleiman also constructed a major Mediterranean fleet, hoping in this way to extend his competition with the Christian West. He strengthened Ottoman control of North Africa, especially Algeria, and frequently raided Italian and Spanish ports. In his later years, Suleiman grew less interested in battle and concentrated on the building of new mosques. But his life remained troubled, as he had to put to death one son to please his favorite wife, leaving her incompetent son as his heir.

Under Suleiman, the institutions of the Ottoman Empire assumed their fullest shape, forming a successful political system long capable of adminstering vast and diverse territories. In theory this was an absolute state, claiming control over all wealth and property in the empire. Annual tax revenue was massive by the standards of Western kingdoms. Though all power officially rested in the sultan, he in fact delegated much authority to his chief minister, the grand wazir. The wazir and other leading ministers were able to accumulate considerable fortunes of their own through bribery and graft, though they had to struggle against rivals and against the sultan's power to retire them—and often to execute them—at any moment.

The provinces of the empire were ruled by governors called "pashas," who paid for their office with an annual fee. A pasha of Cairo was said to have bribed the grand wazir with a large yearly payment in order to hold his lucrative position. Under the pashas, most land outside the cities was parceled out in fiefs to Turkish and other Muslim landlords, who collected revenues and enforced the laws on a local basis. Under a levy, or conscription, system, each landlord was obligated to furnish soldiers to the sultan. Under this decentralized system, regional rulers and landlords were encouraged to milk their holdings for as much revenue as they could. There was no hereditary nobility, since in theory the sultan owned all the land. This fact initially gave sultans control over regional officials who owed their position to the central court, but it also promoted short-term exploitation of the provinces by officials eager to turn a profit while they could still enjoy it. Suleiman did prepare a centralized law code, which served as unifying legal cement for the empire until the 19th century.

The Ottomans expanded the early Arab use of slaves in army and administration. Using slaves of Christian origin in the central bureaucracy, from the viziers on down, bypassed the Koran's prohibition on enslaving Muslims and also integrated non-Muslims who formed a majority in the empire for its first 200 years. Government slaves were carefully educated, alongside the sultans' own sons, and promoted according to merit and seniority. Here was another solution to the government of an agricultural society, different both from Chinese bureaucracy and from feudalism. It made the Ottoman Empire the best governed state in the world well into the 16th century.

The army itself represented the main unifying element. In addition to the landlord levies, sultans like Suleiman directly controlled the force of Janissaries, who were recruited from the families of Christians, particularly in southeastern Europe, in what amounted to an annual slave tax. These boys were taken from their homes at an early age, converted to Islam, and trained to become fierce and able soldiers. They seldom numbered more than 15,000, because the sultans feared that they might otherwise grow too powerful; indeed, Janissary revolts troubled the empire periodically even so. Forbidden to marry, the Janissaries were expected to remain loyal to the sultan alone, from whom they received good pay and many benefits. And until the 18th century, when their fighting spirit declined and their interference in internal politics increased, the Janissaries did indeed serve the empire well. The Janissaries and the estate levies were normally well disciplined and remained an excellent fighting force, particularly in battles with European Christians, which were still seen to an extent as holy wars.

The Ottoman navy, on the other hand, never gained significant strength and certainly could not wrest control of the Mediterranean from Italian and Spanish forces. The empire lacked a large merchant marine, a fact that weakened its effort on the seas. It used slaves as oarsmen, who had little interest in battle save as a chance to escape. Though the navy gained brief prominence under Suleiman, it soon declined and then was virtually eliminated by the defeat at European hands in the battle of Lepanto in 1571. After this point, Turkish naval activities were confined to the eastern coast of the Mediterranean, where they mainly protected existing Ottoman provinces.

Even at its height, the Ottoman Empire displayed some important weaknesses. It ruled over the oldest commercial economy in the world, but it did not sponsor significant economic advance. As the focus of world trade moved away from the Mediterranean, the Empire was obviously at a disadvantage. Great efforts were exerted to sustain the magnificent city of Constantinople (called Istanbul by the Turks). Most farming was done by serfs, who were abundantly exploited by greedy landlords and regional governors. This system did not encourage agricultural productivity. The Turks were not greatly interested in commerce. Most regional trade was conducted by Arabs, Greeks, and Jews, who maintained an active urban economy. The empire's role in the larger world economy declined. Once Europeans learned to sail around Africa directly to Asia, the position of the Middle East as intermediary between Asia and Europe fell off. Trade between the Middle East and Europe lay largely in Western hands, and a growing colony of Western traders emerged in Constantinople.

The empire embraced and encouraged a lively religious life, though the leaders in Islamic scholarship were more often Arab than Turk. The building of mosques and palaces stimulated architecture and crafts, which maintained earlier Arabic styles for the most part, though to some extent Persian influences were also evident. Decorative arts, including rich carpets and fine metal work, flourished. But there was little new literature, particularly in Turkish; Arab poetry continued, but, as in the later days of the caliphate, mainly in a religious vein. Arab schools and universities concentrated primarily on religious instruction and the complicated scholarship of Islamic law. Egypt served as the cultural center for Arab intellectual life, but most Egyptian writers devoted their efforts to compiling older works and commenting on them, or preparing biographies of long-ago Muslim holy men. The rich and diverse cultural traditions of the earlier Arab civilization at its height

This Turkish artifact of the 16th century maintained earlier Islamic styles of art. (The Granger Collection)

were not revived. In the 16th century, Turkish literature began to develop, as sultans encouraged the writing of state histories highly favorable to those in power and as Turkish poets and songwriters copied Persian and Arabic verse. Much Turkish writing was devoted to accounts of the life of the prophet Muhammed and leading dervishes, confirming the heavily religious orientation of Middle Eastern culture.

The Ottoman Empire remained in part a military imposition. Turkish leaders continued to esteem military virtues above all, though they often tempered their commitment to warfare by pursuing religious concerns and the enjoyment of art. The Turks had little interest in the chores of bureaucracy. Most administrative posts under the sultans were held not by Turks, but by East Europeans—mainly Slavs and Greeks—and by Jews. Only a minority of the wazirs were Turkish. Most of the literate bureaucrats were Europeans, Christian Armenians, and Jews. Decentralized rule combined with strong military power held this empire together, though high taxes, forced labor, and military recruitment caused discontent, particularly in southeastern Europe, where the Turks became cordially detested.

Despite its weaknesses, however, the Ottoman Empire enjoyed over three centuries of ascendancy, from its dynamic beginnings in the 14th century until well after the defeat at Lepanto. This is hardly a record of failure, for it compares favorably with the glory days of other military empires such as that of Rome.

Ottoman decline began late in the 16th century, though it became readily apparent only a hundred years later. The quality of individual sultans deteriorated after Suleiman. Many ruled for only brief periods; a few were severely retarded. Many devoted themselves to sensual pleasures, surrounded by large harems of concubines. Palace intrigues and military interference increasingly dominated the Ottoman state, which helps account for the poor political performance of those who became sultans. Periodic reform efforts, to tighten central control and reduce the corruption of regional governors, had no permanent effects, though they helped sustain the regime. Religious and local institutions supplemented the government by providing courts, charity, education and public works — another reason the system survived.

During most of the 17th century, the empire held onto its territory. Its control over North Africa (aside from Egypt) weakened, in part because of the declining navy. North African states became small principalities and were the source of considerable piracy until the 19th century. Yet the Western powers, caught up in their own colonial expansion, had no interest in direct attack on Ottoman lands.

The Ottoman Empire itself made one last attempt at conquest in 1683, in a new assault on Vienna. For three months a huge Turkish army laid siege to this city, until a mixed German and Polish force drove them back. Soon after this, the Austrian Habsburg emperor, in loose alliance with the Russian tsar Peter the Great, attacked the Ottomans. Austrian troops drove the Turks from Hungary, inflicting the worst defeat the Turks had suffered since the early days of the Osmanlis. From this point onward the Ottomans were on the defensive in southeastern Europe and central Asia. In the 18th century, Russian attacks pushed them from the northern coast of the Black Sea, while Austria also gained some territory in Serbia.

During the 18th century, the quality of internal government deteriorated further. Control over provincial governors declined; a few governors even rebelled against Constantinople. Many governors became increasingly corrupt, using their rule as a means of acquiring vast personal fortunes. Taxation, earlier restrained by some central regulations, grew heavier. Popular discontent increased, though there were no vast uprisings. Arab involvement with intense Muslim piety, under the leadership of Sufi mystics, helped limit the impact of protest, expressing hostility to the existing order but through attention to religious rather than political goals.

As the power of the empire waned, European economic penetration of the Middle East began to intensify. Even before, Western traders, led by the French, had won special privileges from the sultans, establishing merchant colonies that were exempt from Ottoman law. French, British, and Dutch groups thrived not only in Constantinople but in Syria and Egypt as well. Western inspiration also had some cultural impact, as Middle Eastern Christians, particularly in Lebanon, sought new ties with the Catholic church. Christian printing presses were set up in Arabic, though they were banned by the Turks for Muslims until 1729.

For the most part, Turkish political leaders and Arab cultural leaders remained uncertain in reacting to the declining strength of their civilization, though officials were aware of specific problems. There was no successful effort at political reform until after 1800. Muslim cultural figures were convinced of their superiority over their European neighbors. No attempts were made, again until after 1800, to translate European scientific or technological works, for this intellectual current seemed irrelevant in Muslim eyes. A few Western doctors were imported by the sultans—which was ironic, because this was an area where Muslim science was fully as good—but the larger disparities with Western Europe were ignored. The cultural blanket of Islamic legalism and otherworldly faith continued to cover this vital civilization, even as both Western and Russian interests in the region increased.

THE MUGHAL EMPIRE

INVASION, CONSOLIDATION, AND DECLINE

India during the 15th century was locked in its recurrent pattern of regional states. The Delhi sultanate, which earlier had provided Muslim rule for much of northern India, was now merely one among many principalities, most of them headed by Hindu princes.

This situation changed as a result of another invasion early in the 16th century, the last echo, in a way, of the great period of Mongol conquests. Babur, a regional chieftain in Afghanistan and a Muslim, was of mixed Turkish and Mongol ancestry. Beginning in 1526 he used the familiar passes through the mountains of northwestern India to mount a war of conquest, within four years bringing a large part of the northern plains under his control.

Babur's conquests benefited obviously from India's political division, as regional states could not join forces effectively. But Babur himself was no ordinary raider. His vision was a new empire, under himself and his descendants, not plunder. He was a bold though often cruel general, a lover of gardening and poetry who wrote a long memoir describing his own life with real sensitivity. He cherished books and liked to select prize volumes from the libraries that came under his dominion. The dynasty he established was called "Mughal," from the Persian word for *Mongol;* from the wealth of Babur and his successors came the English word *mogul.* But this was, at the outset, a regime with serious po-

The Ottoman Empire at Its Height and in Decline, 1683–1923

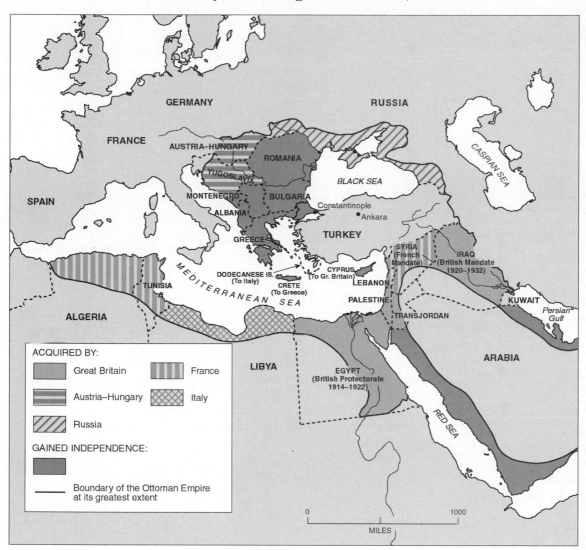

litical purposes, not a luxury-loving enterprise. To solidify his new dynasty, Babur carefully avoided acts of intolerance against Hindus, whose customs he studied closely.

Babur's chief heir, after a brief period of confusion under a weak son, was his grandson Akbar, who took charge in 1555. Initially winning only a portion of Babur's empire, Akbar soon conquered one of the largest empires ever established in India, recalling the old days of the Maurya dynasty. Akbar's achievement gained the awed respect of Europeans, who named him the "Great Mughal." Akbar was brave almost to the point of foolhardiness. As a boy he liked to ride his own fighting elephants; he reveled in the hunt, once killing a tiger with his sword in single combat. He was also an excellent marksman with a gun—and guns spread to India initially through Muslim influence. But Akbar was also a cultivated man, a book collector and a patron of painting and architecture. Mughal culture reached a peak under his rule. Further, Akbar carried tolerance of Hinduism to unusual extreme, marrying a Hindu princess and allowing Hindu women in his court to practice their religion openly, an unprecedented act for a Muslim ruler. He even listened to Portuguese Jesuit missionaries who reached the west coast under his regime, though he never himself converted. Akbar seems to have had a vague idea of sponsoring a new religion that would blend Hinduism and Islam, though this never won significant success.

Akbar's empire built on a combination of great military force and careful administration. His army numbered 140,000 troops at its height, a massive number for the age, far greater than the forces of the leading European powers. At the same time he set up a clearly defined bureaucracy, divided into specialized ministries to deal with finance, law, and military affairs. Akbar's administrative reform drew on practices in Afghanistan that were refined by his Hindu chief minister. Eighteen provincial governors, called subahdars, administered the major regions of his empire. Akbar united virtually the whole of northern India and began the conquest of the Deccan region in the south. His legal system sought to moderate what he saw as some excesses in Hindu customs; thus he attempted to ban sati, the practice of suicide by widows, and he forbade child marriage by insisting on a marriage age of 16 for boys, 13 for girls. Akbar also endeavored to create a common language for his empire, enabling his scholars to produce the synthetic mixture called Urdu, or Hindustani, which provided a vehicle of communication for his bureaucrats and ultimately spread to a large minority of his subjects, particularly Muslims. Urdu forms one of three major languages, along with English, on the subcontinent today. Above all, Akbar and his subordinates developed an efficient system of military recruitment and taxation, the latter based on landed property. Even with the huge demands of his government for revenue, prosperity increased in northern India. Muslim rule provided India not only with stable government, but also with new products such as paper. India continued an active regional trade with southeast Asia in spices and other products, even as Western shipping spread.

Akbar's reign was the high point of Mughal rule in India, yet the empire was to survive until the 19th century. Akbar's immediate successors, though less able than he, maintained the policy of conquest; during the first half of the 17th century, the empire reached its greatest extent through gains in the south. Patronage of the arts continued. Mughal portrait painters flourished, and some influences from Western art crept into their works—as in the halos painted around the heads of the emperors themselves. Mughal art had a distinctive style, different from Middle Eastern tradition, as the use of portraits demonstrates. In architecture, the Muslim heritage, including the use of decorative motifs, loomed larger. Under the emperor Shah Jehan I, who ruled from 1627 to 1658, the great tomb called the "Taj Mahal" was built. Designed by a Turkish architect, it required 14 years to construct; initially intended for Jehan's favorite wife, it also served as a shrine for Jehan himself, and is still rated one of the two or three most beautiful buildings in the world. Thus, in painting and architecture, as in the development of Urdu, the Mughals added greatly to India's artistic and cultural legacy.

The political structure of the empire, however, began to unravel during the mid–17th century. Jehan departed from the tradition of toleration for Hindus. Hindu officials still

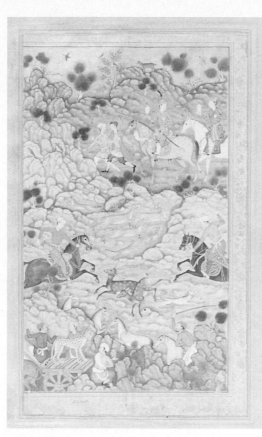

Mughal book painting: late 16th-century hunting scenes. (The Granger Collection)

served in his bureaucracy, and the emperor patronized Hindu poets and musicians, but many Hindu temples were pulled down. Jehan also attacked Portuguese settlements in the east (near present-day Calcutta), though his huge army had great difficulty subduing a force of merely 1000 troops, whose superior weaponry foreshadowed later Western potency on the subcontinent. Many Christian churches were destroyed, and thousands of Christian converts were killed. Taxes were increased to cover growing expenses of the luxurious court. Many peasants were forced off the land through these burdens, and rural banditry became a growing problem.

Tensions increased under Jehan's son Aurangzeb, the last important Mughal ruler (1658–1707). Aurangzeb, who took power by imprisoning his father, did manage to reduce taxation. But he intensified the attacks on the Hindu majority in the name of a fervent adherence to Islamic law. More temples were destroyed, and taxes on Hindus were raised. Hindus who sought bureaucratic service normally had to convert to the Muslim faith. Hindu resistance, not a major factor in most of the empire previously, now increased. This helped to rally regional princes in the south, who prevented the further conquest of the Deccan region. A new Hindu leader in the south, Shivaji, generated

The Mughal Empire in India

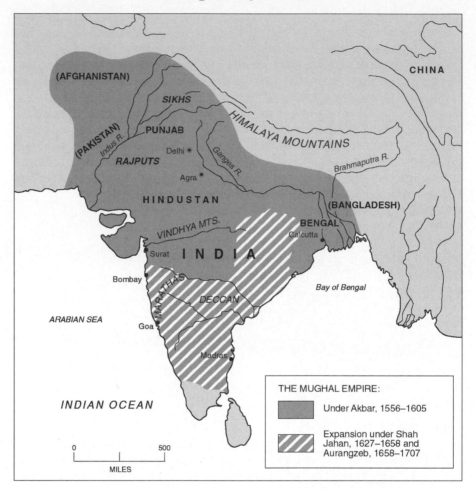

something akin to a Hindu nationalism in forming a new Deccan state against which Aurangzeb battled in vain until his death.

Another important center of resistance arose in the northwest. Here, a new religion had sprung up in the 16th century, in part as a reaction to earlier Muslim influence. This Sikh religion was closely related to Hinduism, though it was held by its leaders to be inspired directly by God. The Sikh faith combined Hindu practices and beliefs with a more activist approach. Sikhs abolished the caste system in their religion, creating a military brotherhood dedicated to a vigorous role in the affairs of this world, including something like a spirit of holy war. The contemplative side of Hinduism was played down, though Sikh temples maintained many Hindu rituals, and belief in reincarnation persisted. As the Mughal Empire weakened, Sikhs set up a regional realm of their own that lasted until 1849. Not only fierce fighters, the turbaned Sikhs were active in business and in agricultural improvements. They formed an important religious minority in India from the 17th century onward, along with the larger Muslim group.

By the time of Aurangzeb's death, India was divided into essentially three major states—the Mughal Empire itself, the largest, plus the new state in the Deccan, and the Sikh empire; several smaller states survived in the south, while European settlements—Portuguese Goa, but also British and French ports—dotted both the east and the west coasts. Within the Mughal Empire itself, Hindus and Muslims were increasingly in conflict. Many Hindus withdrew into their own communities, tightening their religious rituals to preserve their identity in a state they could no longer actively accept. Under Aurangzeb's 18th-century successors, Mughal administration became increasingly conservative and inefficient. Not only did political control became more lax, but India's educational system declined as a result of Hindu isolation and Mughal inattention, and the economy deteriorated. Merchants suffered under the taxation of the later Mughals, who had no love for commerce. Indian technology—like that of much of Asia by the 17th and 18th centuries—stagnated.

In sum, an empire that had begun with great brilliance and promise declined with extraordinary rapidity. Intolerance seems to have been a key to the downfall, along with the

Mughal art: Jahangir embracing Nur Jahan. Compare this to the earlier Indian styles shown in Chapters 3 and 7.

continued ability of most Hindus to retain their faith. In this situation the Mughal rulers were increasingly beleaguered and ineffective.

WESTERN INTRUSION

Growing weakness and division in 18th-century India constituted an unintended invitation to more active European intervention. Western merchant companies were drawn increasingly into Indian political affairs, to provide what they saw as necessary stability for their commercial operations. This was the most important impact of the new world economy on Asia in the early modern period. This motive for intervention was enhanced by conflicts among the European groups for influence on the subcontinent, and particularly by the recurrent battles between England and France. Though European forces were small, their superiority in weapons gave them centralizing power in a divided region.

By the 18th century, Portugal's role in India was minor; the colony at Goa remained, but Portugal was too weak to re-establish other centers after the Mughal attacks. Dutch power was also declining, as the Dutch were preoccupied with administering their important holdings in the Indonesian islands. France and Britain had both established toeholds on the subcontinent during the 17th century, winning port rights by bargaining with local princes. The British East India Company operated a station at Calcutta, which gave them some access to the great wealth of the Ganges valley. The company had enormous influence over the British government and, through Britain's superior navy, excellent communication on the ocean routes. Their French rivals, in contrast, had less political clout at home, where the government was often distracted by purely European wars. The French were also more interested in missionary work than the British, who were long content to leave Hindu customs alone and devote themselves to commercial profits.

French-British rivalry raged bitterly through the middle decades of the 18th century. Each side recruited Indian princes as allies. Outright warfare erupted in 1744, and then again during the Seven Years' War. British officials had become alarmed at growing French influence with local princes. They were also roused in 1756 by the capture of Calcutta, by an Indian official, who imprisoned English captives in a "Black Hole"—an underground chamber originally used as a jail by the English themselves; many English officials suffocated. The East India Company's army recaptured Calcutta and then seized additional French and Indian territory, aided by abundant bribes distributed to many regional princes. French power in India was destroyed, and England was committed, without plan or clear intent, to the administration of the region called "Bengal," which stretched inland from Calcutta. Soon after this, the British also gained the island of Sri Lanka (Ceylon) from the Dutch. Although the British military force remained small, its superior weaponry, including field artillery, had proved decisive in battles with Indian rulers. At the same time, more sophisticated naval power allowed Britain to outdistance its European rivals. Thus, from 1764 onward, a British empire in India was truly launched. Along with Indonesia and the Americas, India became one of the great territorial acquisitions of the West prior to 1800.

The full history of British India did not begin until late in the 18th century, when the British government took a more active hand in Indian administration, supplementing the quasi-government of the East India Company. Indeed, before 1800, British control of the subcontinent was incomplete. The Mughal empire remained, though it was increasingly hollow, as did other regional kingdoms including the Sikh state. Britain gained some new territories by force of arms, but was also content to ally with local princes without disturbing their internal administration, again until after 1800.

But British, and to an extent French and Dutch, commercial activities in India did have an important effect even before the full implications of India's new colonial status were worked out. Throughout the 18th century, much of India was increasingly drawn into the world trading patterns dominated by the West. Like Indonesia, but unlike the Americas, India offered a well-developed manufacturing economy along with a vast population and solid agricultural base. European merchants were eager to exploit India's wealth, but were concerned lest India compete with their own manufacturing capabilities. Early in the 18th century, Britain began to levy high tariffs on the import of cotton cloth. This was one of India's chief industries, but it was just getting started in Britain. By limiting Indian access to a British market, London effectively reduced India's opportunities in world trade. British-made goods, including textiles, were widely sold on the subcontinent, while hundreds of thousands of Indian textile workers began to be thrown out of work. In turn, the Indians exported gold and also agricultural products, such as tea, which were grown on commercial estates staffed by low-paid wage laborers. British agents also took growing command over Indian textile production, dictating wages and conditions to the workers, while the British East India Company claimed Indian gold as a payment for their costs of administration.

These exploitative economic policies were not Britain's final statement on Indian affairs. As the British Empire matured after 1800—and particularly after about 1830—economic relations with India became less one-sided. In this early period, however, India was clearly added to the list of world territories that helped feed European wealth. An 18th-century Indian account showed a clear understanding of what was going on:

> But such is the little regard which they [the British] show to the people of this kingdom, and such their apathy and indifference for their welfare, that the people under their dominion groan everywhere, and are reduced to poverty and distress.

To be sure, some Indians welcomed British rule as an alternative to intolerant Muslim control. And many, particularly those in the independent kingdoms that still, in 1800, governed over half of the subcontinent in loose alliance with British administration, were scarcely aware of the British presence as yet. But the initial impact of European, especially British, operations deepened India's decline from the high point of Mughal rule. The Hindu religion, still the fundamental cultural resource for the majority, had ceased for a time its role in sparking vigorous philosophical and artistic statements. India's schools and universities were inactive. Manufacturing stagnated, and the level of prosperity reached under Akbar was not regained.

Basic structures—the family, the village, and the caste system—still organized daily life effectively. But the subcontinent had suffered yet another foreign-imposed regime, the Mughals, whose ultimate political legacy involved the embittered relations between Hindus and Muslims and its own decline. And as the 18th century drew to a close, India received yet another administration imposed from the outside. British rule relied on superior military technology rather than the sheer numbers of the earlier Muslim forces. The

British concentrated more on commercial purposes, in contrast to the Muslim tendency, at least ultimately, to focus on religious gain. But in many ways the British occupation confirmed what was now a well-established Indian tradition of suffering control by others, secure in the belief that basic local and religious structures could be preserved and unable in any event to offer an effective political or military alternative. It could not be predicted, in 1800, whether experience under British rule would finally break this aspect of the Indian tradition.

CONCLUSION: THE RISE AND DECLINE OF ASIAN EMPIRES

The rise of the great early modern empires in India and the Middle East, dazzling though they were, had not prevented the relative decline of both regions in the face of the rapid change and expansion of Western civilization. Partly because of the persistence of cultural and political traditions, partly because of the institutions of foreign military rule, neither Indian nor Middle Eastern civilization remained actively innovative, in technology or intellectual life, between 1600 and 1800. As one measure, the conditions of most ordinary people, the bulk of them peasants, changed little. Taxes rose, especially under rapacious Ottoman governors, and economic conditions deteriorated somewhat—most obviously in India—but the basic framework remained the same.

This pattern was not totally different from that of China during the same period. Here, too, we will discuss a growing stagnation, even as the West continued to develop rapidly. Here, too, there was relative decline as a result. But in the Middle East and particularly India, the outcome of relative decline was more quickly visible. Neither civilization was able to mount a policy of strict isolation. In both cases, European merchants pressed in with growing numbers. Unlike the Chinese also, the Ottomans were unable to establish any durable agreement with expanding Russian forces, in part because the Russian heartland was closer, in part because Russian appetites for warm water ports and contact with Middle Eastern Orthodox Christians were more vigorous than vaguer interests concerning expansion against China. Yet, despite outside pressures, and despite the example of imaginative individual leaders like Suleiman and Akbar, the Ottoman and Mughal empires were no more eager than the Chinese to undertake significant internal reform. For Muslims, reluctance to think in terms of copying the West, so long viewed as culturally barbarian, was at least as great as in China.

The results of first relative, then absolute, decline began to emerge after 1700. The growing British hold over much of India was the most dramatic sign that internal weakness plus Western ambition was a combustible mixture. But the Middle East was vulnerable as well. In 1798, a small naval expedition under a discontented French revolutionary general, Napoleon Bonaparte, sailed to Egypt and conquered the province after brief fighting. This was a minor episode in the European history of the time, and the French were indeed soon chased out by British naval forces as Napoleon returned to France to pursue grander designs. But to Muslims, the shock waves were profound, as it was realized that even a minor European excursion could now topple a proud Ottoman province. The question of Western threat for the Turks and Arabs and of Western domination for the

Indians was becoming paramount by 1800, despite the important political strengths that had surfaced in the 16th and 17th centuries. Indian and Middle Eastern responses, after 1800, would differ widely. But for a moment both civilizations seemed caught in a similar midposition, among the ancient civilizations, between the expansive surge of the West and Russia and the proud isolation of East Asia.

SUGGESTED READINGS

On the Middle East, L. S. Stavrianos, *The Ottoman Empire: Was It the Sick Man of Europe?* (1957), offers interpretive issues; for surveys, see: Stanford Shaw, *History of the Ottoman Empire and Modern Turkey*, vol. 1, 1280–1808 (1976); Bernard Lewis, *Istanbul and the Civilization of the Ottoman Empire* (1963); and Peter F. Sugar, *Southeastern Europe Under Ottoman Rule, 1354–1804* (1977). On the vital question of Western relations, see H. A. R. Gibb and H. Bowey, *Islamic Society and the West* (1957). For India, see M. Prawdin, *The Builders of the Mogul Empire* (1963); P. Spear's, *India: A Modern History* (1961) and *Twilight of the Mughals* (1951) provide additional insight. On Mughal cultural development, consult Gavin Hambly, *Mughal Cities* (1968).

The Isolation of East Asia

Focal Points

China and Japan both consciously decided to isolate themselves from extensive Western contact and from the emerging world economy. Why did they do this? Did they suffer from this decision in the early modern period? Along with isolation, however, China and Japan embarked on radically different courses from the 16th century onward. China emphasized stability, calling on its elaborate political and cultural traditions. Change came, particularly through growing cities and internal commerce and rapid population increase, but it was not fully acknowledged. Japan, in contrast, redefined a number of its institutions and cultural emphases. Why did Japan and China differ at this point, and what were the implications of their differences for the future?

The response of East Asia to the West and to the new world economy differed greatly from the reactions that developed in Russia during the early modern period. At the same time, the East Asian situation differed from that of the Muslim empires as well. China, Japan, and Korea undertook absolutely no Westernization effort, though Japan briefly flirted with the idea. But there was little intrusion from the West, in contrast to India. Geographically most distant from the West, operating in a culture much more accustomed to proud isolation, East Asia stood apart from the rest of the continent. Yet this was an important period in the region's history, as different sets of trends took root in China and Japan.

Both China and Japan responded similarly to the growing level of international contacts under Western auspices after the 15th century: they chose to try to ignore it. Their decisions were reached separately, for Chinese and Japanese societies, though rooted in some common patterns, remained distinct. Japan decided on isolation quite explicitly, after a brief and intense interaction with Western influence. China's decision came more by default. After an impressive surge toward greater international involvement in the 15th century, China's leaders pulled in their horns in favor of greater concentration on traditional cultural and economic patterns. Westerners were not entirely banned, but were treated as a minor and decidedly inferior intrusion.

The East Asian choice of isolation was in many ways unsurprising. This had long been the most remote of the major European and Asian civilizations, though Japan had of course vigorously utilized influences from China within the civilization's confines. None of the East Asian societies normally sought major expansion, which further limited the relevance of Western example. What was novel after 1450 was that isolation, when it came, flew in the face of the shrinkage of the world—the fact that all other societies were being drawn into an increasing network of contacts at least to some degree. East Asia's option to stand apart was entirely viable, in the sense that the separate societies continued to function well. But the policy raised problems for the more distant future. For East Asian civilization no longer possessed sufficient dynamism to maintain the pace set by other areas of the world, particularly the West, on its own. By standing apart, it fell behind.

While Japan and China were both largely isolated, however, their patterns during the early modern period were not identical. Here the importance of purely regional developments must be recognized, along with the larger relationship to the world economy. Japan changed more than China did, in part through belated utilization of its Confucian heritage. As a result, by the 18th century, Japanese government and society were more vigorous internally than their Chinese counterparts.

CHINA: THE RESUMPTION OF THE DYNASTIES

Mongol rule in China turned out to be no more than a painful but passing episode, lasting from the later part of the 13th century until 1368. Chinese resentment of the Mongols as unwashed barbarians confirmed their suspicions of the world outside their boundaries. But in fact the Mongol episode showed once again the historic assimilating power of Chinese culture. The Mongol rulers used the bureaucracy, rather than destroying it, for the simple reason that they, like earlier invaders, could think of no better administrative system. Kubilai Khan, himself a Buddhist, supported Confucian scholarship, though Confucianists did not return his affection. Trade actually increased, as contacts with Muslim traders expanded. Chinese culture continued to experiment with new forms, particularly new dramatic and musical styles for urban audiences.

While Chinese vitality seemed unabated by Mongol rule, resentment increased, especially when serious flooding pushed the peasantry to revolt. Revolutionary forces drove the Mongols out, to the northern plains of Mongolia, in 1368. A rebel leader, born of peasant stock, seized the Mongol capital of Beijing and proclaimed a new Ming, meaning "brilliant," dynasty, which was to last until 1644.

It was the Ming dynasty that early on experimented with the great trading expeditions through the Indian ocean and then in 1433, pulled back, on the grounds that the effort was too costly for what it yielded to China. The initiative was fascinating, but the decision to return to relative isolation was in many ways more important for China's course during the early modern period. Other expenses, for a dynasty bent on building a splendid capital while protecting China from any Mongol resurgence, helped prompt the decision. But the pullback reflected deeper factors as well, beginning with a preference for traditional expenditures rather than distant foreign involvements. Chinese merchant activity continued to be extensive in Southeast Asia. Chinese trading groups established permanent settlements in the Philippines, Malaysia, and Indonesia, where they added to the cultural diversity of the area and maintained a disproportionate role in local and regional trading activities into the 20th century. But China's chance to become a dominant world trading power was lost, at least for some centuries, with a decision that in essence confirmed the relatively low status of commerce within the official Chinese scheme of things.

To Western eyes, accustomed to judging a society's dynamism by its ability to reach out and gain new territories or trade positions, China's decision may seem hard to understand, the precursor to some inevitable decline. In Chinese terms, of course, it was the brief trading flurry that was unusual, not its cessation. And China did not clearly suffer from the decision to pull back. The government carefully regulated contacts with the West, permitting trade only through the Portuguese-controlled port of Macao. Ming emperors consolidated their rule over the empire's vast territory, though there was more factional fighting in the imperial court than had been true in earlier dynasties. The bureaucracy functioned well, as the Ming sent out representatives to guard against corruption by local officials. Internal economic development continued as well. Industry expanded, with growth in the production of textiles and porcelain. Ongoing trade with Southeast Asia enriched the port cities. Agricultural production and population both increased. Cultural activity focused on summing up expanding knowledge in medicine, agriculture, and technology; on maintaining interest in drama and poetry; and on pursuing philosophical training in Confucianism.

Historians of China have characterized the Ming period in terms of the importance of "change within tradition." The phrase aptly summed up developments under Ming rule, after the trading expeditions ceased. Chinese society evolved within frameworks previously set. There were no intellectual breakthroughs, no basic alterations in social structure, with the continued preeminence of the educated gentry-bureaucrat group. The expansion of trade, and the rise of a group of "overseas Chinese" merchants in Southeast Asian cities with close ties to the homeland, did not shake the earlier social priorities. Family structure remained similarly stable, with emphasis on patriarchal control, reverence for elders and ancestors, and provision of male heirs.

Traditional also was the decline of the Ming dynasty, early in the 1600s. Emperors grew weaker, the bureaucracy more corrupt, while peasant unrest increased under the impact of population pressure. Rebellions and banditry became widespread. A popular rebellion caused the last Ming emperor to hang himself. This internal disorder attracted invaders from southern Manchuria, who in 1644 set up a new dynasty, the Qing (sometimes called Manchu), which lasted until 1912—the last royal house to rule China.

Again traditionally, the Qing (or Pure) dynasty started out with a flourish. The Manchurian emperors were foreigners in the eyes of most Chinese, and they maintained a separate military establishment to support their regime. But on the whole their rule quickly took on familiar patterns, with substantial reliance on the bureaucracy, which remained in Chinese hands, dominated by the educated scholar-gentry. The emperors also encouraged Confucianism. Like most early dynasties, the Qing initially expanded the empire's territory. They pushed the Mongols still farther north and extended the empire into Muslim central Asia; they also took over supervision of Tibet. Finally, they conquered the offshore island of Taiwan, which had previously been ruled by trading officials from a Dutch East India Company. This expansion, directed by the able emperor K'ang Hsi from 1662 to 1722, revealed the successful merger of Manchu military qualities and Chinese administrative skill. K'ang Hsi himself mastered the Confucian classics and sponsored important cultural competitions, endearing himself to the Chinese scholar-gentry class.

K'ang Hsi and his 18th-century successor also worked on increasing government centralization—another common impulse of vigorous early dynasties in the Chinese tradition. Central schools for training would-be bureaucrats expanded, and a Grand Council was set up to direct the bureaucracy and handle the mountain of paperwork resulting from regular reports from local and provincial administrators. Careful regulations provided punishments for local rebellions. Village leaders were held responsible for individuals in their community who committed crimes or tried to evade debts. Chinese society remained the most closely regulated and the most centralized in the world. Local and central administration intertwined, and there was no real separation, as in the Western tradition, between public and private concerns.

During this vigorous period the Qing dynasty continued to supervise European contacts with China. K'ang Hsi negotiated a border agreement with the expanding Russian empire, on the Amur River, that was to last until 1850; this checked Russian expansion into Chinese territory, although the Russians continued to move eastward into Siberia. Small numbers of Jesuit missionaries had been allowed into China since the 16th century, from Western Europe, mainly because they brought useful scientific and technical knowledge, including superior clocks. For their part the missionaries were careful to adopt many Chinese ways, approving ancestor worship and wearing Confucian clothing. In the 18th century the government, growing less secure, began to persecute the small number of Christians.

The Chinese outlook toward limited Western contacts was symbolized by the reaction to the Portuguese community set up on Macao. While some officials wanted to force the Portuguese out, the dominant view was that it was safe to leave them there because they could be so closely supervised; indeed, it would be easier to control them in this one center than to try to monitor their activities on the high seas. As one viceroy put it:

> Our military forces can watch over the foreigners by just guarding the surrounding sea. We shall know how to put them at death's door as soon as they cherish any disloyal design. Now if we move them to the open sea, by what means could we punish the foreign evil-doers and how could we keep them in submission and defend ourselves against them?

Trade and cultural contacts with the West, or indeed with any other civilizations outside the traditional Chinese orbit, thus reached only modest levels by 1800. Some conscious policies of regulating foreign merchants and missionaries combined with great confidence in the superiority of Chinese ways to produce this result. Efforts by Britain and other Western countries to open further trading contacts were consistently rebuffed. An English representative in 1793 was treated as if he brought tribute from an inferior state. He was forced to kow-tow (bowing by kneeling and knocking his head on the floor), as the subject-state envoys from countries like Korea or Vietnam were required to do. And then the emperor, rejecting his argument for more trade, wrote a long, patronizing letter to King George III explaining that China had no need of English goods.

Christian missionary (a Bajan Jesuit) in China, 17th century. Jesuits proceeded cautiously, respecting Chinese culture.

CULTURAL AND SOCIAL TRENDS: SOME NEW PROBLEMS

Although there was no reason to suspect in 1800 that China was on the eve of some unprecedented difficulties, going beyond the usual decline of a dynasty, significant problems in the empire occurred under the Qing even before this point. These problems were not initially political; the institutions of government remained secure. But they raised important issues nevertheless.

In the first place, Chinese culture even under the early Qing seemed to stagnate. The Qing themselves, as foreign rulers, favored traditional expressions as a means of proving their sympathy with Chinese ways; thus the emphasis on the classics of Chinese literature and philosophy, already extensive, increased. By the 18th century most educated Chinese turned to collecting older examples of art and expounding literary criticisms of older works, rather than seeking to create new styles. The amount of cultural effort was great; many bureaucrats and other educated people painted nature scenes or dabbled in calligraphy and poetry writing. But the goal was decidedly uninspired, with trivial themes emphasized and traditional styles rigidly defended. Similarly in philosophy attention focused on expounding past principles and offering extended commentary on what had been written in earlier periods. Thus the earlier Chinese ability to blend reverence for tradition with an interest in promoting new styles and in adding new thinking seemed somewhat stultified.

The Chinese economy, for its part, did not break fundamental new ground either. Revealingly, after the early Ming advances in navigational devices, the Chinese produced no significant technologies during the Ming and Qing dynasties. It was not a matter of decline. As in the arts, Chinese levels of achievement remained high, and Chinese craft products, such as porcelain (which became known simply as *china* to the Europeans), were greatly valued. But an earlier ability to build on past accomplishments seemed to have been lost.

One key symptom of the new outlook toward technology showed in the reaction to European superiority in weapons. The Chinese were perfectly capable, in the 16th and 17th centuries, of building cannons as good as the Europeans had, even though they had not pioneered in the design. But in fact they did not care to; the subject did not interest them greatly, and they were content to assemble inferior muskets and small guns, confident that their strength on the land was sufficient to keep any European threat at bay. To be sure, the Chinese had never been as interested in military as in manufacturing technology, but their earlier creativity in the whole area was demonstrably slipping.

The interruption of China's tradition of innovation in basic technology did not, indeed, prevent continued internal economic development, supported both by the government and by private business interests. During the late Ming and early Qing dynasties, manufacturing, city growth, and internal trade surpassed all previous levels. China's strong production base and extensive market activities help explain why, well into the 19th century, the nation could largely ignore Western goods, leaving Western merchants casting about for items to trade for sought-after Chinese products such as silk cloth and porcelain. But China's economic surge did not bring fundamental economic transformation of the sort that might have generated new manufacturing technology. Much production lay in the hands of rural cottage artisans whose low wages discouraged more elaborate capitalist arrangements. And by the mid–18th century the economy itself began to stagnate, bringing renewed poverty and distress. Why did China not make a fuller turn to new economic forms?

The Chinese upper class had of course always esteemed traditionalism and looked rather scornfully at purely economic activity; yet, while this was a factor, it had not prevented earlier technological or commercial advance. The increasing centralization of the government under Qing rulers, who were more cautious than their Han or T'ang forebears, may have been a cause as well.

One vital and novel ingredient in the tendency toward stagnation in key areas of Chinese society was a rapid increase in population levels, from the late Ming dynasty onward. Between 1600 and 1800, Chinese population probably doubled, from 150 million to 300 million people. China's well-organized agriculture and the strong cultural emphasis placed on high birth rates, in order to produce male heirs in the family, had long encouraged population growth. Many dynasties had previously declined when such growth outstripped available resources, creating greater poverty. Usually, however, population levels would then fall back; but this did not happen during the late Ming and early Qing peri-

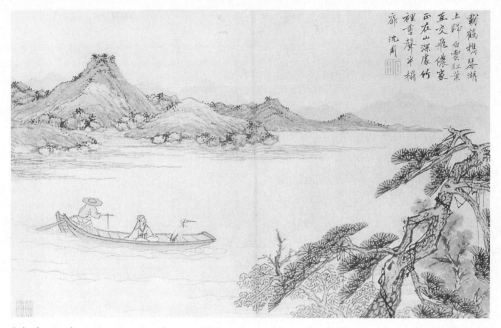

Scholar and crane returning home, 15th century. Note the similarities to earlier Chinese styles (illustrated in Chapter 9).

ods. Agricultural techniques were advanced enough to maintain a large but impoverished population. Cultivation of some crops brought in from the Americas by European traders and missionaries, particularly corn and the sweet potato, added to the agricultural production that could support high population levels. New strains of rice, which grew more rapidly than older varieties, achieved the same end. As a result of these crop changes, China began to shift from a society in which population sometimes outstripped resources, to a society chronically pressed by its population levels.

Population pressure, in turn, had two clear effects, quite apart from the great poverty of many Chinese peasants and urban workers. First, it made political unrest a greater threat than had usually been the case except when dynasties were losing their grip. And second, it diverted resources that might have been used for encouragement of further manufacturing or trade to a desperate effort to sustain the vast population. The empire's economic flexibility was reduced by the need to devote so much labor and land to agricultural subsistence. This may be the clearest cause of the lack of innovation in the economy and possibly even in the culture.

By the late 18th century, massive poverty and slow economic growth began to surface as clear political problems. The Qing government found it increasingly difficult to collect adequate taxes. Collection efforts, along with grinding misery, also began to produce a new series of popular revolts. Peasants in many regions formed secret societies. An uprising by one such society in the 1790s, the White Lotus, was put down only with difficulty. At the same time the Qing dynasty was showing signs of internal decay: military virtues waned among the Manchu generals, who preferred more luxurious living, and court officials became more corrupt, siphoning money off from the state. This kind of decline normally prefaced a period of growing instability, and ultimately the rise of a new dynasty. Greater disorder came, without question, in the 19th century, but for once in China's long history a new regime, not a new dynasty, was the ultimate result.

Stagnation and political problems were not the only feature of Chinese society under the Qing. Some interesting changes occurred in popular culture, as Confucian leaders managed to persuade more and more peasants to abandon older beliefs in magic and superstition, and to use doctors instead of shamans in cases of illness. This shift in outlook, somewhat similar to changes going on in the West in the same period, differentiated China from most agricultural societies, where popular religion had yet to be disturbed. The scholar-bureaucrats also pressed peasants and city dwellers to standardize the worship of local gods and goddesses. The practice of celebrating various deities and building temples to them had persisted from the classical period or before, along with other belief systems, and the government long tried to bend this popular faith toward loyalty to the state. Certainly, in 1800, the Chinese government remained easily able to regulate China's contacts with other cultures. European influence, most notably, remained no greater than it had been two centuries before, and European traders were powerless to escape government supervision. Only developments after 1800 would break this stalemate, to China's disadvantage.

JAPAN AND THE ORIGINS OF ISOLATION

Japanese social forms were less firmly set around 1450 than were those of China, so it is not surprising that Japanese history shows more movement, more basic changes, than did the evolution of its giant neighbor. Yet the Japanese did come to share one basic concept with the Chinese: that the outside world was a risky and inferior place, best kept at bay.

Japan was touched only indirectly by the Mongol invasions. The failure of the two great Mongol attacks bolstered Japanese confidence in the god-protected superiority of their own society even over that of China, which lay under foreign thrall. But the defense effort was very costly to the ruling government of the shogun; it contributed to the fall of this essentially feudal monarchy in 1338. Japan returned to a stage of regional feudal governments, of the warlike daimyos and their samurai supporters. A central government remained in form only. In fact, disorder and warfare, punctuated by some peasant rebellions, continued until 1573. A host of classic campaigns, celebrated in legend and more recently in Japanese films, dotted this period, in which samurai fighting techniques and codes of honor were perfected.

Yet despite disorder, the Japanese economy continued to progress. Because the daimyos were well aware of the importance of prosperous agriculture for their own tax revenues, they promoted irrigation efforts and improved methods of farming. Trade also grew, and the use of banking and money expanded. Daimyo supervision of trade set up a pattern of government-business collaboration that in many ways has remained to the present day.

Japanese culture continued to develop as well, again setting up durable new lines. The Zen form of Buddhism, stressing calm meditation and love of nature, predominated in religion, though there were many Buddhist sects and though Shintoism still guided family ceremonies as well. Zen Buddhism encouraged an interest in ritual, as demonstrations of the simplicity of true beauty and as signs of self-control. Tea ceremonies and flower arrangements were important parts of family and social life. The Zen spirit also influenced art, leading to a focus on simple but dramatic representations of nature.

In literature, adventure stories and poetry continued to dominate. Soon after 1600 a new poetic form, the *haiku,* or 17-syllable verse in a 5-7-5 pattern, became popular. Though this was a new style, it maintained the East Asian tradition of carefully enunciated rules of poetry and an interest in clever play on words. Composing haiku became a favored pastime among all social classes.

By the mid-1500s, however, the Japanese combination of feudal warfare and economic and cultural creativity was breaking down. Feudalism could no longer contain the forces at work in Japanese society. A rising merchant class complicated the feudal pattern. Armies of peasant soldiers were sometimes able to beat samurai swordsmen—just as common bowmen in Europe had ultimately dislodged the feudal cavalry. Furthermore, Portuguese traders reached Japanese shores in 1542 and, while they were initially welcomed by a people who had once before learned from others, their presence encouraged a desire among more conservative cultural and political leaders to develop a stronger government that could regulate the foreign intrusion. And the guns and cannons the Portuguese

Japanese garden style: Sanbro-In Temple, Kyoto, laid out under Hideyoshi at the end of the 16th century. The pond, waterfall, and bridge show the move toward a disciplined nature.

brought obviously threatened the fighting traditions of the samurai. Many regional daimyos tried to ally with the foreigners to gain a weapons advantage; the result, for a time, was simply further disorder. In the long run, however, the advent of gunpowder increased the possibility of greater governmental centralization. As the Japanese quickly learned to manufacture their own muskets, the doom of the full feudal system was sealed.

It came in the form of several brutal wars at the end of the 16th century in which a successful general, Hideyoshi (see p. 359), emerged victorious. Hideyoshi was able to reestablish centralized rule by using the allegiance of the daimyos. Thus the feudal classes remained in Japan but were again overseen by a national administration. After Hideyoshi's death, a general from the Tokugawa family took over the office of shogun and completed the process of centralization. A "great peace" settled on Japan, after more than two centuries of internal warfare.

This new centralization caused a reassessment of Japan's contacts with the outside world. Hideyoshi contemplated a policy of foreign conquest to keep the warlike samurai busy—a policy later renewed by Japan after 1890. But an attempt to invade Korea failed, as Chinese armies supported their vassal government there, and this convinced the new Japanese government to concentrate on its national uniqueness.

Hideyoshi and the early Tokugawa thus turned to what they saw as the problem of Western influence. Initial Western contacts had been welcomed not only for the guns and navigation technology the Westerners brought, but also, among some Japanese, for the religious message of Christianity. Interested in learning from foreign example and impressed by a religion that seemed to accompany military and trading success, several thousand Japanese converted to Catholicism in the port cities where Europeans clustered, during the late 16th century. But Japan's new rulers looked harshly on this development. They feared European power and thought that where Western religion went, political control might not be far behind. When the Spanish government set up military outposts in the Philippines, to enhance the missionary effort there, Hideyoshi's fears deepened. In 1597 he banned all foreign missionaries, crucifying nine of them and 17 of their Japanese followers.

The Portuguese come to Japan, 16th century.

Toyotomi Hideyoshi (1536–1548) was an outstanding military leader who picked up on efforts earlier in the 16th century to tame the power struggles among the daimyos in favor of more centralized, orderly rule. The son of a peasant, Hideyoshi used his military skills to win leadership in Japan, then parlayed even greater diplomatic talents into the creation of a string of alliances with the daimyos that created a central state by 1590. Hideyoshi, unlike most Japanese leaders before or after, dreamed of wider achievements as he contemplated ruling China and even India (despite, or perhaps because of, knowing little about either place). He did launch two abortive attacks on Korea, the last still in progress when he died. More important, Hideyoshi also launched the campaign to limit European and Christian influence in Japan. Hideyoshi's hopes to pass power to his son were dashed as the Tokugawa family seized control and his overseas plans were dropped. Nevertheless, he had contributed greatly to changing the course of Japanese history. His portrait shows the military might and the confidence that spurred his achievements. How does Hideyoshi compare, in achievements and goals, to other great military leaders in world history who rose from the ranks? (The Granger Collection)

Feudal Japan Under the Shogunate, 16th Century

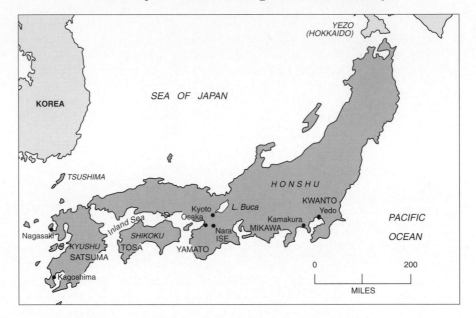

Western weapons seemed at least as great a threat as Christianity. The new central rulers feared the results of independent daimyo access to Western firearms. Rather they sought state control over guns, while also protecting samurai warrior values. To do this, they needed to restrict foreign trade.

The Tokugawa shogunate completed the destruction of Christianity in Japan. It severely curtailed Western trade as well. Only merchants from the Netherlands were allowed in Japan at all—Holland was feared less than Spain or Portugal because, being Protestant, it was not linked to what seemed to the Japanese an ambitious and powerful papacy; and Dutch traders were confined to one isolated, carefully controlled port (Nagasaki). Even Chinese merchants were supervised. In 1635, the Japanese themselves were forbidden to go abroad, and those already overseas were not allowed to return home. Finally, the government prohibited the construction of large, seagoing ships; only vessels for coastal trade were permitted. Japan, even more than China, was cut off from the outside world. A nation that had once eagerly imitated foreign example, and would do so again in the 19th century, pulled back on this occasion. European ways seemed too foreign, and too inferior, to be allowed free play, and attacking outside influence provided a useful way of cementing new national loyalties after the long period of disunity.

The policy of isolation combined with regulation of military technology, now that foreign items could not be imported. The shogunate deliberately turned against guns, preferring to preserve the Japanese social structure. Only a few could be manufactured each year—sometimes no more than nine for the whole country. Even more than in the Ottoman empire, where printing was long shunned, Japan decisively rejected the idea that new technology is good technology.

In isolation, Japan proceeded to construct effective political forms and completed the development of a national culture, sponsoring considerable social change while seeming to maintain older values. Unlike the earlier Kamakura shogunate, the Tokugawa rulers depended less on personal ties with feudal lords and more on an efficient bureaucracy imbued with Confucian values. The warrior aristocracy was given great social prestige, including special privileges in law and special costumes, though in fact there was no fighting to be done. While warrior values and military training continued to describe the samurai ethic, upper-class bureaucrats learned the importance of administrative efficiency and training—Confucian principles that gained ground during the 17th and 18th centuries. This was an important period of cultural change in Japan, as Confucianism, and therefore secular interests, increasingly dominated intellectual life. Rapid spread of Confucian education and literacy disseminated the new cultural interests by the 19th century. Thanks to extensive schooling, literacy (at 25 percent among adult men) was far higher than in any society outside Western Europe and North America.

Though confined to internal trading, merchant activity flourished during the Tokugawa period. The government favored commerce, though it was somewhat scornful of the merchant class. Great trading houses emerged, selling rice, textile goods, metals, and liquor all over Japan; some of these big family firms still operate in Japan today. This was a key period for the development of banking and merchant experience in Japan. Japanese agriculture advanced as well, becoming more technologically sophisticated than any in Asia. Japanese farmers learned better use of crop specialization and fertilization; they also became increasingly accustomed to producing for sale on the market. Although economic growth slowed somewhat after 1700, Japan had the most advanced commercial economy in the world after that of Western society. In another important development, population size was controlled in the 18th century, in contrast to the situation in China. Many peasants practiced infanticide of unwanted—and particularly female—children.

Japanese literature and art remained vigorous under the Tokugawa, who supervised cultural life to prevent disorder. Enthusiasm for haiku poetry and the stylized Nō theater continued. Literacy and book publishing spread. As in China earlier, the growth of cities—particularly the capital city, Edo, which had a million inhabitants by 1700—encouraged a flourishing entertainment industry. Professional women entertainers, called geisha, or "accomplished persons," specialized in singing and dancing for a male clientele. A new dramatic form, Kabuki, developed in the 18th century, more popular in its portrayals than the Nō forms; Kabuki theater remains active in Japan today. Not surprisingly, the varied artistic endeavors and the continuing isolation of Japan produced a heavy emphasis on the nation's uniqueness and superiority, the forerunner of a cultural nationalism that still runs strong in Japan.

Japan thus emerged, by the 18th century, as an unusually diverse society, embracing more internal tensions than did China. Feudal and Confucian elements coexisted: official lack of interest in commerce belied rapid commercial expansion; Buddhist spiritual fervor could strain against a national emphasis on controlled expression and secular education. These tensions contributed to the dynamism of Japanese society, which had unquestionably advanced under the policy of isolation.

Indeed, by the 18th century the policy of isolation was itself slightly relaxed. Some Japanese were allowed greater contact with Dutch traders in the port of Nagasaki; a few scholars learned Dutch and became familiar with Western advances in military technology and medicine. These early exchanges helped prepare the way for fuller Japanese confrontation of Western ways in the 19th century. At the same time they whetted the appetites of those few Japanese aware of the gap between their society and the West; Japanese backwardness in scientific and medical knowledge seemed particularly galling.

Also during the 18th century, however, the Tokugawa shogunate showed some signs of decline. Government leaders became indebted to urban merchants, a situation that forced them to reduce their support of their samurai retainers; the oddity of preserving this warrior group in a bureaucratic, commercial economy intensified. Individual Tokugawa rulers were less capable than their 17th-century predecessors, in a process of dynastic decline similar to that of China. The economy remained prosperous, but the government faced recurrent problems collecting sufficient taxes. Peasant protest increased. Japan did not experience the kind of population pressure that burdened China, though the islands were crowded; but Japan's commercial agriculture resulted in a division between landowning peasants and landless paid laborers, whose discontent produced periodic revolts. The Tokugawa regime was in no sense on the ropes by 1800; there were few pressures for explicit political change, and bureaucratic training and efficiency may even have been improving. Japan's strengths, generated by the important developments of the preceding centuries, would help explain the nation's extraordinary reaction to challenges in the 19th century, when isolation finally had to be abandoned completely. The contrast with the looming crisis in China was marked, but there were some new concerns, and these too help explain why Japan became more open to the possibility of more radical transformations.

CONCLUSION: VITALITY AND TENSION IN EAST ASIA

East Asian history between 1400 and 1800 was no mere record of isolation. Although during this period the civilization was set apart from wider currents of world history, these were centuries of considerable internal change. Change meant new political dynasties, but also new cultural and economic forms, particularly in Japan. It also meant some new problems, such as the population pressure that surged in China. The hand of tradition was strong as well, in Japanese culture and its sense of national identity, in Chinese politics and society more generally.

East Asia's lag behind Western levels of technology and military organization during these centuries would leave the civilization vulnerable after 1800. It might have been preferable had the society assimilated or reacted to European styles more gradually, to the extent necessary to keep pace with European power. This was the sentiment that inspired China's communist leader in 1984 to claim that the Ming-Qing period of isolation—as well as a more recent, brief attempt to insulate China from foreign contact—was a mistake. Yet in our own day it seems clear that East Asian civilization, or at least significant portions of it, has been most successful in developing competitive alternatives to Western ways. In this sense the period of isolation, as a time for solidifying traditions apart from the distraction of handling foreign influences, may not have been totally ill-conceived. Certainly, the decisions to cut off ties allowed East Asian societies to continue to follow their own complex dynamic for a final few centuries, before confronting some of the larger currents of modern world history.

SUGGESTED READINGS

An excellent source collection is W. T. de Bary, ed., *Sources of Chinese Tradition* (1966); close to source reading, offering fascinating insight into Chinese provincial life, is Jonathan Spence, *The Death of Woman Wang* (1979). Larger studies of China in the early modern period include: J. D. Spence and J. E. Wills, Jr., eds., *From Ming to Qing: Conquest, Religion and Continuity in Seventeenth Century China* (1979); Albert Chan, *The Glory and Fall of the Ming Dynasty* (1982); Roy Huang, *1587: A Year of No Significance; The Ming Dynasty in Decline* (1981); Jonathan Spence, *The Memory Palace of Matteo Ricci* (1984) and *The Search for Modern China* (1990); and J. K. Fairbank, ed., *The Chinese World Order: Traditional Chinese Foreign Relations* (1968). On Japan, consult: Peter Duus, *Feudalism in Japan* (1976); H. D. Harootunian, *Toward Restoration: The Growth of Political Consciousness in Tokugawa Japan* (1970); and E. O. Reischauer, *Japan: The Study of a Nation*, 3rd ed. (1981). Noel Perrin, *Giving up the Gun* (1979), is a fascinating account of shogun policies on weapons and trade. On the much-debated, important topic of peasant conditions in the Tokugawa shogunate, see H. Bix, *Peasant Protest in Japan, 1590–1884* (1986).

PART V

The World's First Industrial Period, 1750–1914

INTRODUCTION: THE INTERNATIONAL IMPACT OF INDUSTRIALIZATION

Toward the end of the 18th century, Western Europe began to change in several fundamental ways. Most apparent, a new economic and technological system took shape in Britain that would ultimately replace the dominance of agriculture with an industrial order. British industrialization spread to other parts of Western Europe early in the 19th century and also to the new United States. New political doctrines and institutions also began to emerge in Western Europe and the United States, with fundamental implications about how the state should operate and what kinds of laws and social structures were appropriate. Previous changes in Western culture, plus the profitable position Europe had already won in the world economy, now combined to generate even more more sweeping transformations.

Although these developments initially concentrated in Europe and North America, they had major implications for the rest of the world. Western Europe's power, already on the increase, soared still further, beginning in the late 18th century and extending until 1914. Until 1850 Western Europe even maintained its edge in population growth rates, giving it great human resources (see Table V.1). Never before had a single civilization wielded such worldwide influence.

The world economy, already well defined, gained new importance as well. More parts of the world were drawn into production for export markets that Europeans dominated, while Western manufacturing expanded its output and its impact on sales to other societies. Two changes were particularly important. First, areas like Latin America and India, already producing raw materials, accelerated this emphasis yet fell further behind in living standards because of the need for cheap labor. Western industrialization heightened the consequences of economic dependency for key regions, partly because it displaced even more local manufacturing. Second, areas once barely affected by the Western-dominated world economy, like East Asia and the Middle East, were now forced in.

TABLE V.1   *Estimated Population of the World and of the Continents, 1650–1850 (in millions)*

Continent	1650	1750	1800	1850
Africa	100	95	90	95
Asia (excluding Russia)	327	475	597	741
Latin America	12	11	19	33
North America	1	1	6	26
Europe & Asiatic Russia	103	144	192	274
Oceania	2	2	2	2
World Total	545	728	906	1171

Source: Adapted from Dennis Wrong, *Population and Society* (New York: Random House, 1969), p. 13.

Industrialization also furthered European military advantage in the world by increasing weapons production and innovation. By 1850, Europe could defeat almost any rival on land as well as on the seas.

Overall, two of the key trends of the early modern period—economic and military—thus intensified. European influence escalated in a new imperialism that brought many additional areas under Western control. Variants of Western civilization spread to parts of the world particularly open to European immigrants, notably the United States, Canada, Australia, and New Zealand.

Europe's industrialization did more, however, than enhance pre-existing trends. Western society was itself transformed through the new economic system. New Western beliefs spilled over into the international arena. As the West came to rely more on wage labor supplemented by machines, and as new humanitarian ideals gained ground, Western leaders attacked the institution of slavery worldwide. The Western-dominated Atlantic slave trade ended, and slave systems within the Americas came to an end through the first three quarters of the 19th century. Pressure on African and Middle Eastern slavery also reduced the institution in these areas. The labor systems of many parts of the world, in other words, were dramatically challenged by new Western standards, backed by growing imperialist muscle. Africa had to redefine its world economic role as a result.

New beliefs spread on a global basis. Mass nationalism first arose in Europe itself, as a means of expressing new secular loyalties and supporting political change. Latin American people used a budding nationalist sentiment as one of their motives in demanding independence from Spain or Portugal. By the second half of the 19th century nationalism spread to the Middle East, India, and elsewhere. Nationalism challenged many local and religious attachments. It focused new attention on the state (or on a desire for political independence) and on wider changes needed to make one's nation a viable force in the modern world.

Because of growing Western power and the challenge of industrialization, a wider set of international forces influenced individual societies during the 19th century than had characterized the early modern period. Every society faced the necessity of coming to terms with the expanding world economy and with Western imperialism—the impossibility of isolation, the worldwide growth of market labor instead of slavery or other traditional work systems, and the growing spread of nationalism all signaled the presence of these new international forces. Every society now had to ask questions about what changes must be contemplated in order to gain or maintain independence and to adapt to an industrially fueled world economy.

New international forces, however, did not produce uniformity from one society to the next. Traditional beliefs and institutions continued to shape different responses. One of the reasons for nationalism's success lay in its ability to combine new political impulses and loyalties with devotion to older, distinctive values. Forces within the 19th century itself impacted different societies in different ways. Some places became new colonies; others freed themselves from colonialism; still others faced growing Western intrusion without the indignity but also without the protections of colonial control. As before in world history, tracking the different responses to the growing array of international contacts constitutes a major analytical challenge. On the surface, the extended 19th century seems perhaps the simplest of all the world history periods, not even breaking fully with the trends of the early modern period. The basic menu of this time includes the expanding world economy, Western imperialism, spreading nationalism, and other efforts to adapt to Western-dominated change. But the ways individual societies combined these factors and reacted to them maintained considerable complexity. Careful comparison remains essential. The world by 1914 was much different from what it had been in 1750, but it was hardly more uniform.

Western Civilization	East Asia	Middle East	India and Southeast Asia
c1770 Invention of steam engine by Watt.		**793** Failure of sultan's efforts at military reform.	
1775–1783 American Revolution.		**1798** Napoleon's Egyptian expedition.	
1787 Constitutional Convention, Philadelphia.			
1780 ff. Industrial Revolution.			
1789–1799 French Revolution.			
1793–1794 Radical phase.			
1799–1815 Reign of Napoleon.			
1800–1850 Romanticism in literature, arts.		**1811 ff.** Reforms in Egypt by Muhammed Ali.	
1815 Congress of Vienna.		**1820–1829** Greek war for Independence.	
1820 Revolutions in Greece, Spain.	**1820s** Growing Western trade with China.	**1826** Dissolution of Janissaries by Sultan Mahmud II.	**1825 ff.** Extension of Dutch control over interior of Indonesia.
1830 ff. Rise of liberalism, nationalism.	**1839–1842** Opium Wars in China.	**1828–1833** Russian-Ottoman War.	**1827–1829 ff.** Reorganization of British rule in India, development of Civil Service, new legal codes.
1829–1837 Jacksonian period in U.S.; universal white male suffrage.		**1830** Takeover of Algeria begun by France.	
1830, 1848 Revolutions several European countries.		**1830 ff.** Steamship routes set up in eastern Mediterranean and Persian Gulf by Britain, France.	
1832 British Reform Bill.		**1839** Ottoman reform attempt.	
1848 ff. Writings of Karl Marx.			

Russia and Eastern Europe	Latin America	Sub-Saharan Africa
		1787 ff. Sierra Leone founded as British colony for freed slaves.
	1808 Formation of governing junta in Venezuela.	**1807–1834** Abolition of Atlantic slave trade.
1812 Failure of Napoleonic invasion of Russia.	**1810** Leadership of Mexican revolt by Hidalgo.	
1815 Poland acquired by Russia in Treaty of Vienna.	**1810** Independent government in Argentina.	**1814** Acquisition by British of Dutch South Africa.
	1811 Proclamation of independence; Bolivar leadership.	**1821** Extension of British rule in West Africa.
	1814 Regain of control by Spain.	**1822** Liberia founded as colony for freed American slaves.
	1821 Independence regained in "Gran Colombia."	**1830 ff.** Formation of firmer Bantu governments in southern Africa.
	1814 ff. Wars of independence led by San Martin in Chile, Peru.	
	1821 Proclamation of Mexican independence by conservatives.	
	1822 Pedro emperor of Brazil	
1825–1855 Heightening of repression by Tsar Nicholas I; increase in secret police.	**1823** Independence of United Provinces of Central America.	
1829 Full autonomy gained by Serbia within Ottoman Empire; fuller independence achieved in 1856; complete independence granted in 1878.	**1825–1850** Consolidation of new nations; division of Gran Colombia, Central America.	**1835–1837** Great Trek of Boers; clash with Zulus.
1830–1831 Polish revolt put down by Nicholas.	**1829–1852** Manuel de Rosas caudillo in Argentina.	**1840 ff.** Increased Protestant missionary activity.
1831 Full independence gained by Greece.	**1833 ff.** Santa Anna leader in Mexico.	
	1836 Independence of Texas.	

Western Civilization	East Asia	Middle East	India and Southeast Asia
1859 Darwin, *Origin of Species*	**1850–1864** Tai Ping Rebellion.	**1853** Russian Ottoman War.	**1850 ff.** Development of railroad in India.
1859–1870 Italian unification.	**1853** Perry expedition to Japan.	**1854–1856** Crimean War.	**1852–1853** British war with Burma; growing influence gained by Britain.
1861–1865 U.S. Civil War.	**1857–1859** Second Opium War.	**1856** Ottoman reform attempt; new rights for Christians.	**1855** Growing British influence over Siam; trade opened by treaty.
1864–1871 German unification.	**1867** Mutsuhito emperor of Japan.	**1869** Completion of Suez Canal.	**1857–1858** Sepoy mutiny, India.
1867 Unification, dominion status for Canada.	**1868–1912** Meiji period in Japan.	**1876** Promulgation of Ottoman constitution, guaranteeing individual freedoms, setting up parliament.	**1858 ff.** British reform of government in India.
1870 ff. Spread of compulsory education laws.	**1872** Universal service in Japan.		**1858 ff.** Takeover of Indochina begun by France.
1870–1879 Institutions of French Third Republic.		**1877** Lapse of constitution.	**1861** Establishment of advisory councils, with Indian representation.
1871–1914 Highpoint of Western imperialism.		**1877–1878** Russo-Turkish War; independence gained by new Balkan nations.	**1864** Indians allowed in upper Civil Sevice.
1871 ff. Rise of socialist movement.		**1870s** Growing Western control over Egypt.	**1885** Formation of Indian National Congress.
1879—1907 Alliance system: Germany-Austria (1879); Germany-Austria-Russia (1881); Germany-Italy-Austria (1882); France-Russia (1891); Britain-France (1904); Britain-Russia (1907).		**1881** Occupation of Tunisia by France.	**1885–1886** British takeover of much of Burma.
1881–1889 German social insurance laws enacted.	**1890** New constitution, legal code in Japan.	**1882** British protectorate over Egypt.	**1886** Steel industry begun in India.
	1894–1895 Sino-Japanese War.	**1888** Construction begun on Berlin-Baghdad railway.	**1896 ff.** More formal British control of Malaya (completed 1914).
	1896 ff. Chinese students abroad.	**1896 ff.** Rise of Young Turk movement.	
	1897–1899 Chinese port concessions gained by Western nations and Russia.		
	1899–1901 Boxer Rebellion in China.		

Russia and Eastern Europe	Latin America	Sub-Saharan Africa
	1844–1846 Mexican-American War; occupation of Mexico by U.S.; upper California, New Mexico acquired by U.S.	
1854–1856 Crimean War.	**1858** First Benito Juarez government in Mexico.	**1854 ff.** Expansion of French from Senegal.
1856 Gain of virtual independence by Romania.	**1861–1867** French intervention in Mexico.	**1857–1863** French exploration in Congo basin.
1861 Russian emancipation of serfs.		**1960** German trade station set up in Cameroons.
1864 Abolition of serfdom by Romania; little land obtained by peasants.		**1861** Beginning of British expansion in Nigeria.
1860s–1870s Additional reforms by Alexander II in judiciary, local zemstov government.		**1867** Discovery of South African diamonds; increase in importation of Indian laborers.
1865–1876 Russian conquests in central Asia.		**1875 ff.** Explosion of European imperialism in Africa.
1867 Alaska sold to U.S. by Russia.	**1876–1911** Porfirio Diaz caudillo in Mexico.	**1876** Congo claimed by Belgian king.
1875–1878 War with Ottoman Empire, gain of new territory.	**1880 ff.** Growing commercialization of Latin American economy.	**1878 ff.** New Catholic missions set up.
1878 Independent Bulgaria created.	**1870–1888** Guzmán Blanco caudillo in Venezuela.	**1878 ff.** Expansion of British, French interior expeditions in West Africa.
1881 Anarchist assassination of Alexander II.	**1889** Republic of Brazil; abolition of slavery.	**1899** Nigeria a full British colony.
1881 ff. Growing repression in Russia; attacks on minorities.	**1898** Spanish-American War; acquisition of Puerto Rico by U.S.; protectorate over Cuba.	**1877–1879 ff.** New missionary efforts in east Africa; curtailment of East African slave trade.
1884–1887 New gains in central Asia.		**1879** Defeat of Zulus by British.
1884 ff. Beginnings of Russian industrialization; Sergei Witte the leading minister; completion of trans-Siberian railway.		**1880** Acquisition by French of separate Congo colony.
1898 Formation of Marxist Social Democratic party.		**1884** Organization of German treaties by Karl Peters to gain Tanganyika.
		1886 Discovery of South African gold; development of railway.
		1892 ff. Expansion of East Africa Company into Uganda.
		1890s–1905 Uprisings in West Africa (Ashanti); in Sudan, Tanganyika (Muslims and animists).
		1899–1902 Boer War.

Western Civilization	East Asia	Middle East	India and Southeast Asia
			1896–1899 Revolt against Spain in Philippines. **1898** United States capture of Manila. Defeat of Philippine independence movement by United States.
	1904–1905 Russo-Japanese War. **1910** Annexation of Korea by Japan. **1911** Chinese revolution. **1912** Fall of last (Qing) dynasty.	**1911** Occupation of Morocco by France; takeover of Tripoli (present-day Libya) by Italy. **1918** Collapse of Ottoman Empire.	
1914 Beginning of World War I.			

Russia and Eastern Europe	Latin America	Sub-Saharan Africa
	1903	**1901 ff.**
	U.S.-backed revolt in Panama; independence from Colombia.	Development of railway in East Africa.
1904–1905	**1904–1914**	**1904**
Loss by Russia of war with Japan.	Construction of Panama Canal by U.S.	Great insurrection in German Tanganyika, put down with 20,000 troops.
1905	**1905 ff.**	
Revolution in Russia; peasant reforms and Duma.	Growing U.S. political and military intervention in Central America, Haiti, and Dominican Republic.	
1912–1913	**1911**	
Two Balkan wars.	Beginning of Mexican Revolution.	
1917		
Russian Revolution; abolition of tsarist regime; Bolshevik victory.		

CHAPTER 19

The First Industrial Revolution: Western Society, 1780–1914

Focal Points

The industrial revolution was the dominant development in Western Europe during the 19th century. What was this economic transformation? How did it alter European politics, culture, social structure, and family life? Along with industrialization came a host of new political movements associated in particular with the great French Revolution of 1789. What were the goals of these movements? How did they change European life, and what impact might they have outside Europe itself? New approaches in science and art constituted a third area of innovation. Western Europe was the scene of vast changes during the 19th century, and the focus of inquiry must be on what these changes were and how they related to each other.

THE NATURE OF INDUSTRIALIZATION

The industrial revolution transformed agricultural society much as the Neolithic revolution had once transformed hunting-and-gathering cultures. Associated with this economic and technological upheaval in Western Europe and North America was the development of new political forms, ushered in by a staccato of revolutions in many countries. Industrialization and political change also introduced major shifts in cultural life and basic social relationships, including class structure, family roles, and the locations of people's homes and work. The West did not lose all touch with its traditions in this sweeping process, but it was forced to reshape those traditions it retained.

This chapter deals with the transformation of the West itself, including the causes of change that fed in from previous developments in Western society, before proceeding to its global impact. With industrialization, the West cashed in the social and intellectual currents of the early modern period and the capital it had amassed from its control of world trade, in order to produce a society the likes of which had never been seen in world history.

WHAT INDUSTRIALIZATION WAS

PATTERNS OF INDUSTRIALIZATION

Typically, when we deal with major historical periods within a civilization, political or cultural developments hold center stage. Thus there are centuries during which new political organizations seem to dominate other activities, and other centuries in which new religions, scientific innovations, or shifts in popular beliefs have pride of place. In 19th-century Europe, however, economic change must be grasped in advance of other features; and economic change meant, above all else, industrialization.

In its essence, the industrial revolution consisted of a fundamental shift in technology and power sources. Instead of relying on human and animal power for virtually all production, the industrial revolution substituted fossil fuel power, first by means of coal to drive steam engines and later with electric and internal combustion engines. Along with the revolutionary power sources came new production equipment that could apply power to manufacturing (and later to other activities), with less dependence on human effort. Spinning jennies wound fiber into thread, applying steam or, in the early days, water power through gear transmissions. The flying shuttle was adapted to steam engines for weaving. Hammering and rolling devices allowed application of power machinery to metallurgy. And although, in early industrialization, textile manufacturing and metallurgy, along with coal mining, received greatest attention, engines were also used in sugar refining, printing, and other processes. The new industry of machine building arose to construct the engines, looms, and presses—the new sinews of production. Machine building was greatly aided by the American invention of interchangeable parts, initially introduced for the manufacture of rifles.

The technological breakthrough spread quickly to communication and transportation. The development of the telegraph, steam shipping, and the railway, all early in the 19th century, provided new speed in the movement of information and goods. These inventions were vital in facilitating the new stage in Western penetration of world affairs.

Innovations were applied to agriculture, particularly after 1850, with new harvesting and planting equipment and gasoline-powered tractors. Scientific farming methods also produced artificial fertilizers and new strains of seeds and livestock. Technology also reached offices, through typewriters and cash registers, and homes, with sewing machines and refrigerators, though again the major changes came from the later 19th century onward. By this point virtually all kinds of work had been altered by new equipment and power sources.

Furthermore, technological change was a recurrent process once the industrial revolution was launched. New generations of equipment displaced earlier machines. By the late 19th century, when the United States was taking the lead in technological advances, many power looms were sufficiently automated for one weaver to operate 16 or more looms, in contrast to the one or two looms per worker in earlier decades. Metallurgy was transformed, beginning in the 1850s, by new blast furnaces that increased the capacity for refining iron ore and allowed the automatic reintroduction of minerals to convert iron into steel. Coal mining, though less open to modernization, saw the introduction of engines to move ore and then cutting devices to use in the pits. Clearly, the industrial revolution was no single change in methods, but an opening to successive waves of innovation.

Power loom weaving in a cotton textile mill, 1834.

Along with revolutionary inventions came major changes in economic organization. Manufacturing was becoming concentrated in factories, rather than in small shops. With steam equipment, it was necessary for workers to cluster around the engines. Even apart from technological requirements, there were advantages to be gained from grouping larger numbers of workers: discipline and specialization increased. Finance, too, became more sophisticated. New equipment and factories required growing investments. Banks began to play a greater role in funding industry. Corporations grew, particularly after 1850, to sell shares to large numbers of investors. In industrial economies, big firms assumed a dominant position. Even in sales, small shops increasingly faced the competition of department stores and mail order houses. Thus the characteristics of economic organization were concentration, bureaucracy, and impersonality.

CAUSES OF INDUSTRIALIZATION

The industrial revolution first took shape in Great Britain, where key inventions, including the steam engine, had been introduced by 1780. British developments were quickly copied and other inventions added, so that by the 1820s most of Western Europe and the new United States were involved in the early stages of the industrial revolution as well. Indeed, during the 19th century the United States and Germany caught up with Britain, particularly in their emphasis on coal and iron production. The first industrial revolution was thus a Western-wide phenomenon, despite some interesting regional variations within the West.

The position the West had acquired in the world economy provided an active framework for the industrial revolution. European nations gained large amounts of capital from their colonial trading activities, including the slave trade. Businessmen also learned that there were markets for processed goods, which helped motivate them to devise new and cheaper ways to produce such goods. The privileged position of the West in world trade unquestionably explains why it was this society that first introduced industrialization and why it long maintained an industrial lead over other areas.

The internal causes of the industrial revolution were exceedingly complex, a fact that helps explain why many societies continue to find it difficult to carry through the process the West first introduced. The factors that went into the West's industrial revolution range from a massive population increase, which forced many workers to accept factory jobs simply because they had no alternative, to new ideas and a business mentality that made some industrial entrepreneurs positively eager to introduce risky changes. Material resources and capital constituted other Western advantages in pioneering the industrial spirit. The West's list of industrial causes did not, of course, have to be imitated precisely by other societies that later industrialized, but they did suggest the complexity of the process as well as the reasons why the West, rather than other advanced agricultural economies, took the lead.

Industrialization built on many of the trends in Western society prior to the 1780s. The new technologies were related to the rise of science. James Watt, the inventor of the first manufacturing steam engine, worked closely with scientists at the University of Glasgow. During the 19th century, the link between the economy and science grew closer, as university chemists pioneered in developing new dyes, fertilizers, and explosives. More widely, the outlook accompanying the rise of science promoted beliefs in change and con-

Railroad across the continent: "Westward the Course of Empire Takes Its Way"—Currier and Ives lithograph, USA.

trol over nature that guided many manufacturing innovators even without specific exposure to formal science.

Industrialization required capital and a willingness to take risks. Western experience in colonial trade had encouraged a daring merchant spirit that was now applied to manufacturing. The colonial trade and earlier improvements in agriculture and domestic manufacturing had piled up considerable capital, available for investment in the new equipment. Industrialization also required favorable natural resources, particularly coal and iron ore; parts of Europe and North America had these in abundance, along with rivers and canals that facilitated transport even before the rise of the railroads.

Along with science, an openness to risk and to change, and the availability of capital, a massive jump in population growth spurred the industrial revolution in Western Europe. Beginning early in the 18th century, population began to soar, rising between 50 to 100 percent in all Western nations before 1800. The population revolution was itself caused by relatively peaceful conditions, by a temporary decline in epidemic disease, and, above all, by the introduction of new foodstuffs brought from the Americas. Europeans had initially hesitated to try new foods, but by 1700 they began to convert rapidly, particularly in their adoption of the potato into their diets. Use of new foods caused agricultural production to rise and cut the death rate, which in turn allowed more children to live to adulthood and have children of their own. Hence the population boom in a civilization that, unlike Asia, had not been particularly crowded previously. Population pressure rose rapidly, forcing many people off the land and creating a labor force for the new cities and factories. Population pressure also spurred merchants to take new risks in order to provide for their own growing families. The population revolution thus helps explain the timing of the West's industrial revolution as it combined with the other factors.

In several Western countries, full industrialization also depended on political change. In general, industrialization relied heavily on private capitalists, who built the new factories and offices. But governments played a role as well. In the United States, government provision of free land was vital to the development of the railroad network; in France and Germany, governments built rail systems outright. At the same time, governments had to abandon certain traditional practices in order for industrialization to occur. They could no longer, for example, defend the guild system, which tended to restrict technological innovation and the free movement of labor. Nor could they continue to defend slavery. Political revolutions in France and its neighbors, and the Civil War in the United States, served a vital function in setting up governmental systems favorable to industrialization and in promoting a sense among government officials that industrialization was a good thing. While a host of factors, such as the bitter moral debate over slavery, entered into United States political conflicts, a key ingredient was a clash in visions of how the economy should be organized, with the North urging mobile wage laborers tied to rapid technological change; in the 1861–1865 Civil War, Northern industrial strength provided a vital edge, and in turn after the war United States encouragement of rapid industrialization increased.

Industrialization was no simple development, even in its first, Western home. Many people resisted the changes in habits and the new, materialistic values it required. A complex set of causes, ranging from population growth to the dissemination of modern ideas, was needed to generate wide adoption of the new inventions and forms of organization.

HISTORY DEBATE

Consumerism and Industrialization

Until about fifteen years ago, historians thought they had a good read on the relation between Western industrialization, which was a major new production system, and the advent of a society in which the consumption of goods played a transforming role in defining the economy and personal goals. Industrialization came first, and only later did output reach levels in which people gained both time and money needed for mass consumption.

Major discoveries in recent years, however, demonstrate that a first stage of consumer society arose in places like England in the 18th century. New shops opened, advertising and sales gimmicks gained ground, and ordinary people began to place new meaning on acquiring goods, particularly clothing and furniture. New levels of consumption helped cause industrialization, which then accelerated consumerism to yet a further stage. What historians still debate, however, is why consumerism arose in advance of major new production levels. Enjoyment of products from the world economy, like sugar, played a role. So did prior changes in social structure, which created more fluid boundaries in which people sought to establish identities by wearing stylish clothes. So did a decline in religious fervor. But the precise causation package remains to be established in this new frontier of historical inquiry.

EFFECTS OF INDUSTRIALIZATION

The economic effects of industrialization did not end with the rise of the factory system and the new equipment. Industrialization produced new wealth. With machines, productivity per worker rose rapidly. Even with the equipment available by 1800, a single worker using steam-driven spindles, for example, could produce as much thread as 100 manual spinners. Not all improvements in productivity were this vast, and the new wealth was not evenly distributed. But there was no question that, with industrialization, the West, already a wealthy society by world standards, got richer. Expanding wealth brought major changes in living standards and a desire for further improvements. By the later 19th century the apparatus of a consumer society expanded further, as factories poured out growing quantities of goods. Advertising developed, promoting a new mass press. Shopping gained new attention; even a new disorder, kleptomania, reflected some of these changes.

Industrialization, which had depended on greater agricultural output through new crops, transformed farming in turn. Growing factories and cities required major improvements in the output of food. The average farmer had to produce more, so that an increasing percentage of society could live and work off the farms. New equipment, fertilizers, and scientific techniques promoted the spread of market agriculture. More and more European peasants tried to increase their landholdings and employ landless laborers, to take

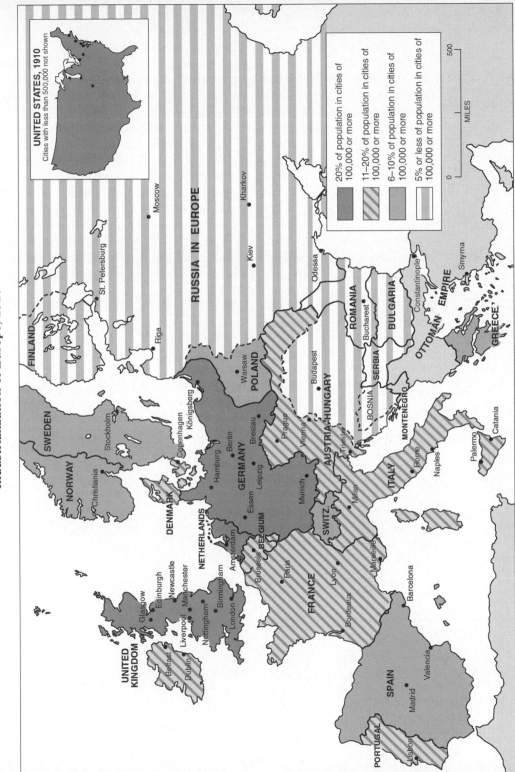

Industrialization of Europe, 1910

UNITED STATES, 1910
Cities with less than 500,000 not shown

20% of population in cities of 100,000 or more

11–20% of population in cities of 100,000 or more

6–10% of population in cities of 100,000 or more

5% or less of population in cities of 100,000 or more

500
MILES
0

RUSSIA IN EUROPE

Moscow
Kharkov
Kiev
St. Petersburg
Odessa
Riga

FINLAND

SWEDEN
Stockholm

NORWAY
Christiania

DENMARK
Copenhagen
Königsberg

POLAND
Warsaw
Breslau

GERMANY
Hamburg
Berlin
Essen
Leipzig
Munich

NETHERLANDS
Amsterdam

BELGIUM
Brussels

UNITED KINGDOM
Glasgow
Edinburgh
Newcastle
Manchester
Liverpool
Nottingham
Birmingham
London
Belfast
Dublin

FRANCE
Paris
Lyon
Marseille
Bordeaux

SWITZ.

AUSTRIA-HUNGARY
Prague
Vienna
Budapest
Trieste

BOSNIA
SERBIA
MONTENEGRO
ROMANIA
Bucharest
BULGARIA

ITALY
Rome
Naples
Milan
Palermo
Catania

OTTOMAN EMPIRE
Constantinople
Smyrna

GREECE

SPAIN
Madrid
Barcelona
Valencia

PORTUGAL
Lisbon

381

advantage of market opportunities. This kind of peasant was still tied to village traditions, but more open than before to production growth and money-making. Some peasants converted to specialization in dairy farming or vegetable production for the cities, buying more processed goods in turn. Finally, particularly after the rise of steam shipping, canning, and refrigeration in the later 19th century, Western Europe looked to other parts of the world for some of its food. Grain imports from Eastern Europe were surpassed by the highly productive commercial farms of the United States, Canada, Australia, and Argentina—where technological change far outstripped peasant levels—and meat was imported as well. Industrialization reduced the size of the agricultural population in the Western world while transforming economic life for those who remained on the farms.

Industrialization also created new needs for management skills and the handling of information. Early factories were small, often run by a single family. But with growth came larger and more complex hierarchies, with supervisors directing the workers, a sales staff, secretaries, and file clerks. Along with the spread of large department stores, the rise of management created an expanding white-collar work force, which by 1870 had growth rates even more rapid than those of factory labor. Like factory workers, white-collar employees were highly specialized and closely supervised according to rules designed to encourage maximum productivity.

Another effect of industrialization was the promotion of cities, and particularly big cities located at transportation hubs, near coal fields, or as banking and political centers. During the industrial revolution hundreds of thousands of people, mostly young, migrated from country to city, prodded by population pressure and seeking new jobs. By 1850, for the first time in history, half of Britain's population lived in cities. By around 1900, the same was true of Germany, France, and the United States. The rapid growth of cities placed huge strains on existing urban structures and governments. Many early industrial cities suffered appalling conditions in housing and sanitation. Gradually, however, aided by industrial wealth, cities improved; by 1850 the worst was over in the West, as cities began to process sewage, pave streets, inspect the quality of food and housing, and provide parks and some other amenities. Adjusting to urbanization—or failing to adjust—was an important aspect of the whole industrialization process.

Closely related to urbanization were changes in health conditions. In agricultural societies, urbanization on the scale now introduced by the West would have been impossible, not only because of insufficient food supplies but also because cities had long bred disease. Indeed, during the first two thirds of the 19th century, urban health was a serious problem in the West, as poverty and inadequate sanitation caused continuing high death rates. But more efficient urban organization, particularly in the provision of better treatment of sewage and purer water supplies, plus related gains in medical knowledge through the development of the germ theory of disease, caused significant health improvements after 1880. Child death rates, especially, began to drop rapidly. Instead of a third of all children dying before reaching adulthood, by 1900 the figure was down to less than 20 percent and falling fast. Here was another important use of the wealth, technical knowledge, and organizational skills wrapped up in the industrial revolution.

The industrial revolution, itself primarily a transformation in technology and economic organization, had wide-reaching effects on where people lived, how healthy they were, how wealthy they were, and what jobs they had. The transformations brought by industrialization were not overnight affairs, nor were they uniform. Early factories were small, and the large factory run by a hierarchy of supervisors and managers was a creature only of the later 19th century. Many groups continued to work along rather traditional lines, well into the industrial revolution. Artisans still produced luxury products and even some necessities such as housing; most women employed in the cities worked as domestic servants, where their jobs still had a traditional flavor. But change, if sometimes gradual and uneven, was the name of the game in the West's industrial century. Even artisans faced pressures to become less creative and more efficiency-minded in their work, while their overall importance was eclipsed by the rising factories. By 1900 most people in the West were not working at the jobs their great-grandparents had performed in 1780; they were not living in the same place; they did not play the same games. In 1780, most people had worked in or near the home; by 1900 most work was separate from home. In 1780, most people had used traditional herbal remedies when ill, viewing hospitals as places where the desperately poor went to die; by 1900 many people in the West were beginning to rely on hospitals and doctors regularly and to believe that many age-old health problems could and should be eliminated. Here were some human measures of the change the industrial revolution had produced.

PATTERNS OF WESTERN HISTORY, 1780–1900

Industrialization was a large, subterranean, often faceless process that altered the shape of Western society between 1780 and 1900. Particularly in its early phases, Western people were not always aware of exactly how their lives were changing. The concept of an industrial revolution itself arose only late in the 19th century, after the most basic changes had already taken place in the West. Along with industrialization, and more noticeable to most articulate observers, came a compelling number of political and intellectual innovations that produced a seemingly endless procession of dramatic events.

THE PERIOD OF REVOLUTION, 1789–1848

The period began with a series of political revolutions, starting with the Revolutionary War in North America in the 1770s, which led to the formation of the United States. Americans, stirred by the liberal political values of the Enlightenment and pressed by new British restrictions on trade and political autonomy, produced the first modern struggle for national independence. They proceeded to set up a republican form of government, with a decentralized federal system and wide male suffrage. U.S. ties to Europe remained close, which enabled Americans to pick up quickly on European industrialization; European investment in the United States also supported economic change and expansion, while growing waves of European immigrants provided much of the necessary labor.

The American Revolution helped inspire a more sweeping revolution in France, starting in 1789. This great event resulted from an absolute monarchy grown inefficient, the power of Enlightenment ideas, and the discontent and confusion brought about by population growth and rising commerce in advance of outright industrialization. The French Revolution was the first of many, in various parts of the world, that would stem from pressures to change that could not be contained within traditional political and social structures. For the French Revolution, though not fully successful, did alter the political and legal framework of French society and, through conquest and imitation, that of much of the rest of Western Europe.

The French had grown restive under an absolute monarchy that was no longer effective and unable to produce meaningful reforms. Many French people resented the powers of the church and the aristocracy. Population pressure added to the discontent, as did the growing popularity of Enlightenment ideas. While France was not yet industrializing, groups of peasants and artisans were already hostile toward the increasingly commercial spirit of many merchants and farmers; they saw revolution not as a blow for new political forms so much as a way to regain older values. This heady brew came to a boil in 1789 when the king, Louis XVI, strapped for funds, had to call a meeting of the Estates-General, the old medieval parliament that had not met for 175 years. Business and professional people, inspired by the Enlightenment, were unwilling to meet as a separate estate, giving greater power to the aristocracy and clergy as the first two estates; and peasants in many parts of France rose against the remnants of manorial obligations. The great political revolution of modern Western history was underway.

The Revolution went through several stages. For two years relatively moderate leaders tried to set up a constitutional monarchy, which would protect the freedoms of the press, religion, and assembly. The idea was to scale down the power of the church, while abolishing serfdom and the guilds, thus cutting away the anchors of traditional social structure. The government divided up many of the estates of the aristocrats, making France a country of peasant owners. The Constitution of 1791 proclaimed the legal equality of all French people, as against the traditional idea that different social groups had different hereditary rights. A parliament was established with the vote confined to the relatively wealthy—a strong hint that middle-class rule, based on money power, was replacing aristocratic rule, based on legal privilege by birth. But, partly because of opposition inside France and attacks by foreign monarchies, the Revolution turned steadily more radical. Many aristocrats and other opponents were killed in what was called, somewhat grandiosely, the Reign of Terror (1793–1794); radicals executed the king and proclaimed a republic. The power of the central government increased over traditional local bodies; every man was allowed a vote. The most important result of the Revolution's radical phase was the organization of a new, mass conscript army—for once citizens were equal, they had equal obligations to serve—which helped the revolutionaries gain new territories in western Germany, the Low Countries, and elsewhere. This successful war spread many of the revolutionary principles to larger parts of Western Europe.

The radical phase of the Revolution was soon overturned, and in 1799 a military dictator, Napoleon Bonaparte, took charge of France. There followed 15 years of recurrent fighting, as Napoleon sought to carve out a European empire. Within France, Napoleon confirmed revolutionary law and promoted new secondary schools to recruit talented bureaucrats. Napoleon's conquests outside France weakened manorialism and advanced the idea of equality under the law throughout much of Western Europe. Wars during the Revolution, and under Napoleon also encouraged considerable popular nationalism. The French, with their new political rights, became enthusiastic about being citizens of France; Germans and Spaniards, angered by Napoleon's invasions, grew more nationalistic in opposition. Nationalism supplemented the efforts of Europe's monarchies to put down the dangerous revolutionary upstart. Britain was a consistent enemy of France, with Austria and Prussia frequent opponents of Napoleon. And the tsar of Russia, now intervening more in Western affairs than ever before, also played an important role in the final alliance that brought Napoleon down. An attempt by Napoleon to invade Russia, in 1812, ended in disaster. As Russian forces retreated, the French armies followed and were subsequently locked in the frozen vastness of a Russian winter; here was a sign of how much Russian military organization and size had changed since the days of the Mongols. The allies finally conquered France and exiled Napoleon in 1814–1815. A glittering diplomatic gathering, the Congress of Vienna, then tried to put Europe's pieces back together.

For the next 30 years, Europe seemed dominated by conservative attempts to contain the forces that revolution had unleashed. Monarchy was restored in France, and some, though not all, of the revolutionary legislation undone. The Catholic church, vigorously allied with the antirevolutionary cause, gained new rights in France and elsewhere—though it never recovered the vast property lost in the revolutionary period. Conservatism was buttressed by a new intellectual current, called Romanticism, which opposed Enlightenment values. Romantic writers and artists wished above all to portray emotion; they disdained the cold rationalism of the 18th century. They adored Gothic styles and medieval adventures. Some Romantic theorists went further, opposing Enlightenment

Romantic nostalgia: Corot's painting of the harbor of La Rochelle, 19th century.

political values in the name of religion or the mystical collective power of the state, which, they felt, should not be hemmed in by constitutions or individual rights.

But while conservativism gained new ground, the old order that had existed before the French Revolution and the Napoleonic Wars could not be recaptured. The Congress of Vienna, for example, did not restore the welter of small states into which Italy and Germany had been divided; it thus encouraged Italian and German nationalists to hope that their respective countries could be unified outright. At the same time, liberals in France and elsewhere wanted to regain revolutionary achievements such as constitutions, parliaments, wider voting rights, and full religious freedom. And a new, small group of socialists began to encourage protest in the name of economic equality. Thus Western Europe was honeycombed by periodic efforts at agitation. Conservative leaders, headed by the tsar and the Habsburg monarchy, with its able minister Prince Metternich, tried in vain to keep the lid on. Revolutions broke out in Spain, parts of Italy, and then Greece after 1820, with the Greeks winning independence from the Ottoman Empire. Again in 1830 revolutions burst forth, leading to a new monarchy in France with a more liberal air, independence and a liberal monarchy for Belgium, and upheaval elsewhere. A final series of revolutions, in 1848, swept over much of Western Europe. It destroyed manorialism in Germany and Austria, encouraged Italian and German nationalists without, however, winning unity, and unseated the monarchy in France, this time for good.

A few Western countries were exempt from the tide of revolution. Britain, though strongly conservative in opposition to the French Revolution and for a decade after 1815, already had a parliamentary system. Popular protests sought political and social liberalization. In 1832 a reform bill gave most middle-class people the right to vote, and other reforms granted fuller religious toleration, even to Catholics and Jews, regulation of women and child workers in the factories, and new powers for city governments to improve material conditions. British politics became increasingly liberal, without revolution. Scandinavian governments also granted new powers to their parliaments and widened the suffrage. In the United States, where revolution had already produced a constitutional republic and protection for individual liberty through the Bill of Rights, further pressures for political change were met, in the Jacksonian era of the 1830s, by reforms such as the secret ballot and extension of voting rights.

The revolutionary era in the West ended with the uprisings of 1848. There has been no major political revolution in this civilization since that time. The assurance of food supplies, prevention of famine, and stronger police forces contributed to the end of Western revolution, as did various political changes. On the surface, the revolutions of 1848 were political failures. Liberal leaders, eager for new rights and parliaments, grew afraid of the demands of the growing urban masses. Urban workers, pressed by the crowding and upheaval of early industrialization, sought economic reform, and a few fought for socialism as a means of creating economic equality. Socialists argued for group control over property and production, often urging governmental attacks on capitalist ownership and capitalist values. Revolutionaries were divided still further in many countries by their nationalist interests. German nationalists, for example, often wanted unity more than they wanted liberal political reforms. Amid these divisions, the forces of the traditional monarchs reasserted themselves, chasing the revolutionaries from Hungary to Italy. In France, a nephew of the great Napoleon won a popular election as president and soon set up a

Bucolic romanticism: landscape by the British painter Constable, early 19th century.

new empire. The new or restored regimes proceeded to create new police forces that helped stamp out political agitation.

THE POSTREVOLUTIONARY ERA AND NATIONALISM, 1848–1871

But political repression was not the whole story after 1848. The revolutions had won new freedoms for the peasantry, in the full abolition of manorialism. Most of Western Europe now became a region of small peasant farmers; and the aristocracy, though still powerful, was weakened. Furthermore, government leaders began to realize that concessions were necessary in the political arena, if a new round of revolution was not to begin. So they granted constitutions and new powers to parliaments, plus a widened suffrage; these changes contented many liberals. Conservatism, in other words, became more adaptable. Two particularly flexible conservatives also worked to meet nationalist demands. In Italy Count Cavour, leader of a regional state in the north, engineered a series of wars beginning in 1859 that freed Italy from Austrian control and unified the entire peninsula. Otto von Bismarck, a Prussian politician, followed by orchestrating three regional wars, from 1864 to 1870, that unified the regional states of Germany. His final war, against France, also led to the downfall of Louis-Napoleon's empire and the establishment of a new republic.

By 1870–1871, then, with the unification of Italy and Germany, political and diplomatic changes in Western Europe had delighted most moderate nationalists. The new nations, and also Habsburg Austria-Hungary, had constitutions with some real protection for personal liberties, including religious freedom; they had parliaments with some real power over the budget. Germany even offered universal male suffrage, though the measure was qualified by a complex voting system. France, newly republican, also confirmed universal male suffrage. These developments, along with continued reforms in other states—as in Britain, where suffrage was extended in 1867 and 1884 so that most men could vote—seemed to satisfy most Westerners sufficiently that basic issues of political structure no longer dominated the scene.

The United States also dealt with a fundamental issue of political structure in the same period, through the Civil War. The preservation of the Union and the abolition of slavery did not end important political divisions in the United States or the continuing problems faced by the black minority. As in much of Europe, political change was qualified by conservative principles. Thus while Germany granted parliamentary rights but kept basic sovereignty in the hands of the monarch, who appointed the chief ministers, the United States abolished slavery but then allowed new kinds of legal discriminations against black citizens after the Reconstruction period. Yet the changes that had been won reduced internal friction, another of the adjustments that brought revolution to an end throughout the West and resolved some longstanding issues of political and legal structures.

Western society had thus gone through several political phases by 1871: outright revolution and upheaval, dominated by the French Revolution and Napoleon (1789–1815); conservative–liberal contest (1815–1848); and consolidation, under the auspices often of flexible conservatives (1849–1871). This last period had produced several sharp conflicts and the bloody American Civil War, which was the first war to reveal the importance and destructive power of armies backed by industrial arsenals. The era of Romanticism had ended in the West, and with it some of the more visionary political efforts; politicians now preferred hard facts and cold steel to enthusiasms either revolutionary or conservative. Bismarck talked of having created the new, united Germany through "blood and iron."

"THE SOCIAL QUESTION," 1871–1914

Between 1871 and 1914, most Western governments were concerned with protecting the gains and compromises worked out earlier. There was no major war within the Western world, though rivalries spilled over into struggles for colonial empires elsewhere. Germany's unification and the consolidation of the United States brought these powers increasingly to the fore, which automatically generated new tensions by altering the balance of forces in the West. One result was a new system of diplomatic alliances, as Germany sought to protect itself by linking with Austria and Italy, while France, eager to regain territories lost to Germany in 1871, gradually constructed its own alliance system with Russia and then Britain. Diplomatic maneuvering among the leading Western powers won growing attention by the end of the century; it would ultimately, in 1914, help lead to unprecedented world war.

The final decades of the century saw two major developments in the internal politics of Western nations. Governments began to react more clearly to the pressures and prob-

Mary Wollstonecraft (1759–1797) was one of the world's first explicit feminists. Her book, *Vindication of the Rights of Women* (1792), applied the doctrines of the ongoing French revolution to women's issues and effectively launched the modern women's movement not only in her native Britain, but throughout the western world. Wollstonecraft was the daughter of a tradesman who abused her mother and squandered his own inheritance. She early rebelled against some of the norms applied to women, and her first writings dealt with the lack of occupations open to them. She frequented radical circles in London, and followed a deliberately unconventional lifestyle—bearing two children out of wedlock. (She died after the second birth; her daughter Mary Shelley is the author of *Frankenstein*.) The shock she roused caused subsequent feminists to shy away from citing her example, until a full century later. The portrait, by John Opie, shows a powerful woman with a trace of sadness. She may have been pregnant with her second child at the time. What combination of personal and more general social forces would prompt such a radical life and outlook at this time?

lems of industrial society, taking on new functions. Many countries followed Germany's example and maintained mass conscript armies even in peacetime. Most countries extended a national system of compulsory education. National—or, in the United States, state—governments also took on new functions in inspecting factory conditions, setting housing standards, and the like; many began to provide health services to the poor. A number of governments, finally, led by Bismarck's Germany in the 1880s, passed social insurance laws, giving some state-sponsored protection against financial problems caused by illness, accident, or old age.

The expanded functions of governments were prompted in part by new political pressures, the second important domestic political development. Socialist parties arose everywhere after 1871. Many were inspired by the doctrines of Karl Marx, who had worked out his theories between 1847 and 1870. Socialist parties urged major reforms to protect working people; their goal was an alternative to capitalism that would provide economic equality. Some advocated revolution to reach this goal, but in fact most Western socialists worked within the political system, seeking to obtain power by majority vote. Careful political organization and wide appeal made socialist parties the strongest single political force in countries like Germany, and an important third force, along with liberals and conservatives, in Britain, France, and (until after World War I) the United States.

The rise of socialism and the new functions of governments made what was called "the social question"—what to do about poverty and working-class demands—the leading domestic political issue of the last decades of the 19th century. Political alignments around this issue overshadowed the year-to-year shifts in parliamentary votes or presidential elections, as this level of politics became relatively routine. Thus, after a series of earlier periods in which the *form* of government had been the leading issue, Western politics settled increasingly into debates about the *functions* of government, the role of government in reshaping (or preventing the reshaping) of society; and, with growing urgency, about the role of government in international affairs, as the armies and arsenals of the Western nations were mobilized around a tense network of diplomatic rivalries. Some observers judged that divisions over the social question encouraged Western governments to think in terms of diplomatic initiatives that could unite their nations and distract from the new signs of unrest.

WESTERN POLITICAL INSTITUTIONS IN THE INDUSTRIAL REVOLUTION

The age of revolution in Western society recalled earlier political traditions in this civilization by calling for new balance against the power of the monarchy. But this traditional impulse was reshaped by new political ideologies and by the demands of an industrializing society. The result was a new kind of government, neither medieval nor absolutist in structure.

Nationalism constituted one new force, fed by revolutionary beliefs in popular government and by reactions to French invasions. Nationalists argued that the state should be linked to a single basic culture—a "national" culture, that should override minority differences within the society and should clearly delineate each nation in relation to others. Nation-states were partly invented—national cultures were not in fact so clearcut—but the association of state with a dominant language, literature, and history proved to be a powerful mix, first in Europe, then elsewhere in the world. Nationalists could either call for attachment to existing territorial states—as in revolutionary France—or, as in Germany, they could claim ethnic cultural unity and urge its political expression. In Europe, nationalism fed the longstanding military and economic competition among states, and ultimately encouraged a growth in state power.

Liberalism also became a major political force throughout the Western world. Liberals believed that governments should be controlled, not by institutions such as the church or groups such as the aristocracy, but by constitutions and assurances of individual rights. Their efforts led to the establishment of wide freedoms for religious practice, assembly, and the press by the 1870s; even trade unions won the right to organize and strike. Liberals also believed in the importance of powerful parliaments, elected by at least part of the population and representing not estates, as in the medieval institutions, but the whole nation.

While liberalism was shaped particularly by Enlightenment values, including the beliefs in progress and in human rationality and improvability, it was also affected by ongoing industrialization. Some liberals argued that the poor should fend for themselves. But social problems created by difficult factory labor and crowded cities prompted most practicing liberals to advocate some limited social reforms, as in regulating the work hours of women and children. The growing political awareness of the urban masses also pressed many liberals to accept a democratic voting system.

The result of liberal and popular pressure, through the decades of revolution and reform, was a new structure for most Western states. By the 1870s the Western political framework involved parliaments, based on wide voting rights, that served as the source of most legislation and acted as a check on executive authority. Monarchies had either been abolished, as in France, or reduced in power. The political activities of Catholic and Protestant churches had been radically scaled down, and most governments no longer judged that they had significant religious functions. It is important to realize that Western governments varied in the extent to which they had converted to liberal goals; the new German state, for instance, was notably less liberal in structure and intent than the governments of France, Britain, and the United States. And there were important political movements in many countries that opposed liberal values in the name of older principles of monarchy and aristocracy. Nevertheless, despite variety and opposition, liberal values had significantly reshaped Western politics during the 19th century, among other things creating more similar political forms among the major Western states than had existed during the 17th and 18th centuries.

One key result of the development of liberal institutions was the rise of modern political parties, designed to organize members of parliament and to campaign for popular votes. In the United States both major political parties espoused broadly liberal goals, though they differed significantly at important points of American history—for example, on the issue of slavery. In most European countries, liberal political parties competed with more conservative groups. By the 1870s most conservative parties had added nationalist appeals to their political arsenal, using this new force to advocate a strong state and military apparatus. Nationalism also gained force from the disruptions brought by industrialization. As people moved to the cities from their local villages, they were open to new loyalties, and a fascination with national achievements often served this purpose well. Finally, particularly after 1870, socialist parties began to grow, adding a new element to the political spectrum of most Western countries. Socialists were wary of nationalism and found liberalism too limited, though they largely accepted the importance of parliamentary institutions. Socialists pressed for major legislation on behalf of working people, and their revolutionary rhetoric often frightened liberals and conservatives. Nowhere, by 1914, had socialists won major positions in government, but their growing power helped generate new legislation to deal with the social question.

Western politics, then, involved not only new political institutions but also a multiparty system embracing a wide variety of political opinions. These views, expressed through a host of new "isms"—liberalism, socialism, nationalism, and formal conservatism—coexisted uneasily, and some politicians questioned the ability of the parliamentary system to manage all the forces it had unleashed. But most groups accepted at least tentatively the possibility of working within the system, seeking to win enough votes to carry through the measures they sought. Continuing changes in voting rights opened the way to additional issues. A rising feminist movement in many countries by 1900 pressed for granting the vote to women; this was mainly an issue for the future, but several American states had granted female suffrage, and Scandinavian governments did so shortly after 1900. Here was an important extension of the idea that basic political power should rest with the people themselves, expressed through equal voting rights.

Along with new constitutional structures and parties, the modern Western state assumed important new responsibilities and the personnel to carry them out. Some old functions were of course dropped or reduced, including support of a single official religion and of aristocratic privilege. Governments after 1848 had stopped defending the rights of groups such as guilds to set work rules. But the new tasks of government were more extensive than those that were abandoned; one sign of this was that government staffs and budgets grew steadily, with rare exceptions, through the 19th century.

Western nations now clearly recognized their duty to encourage economic growth. Some used tariffs to protect particular industries. All supported the spread of railroad and canal networks. Governments also took on the function of mass education. All Western governments by the 1870s not only operated primary and secondary schools but required attendance at least to age 12. Schools had as their role the teaching of useful economic skills to promote agricultural and manufacturing productivity. They also vigorously preached national loyalty, instilling the national literatures and histories as a means of creating a new consensus among citizens. Mass education was a new phenomenon, and levels of literacy, reaching 80 to 90 percent in Western society by 1900, had no precedent. The idea of the state, rather than the churches, serving as main educator was also novel. Governments also gained new contact with citizens through the practice of universal military conscription. The draft was used only in wartime by the United States and Britain, but even here military forces grew larger than ever before. Where most male citizens spent a period in military service, as in France and Germany, they experienced firsthand the new power of the modern state—and, of course, had yet another occasion to learn national loyalties. Finally, as we have seen, governments began to take on responsibility for providing some protection for the health and well-being of all citizens. Laws regulating working conditions and consumer rights, efforts to build sewers and other public health facilities, and social insurance measures were important signs of the new welfare functions of the Western state.

To meet the new demands on it, the Western state not only expanded its bureaucracies but also began to recruit according to talent. Secondary schools in many countries served particularly to train future bureaucrats. All Western governments introduced civil service examinations by the 1870s—imitating practices long ago developed in China. While most upper bureaucrats still came from the aristocracy and wealthy business and professional groups, there was a new chance for ordinary people to rise on the basis of school achievement and test results.

The Western state, as it had emerged by 1914, embodied some interesting tensions. Liberal structures implied controls on government power, through bills of rights and parliamentary limits. Yet government functions and bureaucracies had grown, often with the blessing of liberals themselves. This tension was, in important ways, a restatement of older Western ambiguities about the state. It also reflected the fact that different political groups disagreed about what the state should do. The tension over the state and its limits would continue to color Western history in the 20th century.

WESTERN CULTURE IN THE INDUSTRIAL CENTURY

The 19th century produced a bewildering variety of intellectual movements. Major novelists abounded: Dickens, Jane Austen, and many others in Britain; Hawthorne, Melville, and others in the United States; Balzac, Zola, and others in France. Poetry was slightly less important, as was drama, but here too literary production soared, and with it a host of new styles. In the arts Romantic painters focused on pastoral scenes, and then, in the last decades of the century, impressionists challenged old traditions of literal representation in their attempt to use the canvas to convey the essence, rather than the surface reality, of what the eye sees. Interestingly, the 19th century did not produce a distinctive architectural style; revived Gothic buildings predominated, but there was also classical and even Byzantine imitation. Science continued its advance, with major strides in biology, notably Darwin's theory of evolution; in electricity and magnetism as well as other aspects of physics; discovery of the germ theory in medicine; and important innovations in applied chemistry.

Industrializing society, as it generated growing wealth, almost naturally produced a growing array of cultural expressions. New money built new churches, new public buildings, new art galleries, and new laboratories. Industrial technology directly aided science, in promoting devices such as the X-ray machine or more powerful telescopes. New wealth also supported growing numbers of artists, even if many of them struggled lifelong with poverty. Inventions such as the camera and discoveries in optics also powerfully influenced artistic styles—impressionism rebelled against the camera's literalness, at the same time using new knowledge of how the eye receives color. Rising literacy along with growing wealth supported new legions of writers; authors like Dickens directly serialized their novels in middle-class newspapers, where payment by the word encouraged a rather long-winded writing style.

The role of religion in determining the intellectual agenda continued to decline. Christian faith remained important in the 19th century, even as the political role of the organized churches waned. Many new churches were built, and Western society funded a vast missionary effort. In the United States, religion retained a particularly lively function, as revivals and immigrant churches powerfully shaped American culture. Religion faded more definitively as a popular force in Europe, where nationalism and socialism provided competing loyalties; here, too, however, Christianity continued to sustain many people. But as a formal intellectual force, religion was less vigorous even than in the age of Enlightenment. Few leading writers cared greatly about the nature of God or the fine points of theology.

For Western society continued to reshape its intellectual heritage. This effort involved two major elements: first, ongoing work within the rationalistic, scientific tradition of the Enlightenment, and second, a vigorous artistic statement that new styles were essential to capture the meaning of life and provide an alternative to scientific modes of thought.

The Enlightenment heritage persisted, as we have seen, in political theory. Liberal writers modified Enlightenment beliefs. They no longer argued in terms of natural right, preferring instead to talk in terms of what was useful. But they maintained the old faith that individuals were rational, that education was good, and that scientific and industrial progress was desirable. Most socialists also maintained Enlightenment beliefs. Karl Marx, the leading theorist of the entire century, used a historical rather than a strictly rationalist basis for his grand scheme. To Marx, history changed on the basis of who controlled the existing technology, or means of production. Class struggle resulted, with those in control fighting those below. In modern society, the middle class had wrested power from the aristocracy, but had created a new class enemy, the propertyless proletariat, or working class. This class would grow until revolution became inevitable. But once the proletarian revolution had occurred, an Enlightenment-style utopia would result. The state would wither away, as each individual would be able rationally to determine his or her own interests; goods would be distributed according to need; class struggle would vanish once the vestiges of the middle class had been eliminated. More prosaically, most socialist theorists agreed with liberals about the basic goodness and rationality of humankind and the importance of material progress, education, and science.

In addition to liberal and socialist theory, the rationalist tradition was also kept alive through scientific inquiry. Indeed, as scientists learned about new fertilizers and new health measures, science became more firmly linked than ever before with the idea of progress on this earth. On the more theoretical level, science advanced on every front. The great contribution was Darwin's evolutionary theory. On the basis of careful observation, Darwin argued that all living creatures had evolved into their present form through the ability to adapt in a struggle for survival. Biological development could be scientifically understood as a process taking place over time, with some animal and plant species disappearing and others evolving from earlier forms. Darwin's ideas clashed with traditional Christian beliefs that God had created humankind directly, and the resulting popular debate, on the whole, weakened the intellectual hold of religion. The picture of nature that Darwin suggested was far more complex than the simple natural laws of Newton. Nature worked through random struggle. But Darwin confirmed the idea that scientists could advance knowledge, and his theory was compatible with the idea that natural laws encouraged progress.

The social sciences also continued to advance, on the basis of observation, experiment, and rationalist theorizing. Great efforts went into compilations of statistical data concerning populations, economic developments, and health problems. Sheer empirical knowledge about the human condition had never been more extensive. At the level of theory, leading economists tried to explain business cycles and the causes of poverty; social psychologists studied the behavior of crowds. Toward the end of the century the Viennese physician Sigmund Freud began to develop his theories of the workings of the human unconscious, arguing that much behavior is determined by impulses but that psychological problems can be relieved by rational understanding. Like many of the scientists, social scientists were complicating the traditional Enlightenment view of nature and human nature by studying the animal impulses and unconscious strivings of human beings. But they continued to rely on standard scientific methods in their work, believing that human behavior can be put into rational categories, and most of them asserted that ultimately human reason would prevail, as manifested in appropriate economic, political, or personal behavior.

The artistic vision developed by the 19th century was rather different. To be sure, many novelists created realistic portrayals of human problems, believing that their efforts could contribute to reform. Artists, as we have seen, were aware of scientific discoveries. Beginning with Romanticism, however, many artists looked to emotion, rather than reason, as the key to the mystery of humanity. They sought to portray longings and madness, not calm reflection. They also deliberately endeavored to violate traditional Western artistic standards. They proclaimed their freedom from old rules of the drama or poetry. This impulse was taken up, after Romanticism declined by 1850, by new artists who attempted to defy literal representation itself. Leading poets shunned conventional rhymes and meters, writing abstract, highly personalized statements. Artists and sculptors sought suggestive images, while later 19th-century composers began to work with atonal scales that defied long-established conventions in music. Some artists talked of an art for art's sake—that is, art that had it own purposes, regardless of the larger society around it.

The new split in Western culture, between rationalists and nonrationalists, had institutional overtones. By the late 19th century, most scientists and social scientists worked in or around universities. Western universities, in some eclipse since the end of the Middle Ages, now revived as great research centers that also trained the society's elite. This model of the university developed first in Germany and spread quickly to France, the United States, and to a lesser extent Britain. Many artists, in contrast, worked outside any institutional apparatus. Artistic communities, called "bohemian" by respectable middle-class observers who distrusted the artistic life style, developed in most major cities, with the community in Paris the most glittering. Most artistic patrons preferred older styles, particularly in painting and music. But the modern art impulse continued to grow, its lack of clear standards and its defiance of ordinary taste and tradition clearly expressing an important ingredient of Western culture in the modern age. It was revealing that in an age of great economic change, Western culture did not rely simply on existing artistic traditions as an anchor. The same individualism and secularism that helped spur business competition spilled over into culture, prompting many artists to seek alternatives to ordinary values, scientific modes of inquiry, and the ugliness of the industrial environment itself.

INDUSTRIAL SOCIETY

Industrialization left a decisive mark on the shape of society in the Western nations. In combination with the legal changes ushered in by the decades of revolution, it produced a new social structure. Position in society was increasingly determined by amount of property and money earnings, plus the level of education achieved. Older measures, such as birth, legal privilege, and purely landed estate, declined. In this new social structure, wealthy business executives and professional people gained growing prestige, at the expense of aristocrats and old merchant families. In the United States, where an aristocracy had never seriously existed and where the Civil War cut into the planter class in the South, the middle class reigned supreme. In most European countries aristocrats continued to wield cultural and political influence, but they no longer monopolized the summit of the social pyramid. Middle-class culture, evincing a broadly liberal faith in science and education and a passion for respectable, restrained behavior, increasingly set the social tone. The ranks of the middle class grew, with the expansion of business and the rise or expansion of professions, such as engineering, law, and medicine, in which individuals could claim unique expertise on the basis of special knowledge, training, and licensing.

The second leading social class of modern Western society consisted of the urban workers, particularly in the factories. This group, far larger than the middle class, had scant property and much lower earnings. It did not accept all middle-class values, but was influenced by their powerful expression in popular media, notably books and newspapers, and the schools.

Not everyone fit into the basic middle-class/working-class division of industrial society, even aside from the important remnants of aristocracy at the top. Artisans clung to older values, in some countries even hoping for a restoration of the guilds; they merged only gradually and incompletely with the new working class. The rural population, still massive, continued to reflect distinctive features of peasant tradition and agricultural life. Even here, however, a division increased between peasants or farmers who owned their land and who employed others, on the one hand, and a growing number of landless laborers, on the other.

The rise of white-collar workers added another, newer complexity to the modern Western social structure. Like workers, secretaries and telephone operators owned little property. While they needed some education, they could not claim professional status. But white-collar workers shared styles of dress and values with middle-class people. They liked to think—usually incorrectly—that they or their children could rise into managerial or professional ranks.

Family life was powerfully affected by industrialization. Family responsibilities changed, although gradually. The family ceased being the main center of production, as work moved outside the home. But the family gained or enhanced some other functions.

It served as a consumer unit; most major purchases were effected within the family, and a new division of labor freed some family members—mainly housewives—for the important and time-consuming tasks of shopping, now that families did not make most of their own goods. Much leisure time was spent in families. Holidays more and more became family occasions rather than community affairs. The idea of family vacations spread, first in the middle class and then, in the form of daylong excursions, to workers. The family also became the center of emotional gratification. Family members were supposed to love each other. While this ideal of family life was articulated most directly by the middle class, who believed that the family should be a haven against the stress of the outside world, workers too reflected similar sentiments. Courtship became increasingly romantic; at least in the working class the importance of sexual pleasure deepened. Ironically, this emphasis on emotional satisfaction produced a noticeable growth in the divorce rate, with the United States taking the lead. As families declined as units of economic activity, it became more possible and perhaps more necessary to dissolve marriages that were not providing personal gratification.

Changes in family functions had vital implications for the roles of family members. The man was increasingly seen as breadwinner, his responsibilities mainly expressed in earnings on the job. Married women were largely kept out of the formal labor force; in the middle class, even most girls did not work. According to middle-class family ideals, women were to serve as cultural adornments and moral purifiers within the family. This gave them a new significance, as women in fact came to dominate child rearing and the household more fully than before; but it also removed them from many public activities, since women lagged behind men in political rights. Industrialization raised important questions about women's roles. Women were given new esteem, and their educational gains were more rapid than those of men though women started from a lower base. In the working class, moreover, women were vital to the labor force, as girls worked in factories, as domestic servants, and later as clerks and public school teachers. But in day-to-day activities married women were increasingly separate from men. The rise of feminist movements, seeking expanded rights and opportunities for women, reflected the anomalies of this aspect of the Western family.

Attitudes toward children changed as well. Most middle-class children were expected to learn, not earn. Working-class children, on the other hand, were essential to the operation of the early factories, maintaining the traditional assumptions that children should contribute to the family economy. But many people from all classes objected to the factory conditions to which children were exposed, particularly the frequency of accidents; in fact as machines became more complex, children's usefulness declined. Moreover, the advent of compulsory education took most young children out of the labor force. Most adolescents still worked in 1914, though in the United States the spread of high school education began to recruit a growing minority of working-class youth. Parents became concerned with fostering their children's learning ability. They also increased the emotional expectations they had of children, hoping that affection would compensate for the fact that offspring had become economic burdens. At the same time, parents' roles in children's lives decreased, and interaction among young people in schools created the beginnings of separate generational cultures by the end of the 19th century. Being a child in the industrial West was different from being a child in a traditional agricultural society, but it was not necessarily easier.

The final impact of industrialization on the family was demographic. In what is called the "demographic transition," Western families quickly reacted to the population boom of the 18th century by cutting their birth rates. Birth rates began to fall gradually in the United States and France as early as 1790. The middle class led in the demographic transition. Middle-class culture emphasized the importance of sexual restraint, and most middle-class people married fairly late. Gradually birth rate limitation spread to the working class and the peasantry, though under the new demographic regime, poorer families on average had larger families than the middle class—the reverse of traditional patterns. With children now an expense, and with parents expected to provide careful supervision and training to children, large families began to decline. By 1914 the average Western family had only three to four children. By this point the medical advances that would almost eliminate deaths in childhood were underway, making birth control even more imperative. Most families relied mainly on sexual restraint for this purpose, though new contraceptive devices became more common, particularly after the vulcanization of rubber in the 1830s; abortion also increased. Thus by 1914 the industrial, demographic regime was clearly in place in the West, with lower birth rates than ever before in human history, combined with low child death rates as life expectancy steadily rose. This new demography produced important changes in family life and in the roles of women, now that mothering required less effort than before; it also produced considerable tension given the need for sexual restraint. The new demography had wider consequences too, as the population of the West began to decline in relation to that of other parts of the world.

Despite all the changes, the family thrived in Western society, adapting new purposes and roles as old ones dwindled but also maintaining some function as traditional anchor. Change itself was often concealed. As new household equipment made women's work easier, standards of household cleanliness increased so that the effort involved in fact remained the same. The decline in the birth rate was greeted by praise for mothers—the United States Congress, for example, enacted Mother's Day soon after 1900. Of all the traditional institutions from agricultural society—village, guild, even church—the family survived best. But it did change, and Westerners worried out loud about the stability of this basic institution—as they worry still.

Along with social structure and family, popular culture altered its shape under the effects of industrialization. Growing literacy, exposure to political campaigns, and increasing wealth—at least, for most by 1914, a slight margin above subsistence—all had an impact. Ideas about the value of education, science, and technology spread more widely, and the gap between popular and elite values narrowed by 1914.

But industrialization imposed strain, and ongoing changes in technology and business organization continued to do so. The nature of work shifted, and probably its quality deteriorated. Before the industrial revolution, work for most people had been a social act, punctuated by gossip and naps, accomplished in a family context. With the rise of factories and offices, work was not only taken out of the home, but it became increasingly regimented. Shop rules forbade singing, chattering, or wandering around. The pace of work quickened, as it was subjected to clock time. In addition, more people were supervised by strangers than ever before; and they performed specialized tasks, rather than seeing whole products.

These changes were hard to assimilate, and many would argue that they have not been fully assimilated even now. In the early stages of the industrial revolution, particularly before 1850, the impact of new work forms was intensified by the rapid decline of popular leisure traditions. Festivals virtually vanished. As communities dissolved through migration to the cities, these highly local events were hard to maintain. Furthermore, the middle class disapproved of festivals as threats to public order and wastes of time; the newly created police forces actively discouraged such public gatherings. Middle-class leisure consisted chiefly of useful activities, like family reading or piano playing, that would show cultural achievement and train the young. This utilitarian definition of leisure was not accepted by many workers, but they had few alternatives. Tavern drinking became one of their major pastimes (one that middle-class temperance reformers fought in vain) because it provided a shadow of former sociability.

Many workers protested the changes in their lives. The decades of revolution depended heavily on working-class protest in the name of older work values, with artisans taking the lead. Workers also sought to cushion the impact of industrialization on their own lives, by taking time off from the job or changing jobs with great frequency, to the fury of middle-class managers. Gradually, however, workers found an avenue of adjustment in the concept of instrumentalism; they recognized that they could not control the quality of their work but would accept this situation for the sake of rising earnings. Work became an instrument to other things. After 1850, working-class protest, though it increased as workers became better organized, largely moved away from the attempt to control the job itself, to a demand for shorter hours and higher pay. It looked forward to new economic benefits, rather than backward to older values. At the same time new recreational outlets arose. Popular reading, vaudeville theaters, and professional and amateur sports proliferated in Western society after 1870, for various social groups. The new leisure was highly commercialized, part of the growth of a consumer society. Sports also served to train people for work discipline, as they learned team cooperation and obedience to the new rules imposed on every modern sport; and they served to condition possible future soldiers. Some critics at the time and since have blasted the new mass taste, bent on pleasure seeking and physical release, and wondered if leisure was as satisfying and expressive as it should be, given the limits of industrial work. Whatever its quality, mass leisure was a modern creation and a vital part of the new culture spawned by industrialization. And some games, like soccer football, first developed in industrial England, would spread around the world much faster than industrialization itself.

CONCLUSION: GAIN AND STRAIN IN INDUSTRIALIZATION

In 1900, heralding the advent of a new century, many Western newspapers looked back on the past century and found it satisfactory. Improved health conditions, new wealth, greater political freedom, more education—things were fine and getting better. Great change had unquestionably occurred, but by 1900 many people were becoming accustomed to novelty, bolstered by their belief in progress. Only a few groups in Western society, such as the new immigrants to the United States, were confronting urban, industrial life for the first time.

But change had brought strain as well as apparent progress, and it continued to do so. An aristocratic German general, a Catholic bishop, and an old-fashioned New England intellectual would take issue with the idea of progress, seeing the values that were lost as more important than the material gains. From other vantage points many workers, particularly those who could find no meaning at all in their work, and many feminists would also quarrel with the idea of progress, though they might hope that their day would still come.

The strains of Western society spilled over into the West's world role. Industrialization brought new power to Western society, which it used to gain fuller control over more areas of the world than ever before. But the use of power was conditioned by the need to alleviate tensions at home from those who looked back to a better past and those who pressed for more radical reforms for the future. The combination of power and uncertainty produced the great wave of European imperialism, which brought Western power to every corner of the globe. Imperialist expansion reflected business success but also the desire of aristocratic officers and Christian missionaries to find new arenas for their version of power.

In turn, groups from China to Latin America, though proud of their own cultures, recognized that they had to copy some aspects of industrial society if they wanted to prevent total Western domination. A key question was, which aspects of the Western industrial process had to be, and could be, imitated: was it just the military technology and organization, or the wider economic revolution, or did Western-style politics, or art, or changes in women's roles also inextricably enter the process? Western history between 1789 and 1914 had brought profound transformations to one of the world's major civilizations; it also set up a complex model for others to ponder.

SUGGESTED READINGS

Fine studies of the early industrial period are Phyllis Deane, *The First Industrial Revolution* (1980) (on Britain), and E. J. Hobsbawm, *The Age of Revolution: Europe 1789–1848* (1962) (on Europe generally). See also Peter N. Stearns, *The Industrial Revolution in World History* (1998). A more general survey of the social history of the period is Peter N. Stearns and Herrick Chapman, *European Society in Upheaval: Social History Since 1750*, 3rd ed. (1992); more interpretive is Barrington Moore, *Social Origins of Dictatorship and Democracy* (1966). For more specialized aspects of industrial change, see: L. Tilly and J. Scott, *Women, Work and Family* (1978); E. A. Wrigley, *Population and History* (1969); F. D. Scott, *Emigration and Immigration* (1963); and E. P. Thompson, *The Making of the English Working Class* (1963). On leading developments in political history, a useful volume is R. R. Palmer's *The Age of Democratic Revolution: A Political History of Europe and America 1760–1800* (1964); a good text survey is John Merriman, *Modern European Civilization*, v. 2 (1996). See also: Harvey Graff, ed., *Literacy and Social Development in the West* (1982); Albert Lindemann, *History of European Socialism* (1983); and David Kaiser, *Politics and War: European Conflict from Philip II to Hitler* (1990).

New Societies: The West on Frontiers

Focal Points

The 19th century saw the development of important societies in North America, Australia, and New Zealand. These societies were largely populated by Europeans and maintained close contacts with European patterns. However, they were also affected by frontier conditions and by interactions with other minorities, indigenous peoples, and, in the case of the United States, Africans who had been imported as slaves. Abundant land encouraged commercial farming; there was little peasant agriculture. What were the main features of these new societies? How did they differ from West European patterns? The economic influence of these societies increased steadily, as they developed commercial agriculture and mining and, particularly in the United States, an important industrial base. What other impacts did the rise of a "frontier West" have on the world at large?

COMPARISON WITH WESTERN EUROPE

The rise of the West, including its dynamic industrial and strong population growth through much of the 19th century, fed several overseas regions that received the majority of their populations and much of their political and cultural inspiration from Europe. The new United States, Canada, Australia, and New Zealand built on Western traditions, but they had to combine these with their contacts with more diverse peoples—native inhabitants, plus, in the case of the United States, African slaves and a small but important stream of Asian immigrants. These countries also faced frontier conditions long since eradicated from Europe, and in this respect they more closely resembled contemporary Russia and Latin America. These growing centers became increasingly important in world history from about 1870 onward, when their economic growth generated growing agricultural (and, in the case of the United States, industrial) exports.

The Western frontier societies differed from Europe in key respects. They did not have an established aristocracy or a peasant class. Innovative, market-minded farmers increasingly dominated the agricultural sphere. They were not as wealthy as their European counterparts, though their standards of living were high; they depended greatly on capital investments from Europe. These people were not as culturally creative as Europeans, looking to them for most basic styles, though a regional art and literature took shape during the 19th century (mainly in the United States). The frontier peoples escaped some of Europe's political tensions, establishing democracy relatively early, but they faced specific political problems of their own—as, for example, in the American Civil War between the antislavery North and the slaveholding South.

The Western frontier societies also followed many of the same trends Western Europe did during the 19th century, being affected by liberalism, nationalism, and (to a lesser degree in the United States) socialism. They underwent a demographic transition that cut their birth rates. Family patterns and women's roles were defined in similar fashion. Western-style science held a firm place, along with currents derived from Romanticism. Industrial technologies spread quickly. Canada, New Zealand, and Australia relied heavily on mineral and/or agricultural exports, but they were well rewarded because of their rich resources and their use of advanced technology. Canada, as its vast territory was linked by a rail network in the later 19th century, also began an industrial revolution of its own, and Australia and New Zealand had important regional factory centers. The United States, importing its first equipment from England before 1820, began industrializing rapidly, particularly as it participated in railroad and heavy industrial development. On the basis of its economic power and political independence, the United States even began joining in European-style imperialism by the 1890s, taking over islands in the Caribbean and assuming rule over the Philippines and other Pacific island territory.

Residents of the Western frontier societies—aside from the native peoples whose numbers and power declined rapidly—had something of a love-hate relationship with Western Europe. They recognized their affinity and dependence and in many ways felt part of Western civilization, though the term was not yet used; but they were also proud of their differences and realized that their tasks of settlement and state-building differed from those of the mother countries. The United States also maintained a tradition of isolation from Europe's diplomatic squabbles, while it tried (not always successfully) to discourage European intervention in the Western hemisphere from the Monroe Doctrine (1823) onward.

THE UNITED STATES

After the American Revolution, the constitutional structure of the new United States was established in 1789. The republic launched a period of consolidation—interrupted by the 1812 war with England—and westward expansion, as the new nation acquired the Lousiana Purchase from France in 1803. Democratic voting systems, with rights for free males, were widely completed by the 1820s. The nation's federal system led to a fairly weak central government, and many major developments were the result of state action or business initiatives. Thus the Erie Canal, which helped link the Midwest with the East coast, was sponsored by New York State. Yet the federal government was heavily involved in further westward expansion and warred with Mexico to confirm its acquisition of Texas in the 1840s. Within the federal government there was also the growing tension between the Northern states and the slaveholding South, which culminated in the Civil War.

American culture began to take shape before the Civil War, personified by many New England writers and thinkers and a smaller group of painters and musicians. Also before the Civil War, new waves of European immigrants, particularly from Ireland and Germany, added to the size and mix of the American population.

The North's victory in the Civil War led to a new period of consolidation. Efforts to reform the South, beyond the abolition of slavery, were largely abandoned by 1877, as the United States settled into a succession of undistinguished presidencies and relatively modest basic divisions between the two major political parties. Settlement of the western territories continued, amid recurrent Indian wars. The pace of industrialization increased, and labor agitation led to new unions, strikes, and occasional political assassinations. Waves of immigration from southern and Eastern Europe brought much-needed labor to the nation's growing industries, while by 1914 a growing migration of African Americans from the South fed urban populations as well.

United States entrance into the world economy, as more than a source of cotton or an investment opportunity, began in the 1870s. Massive agricultural exports combined with significant industrial ventures abroad. Several American companies, like the Singer Sewing Machine Company and International Harvester, set up subsidiaries in Europe and Russia. American arms manufacturers sold weapons abroad after the Civil War's end, including among their clients newly opened Japan. Although still importing technologies from Europe in such industries as the manufacture of chemicals, the United States contributed a host of inventions, including major developments in the uses of electricity. Even more significant were American innovations in the management of labor, where the democratic society sponsored new ways of regimenting large groups of workers. American initiatives in time and motion studies, designed by industrial engineers to speed the work process, and then the assembly line, spread widely to other industrial societies after 1900.

The United States' diplomatic expansion showed not only in imperialism, but also in growing involvement in other international issues; it was President Theodore Roosevelt, for example, who sponsored the conference ending the 1904–1905 war between Russia and Japan. American cultural influence was more modest outside its borders, though the introduction of the skyscraper in Chicago soon after 1900 showed a new potency in the marriage of art and technology. Individual American artists and scientists went to Europe to learn, and sometimes made a mark as imitators, but in this area the United States remained largely a borrower.

NEWER EUROPEAN SETTLEMENTS

At the same time as the United States expanded, Canada, Australia, and New Zealand also filled with immigrants from Europe and established parliamentary legislatures and vigorous commercial economies that placed them effectively in the general dynamic of Western civilization. Like the United States, these new nations looked primarily to Europe for cultural styles and intellectual leadership. They also followed common Western

HISTORY DEBATE

Exceptionalism

For over a century most approaches to United States history have emphasized the distinctiveness of the American society—its performance as an "exception" to the norms of European history (or, presumably, any other history). American exceptionalism features arguments that the United States was unusually democratic, or unusually open to social mobility, or unusually free from political division. An exceptionalist argument can also be used in a less benign fashion: the nation as unusually racially divided or harsh to factory workers. Exceptionalism is of course a comparative statement, though many historians have not bothered to compare. Should the United States be regarded as a separate civilization? If so, how can one account for similar dates and patterns of industrialization, demographic transition, feminism? Should the United States be regarded as a somewhat unusual but definite part of Western civilization? If so, how can one account for the unusual per capita rates of American violence (well above European levels from the late 18th century to the present), the unusual hostility to the state as an active force in society? The comparative problems run deep, and they have not been resolved.

For world history, the ongoing debate over American exceptionalism raises additional issues. If the United States differs from Europe, how much does it resemble other frontier societies, like Australia or Latin America? As the United States gained a growing world role (particularly in the 20th century) did it behave differently from previous European great powers, like Britain, and if so, how? Finally, did the United States grow more or less different from West European nations, as it became more industrial and a great power, and as Europe became more fully democratic?

---

patterns in such areas as family life, the valuation of women, and the extension of mass education and culture. Unlike the United States, however, these nations remained part of the British Empire, though with growing autonomy.

Canada, won by Britain in wars with France in the 18th century, had been preserved from the contagion of the American Revolution. Religious differences between French Catholic settlers and British rulers and settlers troubled the area recurrently, and a number of uprisings occurred early in the 19th century. Determined not to lose this colony as it had lost the United States, in 1839 the British began to grant increasing self-rule. Canada set up its own parliament and laws, while remaining attached to the larger empire. Initially this system applied primarily to the province of Ontario, but other provinces were included, creating a federal system that describes Canada to this day. French hostilities were eased somewhat by the creation of Quebec, a seperate province, where the majority of French speakers were located. Massive railroad building, beginning

SHEEP-WASHING IN AUSTRALIA.

This picture. of sheep-washing in the Australian outback, shows one of the export staples of the Australian economy and of the nation's frontier expansion, from the 19th century onward.

in the 1850s, brought settlement to western territories and a great expansion of mining and commercial agriculture in the vast plains. As in the United States to the south, new immigrants from southern and particularly Eastern Europe poured in during the last decades of the century, attracted by Canada's growing commercial development and spurring further gains.

Britain's Australian colonies originated in 1788 when a ship deposited convicts to establish a penal settlement at Sydney. Australia's only previous inhabitants had been the aborigines, a hunting-and-gathering people who were in no position to resist European settlement and exploration. Unfamiliar European-imported diseases and guns took a predictable toll. By 1840 Australia had 140,000 European inhabitants, based mainly on a prosperous sheep-growing agriculture that provided needed wool for British industries. Exportation of convicts ceased in 1853, by which time most settlers were free immigrants. Discovery of gold in 1851 spurred further pioneering, which led to a population of over one million by 1861. As in Canada, major provinces were granted self-government with a multiparty parliamentary system. A unified federal nation was proclaimed on the first day of the 20th century. By this time considerable industrialization, a growing socialist party, and significant welfare legislation had occurred.

New Zealand, discovered by the Dutch in the 17th century and explored by the English in 1770, began to receive British attention after 1814. Here the Polynesian hunting-and-gathering people, the Maoris, were well organized politically. Missionary efforts converted many of them to Christianity between 1814 and the 1840s. The British government, fearful of French interest in the area, moved to take official control in 1840, and considerable European immigration followed. New Zealand settlers relied heavily on agriculture (including sheep growing), selling initially to Australia's booming gold-rush population and then to Britain. Wars with the Maoris plagued the 1860s, but after the Maori defeat generally good relations were established, with Maoris winning some representation in Parliament. As in Canada and Australia, a parliamentary system was created that allowed the new nation to rule itself as a dominion of the British Empire, without interference from the mother country.

Like the United States, Canada, New Zealand, and Australia each had distinct national flavors and national issues. These new countries were far more dependent on the European, particularly the British, economy than was the United States. Industrialization did not overshadow commercial agriculture and mining, even in Australia, so that exchanges with Europe remained unusually important. Nevertheless, these countries followed basic patterns of Western civilization from this point onward, from political forms to key leisure activities. Currents of liberalism, socialism, modern art, and scientific education, which described Western civilization to 1900 and beyond, thus largely characterized these important new extensions.

It was these areas, finally, along with the United States and parts of Latin America, particularly Brazil and Argentina, that received new waves of European emigrants during the 19th century. Though Europe's population growth rate slowed after 1800, it still advanced rapidly on the basis of previous gains—that is, as more children reached adulthood and had children of their own. Europe's expansion was in fact greater than Asia's in percentage terms until the 20th century, and Europe's export of people helped explain how Western societies could take shape in such distant areas.

CONCLUSION

The extension of Western society through most of North America as well as Australia and New Zealand depended on the fortuitous absence of large previous populations, compounded by the continued ravages of Western-imported diseases on the indiginous people. Other parts of the world, more thickly inhabited, had quite different experiences under the impact of Western influence and some outright settlement. The spread of the West also reflected the new power of Western industrialization. Huge areas could now be settled quickly thanks to steamships and rails, while remaining in close contact with the Western home base in Europe. The expansion of the West revealed the power of Western values and institutions, as colonists deliberately introduced most of the patterns that had prevailed in Europe, from parliaments to Western-defined standards for women and children.

SUGGESTED READINGS

On U.S. history, in addition to several excellent recent textbooks with good reading lists (e.g., Gary Nash and Julie R. Jeffrey, *The American People: Creating a Nation and a Society* [1990]; and James K. Martin et al., *America and Its People*, 2nd ed. [1992]), see Eugene D.

Genovese, *Roll, Jordan, Roll: The World the Slaves Made* (1974); Thomas Cochran, *Frontiers of Change: Early Industrialization in America* (1981); Steven Mintz and Susan Kellog, *Domestic Revolutions: A Social History of American Family Life* (1988); and Albert W. Niemi, *United States Economic History* (1987).

On Canada, Australia, and New Zealand, see: J. M. Bumstead, *A History of Canada* (1992); Alastair Davidson, *The Formation of the Australian State* (1991); Charles Wilson, *Australia, 1788–1988: The Creation of a Nation* (1988); and Miles Fairburn, *The Ideal Society and Its Enemies: Foundations of Modern New Zealand Society, 1850–1900* (1990).

CHAPTER 21

Western Imperialism in Africa and South Asia

Focal Points

European industrialization, supplemented by the growing industrial power of the United States, inevitably transformed the world economy. Merchants poured out from the industrialized nations, seeking markets and raw materials all over the world. Pressure to participate in world commerce increased everywhere. Previously isolated economies, like Japan, now had to play ball with the West. Economies already exporting to the West now had to do even more; this was the case in Latin America. The attack on the slave trade added another force for innovation. Industrialization also prompted the West to acquire new colonies, particularly in Africa and Asia, and to intensify its colonial control of places like India. Ironically, Western nations did not do most of their trading with their own colonies, but they nevertheless sought secure resources and military bases. For the areas involved, new Western control brought massive change. How did heightened colonialism affect India? What was the impact of Western domination in Africa? What kinds of resistance to the West developed? Think of Western intrusion and national resistance as forces for change. How was India different, as a result, in 1900 from what it had been in 1780? How was Africa beginning to alter its previous patterns?

CHANGING THE WORLD ECONOMY

Even aside from the new frontier societies, the industrial revolution greatly changed the relationship between Western civilization and the rest of the world. New patterns became most obvious toward the end of the 19th century in the frantic burst of imperialism, but in fact events had been taking shape for many decades as industrialization's impact took hold.

The links in the world economy expanded steadily. New and speedier shipping played a vital role, making the crossing of the oceans a matter of a week or two rather than months. At the same time, railroads reached into continental interiors. More rapid communication, provided by the telegraph and later the telephone and the wireless, transmitted unprecedented information about business conditions around the globe. Levels of international trade rose as a result. By the 1830s, many industrial concerns were opening branch offices in major cities in various parts of the world.

Along with great increase in volume came some alterations in the nature of the world economy. The industrial revolution gave the West new quantities of manufactured products to sell, including factory equipment, locomotives, and steamships. The West had already sold manufactured goods to other societies, but its capacity was now literally revolutionized, as was its intense need to find available markets for its soaring output. Europe and North America also had capital to export, particularly after about 1850. Earnings from early industrialization begged for profitable investment outlets; while the domestic economies provided some of these, there was an avid search for opportunities, at higher interest rates, in less-industrialized areas. The development of the U.S. West, including the rapid expansion of a railroad network, owed much to British and French investment, but significant capital also went to Latin America, Africa, and Asia—at a price. Levels of Western investment in Russia also increased rapidly.

New Western opportunities to export industrial products and capital were matched to some extent by growing needs for imports. Slaves were no longer necessary. The transatlantic slave trade was abolished between 1807 and 1834, mainly on British initiative; at the latter date, slavery was ended in British colonies. In succeeding decades, slavery was abolished in the Americas and elsewhere. On the other hand, nonindustrial societies intensified their commitment to food exports, as Europe's urbanization and growing wealth increased the market both for staples, like wheat and beef, and for specialty products, like coffee and sugar. The need for raw materials became even more intense. Western transportation and recreational requirements opened a wide market for rubber, for example, which could be produced only in tropical areas. Growing production of steel made certain rare alloys vital, while other metals (such as copper) and chemicals were sought outside the West as well.

In basic outline, with the important exception of the end to massive international slave trading, the world economy proceeded on lines previously established: the West supplied more expensive manufactured products, while most of the rest of the world exchanged food and raw materials. The earlier result—a fundamental economic advantage to the West—persisted as well, particularly because until 1900 most of the world's trade was handled by Western ships and merchant firms. But the new volume of economic exchange made the disparity between the West and most other civilizations far more significant than it had previously been. Spurred by Western merchants and capital, producers in other regions found themselves more deeply affected by the world economy than ever before. Huge numbers of Latin American peasants, for example, were now drawn into production of coffee or of hemp for ropemaking, and away from their traditional village agriculture. The influx of Western capital into mining, transportation facilities, and market agriculture literally around the world also increased the direct involvement of millions of people in the international economy.

The solidification of the world economy was recognized and furthered by new European-sponsored economic arrangements, from the 1850s onward. International regulations facilitated telegraphic links; the new Postal Union systematized worldwide deliveries of mail.

The expansion of the global economic structure under Western control was a basic force in world history through the 19th century, bearing on all other civilizations. Its im-

HISTORY DEBATE

The End of Slavery

Slavery had existed from early civilization, though its importance varied. Western colonialism in the early modern period carried the institution to new levels, particularly in the wholesale import of slaves to the Americas for commercial purposes. Why, at the height of Western power, did the institution come under attack and finally decline?

Historians have developed two lines of argument. The first emphasizes changes in Western culture, toward greater humanitarianism. A new Christian reformist surge (particularly in new denominations like the Society of Friends [Quakers] and Methodists) and the ideals of the Enlightenment made bondage abhorrent. Formal abolitionism developed in the late 18th century as a result, and led to the legal measures. The second argument scoffs at intepretations so friendly to the West. Many historians argue that slavery was attacked because population growth made it easier to employ cheap wage labor, dismissible at will, than to maintain slaves, while antislavery campaigns also served to distract from abuses of workers in the new Western factories. Only these motivations might account for the striking shift of the world's leading slave-trading society to a society piously insisting that slave systems everywhere be dismantled. Obviously, both explanations may be partly right, but the combination continues to inspire debate.

Other debates are related. Why did attacks on serfdom, in places like Russia, parallel the antislavery debates? Is this a case of cultural diffusion, making non-Western societies embarrassed about their own compulsory labor systems, or did special Russian factors predominate? Did slavery fully end? Remnants existed in Africa and the Middle East for some time. In the 20th century, American and other corporations might subjugate foreign workers—like Filipinos on American-held Pacific islands—by making them work for a paltry wage, amid long hours and stern discipline, threatening them with exportation as well as dismissal if they did not bow down. Latin American estates forced acceptance of low wages by requiring workers to go into debt at company stores. Firms in Japan around 1900 and, later, other Asian societies bought child workers or women from families, forcing them to work according to employer dictates. The decline of slavery was a major world history change, but echoes of the institution persist.

pact was enhanced by the new surge of outright imperialism, based on growing European appetites and new military technology such as the repeating rifle. Western European nations and the United States gobbled up huge chunks of territory, from the islands of the Pacific to the interior of Africa. Land previously acquired, particularly in India and Southeast Asia, was now more closely controlled, as Europeans had both the military and organizational means and the economic need to go beyond port cities and loose alliances with regional governments in the interior. The expansion of Western empire and the changes in its nature bore most heavily on three non-Western civilizations: sub-Saharan Africa, India, and Southeast Asia. But the threat of imperialist control, along with the expansion of the West's world economic role, affected all civilizations by 1900, sharpening the problem of what to do about the power and example of the West. This chapter deals with the new imperialism and the areas it most directly touched; the following chapters consider the varying reactions of other civilizations, to what became, by 1900, a set of common themes in modern world history.

THE REASONS FOR IMPERIALISM: MOTIVES AND MEANS

At the end of the 18th century, the empires of Western nations consisted of North and South America, save for the newly independent United States; India, though the process of British control had yet to be completed; the islands of Indonesia; and scattered port holdings, particularly in parts of sub-Saharan Africa. The bulk of the Latin American empire was lost soon after 1800, through wars of independence, though this civilization remained closely tied to the Western economy.

By 1900, Western empires included all the 1800 holdings outside Latin America plus most of the mainland of Southeast Asia, as the French conquered Indochina (present-day Vietnam, Laos, and Cambodia), while Britain took over Malaya and effectively controlled Thailand and Burma; plus the entire continent of Africa with minor exceptions, the most important of which was the proudly independent kingdom of Ethiopia; Australia and New Zealand; and the various Pacific islands including Hawaii, Samoa, and Tahiti, which were divided mainly among British, French, German, and United States possession. Western nations also had virtual colonies along the coast of China, holdings on the eastern coast of the Arabian peninsula, and growing influence in Persia, Afghanistan, and parts of the Ottoman Empire. Britain proudly claimed that the sun never set on its empire, because of its worldwide span, and to many other Westerners the world seemed, for all intents and purposes, a Western holding. Never before had so much territory been acquired in so little time.

During the 19th century, moreover, the Western idea of empire changed. Most earlier colonies had been regarded primarily as market outposts. Catholic powers, notably Spain and Portugal, had thought also in terms of Christian conversion, which extended European control in Latin America and the Philippines. British colonization of the East coast of North America had also formed an important exception to the common pattern. Outside the New World, limited control for trading purposes described the Western approach. After about 1800, this began to change rapidly. Trade alone was not enough when new market agriculture, transportation networks, and investment outlets had to be established. The redefinition of the world economy alone suggested more extensive penetration. Furthermore, Europeans and North Americans began to develop a greater sense of cultural superiority. Protestant groups now joined Catholics in seeking missionary contacts. More generally, Westerners began to claim a clearer mission to bring civilization to the peoples of the world—civilization, of course, being as the West defined it. The English poet, Rudyard Kipling, described a widely held sentiment in arguing that the West had such superior moral and political values that it had a responsibility—the "white man's burden"—to reshape the rest of the world. Missionaries brought not only Christianity but Western styles of dress and some schooling and medical care. Business managers, convinced of the inferiority of "native" ways, tried to tell non-Westerners on how to work and organize. Imperial governments sought to redefine marriage customs, caste systems, and tribal politics. In both old colonies and new, European imperialism now meant an effort to establish effective government and supervision over wide areas.

Why did Western imperialism change and push into so many new parts of the world? The West's growing technological sophistication played a major role though colonialists also played on ethnic and other divisions in the societies they conquered. European imperialism in Africa can be explained in large part by the ability of Western ships, steam-propelled, to navigate up the previously impenetrable African rivers. This allowed contacts with the interior that no people, including Africans themselves, had ever before achieved. Steam-driven iron boats were also basic to European penetration of China. Western facility in weaponry continued to increase, even as Africans and Asians gained access to old-fashioned rifles. By the late 19th century, Western soldiers were armed with repeating rifles, which did not require separate reloading and thus represented a huge advantage. The introduction of the machine gun was another fundamental step. Winston Churchill, later the British prime minister, described an 1898 battle near the Upper Nile, pitting a small British force armed with 20 early machine guns against 40,000 Muslim troops:

> The infantry fired steadily and stolidly, without hurry or excitement, for the enemy were far away and the officers careful. Besides, the soldiers were interested in the work and took great pains. . . . And all the time out on the plain on the other side bullets were shearing through flesh, smashing and splintering bone . . . valiant men were struggling on through a hell of whistling metal, exploding shell, and spurting dust—suffering, despairing, dying.

When the battle ended, 11,000 Muslims and 48 British soldiers were dead, and the British had conquered the territory now known as the Sudan.

If technology, backed by medical advances that allowed Westerners to avoid many tropical diseases, accounts for a key part of the Western advantage, particularly in Africa but to an extent elsewhere, it does not explain the motives for the new imperialism. Gains brought by the industrial revolution, including technology but also improved organization, better health care, and expanded literacy, fed the growing belief that the West was superior to the rest of the world, with a right and duty to rule. This attitude now combined with Christian beliefs in religious superiority, a current that had been evidenced in earlier Western expansion attempts from the Crusades onward. Economic motives played a prominent role as well. Not only were Europeans eager for markets and raw materials; they were also anxious about the stability of their own changing economy. Even confident United States business leaders sought secure markets and supplies through colonies or, in Central America, semicolonies. Many people believed that domestic sales and supplies were insufficient for an economy that depended on growth. They also saw imperialism as a way to excite and divert ordinary people who might otherwise join in social protest— and indeed imperial conquest did arouse popular passions in Europe and the United States, aided by the stirring headlines of the new mass press.

Certain groups in the West, left behind in the rush to industrialize, found solace in their empires. Aristocrats, increasingly displaced at home, could win prestige as imperial bureaucrats, living the good life while ruling the natives. Christian missionaries sometimes found greater joy in preaching to the heathen than in dealing with the gradual decline of religion in their own lands. Individual adventurers, tired of the increasingly bureaucratic life of industrial corporations, found excitement in seeking fame and fortune in distant places. In various ways, then, imperialism expressed social tensions generated by industrialization, as well as the power that the industrial revolution provided.

The most direct factors in the imperialist scramble, however, were the claims and rivalries of the national states in the West. Nationalist loyalty motivated many explorers and adventurers, like the German Karl Peters, who staked Germany's claims to Tanganyika in eastern Africa, because of his desire to see his country assume its rightful place among the great powers—and who operated at first without state backing. Patriotic assertions prompted European governments to intervene to protect individual missionaries or business entrepreneurs, who could not be tampered with lest national honor be impugned. Above all, chauvinist rivalries spurred new states to claim a share in imperial glory and old states to protect their existing holdings through expansion. Britain acquired many new colonies—such as Egypt, which guarded the quickest route to India after the building of the Suez Canal—to defend old ones against possible competition. France sought additional territory in North Africa to protect its first North African colony, Algeria. New entrants to the imperialist game included Italy, which won important territory in North Africa; Belgium, which acquired the vast Congo region; Germany, which displayed its greatness by taking possession of two major African colonies plus areas in China and the Pacific; and the United States, which tended to oppose imperialism in principle, in part because of a long preoccupation with overland expansion to the west and in part because of the national experience as a colony, but which in fact acquired extensive Pacific holdings, including the Philippines, won from Spain in the Spanish-American War in 1898, and several West Indian islands, most notably Puerto Rico. The entrance of new imperialist nations heightened a growing French desire, after 1871, to gain colonies to compensate for defeat at Germany's hands back home in the Franco-Prussian War. The various pressures for conquest, which developed particularly after 1870, added to the belief that every available territory should be swallowed as quickly as possible, for the sake of national security and national glory. Ironically this same spirit of heedless rivalry would later intensify conflict in Europe, when, after 1900, the available lands were taken and attention returned to competition nearer home.

IMPERIALISM IN INDIA AND SOUTHEAST ASIA

The new European imperialism focused particularly on conquering relatively populous territories that had important traditions of their own. It involved, in other words, ruling millions of other people and encountering considerable resistance in the name of established values. Most of the new colonies received European administrators and some business entrepreneurs, missionaries, doctors, and teachers, but few ordinary settlers. Important Italian immigration occurred in parts of North Africa, and some Europeans

Fight between the German army and native troops in Tanzania: early 20th-century African art.

established themselves in the rich agricultural lands of East Africa as a new and privileged minority, but these were exceptional patterns.

European imperialism in Asia was completed—with the British conquest of India and extension of influence to Thailand and Burma and the French takeover of Indochina—without in any sense drawing these regions into the orbit of Western civilization. Revealingly, Christian missionary efforts in India and Southeast Asia had little success, winning only small minorities of converts—a clear sign of the continued validity of traditional cultures. But the new imperialism had a vital impact nevertheless. In India, Britain's rule had far more sweeping consequences than most previous periods of foreign control, including the recent Mughal empire. Indeed, India and Dutch Indonesia became showcases for the kind of penetration that 19th-century imperialists sought. With such penetration, in turn, came important resistance, which itself set up new patterns while confirming some older cultural values. One vital result was that British rule lasted a considerably shorter time than had previous foreign occupations. This fact suggests some interesting features of the British commitment, which never evolved into a fully Indian regime, while also revealing important changes in the Indian political tradition itself, which became less tolerant of foreign rule.

INDIA

As Britain completed its conquest of India during the first half of the 19th century, it began also to take a more active hand in Indian affairs. Control by the British government substantially replaced that of the East India Company, and at the same time the respect British officials had for Indian culture declined. India became a place to change, to Westernize. Thus laws (not totally unlike those of the early Mughals) sought to limit child marriage and religious sacrifices; Hindu converts to Christianity were rewarded with government jobs.

British rule during the bulk of the 19th century had a substantial impact on Indian politics. The very fact of unification of the entire subcontinent was a major development. British rule permitted considerable autonomy for individual areas, with regional princes allowed to maintain governments under British advisors, but a uniform code of laws was imposed over the entire country, derived from British precedent. Administration became steadily larger and more efficient. Direct taxation, based on land values, replaced earlier regional collection. Britain established tax levels it regarded as equitable; but the fact that it gathered taxes directly, rather than using regional lords and village headmen, who might determine how much their clients were able to pay, meant that tax exactions tended to rise—the source of considerable discontent from Indians who were unaccustomed to dealing with government without intermediary patrons. Britain also established a civil service, based on an examination system. Top officials were always British until 1864, and mainly so thereafter, but lower-level officials were drawn from high-caste Hindus, who thus gained experience in coping with Western administrative ideas.

British rule had considerable cultural impact as well. Though relatively few Indians converted to Christianity, new missionary pressures prompted Hindu leaders to re-examine their own practices. They tended to downplay the worship of lesser gods, though this custom continued at popular levels, and to emphasize the monotheistic elements of Hinduism. This reaction was similar to that which had greeted earlier Muslim influence. It involved an attempt to adapt traditions to the standards of India's new leadership.

Still more important, for Indian culture, was a British-sponsored school system, seen as vital to reverse the decline of Indian education that had occurred under the later Mughals. British-sponsored secondary schools and universities were bent on teaching Western values. As one British liberal put it: "The great end should not have been to teach Hindu learning, but useful learning." This meant increased emphasis on science and technology, not totally foreign to Indian traditions in any event, and modern (mainly European) history. Many schools taught in English, which meant that English became a second language to many upper-caste Hindus and Muslim leaders.

Economic development was another British target. During the 1850s the British began to construct railroad and telegraph systems. The new facilities aided the administration and military control of the vast country, but they also brought some prosperity. The governor general stated, in 1853:

> A system of railways . . . would surely and rapidly give rise to the same encouragement of enterprise . . . and some similar progress in social improvement that have marked the introduction of improved and extended communication in various kingdoms of the western world.

By 1900, India had over 26,500 miles of rails, plus a number of new roads and canals. Britain also encouraged better agricultural methods, again along Western lines, and some industrial development. The subcontinent was no longer seen as a colony simply to exploit, but as a place where substantial economic activity could be pursued.

Socially, in addition to attempting to modify some family traditions through law, the British sought to change the caste system. Britain allowed different castes to mix in prisons and on trains, and lower-caste members could sue upper-caste people in British courts.

The British presence had mixed results. Many measures did not reach the Indian masses, who remained largely illiterate and wedded to traditional family and religious practices. The caste system persisted for the most part. On the other hand, some Indians, particularly those educated in the upper schools, welcomed aspects of the Western occupation. Rammohun Roy blasted traditional education and praised the British for promoting "a more liberal and enlightened system of instruction, embracing mathematics, natural philosophy, chemistry, anatomy, with other useful sciences."

Important resistance developed as well. Many Indians detested the more efficient tax collection, looking back fondly on the days when they could count on the informal patronage of local elites. Upper-caste Indians resented attacks on the caste system, while many lower-caste people also preferred traditional demarcations, disliking what they saw as demeaning treatment of the upper castes. Hindus and Muslims alike were suspicious of Christian missionary efforts and aspects of the new schools. Muslims also resented British preference for Hindus in government posts; they increasingly saw themselves as a beleaguered religious minority rather than, as in many past centuries, a ruling group. From various sources, then, tradition encouraged hostility to the new Western administration.

This antagonism led to one of the great 19th-century uprisings against Western imperialism. The Sepoy rebellion of 1857 pitted Indian soldiers in the imperial army, numbering about 200,000, against 16,000 British troops stationed on the subcontinent. Many

British colonial officials at Delhi. A herald reading a proclamation that declares Queen Victoria empress of India. (The Granger Collection)

sepoys were of high caste and resented British officers. They also were disgusted by European customs such as eating beef; they insisted on traditional religious practices, for which the British refused to provide facilities. The incident that touched off the revolt was the greasing of bullets to fit in a newly introduced rifle. Animal fat was used for grease, and rumors spread among Hindu troops that the grease was from cows, among Muslims that it was from pork—in both cases highly offensive. Mutiny resulted, and for a time the rebels held the city of Delhi and much of north-central India, massacring many English families. British reinforcements broke the mutiny in 1858, aided by the fact that most Indian civilians had not joined the protest.

Britain responded to this challenge by introducing limited political representation for Indians, through local governments; they also established an advisory legislative council. Thus some Indians gained new experience in parliamentary forms. Britain also ruled that no native of India should be barred from any job or office because of skin color or religion, and while Indians advanced only slowly into the upper reaches of bureaucracy, there were some gradual improvements. The number of Indians with civil service experience grew steadily. Britain also increased centralized supervision of the Indian regions, encouraged English-language education, and attempted new social reforms including the abolition of slavery (never a very extensive institution in India since the classical age). In other words, pressures to Westernize intensified, as Britain stepped up its efforts to alter its colony without undue repression.

During the later 19th century, moreover, the Indian economy began to develop in new directions. Many estate owners and peasants were encouraged to grow crops for a world market. During the American Civil War, for example, the production of cotton in India increased to compensate for the decreased availibility of cotton in the American South. Some factories also were opened, in textiles and metallurgy, and directed by Indian entrepreneurs using equipment imported from Britain. In 1886 Jamshedi Tata, an Indian from a wealthy Bombay family, set up a large steel plant in western Bengal, near India's richest coal and iron deposits. While still dependent on imported machinery, the Indian steel industry was beginning to export some of its products soon after 1900. Industrial development remained rather localized, and no full industrial revolution was underway; but change was taking place.

Economic transformation was a double-edged sword in India, however. British efforts to encourage higher agricultural production, including the sponsorship of large irrigation projects to reduce traditional problems with periodic droughts, stimulated rapid population growth in an already crowded country. Government attempts to introduce some Western medical procedures, through innoculations and sanitary reforms, worked to the same end. India's high birth rate, caused by a traditional desire to have enough sons to protect parents in their old age, rose further, and the death rate, though still high by Western standards, declined. Population growth seriously limited the effects of economic development, as did continued competition from British factories that displaced hundreds of thousands of traditional manufacturing workers; the prosperity of the average Indian did not increase.

Many Indian traditionalists continued to resent British practices. At the same time a new opposition force emerged among educated Indians concerned about their own national identity but also converted to key Western political and educational values that, in their view, argued against undemocratic foreign rule. Several Indian newspapers sprang up, conducting lively political discussion. The first Indian National Congress, with Hindu

Railroads in India: change in an established civilization. This is a railroad station near Calcutta, 1867.

and Muslim delegates drawn mainly from the ranks of civil servants, met in 1885. Its initial demands were modest, focusing on greater opportunities for Indians in the imperial bureaucracy. From this base, a nationalist sentiment spread among educated groups, particularly Hindus. This was a new loyalty in Indian history, cutting across caste, regional, and to some extent religious lines. Nationalism encouraged Indians to think in terms of growing political freedom as well as a culture independent of Western influence. Successive National Congresses became increasingly vigorous in requesting reforms. They focused not only on civil service jobs, but also on British economic control, seeking an India that could advance to the ranks of industrial nations on its own. A 1910 speaker stated: "India has come to be regarded as a plantation of England, giving raw products to be shipped by British moguls in British ships, to be worked into fabrics . . . to be re-exported to India by British merchants." Here was a resentment of the Western-dominated world economy that would echo through the 20th century in many civilizations.

Indian nationalism imitated European, and particularly British, political beliefs, while insisting on India's special qualities. Nationalist leaders opted for an inclusive definition of nationalism—including various religious, racial, and social groups—unlike the narrower ethnic nationalism that had developed in Germany. Key questions of precise definition, however, were papered over by the obvious need to reduce British control.

Before 1900, Indian nationalism did not pose a major threat to British rule. Periodic riots by peasant groups, against taxes or census taking (seen as a government trap to raise taxes), or in the name of traditional religion, were a greater problem, resulting in the assassination of several British officials.

India by 1900 was by no means Westernized, but it had altered substantially both because of British initiatives and because of the new interests of Indian leaders themselves, particularly in education, nationalist politics, and industrial management. Indian cultural vitality had in many ways increased, spurred by the revival of Hinduism and active use of traditional artistic and literary styles. At the same time gaps had opened between Indian leaders, mostly upper caste in any event and now exposed to Western ideas and Indian nationalism, and the masses of Indians who revered traditional forms and who saw changes largely as impositions—new taxes, new and often poorly paid wage labor—by British or Indian masters.

SOUTHEAST ASIA

Many developments in Southeast Asia resembled trends in India—as had long been the case. The regional politics of this area continued, as different European powers controlled different countries. There was no substantial redrawing of the religious map, though a minority of Southeast Asians, particularly in French Indochina, converted to Christianity. In Dutch Indonesia, the government built railroads and created a Dutch-language education system for the elite, along with a growing bureaucracy and a new tax structure. New laws attempted to regulate the planters' use of native labor on the large estates devoted to export production. Essentially manorial controls, involving substantial rights over peasant labor, were converted after 1870 to a wage labor system.

Particularly during the second half of the 19th century, increasing numbers of Southeast Asian peasants were drawn into a market economy, employed as workers producing goods ranging from spices and tea to rubber, for sale on the world market. Many of these goods commanded relatively low prices and the system depended on low wages.

Imperial governments, as in India, began to introduce Western-style administrative measures. Bureaucrats busily collected census data. The independence of local leaders, including village headmen, was reduced. New police forces attempted to regulate crime and local unrest. As in India, more efficient administration and some agricultural improvements drove population up, putting new pressure on available land.

Yet, while traditionalists bitterly resented many European impositions, there was little systematic protest against imperialism before 1900. Nationalism was slow to surface, though soon after 1900, Indonesian civil servants sought greater equality with Dutch officials. Some local peasant uprisings occurred, expressing land hunger and resentment against tax collection, and in Indonesia a movement to renew Islamic fervor took shape. But the main wave of protest against European control, as in India, still awaited the future.

IMPERIALISM IN AFRICA

New Western penetration of sub-Saharan Africa became a dominant force only after the 1860s. During most of the 19th century, African history essentially followed an established route, with scattered innovations, though economic changes were significant. In the northern region, below the Sahara Desert, Islam continued to spread through the popular missionary and holy war movement that had taken shape in the later 18th century. A literature began to develop in Swahili, East Africa's written language linked to Islam. Later in the 19th century, the dissemination of Islam was furthered by Western imperialism, for Islam was seen as a vital, well-organized religion that had the merit of not being Western. Even before this, Islam attacked many African cultural traditions as superstitions, in the regions it touched, much as Western and Middle Eastern popular beliefs had been challenged by monotheism some centuries before. This process in turn helped launch a painful and exciting process of African redefinition to which Western imperialism would ultimately contribute as well.

In West Africa, before the imperialist orgy, Britain and France gradually acquired new port territories; Britain, for example, took over the key city of Lagos, in what is now Nigeria; France, the city of Dakar, in Senegal. In European-controlled port cities, a small number of Africans converted to Christianity and had other contact with Western values. Some began to think in terms of developing African states along liberal political lines, though this remained as yet a dream. The West African economy was badly disoriented by the end of the slave trade, while Western abolitionism brought new ventures to the interior as expeditionary forces sought to root out remaining slave traders. The end of the international slave trade also brought efforts to compensate by novel exports. Slave shipments to the Middle East continued, but a new export agriculture also developed, featuring crops like peanuts and palms (used for vegetable oils). The response of Africans to new markets has been called a "peasant revolution." While some Africans benefited from this development, enslavement within the continent increased, and the economic position of women also deteriorated; growing use of women as slaves enhanced patriarchal systems. These changes foreshadowed the greater intensification of world economic exploitation of Africa under imperialism. Finally, two small states were formed, Liberia and Sierra Leone, by freed slaves from the United States and from British West Indian colonies, respectively. The freed slaves formed an elite governing group, which was heavily influenced by American and British governments, over the African majority in these states; here was another source of new Western influence in this region.

Greater change occurred in southern Africa. Migration of Boer settlers from the Cape province increased when Britain acquired control of this colony from Holland during the Napoleonic Wars. Boer farmers conducted many battles with African forces through the 1830s, gradually pushing forward their own zone of settlement. At the same time Bantu groups north of this zone faced crowded conditions because of their own population growth. The result was the formation of a number of tightly knit regional monarchies, organized along the traditional lines of divine kingship with highly ceremonial rule. Some of these kingdoms, such as the Zulus in Natal (now a state in South Africa), developed well-organized military forces, able to hold their own not only against other Bantu states but against the Boers as well until the late 1880s.

In sum, most of sub-Saharan Africa continued patterns of regional government, mainly under divine kingship, and traditional religion well into the later 19th century. Scattered European gains, more export-oriented farming, and the growth of Islam constituted new forces in some regions. On the other hand, there was no sweeping technological or political transformation.

Then came the new imperialism, bursting into this civilization with full force after 1870. To many European leaders, as well as to many Africans, its force seemed bewildering; the British foreign minister lamented in 1891, "I do not know the cause of this sudden revolution, but there it is." And there it was, indeed. By conquest and negotiation, by

Imperialism in Africa

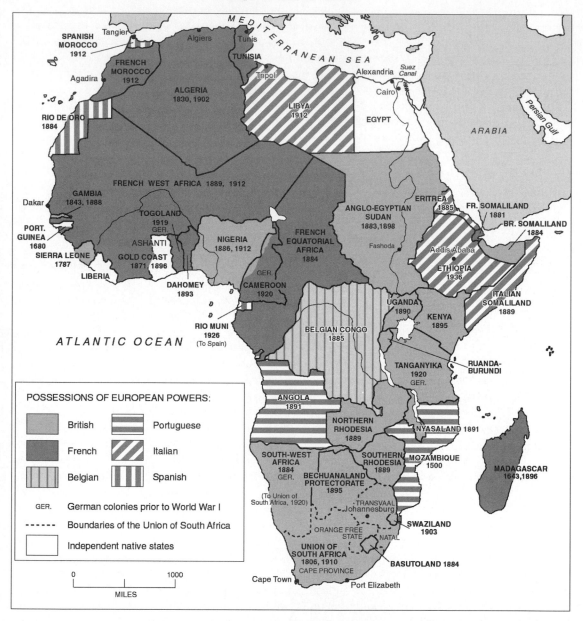

POSSESSIONS OF EUROPEAN POWERS:

British

Portuguese

French

Italian

Belgian

Spanish

GER.   German colonies prior to World War I

- - - - -   Boundaries of the Union of South Africa

Independent native states

0   1000

MILES

1900 Britain had developed an extensive empire in West Africa, including Nigeria, and a north-south axis running from South Africa toward Egypt and embracing the modern nations of the Sudan, Kenya, Uganda, Zambia, and Zimbabwe. The British also conquered the Boer states north of its Cape Colony through the bloody Boer War of 1899–1902, forming a united South African state with a large European minority. France concentrated on an east-west effort from its holdings in Senegal, winning control over most of the territory just south of the Sahara. Belgium had the Congo, Germany possessed Tanganyika and Southwest Africa; and Portugal increased its control over Angola and Mozambique.

These new empires were not won without hard fighting. France and Britain both faced bitter resistance from Muslim forces below the Sahara, leading to battles such as the one Winston Churchill described (see p. 413). Full subjugation of this region occurred only in the late 1890s, because Muslim armies were well organized, if poorly armed, and filled with a spirit of jihad, or holy war, against the intruders. In both their colonies, Germans met with vigorous African resistance, which was put down only by brutal massacres in which tens of thousands of Africans were killed. European intervention was compounded by frequent insensitivity toward local customs, as the imperialists tried to export or destroy religious symbols and some of the ceremonial apparatus of divine kingship; in West Africa, for example, a British governor provoked a war when he tried to seize the traditional Golden Stool of the Ashanti king, to send back to Queen Victoria.

The consequences of new European rule in Africa were dramatic, though colonialism by no means overturned all African customs. As in India, Western institutions were only one among many forces at work. Furthermore, by 1914 the European regimes were barely in place, and much of the impact of the West would become clear only later. Different imperialist countries followed somewhat different policies in their colonies. France, for example, was eager to educate an African elite in Western ways, whereas Britain concentrated more on basic education and medical care for a larger number of people while discouraging the formation of a new elite. But some main lines of development were emerging by 1914, across the new political divisions of the continent.

The first consequence was the new political units themselves. Africa had always been divided, but now it was chopped into states artificially created by accidents of European competition and timing. None of the colonial states had any clear precedent. Many mixed different tribal, language, and religious groups that had long been rivals. A few regional kingdoms persisted under British supervision in southern Africa, and Ethiopia remained independent, defeating Italy in an 1896 war; otherwise, however, the map of the civilization was entirely, and from an African standpoint arbitrarily, redrawn. European administrations tried to impose Western concepts of property law, sanitary regulation, and police on their new domains. Few Africans by 1914 were included in the new imperial bureaucracies.

The cultural impact of the Europeans was initially limited. Intense missionary activity created an important Christian minority in many parts of Africa, which added to the culture's religious diversity. But most Africans remained polytheist or, in the north, Muslim. Some combined Christianity with traditional beliefs, like the witch doctors who converted but still prayed for protection to other spirits, relying on Christianity for favor in the afterlife. Knowledge of a European language spread among an educated minority, along with growing familiarity with Western science and some Western political ideas.

The economic impact of the Europeans was far greater than their cultural influence. The new rulers were eager to make their colonies pay. Small numbers of white settlers claimed the most fertile land, a process already established in southern Africa and now applied to East Africa as well. Colonial administrations imposed new taxes, which forced many Africans to seek paying work on European-owned plantations and mines simply to

AUTHOR

38. John Mensah Sarbah

European imperialism created complex pressures for new African leaders. John Mensah Sarbah (1865–1910) chose a path of utilizing Western standards in defense of African rights. A member of the Fante tribe on the Gold Coast, in the area now known as Ghana, Mensah Sarbah was a scholarly man who trained in English law and was the first African from his region to be admitted to the English bar. Mensah Sarbah used English constitutional arguments to claim that the British had no right to rule the Gold Coast and were consistently violating established African laws. He actively urged expanded responsibilities for educated Africans who could preserve Africa's traditional communal virtues. His multivolume *Fanti National Constitution* (1906) followed from his elaborate research on customary law. He also founded several organizations designed to protect traditional African rights to land ownership, and his arguments did secure African land titles in British legislation of 1898. Mensah Sarbah thus worked in two worlds, an early example of a leader striving for a combination of Western methods and African goals. Was this a more effective approach than outright violent opposition to imperialism?

obtain money in an economy that had previously relied heavily on barter. Colonial officials in some cases requisitioned labor directly, enforcing their demands by brutal physical punishments including dismemberment. In general, Africans working the mines and the estates suffered harsh conditions—including additional brutal physical punishments—and of course low pay. Europeans did improve port facilities and other aspects of the communication and transportation system, though there was much less railroad construction, in the difficult African terrain, than in India or Southeast Asia. New medical facilities to combat traditional tropical diseases were also of some benefit, and the African population began to increase. Still, by 1900 and even beyond, the main economic results of European control were largely exploitative, as Africa supplied food and minerals—copper from the Congo, gold and diamonds from South Africa—to the Western market from the sweat of miserably paid labor gangs.

Most Africans, however, were not directly caught up in the institutions of imperialist rule. Village agriculture changed slowly, and other village institutions persisted; European ability to reach most Africans directly was quite limited in a vast and diverse continent where, even with European technology, communication remained difficult. At the same time, the recency of European conquest hampered ongoing African reaction. Nationalist movements and other forms of resistance would come, but by 1914 the bloody defeat of initial opposition efforts was a setback to further response.

COMPARING COLONIES

Colonialism brought many similar experiences to otherwise different societies. Foreign rule raised some common issues, as did the subjection to an economic system dominated by industrial Europe. But colonies often differed, depending on prior culture and institutions and variations in European policy.

India, with a major religion of its own and extensive experience of outside control in the past, adjusted its culture more selectively than did Africa; there were fewer Indian religious conversions. Indian civilization also had a longer time to come to terms with Western control, in comparison with the shock exposure of Africa. Sub-Saharan Africa, by 1900, was beginning to experience more systematic loss of traditional values, particularly in some areas where Christian missionaries made headway. The rawest economic exploitation of India occurred around 1800. But in Africa, European exploitation of resources and labor stepped up from the 1890s onward. Competition among European states also affected conditions in Africa, in contrast to India by this point. While beliefs in European racial superiority affected policies everywhere, the impact was sharper in Africa than in India. Differences affected experience during the 19th century itself, and also reactions later on, when independence became a possibility.

European imperialism had a worldwide impact, as threat if not always fact. The balance of power among the civilizations of the world was dramatically shifted not only by European control of major civilizations—India, Southeast Asia, and Africa—but by the extension of essentially Western societies to North America, including the U.S. Western frontier as well as Canada, and to Australia and New Zealand.

In India and Southeast Asia, and ultimately in Africa, the fact of European control shaped vital questions of change and adaptation. New Western rule, efficiently administered, brought major innovations, including new political boundaries and new levels of commercialization. It was clear that these societies were not going to become Western. Their traditional cultures were too deep-rooted, their populations and territories too vast; European ambivalence between wishing to reform the natives and seeing them as inherent racial inferiors, as children to be disciplined by wiser Western parents, also limited the Westernization process. But European occupation did provide direct tutelage in Western ways, allowing leaders in southern Asia, and later in Africa, to decide what they wished to copy, what they wanted to reject. One concept to assimilate, if only to give shape to what may have been an inherent desire for independence, was nationalism, as was already evident in India. In nationalism, leaders attracted to some Western patterns, and others eager simply to restore preimperialist traditions, could at least briefly join in a fervent demand for independence. Imperialism clearly generated its own resistance, and this interplay would dominate much of the history of the 20th century.

But imperialism also uprooted a host of traditional economic, social, and cultural modes. Independent India or Africa would not go back to preimperialist ways of life. Imperialism brought new political problems in uniting or dividing earlier units. It brought economic benefits, in the form of improved transportation and agricultural methods, along with harsh use of local labor and the integration of the colonies into a Western-dominated world market. Population growth posed its own new challenge to the economies of Africa and southern Asia. Limited medical advances, such as inoculations, swamp-draining, and other disease-control measures, had tremendous impact, just as Western population growth was ebbing. In 1914 the major question for Indian or Nigerian or Indonesian leaders was clearly focused: how to deal with Western rule. But imperialism raised wider political, economic, and cultural concerns also, which would outlast the struggle for independence in setting an agenda for world history for the 20th century and beyond.

Many similar issues would also affect those parts of the world not subject to full imperialist control, such as China and the Ottoman Empire, or newly freed from it—the Latin American case. Would outright imperialist rule help or hinder a civilization in dealing with problems of population growth, imbalance in the world economy, and new political tensions? Was India, to use the clearest instance, better off for having an intense if relatively brief experience of Western rule, than China, which faced Western depredations without the possible benefits of Western influence? Imperialism provided a shock to the civilizations that came under its full sway in the 19th century; its impact and the reactions it provoked conditioned the history of these areas even after independence was won.

SUGGESTED READINGS

Excellent general surveys of 19th-century imperialism and its causes include: Winifried Baumgart, *Imperialism* (1982); D. K. Fieldhouse, *The Colonial Empires* (1968); and Bernard Porter, *The Lion's Share: A Short History of British Imperialism 1850–1970* (1975). See also C. H. Peake, *European Colonial Expansion since 1871* (1941), and the imaginative

Michael Adas, *Machines as the Measure of Men* (1989). On specific areas and imperialist powers, W. Baumgart, *Imperialism: The Idea and Reality of British and French Colonial Expansion* (1982), is an excellent discussion. On Africa, worthwhile sources include: Colin Turnbull, *The Lonely African* (1971); A. Moorehead, *The White Nile* (1971); Woodruff D. Smith, *The German Colonial Empire* (1978); Walter Rodney, *How Europe Underdeveloped Africa* (1982)—a vital study; R. P. Masani, *Britain in India* (1961); and M. D. Lewis, ed., *The British in India: Imperialism or Trusteeship?* (1962). See also C. A. Bayley, *Indian Society and the Making of the British Empire* (1988). On peasant resistance, see J. Scott, *The Moral Economy of the Peasant: Rebellion and Subsistence in Southeast Asia* (1976).

CHAPTER 22

The Middle East and China in the Imperialist Century

Focal Points

China and the Ottoman Empire were two great states that had to consider a variety of changes under Western pressure. Unlike Africa and India, they were not, for the most part, directly taken over as colonies. Their position in the world did, however, change greatly from what it had been during the early modern period. What were the major signs of new Western impact? What were the principal responses of Chinese and Ottoman leaders, and were they adequate to the Western challenge? Neither China nor the Ottoman Empire managed to recover their former vigor during the 19th century, but Ottoman leadership on the whole reacted more fully. In what ways was China more damaged by Western exploitation and internal decline? What were the most significant Ottoman adjustments?

CHANGE AND RESISTANCE

The Muslim Middle East and China, though quite different still as civilizations, displayed similar reactions to the heightened pace of the world economy and the threat of Western imperialism during the 19th century. Neither the Middle East nor China came fully under Western control, in part because of the continuing strength of their governments and in part because Western rivalries canceled each other out, so that no one imperialist power could win predominance. Their patterns thus differed from those of southern Asia and sub-Saharan Africa. But both areas lost territory and both increasingly felt the threat of further takeovers. Yet the Middle East and, particularly, China responded sluggishly to the transformation in the wider world during most of the 19th century, and both lost further ground as a result. Change came, but haltingly. Traditionalist leadership and a long habit of looking down on foreigners, in the Chinese case, or Westerners, in the Muslim case, delayed vigorous reactions. Late in the 19th century, however, new forces built up in both societies ardently seeking fundamental reforms that would make their societies more competitive with the West and more like the West in certain ways. This outlook set the stage for a much more active period of development during the 20th century.

China and the Middle East, then, represented during the 19th century a pattern somewhat in between the societies under outright imperialist control, like India, and those that were stimulated during the century itself to radically new kinds of responses. Ironically, it was China's East Asian cousin, Japan, that provided the most successful example of the latter type of approach, which means that China and Japan diverged increasingly in their paths despite shared traditions. Latin America, which was another "in-between" case, must be handled separately from China and the Middle East because its civilization was still in formation during the 19th century; but in terms of its relation with the Western imperialist forces, the Latin American experience had some points in common with the two societies studied in this chapter.

THE MIDDLE EAST

THE ATTEMPT TO MODERNIZE EGYPT

The Middle East began the 19th century with a fascinating initiative, though one that ultimately failed. The Ottoman Empire had been rocked, in 1798, by Napoleon's successful invasion of Egypt. When Napoleon was forced out, by British pressure plus Napoleon's own ambition, an Ottoman military officer named Muhammed Ali took over Egypt as a virtually independent ruler, and indeed the Ottomans never did fully regain control of this vital province. At points, Muhammed Ali also conquered areas of the Arabian peninsula adjacent to Egypt, though he was blocked not only by Ottoman resistance but also by British fear of any strong power in this region so close to key routes to India.

As ruler of Egypt, Muhammed Ali represented one of the first non-Western leaders, and certainly the first in the Middle East, to adopt a self-conscious mission to modernize his society in Western terms. Unlike Peter the Great, Muhammed Ali never visited the West, but he greatly admired Western achievements and also realized that he must try to match some of them if he was to preserve the independence of Egypt. Under his sponsorship Western, and particularly French, advisors flooded the country to aid in education, technology, and science as well as military affairs.

Muhammed Ali saw the need to alter traditional economic patterns. Though unable to spur outright industrialization, he did introduce agricultural improvements and, in particular, developed an active export market for Egyptian cotton. The hold of landlords, traditionally uninterested in innovation, was weakened. Muhammed Ali also established a printing press and sponsored the translation of many Western books on science and technology into Arabic. In addition to using Western teachers, he sent a number of Arabs to study abroad. French became a second language to educated Egyptians. Yet Muhammed Ali was unable to break through either the hold of tradition on much of Egyptian society or the limitations imposed by Western dominance of the world economy. Egypt became increasingly dependent, for export earnings, on the Western market for cotton; it thus had to compete with other producers of cotton, including the U.S. South and India, and it did not always win favorable prices. Its export earnings were frequently insufficient to pay for the machines and military equipment that Muhammed Ali sought, so that his regime was increasingly forced to go into debt to Western banks. Here was a tragic irony, repeated many times in many countries, in the Middle East and elsewhere, throughout the 19th and 20th centuries. Governments seek to modernize, adopting new armaments, industrial machinery, and often an array of public buildings and urban amenities. But these innovations, designed to spur independence, cost money, at a time when the economy remains sluggish. Hence the temptation to borrow, which gives foreign banks new powers to supervise policy in the interest of protecting their loans. Muhammed Ali, in sum, managed to change Egypt, but he saw Western control steadily increase; by 1849, when he died, he was bitterly disappointed with the limits of his achievements. His efforts stand more as an early example of an attempt to adapt in response to Western standards than as a successful revitalizing force.

Furthermore, the bulk of the Middle East remained largely immune to Muhammed Ali's influence. The Ottoman Empire reacted to growing Western pressure and the de facto loss of Egypt in much more limited terms. The sultans established somewhat more centralized controls over great estates, in the interests of ensuring higher tax revenues. The sultan Mahmud II (1808–1839) broke up the corrupt Janissary corps. This group had long since lost its military skills and morale, and had turned to political intrigues while living well from state revenues. Mahmud II created a separate, modern artillery corps armed with European cannon; on this base he was able to eliminate the Janissaries and develop a new officer group eager to rival Western military organization and technology.

DECLINE OF THE OTTOMAN EMPIRE

These reforms, focusing on military structure primarily, were not sufficient to revive the decaying Ottoman Empire or to limit growing Western strength in the region. Important provinces of the empire were lost during the first half of the 19th century. Not only Egypt (though it technically remained a province until 1914) but the North African states of Algeria, Tunisia, and Libya (Tripoli) became independent; these last regions had never been fully integrated into the empire in any event. Piracy from the North African shores provoked military response from Europe and also from the United States, which attacked the "shores of Tripoli." In 1830 France began an outright conquest of Algeria, the first of many European takeovers in this area. On the Arab peninsula new, religiously inspired rebellions against the Ottoman Empire broke out, though with the help of Muhammed Ali they were put down. Finally, the European provinces of the empire became increasingly restive, inspired by the example of liberalism and nationalism in the French Revolution. In 1820, a major war for independence broke out in Greece, which after a decade, and with wide if informal support from Western Europe, won its independence. Nationalist agitation also stirred in Romania and Serbia, putting new pressure on the Ottoman regime.

West European economic influence in the Middle East intensified during the first part of the 19th century. Outside the boundaries of the Ottoman Empire, on the east coast of the Arabian peninsula, Britain established a number of protectorates to limit piracy. London set up steamship routes between India and eastern Arabia; by the 1830s, Britain and France operated steamship routes across the Mediterranean to Egypt and the Ottoman Empire itself. Thus Middle Eastern shipping and foreign trade lay increasingly in Western hands. British companies even operated some river shipping within the Ottoman Empire. Western economic power severely limited the revenue capacity of the Empire, which was barred from taxing foreign enterprise. World economic position, in other words, greatly constrained Ottoman political response.

Finally, pressure on the empire continued from yet another traditional source—the surging Russian empire. Several regional wars occurred between Russia and the Ottomans during the first half of the 19th century, resulting in loss of territory. Russia could have gained still more save for the intervention of France and Britain, who now had their own stake in this region and feared Russian dominance. The Crimean War of 1854–1856 resulted from British-French opposition to further Russian expansion in the Mediterranean, and indeed the Russians were defeated. Another Russo-Turkish war occurred in 1877–1878, and again only Western intervention prevented Russian dismemberment of the empire, which lost new territory even so.

By this point, the Ottoman Empire itself was little more than the puppet of forces beyond its control. The empire was not fully carved up only because the Europeans and Russians could not agree on the spoils; each power feared that the others would gain too much. The Middle East was too close to Europe to allow the kind of free-for-all that ultimately occurred in Africa; the danger of all-out war was too great. So the empire survived until 1918. Various sultans continued to tinker with reforms. Occasionally they granted constitutions, in an effort to follow Western patterns, but in fact the rule of the sultan and the bureaucracy remained unchecked. Military reforms were more serious and concentrated much of the impetus for change within the ranks of the armed forces. Many Ottoman officers were trained in Europe, and European—particularly German—advisors were brought in to improve technology and modernize military administration. But the Ottoman army remained weak and relatively backward, in part because military reforms were unable to transcend the loose political organization and largely agricultural economy. Tax revenues and morale were both inadequate to provide new vigor to the Ottoman state as a whole.

Hence the empire continued to lose territory on its fringes and to suffer growing Western economic penetration. Nationalist uprisings in the Balkan area, supported by Russia and some of the Western powers, produced a network of small, independent states by the end of the 1870s: Serbia, Romania, and a few still smaller states joined Greece. As a result of further Balkan agitation, which led to an independent Bulgaria, the Ottoman Empire had, by 1914, lost almost all hold in Europe, save for a patch of territory including Constantinople.

Direct imperialist conquest in North Africa also continued, though this region, of course, had already been lost to the Ottomans. In 1869 a French company completed construction of a canal through the Isthmus of Suez, the narrow strip of land that had connected North Africa and the Middle East. By using the new Suez Canal, European ships could save immense time in reaching the Indian Ocean, by sailing from the Mediterranean to the Red Sea rather than around Africa. Egypt's importance increased because of its new strategic position. Britain, anxious as always to safeguard its interests in India, began to interfere more and more in Egyptian affairs, mainly to preempt French influence. Heavy Egyptian debts to British banks provided an obvious opening. Britain was able to buy controlling shares in the Suez Canal and then, in the 1880s, established a protectorate over the Egyptian government; the Egyptian ruler became virtually a figurehead. In response, France took over outright control of Tunisia, and soon after 1900, Italy

The opening of the Suez Canal: the French Empress Eugénie on her way to the ceremonies.

gained Libya; France captured Morocco. All of Muslim North Africa lay in European hands.

To the east of the Ottoman Empire, British and Russian representatives divided influence over the kingdom of Persia, while direct British hold over the small states of the eastern Arab coast continued. Within the empire itself, European interests gained increasing economic power. German businesses, backed by the government, constructed a major railroad linking Berlin to Baghdad. French and English merchants bought quantities of luxury items. In Turkey proper, a number of rug factories were set up, utilizing machines imported from the West and displacing many traditional handworkers, to fill the growing markets of Western Europe and the United States, where Turkish carpets and other furnishings became the rage in middle-class homes in the later 19th century. While some Turks and Arabs gained experience and wealth as factory owners or agents for Western companies, the new industry rested heavily on low-paid labor, and its basic directions were determined by Western merchants, not those in the Middle East itself. The Ottoman Empire, bounded by Western colonies, new and aggressive Balkan nations, and the ambitious Russian state, was no longer master in its own house.

THE RISE OF NATIONALISM

Although the Ottoman government proved unable to respond successfully to these new developments, several important events occurred that would shape Middle Eastern history in the 20th century. A strong current of Arab nationalism began to emerge, directed both against European imperialists and against the hold of the Ottoman state. In Turkey, a modernizing movement arose among younger army officers. Finally, some efforts were made to rouse new Muslim fervor.

In contrast to India, a large Middle Eastern nationalism did not take clear shape, though there were efforts to encourage patriotic loyalty to the Ottomans. Nationalism increasingly meant particularism, associated with a smaller region, like Egypt, or an ethnic-linguistic group, like the Turks.

Arab nationalism developed most vigorously in Egypt, where Muhammed Ali had first opened the way to growing European influence and example. The nationalism in fact emphasized Egypt more than Arabs in general, where a full nationalist statement would not emerge until the early 20th century. Many educated Egyptians followed Muhammed Ali's goal in wanting to create a modern state and economy, along something like Western lines, but they also wanted a proudly independent Egypt, inspired by the same nationalism they saw in Western Europe. Nationalism was a new force in the Middle East (as in India), in its quest for loyalty to secular states and to specific peoples instead of Arabs or Muslims in general; its newness for a time limited its appeal, particularly to peasant masses, but it did have the great merit of focusing attention on twin goals of independence and political change. As the Egyptian government grew weaker and more indebted toward the middle of the 19th century, nationalist opposition increased. It was inflamed still further by the British takeover. Britain regularized Egyptian finances and helped sponsor some railroad construction and a massive dam on the Nile at Aswan, which increased the amount of water available for irrigation in agriculture. London also abolished slavery in Egypt and expanded the school system. But these reforms did not daunt the new nationalism. Egyptian nationalists resented economic controls that, in their view, prevented full industrialization. They also resented the lack of political rights and the arrogance of many British colonial administrators. As educated city dwellers, the nationalists could easily see the privileged position and luxury of foreigners in their country.

Arab nationalism also sprang up elsewhere in North Africa, in response to new imperialist regimes. In Tunisia, for example, the French built port facilities, rails, and a telegraph and telephone system; they also introduced new schools and hospitals. But they did not encourage much industry and were careful to retain control of most export trade. A handful of French settlers took over some of the most fertile land in the country. These developments, as well as the gap between French and Tunisian culture, were more than enough to stimulate nationalist concerns. As in Egypt, North African nationalism before 1900 mainly took the form of political rallies and newspaper diatribes—themselves new political experiences for the Arabs involved. Little nationalist rioting occurred. But there was no question that a new political force was surging in this ancient region.

Some Arab nationalism also spilled over to the Ottoman Empire itself. A number of governors of Arab provinces, including the one that contained Mecca, flirted with nationalism; their loyalty to the sultan was questionable by 1900. In 1913, Arab nationalists were able to meet in Persia to discuss independence for Iraq.

Other kinds of nationalisms also entered the field. A movement among European Jews, called "Zionism," arose in the later 19th century in response to European patriotic claims and new kinds of intolerance against the Jews. The Zionists argued that Jews should re-establish their homeland in Palestine, and by 1914 a number of Jewish settlers were entering the area. This current had no great political consequences as yet, but it would prove vital in the region's future.

Further north, in the Ottoman heartland, more serious reform currents from the early 19th century set the basis for Turkish nationalism. Even though the Ottomans lost the ability to rule their empire vigorously, they did introduce changes affecting Turkey proper. The strengthening of the military, following the courageous dissolution of the Janissaries, brought many Turkish officers into contact with Western training. University education was reorganized on Western lines, and the government launched new postal and railway services in Turkey. These changes were important, but they whetted appetites for more. Muslim leaders clashed with the Westernizing elite, and Sultan Abdul Hamid re-established authoritarian rule after 1878. This was the context, around 1900, in which a number of younger army officers began to push for reform of the sultan's government and modernization of the empire. This movement of "Young Turks," as they were called, sought political rights, along lines promised in a constitution of 1876 that the sultan had quickly withdrawn; they wanted an end to political corruption and a more vigorous foreign policy. They demanded new limits on European economic activities in their land. As one Young Turk put it, "We follow the path traced by Europe . . . even in our refusal to accept foreign intervention." Young Turks participated in a number of violent attempts to overthrow the sultan's government, though without initial success.

The Young Turk movement was long unclear as to whether it wanted to revive the Ottoman Empire or to form a modern nation-state in Turkey. It talked mainly of the empire, but it relied so heavily on Turkish pride and the imposition of Turkish force that its implications were in fact more narrowly nationalistic. The movement proved, in fact, to be the basis for the modern Turkish nation that emerged after the larger Ottoman Empire collapsed.

In 1914, the Middle East was caught between the pressures of imperialism and the structures of the Ottoman state, on the one hand, and the forces of a modernizing nationalism on the other. These latter forces, including the Young Turks, constituted a vital new ingredient in the region, a sign of Europe's great influence but a symbol also of a vigorous desire for independence. Nationalism was not a native Middle Eastern product. The idea of cutting the region up into separate states, which even most Arab nationalists suggested in their concentration on Iraq, or Egypt, or Tunisia, had some precedent in earlier periods of regionalism in the Middle East, but it ran against the Islamic as well as the Ottoman tradition. The nationalists were not worried about precedent, however. They wanted not only independence, but a new society, however vague their definitions. They often embraced a reformist version of Islam, but they were positively hostile to the traditional social structure and educational system of their region. They wanted new political regimes, not only independent but possessed of parliaments and voting rights. For them, as many admitted, the West was both the example and the enemy.

Most people in the Middle East were still peasants and only vaguely affected by the new currents. They remained faithful to Islam, educated in the laws and ceremonies of the Koran. Some were drawn into new economic endeavors, like the rug factories or the cotton estates, but most continued to work by traditional methods and to rely heavily on village institutions. No serious change occurred in the lives of Middle Eastern women, still largely isolated in extended family households according to Muslim law; even in the upper classes, few women came into contact with Western ideas, as even imperialist regimes did not try to alter this basic feature of Islamic life. A few Muslim leaders talked of trying to adapt the religion to modern life, and to use Islam as a unifying force for the whole civilization against Western pressure and nationalism alike. Islam was not an unchanging force, though it embraced strong traditionalist elements. Several religiously inspired revolts broke out against Europeans in North Africa, and Muslim belief in the superiority of their religion continued unabated, easily sufficient to doom Christian missionary movements in the region. Islam here conveyed anger and anxiety, a role that was to continue in the 20th century.

CHINA

China at the end of the 18th century had been able, proudly if not entirely realistically, to shun Western bids for a reduction in the empire's isolation, which remained far more complete than in the days of Mongol rule, when Western travelers like Marco Polo had roamed widely through the vast country. The Chinese economy remained at this point largely self-sufficient, despite modest exports in return for gold. The Qing dynasty, though past its prime, was still functioning fairly smoothly at the head of the fabled bureaucracy.

A mere 40 years later China was forced to open its borders to new Western trading and cultural activities, as a result of one of those imperialist wars barely noticed in Europe, involving handfuls of Western troops, which dramatically revealed the new balance of power between a declining imperial China and the industrial West.

From the 1820s onward, Western traders became increasingly insistent on gaining access to the vast Chinese markets and the products of Chinese artisans. As they became better established in other parts of Asia, such as India, they gained new knowledge of the profit potential of greater Chinese trade. Growing wealth at home spurred new demand for Chinese vases, porcelain, and other artifacts. At the same time, the Qing dynasty lost vigor rapidly, in a process familiar in Chinese history but now fatefully juxtaposed against the new Western strength. Local rebellions began to increase early in the 19th century. A major uprising, the Taiping Rebellion, burst out in the 1850s. Led by a man who claimed to be the younger brother of Jesus Christ, the rebels sought traditional peasant goals: lower taxes and more land. Peasants were pressed by rapidly rising population; simultaneously, the efficiency of the central government declined. The bureaucracy could no longer collect taxes effectively, and the quality of the imperial army deteriorated. This made unrest harder to put down and harder to prevent. The government struggled for years with the Taiping rebels, finally requiring Western military support to win out. Increasingly, the government was forced to rely on locally trained militias, but these forces, newly armed, often turned against the emperor as well, stepping up rebellion and banditry.

The first clash between a waning empire and the greedy West occurred in the Opium War of 1839–1842. British merchants in India had been exporting opium for sale in China. Ironically, they still had trouble finding goods that would appeal to the Chinese market, because of the adequacy of traditional Chinese manufacturing; factory-made textiles, for example, had little appeal. So opium was seen as a vital exchange item that would allow the West to pay for Chinese goods without offering valuable gold. But the Chinese empire objected to the opium trade. Opium use was not traditional in China, and there was widespread knowledge of its harmful effects. Furthermore, the government continued to treat British representatives as annoying inferiors. A government effort to seize all opium in the harbor of Canton led to a fight with British sailors and an attempt to prohibit all British trade in the area. War followed, as the British blockaded the entire coast; the Chinese were powerless to resist because they had no effective navy. The Chinese finally yielded, paying for all British property they had destroyed, opening several ports including Canton and Shanghai to British merchants, and giving Britain the island of Hong Kong.

The defeat in the Opium War was a bitter blow to Chinese leaders, who would long remember not only the loss but the fact that Britain was willing to fight for the right to export a substance that drugged many Chinese people. But bitter memories did nothing to stop further Western penetration. On the heels of British gains came France and the United States, demanding new trading rights. By 1850, foreign colonies existed in a number of ports. A second war, in 1857, led to the opening of still more ports and additional rights that allowed Westerners to trade and conduct missionary activity even in the interior. An Anglo-French army pushed to Peking, driving the emperor from the city, in order to enforce these concessions.

These early imperialist advances did not alter the basic direction of Chinese policy. The Chinese leadership still believed that traditional ways were best, seeing Western gains as temporary setbacks like other brief invasions that had occurred earlier in Chinese history. No new measures were taken either to imitate or to counter Western developments. For their part, Western nations, led by Britain and France, were learning that China was a weak empire, not all that different from the Ottomans in basic strength, and hence an easy victim for any modern state with a good navy. Ironically, by the middle of the 19th century, the Chinese government was not particularly interested in copying

British East India boats destroy Chinese junks in the Opium Wars period, 1841. Nineteenth-century line engraving. (The Granger Collection)

Western military technology—in contrast even to the Ottoman regime. Chinese officers regarded technology as uninteresting, treating engineers with contempt as social inferiors. The reverence for tradition and for cultural as opposed to military or business concerns in the Confucian value system, plus the weakness and real poverty of the imperial administration at this point, combined to make innovation seem both undesirable and impossible.

Yet, beneath the level of imperial administration, China was changing. Population growth continued, creating great land hunger on the part of many peasants. A relatively small number of peasants even sought solace in emigration—an unusual recourse in Chinese history—as they were recruited by railroad or estate bosses in the United States and some parts of Latin America. This movement, however, put no real dent on continued unrest at home. At the same time, Western influence affected some Chinese as well. Missionary efforts converted small groups of Chinese to Christianity and promoted some wider interest in Western ways. More important, Western business activity in the open, or Treaty, ports helped sponsor wider economic development on a regional basis. The ports grew rapidly in population and wealth; they stimulated market agriculture and some manufacturing, even a few mechanized factories, in the surrounding countryside; and they gave some individual Chinese business executives experience with Western commercial methods and profit-making zeal. A few entrepreneurs and Christian converts began to gain experience abroad, even attending foreign universities, though this was as yet the merest trickle against the barrier of centuries of isolation.

Western imperialists remained uninterested in trying to take over China directly, which would have been a difficult task and which was unnecessary given their new access to Chinese trade. They even aided the Qing dynasty in putting down the Taiping uprising during the 1850s; Western regimes preferred a weak imperial administration to outright disorder. Given growing unrest over land hunger, taxation, and corruption among many officials, the Qing dynasty became increasingly dependent on European—particularly

An English church in Shanghai, late 19th century: transporting Europe to China as literally as possible. Compare this style to the Jesuit approach in China, illustrated in Chapter 18.

British—assistance during the second half of the 19th century. Western advisors were employed to improve the army and also to increase efficiency in tax collection—a real paradox for an empire with the greatest bureaucratic tradition in the world. Use of Western advisors signaled an awareness of a need to change. Some Chinese officials grew more interested in Western weaponry—as one writer put it, "Learn the technology of the Barbarians in order to control them." But there still was no commitment to significant reform. Indeed, after the Taiping Rebellion was finally crushed in 1864, the government bent most of its efforts to restoring the prestige of the emperor and traditional Confucian principles. The government even tore up a rail line built by private interests in the 1870s, in hopes of maintaining traditional ways. This showed a firm desire to avoid Westernization—indeed, some clashes with Christian missionaries occurred—but no grasp of what to do to keep the Westerners out. Furthermore, revival of traditional culture did not effectively deal with internal problems, as bureaucratic corruption increased and regional officials became harder to control. Some economic change occurred, in part because of Western influence in the port cities, but most Chinese manufacturing continued with traditional, hand-labor methods. The Chinese imported machine-made thread from Europe and the United States, but continued to weave cloth manually. A handful of Chinese bankers and merchants built prosperous enterprises in the port cities, but most economic patterns stagnated. Products exported to the West, like tea and craft goods, were generated by small-scale operations, not the big estates characteristic of India or Southeast Asia. China was moving only slowly toward the new principles of world commerce.

China, in fact, was faced with a situation that had no precedent. With the lone exception of Buddhism, foreign influence had never been seen as a source of inspiration—only as a nuisance to be outlasted through superior Chinese traditions. Most other cultures, including Japan, India, and even the Ottoman Empire, had more experience with selective borrowing. Chinese politics had long stressed not only tradition, but the prevention of conflict; they were not well suited for promoting change. Bureaucrats saw no particular reason for new, Western-style efficiency, since they defined bureaucratic talent more in terms of cultural interests and promotion of harmony. The expansionist, profit-seeking values of Western-dominated trade also came hard to Chinese tradition, despite the vigor of many Chinese business executives even in the past. An old Confucian adage held: "Acknowledgement of limits leads to happiness"—and this was hardly the capitalist spirit. Added to these cultural impediments were the growing weakness of the reigning dynasty and the stark pressure of rapid population growth, which diverted resources and political attention from other issues. Thus during most of the 19th century, China changed less rapidly not only than the West or Japan, but also than colonial India or Turkey.

And lack of change, in the context of 19th-century world history, meant invitation to imperialism. France's conquest of Indochina from the 1850s onward was a blow to Chinese prestige, as Vietnam had long been an imperial protectorate. Russia, again on the prowl, took over some territory in northern China in 1860.

But the huge blow came in 1894–1895, in a war with Japan. The Sino-Japanese War was triggered by a rebellion in Korea. Both Japan and China intervened to suppress this revolt. China had long treated Korea as a vassal state, while Japan, now rapidly industrializing, sought new spheres of influence. Both China and Japan also wished to prevent Russian action in Korea. But the two nations attacked each other as well, and Japan, with

China and Japan in the 19th Century

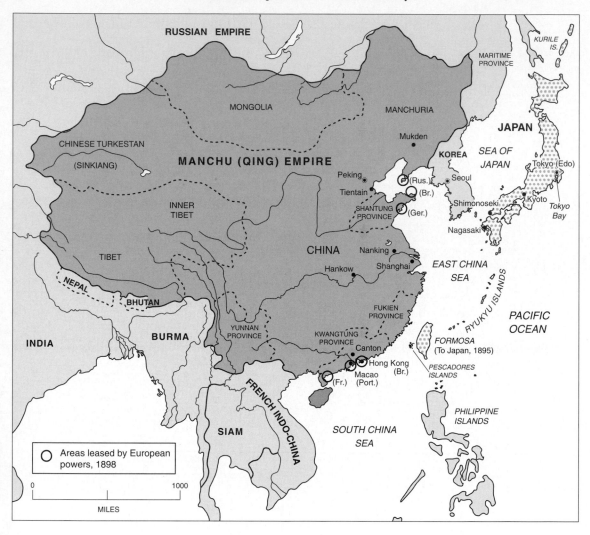

a modern navy, easily won—to the astonishment of literally the whole world outside of Japan. China was forced to yield not only Korea but the island of Taiwan to the Japanese, plus the Liaotung peninsula. This region was regained only by the intervention of the Western powers, who wanted no Japanese influence in China proper. China was shown to be a hollow shell, unable to fend off its much smaller Japanese rival. This fact, plus concern about Japanese gains and the hot rivalry among the European states, which had by now chewed up most of Africa and were looking around for new pastures, produced a scramble for Chinese holdings.

The result, by 1900, was a series of new treaties giving France, Germany, Britain, and Russia long-term leases on a number of key ports and surrounding territories. This was not

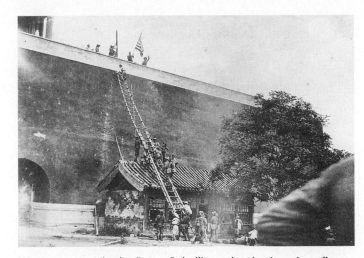

Western troops in the Boxer Rebellion raise the American flag on the Great Wall.

outright imperialist annexation, but it amounted to much the same thing as the imperial governments set up their own local administrations. Russia also seized some additional northern territory outright. Western nations proceeded to expand their business influence from their new centers, building rail networks and setting up river shipping toward the Chinese interior.

At last, China tried to react. A new young emperor, Kuang-hsu, ordered military reforms, railroad building, and extension of education. But Tzu-hsi, the widow of the previous emperor, seized power in 1898 and canceled these reforms, executing several of the leaders of the Westernization movement. Tzu-hsi believed that China could still go its own way despite the foreigners. She gave secret support to a society called the Righteous Harmony Fists, or Boxers, who began killing Europeans and Christian Chinese in 1899. The Boxer Rebellion was suppressed fairly easily by a combined European-American military force, and China was required to grant additional legal privileges to foreigners, making them immune from Chinese jurisdiction virtually throughout the country. Tzu-hsi herself set up a Western-style military structure and updated the education of imperial bureaucrats.

But by this point, shortly after 1900, it was clear that the waning Qing dynasty could not master the three forces bedeviling China: internal problems of decline and population growth; imperialist pressure; and a new force among Chinese who were aware of Western ways and eager to "modernize" their country along partially Western lines. For, from 1896 onward, a flood of Chinese students began to attend schools in Japan, Europe, and the United States, to gain access to the knowledge that their country so painfully lacked. They wanted to learn new technology, new science, and to an extent new organizational methods. In the process they also learned about new political ideas, including nationalism but also liberalism, democracy, and socialism. There was no full agreement on what the new China should look like. Some reformers wanted only limited imitation of the West, in purely practical matters; others wanted a full parliamentary regime, new roles for women, an attack on Confucian tradition. But there was agreement that change was essential and, increasingly, a sense that the existing regime had to go. Students returning from experiences abroad were joined by other students influenced by missionary schools or simply impressed by the growing flood of translations of Western science and literature. Forced finally by defeat to open the gates to change, it was clear that China's old regime could not contain the resulting flood.

CONCLUSION: THE NEED FOR FURTHER CHANGE

Even more clearly than the Ottoman Empire, China was poised on the brink of revolution by 1900. Population pressure caused more internal unrest in China than in the Middle East, while the intellectual minority, newly aroused by Western ideas, was more excited in China than in the Middle East, where Islam continued to operate as a brake on enthusiasm. Both areas, of course, suffered from weak imperial administrations and from infuriating levels of interference from the Western powers and Russia. The resulting mixture was too unstable to last, and it did not survive. Revolution was to break out in China in 1911, ending the Qing dynasty the following year and installing a republic in its stead—ending the world's oldest imperial government. The Ottoman Empire crumbled in the aftermath of World War I, and the political cohesion of the Middle East was shattered as well. Both these developments strikingly revealed the tensions that had built up as a result of internal change and external pressure, particularly during the last decades of the 19th century.

SUGGESTED READINGS

On the Middle East, see: W. R. Polk and R. L. Chambers, eds., *Beginnings of Modernization in the Middle East: The Nineteenth Century* (1968); H. A. R. Gibb, *Modern Trends in Islam* (1947); Alan Palmer, *The Decline and Fall of the Ottoman Empire* (1992); and M. G. S. Hodgson, *The Venture of Islam* (1971). See also David Kusher, *The Rise of Turkish Nationalism* (1977), and P. J. Vatikiotis, *The History of Egypt* (1985). On China, an excellent short survey is M. Gasster's *China Struggles to Modernize* (1983); relatedly, see Gilbert Rozman, *The Modernization of China* (1981), and Jonathan Spence, *The Search for Modern China* (1990). See also: Immanuel C. Y. Hsu, *The Rise of Modern China* (1970); Mary Wright, ed., *China in Revolution: The First Phase* (1968); and Li Chien-nung, *The Political History of China, 1840–1928* (1956). A useful source collection is Ssu-yu Teng and J. K. Fairbank, *China's Response to the West: A Documentary Survey, 1839–1923* (1954).

CHAPTER 23

The Development of Latin American Civilization

Focal Points

Two main developments shaped Latin America during the 19th century. First came the wars of independence, which were part of the great revolutionary upheaval of the Atlantic world in the late 18th to early 19th centuries. How did the goals of independence relate to new political movements in the United States and Western Europe? What were the results of independence? Why was it difficult to form stable political societies after colonial controls were removed? Second was the force of the world economy dominated by Western Europe and the United States, which undermined most Latin American manufacturing and (particularly after 1870) pressed for greater involvement with commercial agriculture and mining that would generate cheap exports. How did the effort to define new political systems and the pressures of the world economy combine in Latin America? How did they shape particular political movements such as liberalism, for example in relationship to the Latin American masses? The 19th century also saw new efforts to define a Latin American culture: What were the principal directions here?

PATTERNS OF LATIN AMERICAN HISTORY

During the century of imperialism, Latin American nations won independence, and the civilization as a whole further defined its identity. Latin America was seriously affected by the currents of imperialism, despite the newly achieved independence, and it was even more severely constrained by the West's domination of the world economy. Ironically, Latin America's failure to free itself from dependence on Western-controlled economic patterns was one of the signs that the civilization differed from that of the West. In politics and culture, Latin American leaders combined a deep devotion to many Western styles and values with some distinctive features that resulted from the civilization's racial diversity, its own colonial past, and the social structure that stemmed from a semicolonial economy. Thus Latin America emerged as a civilization unusually tied to the West, not only through imperialism and economic dependency but through shared religious and political ideas—but one that forged its own character by blending Western contacts with other currents. The result was a distinctive combination, in the 19th century and after.

Latin American history through the 19th century completed much of the basic framework of this newest of the world's major civilizations. One of the key challenges to 19th-century Latin America was the formation of new nations, where no clear precedent served to guide. These new nations were inevitably concerned with the establishment of territorial boundaries and with generating a leadership that could function despite the lack of prior political tradition. Hereditary rule, for example, made little sense in this context because there were no indigenous ruling families: previous Indian regimes had long since been destroyed, and government from Spain and Portugal was now ended as well. Along with new leadership, the nations had to set up legal structures and work to establish some kind of national loyalty. These were difficult tasks, yet for all their undoubted political problems the new countries of Latin America achieved some success during the 19th century. Other emerging nations in the 20th century would face similar challenges and would adopt solutions like those pioneered in Latin America.

THE WARS OF INDEPENDENCE

The 19th century began with the wars of independence from Spanish rule. Conflict broke out at several points in 1810, and the drive for independence was essentially completed by the mid–1820s. There followed another 30 years of consolidation, when the boundaries of the new nations were largely set, amid considerable strife, and key outlines of internal politics established. This was a period of economic hardship throughout most of Latin America, as the wars of independence disrupted earlier trade patterns and consumed substantial tax resources. It is vital to realize that the countries of Latin America were formed in a harsh economic context, when material distress heightened possibilities of discontent and disorder. After 1850, economic conditions tended to improve, as the civilization underwent extensive commercial development—though this same development brought new hardship to important segments of the lower classes. Further imbalance divided a wealthy minority of landowners and merchants from the low-paid masses, even though slavery was abolished. Political instability did not end in this final 19th-century period, but it did follow some clearly established lines. The late 19th century also saw new pressures from the world outside, in the form of imperialist thrusts from Western nations, particularly the United States, and a massive wave of immigration from southern Europe.

The wars of independence—unquestionably the most dramatic events in Latin America's 19th-century history—had several causes. Example was one. The revolution that had produced the United States showed that European colonial authority could be defeated. The French Revolution of 1789 also provided an example of the principles of political liberty and nationalist loyalty. Latin American leaders, particularly those drawn from the creole class, racially European but native to Latin America and often possessed of considerable education and wealth, were keenly aware of what was happening in the Western world, and the new examples were inspirations.

The French Revolution and its Napoleonic aftermath, indeed, provided an opportunity for Latin American leaders. Spain, with a somewhat inefficient government already, became distracted by the new danger on its northern borders, as the Spanish monarch sought to prevent revolutionary contagion in his own land. Then Napoleon's armies invaded Spain, briefly setting up a regime that controlled most of the country. Neither this regime nor the beleaguered Spanish king Ferdinand had much time or resource to keep Latin American colonies in line. Ferdinand regained his throne in 1815, but by this point the drive for independence was well established. A later Spanish revolution, in 1820, led in fact by discontented troops about to be sent to put down colonial unrest, provided additional diversion that allowed independence to be completed.

Example and opportunity were fed by serious grievances. In many regions the colonial economy had depended on extensive slave-holding, and the slaves were restive during the later 18th century. Material conditions and discipline were harsh. Many slaves expressed their discontent by fleeing; by 1800 over a quarter of all black slaves in Venezuela were fugitives, hiding out in self-governing communities in the jungles and mountains. Slave revolts also peppered 18th-century history in Latin America. In 1796, Toussaint L'Ouverture, a black leader in the French West Indian colony of Haiti, proclaimed outright independence. L'Ouverture, inspired by French revolutionary doctrines and eager to use France's own distraction by war and revolution, not only ended Haitian slavery but also set up the first black republic in the New World. Because most West Indian islands remained under Spanish, French, British, or Dutch control through the 19th century and beyond—though slavery was abolished during the middle decades of the century—Haitian independence did not have widespread repercussions. But pressure from discontented slaves was a more serious factor in the Caribbean and in Latin America around 1800 than it was in the United States.

Indians and mestizos also had grievances. Many were bound to labor on haciendas run by creoles, Spanish officials, or the church, or to work in the silver mines. Discipline was harsh, and there was little legal freedom. Most workers were forced to buy goods from estate stores and so suffered both material misery and lack of economic options. Revolts by Indian and mestizo estate workers had broken out in the 1770s, centered at first in Peru and spreading to Colombia. The insurrections attacked both the estates system and the high taxes levied by Spanish administrators. These uprisings, though winning initial success, were ultimately defeated by a combination of military force and trickery. However, they did spur a desire for greater freedom from Spanish rule.

At the top of Latin American society another set of grievances existed. Creoles, often aware of Enlightenment ideals, resented their lack of political opportunity. Though creoles had been used in colonial administration early in the 18th century, after 1750 Spain cut off this channel, returning to a policy of appointing only Spanish-born officials. These officials often disdained creoles, which added to the resentment. Creole merchants and professionals, moreover, disliked Spanish taxes and economic restrictions, which prevented legal trade with the more prosperous nations of Western Europe. As in the United States earlier, revolt was fueled by regulations that seemed excessive and also arbitrary, since they were set without consultation, for the benefit of the mother country. It was creole leadership that largely sparked the independence drive. Indian, slave, and mestizo dissatisfaction did not play a direct role, save in Haiti, in part because popular revolts had been so recently put down. The Latin American wars of independence were not, then, truly popular uprisings, calling social as well as political institutions into question. And while the resulting regimes changed some economic conditions, abolishing slavery in a

Latin American Independence

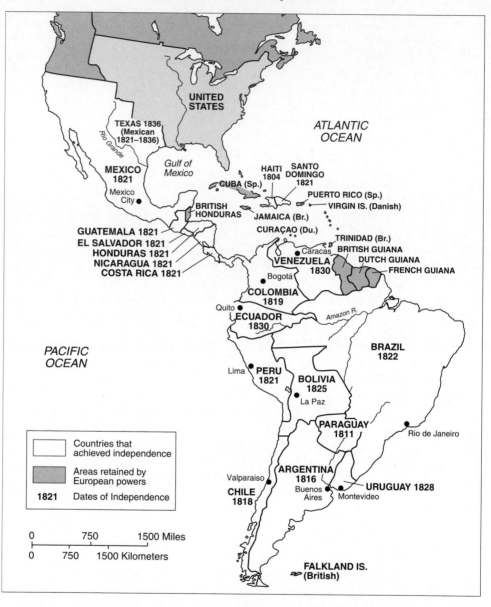

few cases, such as Mexico, and weakening the estates system for a time, the social system of colonial Latin America, with its pronounced divisions between creole owners and mestizo, Indian, and black workers, remained largely intact.

The first blow in the war for independence occurred in Venezuela in 1810, when the Caracas city council debated whether it owed loyalty to the new Napoleonic regime in

Mexican *hacienda* owner with overseer, 1830. (The Granger Collection)

Spain. The council decided on disobedience and urged other city councils to do likewise. King Ferdinand's rump government in Cadiz, Spain, was greatly displeased by these actions, even though they were technically directed at his French enemy; he declared the new regimes in revolt and ordered death to the leaders—an order he was powerless to enforce. The new administration in Venezuela promptly set up its own army and proclaimed its independence, drawing up a constitution modeled on that of the United States and the French Declaration of the Rights of Man. Spanish forces were able to put down this regime in 1812, but their harsh retaliation against early leaders roused further opposition. Simón Bolívar, a wealthy creole trained in the Spanish army and deeply imbued with Enlightenment ideas (see p. 448), now took leadership of the northern independence movement, rather like George Washington in North America, with whom he was often compared. Several years of fighting ensued, in which Bolívar assembled an army composed of many former British, Irish, and German soldiers, along with creole nationalists and some Indian troops. By 1819 Bolívar was strong enough to defeat the Spanish army; he proclaimed a new republic, called Gran Colombia, which united Venezuela and Colombia. Spanish attempts to recapture this nation, hampered by its own 1820 revolution, ultimately failed. Bolívar's armies invaded Ecuador, adding this province to his country.

In 1810, independence movements sprang up in the south as well. In Buenos Aires, a provisional regime was formed with a strong liberal element. An army was organized, ultimately under the leadership of another able creole general, José de San Martín. This army established a full-fledged government in Argentina and also aided the independence

Simón Bolívar (1783–1830) was a classic independence leader in Latin America, often compared to George Washington in the North. Like Washington, Bolívar was born into the upper classes, a wealthy creole officer with close intellectual ties to Europe. He gained a passion for national freedom and republicanism, and his fervor plus real military skill catapulted him to leadership of the Caracas-based independence movement in 1810. He was able to mobilize diverse support and won a series of victories against the Spanish in Venezuela, Colombia, and Ecuador between 1817 and 1822. Running the new country, Gran Colombia, was more difficult, however, and as it broke up into smaller nations Bolívar became bitterly disillusioned."America is ungovernable," he said, and "those who have served the revolution have plowed the sea." His principles remained firm, nevertheless, and he (again like Washington) refused popular efforts to crown him as king. Why is it often easier for individuals like Bolívar to mobilize forces for national independence than to govern the new nation after victory?

movement in Chile. Again, Spanish attempts to recapture these territories after 1815 were defeated, and the rebel armies also invaded Peru.

The final center of the independence movement took place in Mexico and Central America. Two priests, Miguel Hidalgo and José Morelos, led a lower-class rebellion of Spanish-speaking Indians and mestizos against the constraints of the hacienda system in 1810. Some Indians even talked of an Aztec government. The violence of the lower-class rebellion persuaded Mexico's creoles to remain loyal to Spain until 1820. At this point, however, Spain's own weakness convinced the creole elite that they should take matters in their own hands, lest they prove powerless against further social upheaval. Hence they supported an independent Mexico, hoping to create a monarchy that would attract a European prince. Finding no takers, a conservative Mexican emperor was crowned in 1822. Here was a clear case of the determination of creole landlords to defend their own elite position, which severely limited the social impact of freedom movements. Mexico's choice also foreshadowed political patterns in other Latin American areas, when strongman rule would be seen as an essential support for the elite against possible lower-class radicalism.

Independence for the Central American areas south of Mexico initially assumed more liberal lines. Centered in Guatemala, the movement proclaimed a United Provinces of Central America in 1823, with a constitution closely modeled on that of the United States.

No war was needed to bring independence to the final major nation of Latin America, Brazil. Threatened by Napoleon, the Portuguese ruler had fled to Brazil; when he was able to return to Portugal, in 1815, his son, Pedro, remained as regent. Portugal then tried to reimpose colonial controls over Brazil, but Brazilian leaders, now accustomed to a government based in Rio de Janeiro, resisted. Pedro joined this movement, proclaiming Brazilian independence in 1822 with himself as emperor.

By 1825, then, virtually all of Latin America was free from colonial rule. Small European holdings persisted on the northeast coast of South America and in one part of Central America; and of course the bulk of the West Indies remained in European hands. But the spirit of freedom prevailed elsewhere.

THE PERIOD OF CONSOLIDATION

Following the heady activity of the liberation movement, the period of consolidation set in. Between 1825 and 1850 a number of the original nine new nations of Latin America split apart. Bolívar had cherished some hope of a political union among all the regimes, but this was clearly impossible because of disagreements among independence leaders, some of whom wanted to set up monarchies while others sought liberal republics. Similar kinds of disputes, plus personal rivalries, then divided even the original states. Gran Colombia fell apart by 1830, splitting into Colombia, Venezuela, and Ecuador. A brief union between Bolivia and Peru failed, in part because the stronger states of Argentina and Chile sought to avoid a powerful neighbor. The United Provinces of Central America had dissolved into five small states by 1840. Finally, a number of border clashes between some of the new nations marked this early period.

The period of consolidation also saw considerable instability in internal politics. Liberals won most governments, advocating free trade and a federal government system, but their policies were too idealistic. Debates soon surfaced between central government advocates and federalists. Mexico, for example, seesawed between the two systems, with one leader, the colorful general Santa Anna, taking contradictory positions at different points. Liberal rulers sought parliamentary institutions and religious freedom, while conservatives wanted to protect the church and the upper classes; the latter controlled most regimes between 1830 and 1870. Many new governments were hampered by the lack of extensive political experience of the creole group. Because Spanish administrators had so systematically excluded the creoles, save at the level of city councils, few leaders could be found who had a full sense of how to operate a government. In this situation military leaders, drawn from the independence armies, often played an unusually large role. They had a power base and organizational skills. They also characteristically enjoyed landlord support, which was eager for forceful military action against peasant unrest. But factional fighting plagued the military as well, leading to frequent coups and revolts. During the 19th century, for example, Bolivia experienced 60 revolts and coups, Venezuela 52. Lack of previous political activity, the important role in internal politics taken by the military, and the obvious lack of agreement on political principles ensured considerable instability for most Latin American nations. Even Brazil, ruled calmly enough by Emperor Pedro and then his son until 1889, ultimately produced this pattern, as a republic was proclaimed that soon generated battles among liberals, conservatives, and army leaders.

By 1850, however, despite instability and dispute, many new governments managed to establish some key institutions. New legal codes were hammered out, based largely on Spanish precedent. A number of countries opened school systems and took on the function of developing port facilities and other public works. Few regimes set up particularly effective bureaucracies, and personal corruption played a frequent role in Latin American affairs; but the military hierarchy helped compensate for weakly developed civil administrations, and the promotion of military and police functions was obviously vital to the preservation of public order, in turn a cherished goal of the creole landlords and also church officials.

While political instability by no means ended after 1850, it is possible to see some changes by this point, as initial consolidation was completed. Some individual nations emerged from early disputes with a forceful government ready to pursue vigorous policies. By 1840, for example, Chile had settled several key issues of political structure, and during a series of administrations under capable presidents, it was able to expand the education system, offer wider voting rights for parliament, and open new lands in the south through the defeat of Indian groups. A number of governments had also abolished slavery, though the institution would survive in Brazil until 1888.

More impressive than internal political consolidation was the achievement of relative stability in foreign affairs. Many Latin American states remained rivals, sometimes contesting border areas. Britain prompted the creation of Uruguay in the 1820s as a buffer between Argentina and Brazil. But the Latin American map remained quite fixed after 1850. The only major changes, all provoked by the United States, saw massive loss of territory by Mexico (Texas, the U.S. Southwest, and California). Later, a semi-independent Cuba was established, after the Spanish-American War in 1898, and then an independent Panama, also under United States influence, was carved from Colombia to promote United States control of the canal dug through the isthmus there. A few wars dotted Latin American history in the later 19th century. Paraguay took on Argentina and Brazil in the 1860s, provoking great devastation, and Chile warred with its Andes neighbors in the 1870s, taking Bolivian and Peruvian territories. But for the most part Latin America was free from major strife between nations—far freer, certainly, than Western Europe at the same time. The concentration of military leaders on their often repressive internal political role distracted from foreign adventurism.

LATE-CENTURY TRENDS: DICTATORSHIP, IMMIGRATION, AND WESTERN INTERVENTION

No single political pattern describes Latin American developments during the late 19th century, but one significant trend was the tendency toward strongman rule. Venezuela, for example, went through three constitutions after 1870, but in fact was ruled mainly by a series of dictators, of whom the most successful was Antonio Guzmán Blanco. Mexico experienced a dizzying succession of changes before also settling into dictatorial rule. The final defeat of General Santa Anna had ushered in a period of liberal government under the Indian leader Benito Juárez. Juárez sought to reduce the power of the church in Mexican affairs and to extend a secular system of education; he also wanted to cut down landlord influence, though he pressed less vigorously here than he had initially promised his

Benito Juárez (1806–1872) was one of those rare but particularly significant individuals in world history who rose from humble origins to gain an important role in society that helped shape events. Juárez was a Mexican Indian who gained an education in law and became a state governor. He was an avid liberal, eager to cut the privileges of church and army and to promote economic change. After a Liberal revolt in the 1850s, Juárez became president of Mexico and undertook a sweeping reform program including sale of Church property. He also backed a land reform act that restricted traditional communal land holdings among Indians in favor of private property; his hope was to spur modern, independent farming, but in fact the lands were often bought up by speculators, leading to increased landlessness. Conservative reaction chased Juárez from power and brought a French-backed emperor whom Juárez opposed in the name of Mexican independence. Juárez returned to office but became increasingly autocratic in reaction to the previous period of instability. Juárez's personality and goals had made him a national symbol by the time of his death in 1872, as this 1920s mural by Diego Rivera suggests. His legacy, however, was more mixed than he would have wished. A period of strong government and economic growth followed Juárez, but social reform for the groups from which Juárez himself had risen proved more elusive. Why do leaders like Juárez sometimes fail to help their own people, despite a sincere desire to do so?

Indian supporters he would. Even so, his efforts roused the opposition of conservatives, who called for help from France. During the 1860s, when France was eager to gain new empire and while the United States was divided by Civil War, Mexico was ruled by an Austrian duke backed by French armies. But the armies left and liberal insurgents captured and executed the hapless duke. Juárez returned, and with him another series of important liberal reforms. But on Juárez's death, a strongman regime was installed, under Porfirio Díaz, which lasted from 1876 to 1911. Díaz radically curtailed political rights, arranging for the assassination of major opponents. Even in Colombia, where a parliamentary regime had usually prevailed, a brief series of strongman governments took over after 1900.

The tendency to strongman rule, amid considerable shifting of regimes, was only one of the major trends in Latin American history during the second half of the 19th century. Liberals returned to power in most countries, after the decades of conservative rule. They were eager for economic development and freer trade, but their policies were more authoritarian than before. Hence a number of strongmen were actually liberal in orientation, like Porfirio Díaz in Mexico. Many regimes held regular elections but with very restricted voting rights, creating what some historians have called "oligarchic democracies."

A third theme, steadily accelerating after 1870, was a surge of commercial development. Estate agriculture spread, as Latin American leaders sought to take advantage of new European markets for beef and coffee. Extensive mining resumed: a silver boom arose in Mexico, while extraction of copper and other products took hold along the Andes. The economic expansion was encouraged by increased foreign investment in Latin America. It was also supported by the interest taken by a number of Latin American governments, including dictatorships such as that of Guzmán Blanco in Venezuela, in extending roads and rail networks to the interior.

In several regions a massive new wave of immigration provided the backbone for the commercial upswing. Many governments promoted immigration, often inspired by a belief that Indian and black labor could never be suitably trained to the ways of a modern society. The Argentine constitution even included a provision that "the Federal government will encourage European immigration," and by 1895, with three-fourths of all adults foreign born, it had a far higher immigrant percentage than the United States. The end of slavery in Argentina and Brazil, by the 1880s, created a new need for labor. Freed slaves encountered far less thorough discrimination in Latin America than in the United States. More intermarriage occurred, as blacks added to the mestizo population; and light-skinned mestizos were not considered "colored" or black. However, considerable prejudice continued against dark-skinned former slaves and against Indians. This created a favorable climate for use of immigrant labor, which in fact squeezed the job opportunities of former slaves in a number of regions. Latin American interest in immigration peaked just as population pressure in southern Europe crested. Hence, while some immigrants came from Britain and Germany, often bringing capital and organizational skills, the majority came from Italy, Spain, and Portugal. A small number of Asians, from China and Japan, also arrived. Immigrants provided labor for the expanding economies and for the rapidly growing cities. They also represented new markets for the foods produced by estate agriculture. Many settlers adapted readily to Latin American life, often intermarrying with Indians and mestizos. While immigrants promoted some European ideas, such as socialism, in the main they accepted local beliefs, aided by the fact that most shared Catholic religious interests with their new compatriots. Immigration thus brought important changes to Latin America, but it did not overturn established political or cultural patterns.

New problems with Western powers constituted the final major factor in late–19th-century Latin American history. Western nations had not left Latin America alone during the consolidation period; their businesses had a major impact on economic life. Britain, which ruled the seas, also blocked the slave trade. France and occasionally Britain interfered militarily, and both Britain and the United States also officially discouraged outside intervention, though the United States gobbled approximately half of the territory of Mexico between 1830 and 1860, through the annexation of Texas and other lands won by war.

From the 1870s onward, however, foreign intervention increased. Heavy Western investment brought government action to enforce debt payments. British and French ships frequently threatened Latin American ports to compel fiscal reforms. United States ventures were still more significant. In addition to strong U.S. nationalist and imperialist sentiment, North American corporations acquired extensive estate and mining holdings and often called for military and diplomatic support against local reformist pressures. United States influence bore particularly heavily on governments in Mexico and Central America, though there were also important conflicts with Chile and other states. Through the war with Spain, the United States acquired the island of Puerto Rico directly, and a protectorate over Cuba. The building of the Panama Canal brought new pressure, leading to Panamanian independence from Colombia, under United States auspices. And shortly after 1900, the United States began a policy of frequent military intervention in unstable countries in Central America and the West Indies, out of concern for its business interests in these regions. The problem of dealing with Western nations, especially the United States, began to rank high on the agendas of all Latin American states.

Events during the 19th century, and particularly after 1850, had carved a number of distinctive regions within Latin American civilization. The great states of the south—Argentina, Uruguay, Chile, and Brazil—took the lead in the new prosperity of the late 19th century. They were most active in commercial development, and they also encouraged the highest levels of immigration. Several states, led by Argentina, prided themselves on their European airs. Buenos Aires became almost Parisian in its elegant boulevards, while stylish French and English shops served the wealthy classes. Although Brazil had large black and Indian populations, the southern states were overall more European racially than was Latin America as a whole.

A second group of countries covered the Andes region—Bolivia, Peru, and Ecuador. Here, the percentage of Indian population was highest, and the poverty greatest. Political instability and military rule were also somewhat more pervasive in this region than in Latin America generally.

Mexico, Central America, Colombia, and Venezuela all had sizable Indian populations, though the majority was mestizo. This region enjoyed some commercial expansion in the late 19th century. It was also the region most vulnerable to imperialist pressures, a major factor in the development of both foreign and economic policy.

Latin American regionalism, though significant, took shape amid a number of roughly common developments, from independence onward, and amid some widely shared patterns of politics and cultural life.

The European look: section of Buenos Aires in the late 19th century.

POLITICAL INSTITUTIONS AND VALUES

The instability of Latin American politics became notorious in foreign eyes, particularly in the United States. Frequent violence and the collapse of one regime after another encouraged people in the United States to look down on the Latin American political style, because stability and consensus on basic values seemed a hallmark of United States political life, at least after the devastating Civil War. Latin American politics were certainly distinctive, responding to factors rather different from those that described Western politics in the same period.

Politically active groups in Latin America tended to divide, from independence onward, between liberals and conservatives. A small, mainly intellectual socialist movement arose in some places toward 1900, but it had yet to win political significance. Liberals, strongly influenced by their Western counterparts, stood for genuine parliamentary governments, constitutions, and civil rights, and reduction of the power of the Catholic church. They welcomed economic development and sometimes considered limited social or land reforms; they were eager to extend education. On the other hand, they had little commitment to social reform, often scorning or repressing peasant and Indian values, and they supported elite economic interests. After 1870 they increasingly urged strong governments that could back economic developement and also regulate aspects of popular behavior the liberals found unruly.

Conservatives, often attracted in the early days by ideals of monarchy, distrusted parliaments. They directly backed the power of the dominant landlord class and were less interested in commercial or industrial development than were liberals. They also stood in firm defense of the rights of the Catholic church, which maintained a powerful role in education and possessed considerable wealth and land.

Disputes between conservatives and liberals helped account for political instability. Where they were not clearly resolved, as in Colombia and Venezuela in the late 19th century, regime changes were particularly frequent. Generally, however, liberal victory in the 1870s ushered in a period of greater political calm—it has been compared to the general triumph of democratic regimes in Latin America in the late 20th century. Liberals rarely gained a popular following, but they did ally with business interests and a growing urban middle class in promoting not only commercial expansion but also European-style urban renewal projects and efforts to improve public health and to crack down on prostitution.

Accompanying liberal and conservative conflicts, the frequency of strongman rule was also characteristic. *Caudillismo,* derived from the Spanish word for "leader," described this governmental form. Caudillos usually favored the conservative bastions of church and landlord but sometimes represented the liberal camp. Their tactics often cut through some of the conservative–liberal debate, if only by force. At times, some even worked for reform, scaling back church prerogatives and seeking economic development. By reducing liberal attacks on Indian or mestizo traditions, and by offering public works, some conservative caudillos won ardent mass support. But all caudillos relied on force. They forbad political opposition, regulated schools and newspapers, and used jails, police, and firing squads with abandon. Some, without question, were simply corrupt, lining their pockets and those of their cronies. Porfirio Díaz, the last Mexican caudillo, in addition to brutalizing his political opponents, encouraged landlords and United States investors to take over vast stretches of Mexican land, receiving extensive kickbacks in return. His government, indeed, sold off literally 20 percent of all the land in Mexico, much of it previously held by Indians and mestizo villagers.

In the 19th century, Latin American politics had little contact with the masses, save at times to exploit them. Few liberals were ardent democrats; they shared a distrust of Indians and blacks. Liberal constitutions gradually increased the suffrage, but few liberals favored democracy; hence mass political action was not an important feature of Latin America in this period. Liberals, indeed, were in some ways less sympathetic to mass interests than were conservatives, which helps explain their limited popularity. Liberals stood for individualized property rights; they wanted rationality and intense work habits; they typically sought to attack tradition, including, of course, popular religious customs. Liberal caudillos like Porfirio Díaz brutally suppressed incipient trade union movements among urban workers. Other caudillos at times developed political symbols and public works projects that did have mass appeal. Even before 1850, for example, an early Argentine caudillo, Manuel de Rosas, won considerable popular support by requiring church prayers for his regime, and by putting his picture and his political symbol, a red rose, in every possible public place. De Rosas and many other caudillos, particularly in the decades of consolidation, often helped build a national consciousness among elites and masses, even when they were by Western standards unusually repressive. The tensions between the articulate political forces in Latin America and the somewhat separate masses were one of many traditions established in the 19th century that would affect Latin American politics into our own time.

Most Latin American governments remained weak in the 19th century, even when caudillos officially claimed great power. Ability to regulate landlord or foreign business interests, or even, in some cases, roving bands of criminals was limited (as was true to some extent in the United States). This was the context in which, after 1870, liberals often advocated greater state powers in the interests of economic development, government-sponsored education, or regulating Indians.

CULTURE AND THE ARTS

The Catholic church continued to provide one of the key cultural bonds throughout Latin American civilization. The institution operated schools and charitable facilities for the poor, in addition to maintaining its political role. Church ceremonies and buildings provided aesthetic as well as spiritual experience for Latin Americans from almost all social classes and racial groups. Latin America thus remained largely separate from the assaults on religion as an intellectual and cultural force that arose in Western civilization during the same period, though liberals generated fierce attacks on the church as an institution. Debates such as that over Darwin's theory of evolution, in its implications for Christian belief, had little echo in Latin America. Indeed, Latin American culture, even at elite levels, remained relatively uninterested in science. Although in most countries universities were established by 1850 that gradually developed some scientific and medical training, science remained less prestigious in this civilization than in the West, its contribution to overall outlook less great.

Latin American culture was framed not only by religion but by class structure. A considerable gap divided educated Latin Americans from the largely illiterate masses. A few governments, particularly in the southern region or under regimes such as that of Juárez in Mexico, made strides in promoting literacy. Argentina, with a 22-percent literacy rate in 1876, jumped to 50 percent by 1895—the highest of any Latin American nation. These developments, along with growing prosperity, help explain why cultural activity stepped up in Latin America during the later 19th century. But most formal intellectual activity still played to what was, by Western standards, a limited audience.

Culture was also shaped, again especially in the southern region, by the immense popularity of Western modes. Latin America developed no architectural style of its own in this period, in part because those who could afford major building projects thought in terms of replicating what they had seen in Paris or Madrid. Many artists and writers patiently reproduced European-style portraits and novels for a ready, wealthy audience. And even intellectuals who cultivated originality did not think in terms of an entirely independent Latin American culture, as they kept careful tabs on European, and particularly French, styles.

Yet formal culture, especially in literature, did achieve a distinctive tone. Poetry played an important role. Many poets were retained on university faculties, and, in general, poetic expression became more vigorous in Latin America, in comparison with other literary output, than in the West. A number of women writers contributed to the impressive body of work in poetry. Using Romantic styles, a number of poets and novelists also tried to create a sense of popular themes and concerns in their own civilization. They wrote of the frontier, of Indians, of slave life. Many were politically radical, seeking to use literature to spur social reform. They were joined by many historians and folklorists, who strove to describe the special features of the Latin American experience and its racial diversities. Finally, a number of writers, both conservative and radical, sought to convey something of the spirituality of life, and particularly Latin American life. In the 1890s one Uruguayan novelist, Enrique Rodo, who achieved wide popularity in the Spanish-speaking countries, wrote stories vaunting the special virtues of his civilization over what he saw as the deadening materialism and mediocrity of Western culture, most notably in the United States.

Along with formal culture, a vigorous popular art continued to flourish. Many Indian weavers and potterers used traditional themes, designs, and vivid colors in their work. Festivals, even when organized around Christian celebrations, provided Indians and former Africans with an opportunity to participate in lively folk dances. Popular dance music, using Spanish instruments such as the guitar but traditional Indian or African melodies and rhythms, included the fast-paced tango and samba—styles that would later have influence in Western popular culture as well.

Overall, despite the limitations of poverty, illiteracy, and frequent political repression, a vibrant cultural life emerged at various levels of Latin American society. As in politics, Latin Americans worked toward a distinctive amalgam of Western styles and their own customs and values. Artistic expression became a vital facet of the maturing civilization.

ECONOMY AND SOCIETY

Economic and social patterns in Latin America most clearly separated this civilization from that of Western Europe and the United States, and indeed accounted for many of the distinctions visible in politics and culture. For the most dynamic sectors of the Latin American economies arose as suppliers to the West; manufacturing remained weakly developed throughout most of the 19th century, except for peasant production of cloth and other simple items for local use. Since colonial times, Latin America's great export facilities had been geared for the selling of goods in the Western-dominated world economy; this orientation remained after independence, which helps account for the long hold of slavery in a few states such as Brazil. As many regions became commercially active in the second half of the century, Latin American dependence on Western markets and on a low-paid labor force actually increased.

The first half of the century produced bleak economic news for much of Latin America. The wars of independence disrupted previous economic activities. Because few of the

HISTORY DEBATE

Is Latin American Western?

In 1997 a large number of Latin American historians, mostly but not exclusively from the United States, debated on the Internet whether Latin America should be judged a "non-Western" civilization. A few argued that Latin America should be included with the West because it shared a Western language and active participation in a common literary and artistic culture. Latin America is also the only society outside Western Europe and the United States/Canada/Australia/New Zealand where political liberalism gained a wide hold in the 19th century.

Others, however, objected. Some argued that parts of Latin America—a city like Buenos Aires, a group like the middle class—were Western, but other key parts—the poor, or a city like Tucuman—were not. Costa Ricans may view themselves as Western, but the Quechua speakers in the Andean highlands would not. The majority of the debaters argued that the solution to the question was not to decide whether Latin America was Western or not, but to argue that the term Western should be avoided. The term was loaded to mean "superior," and it did not reflect an accurate picture of any society. They further attacked the related tendency to lump many civilizations in a "non-Western" category, as if not being Western was a coherent descriptive feature. Finally, they argued that Latin America should be seen as a syncretic civilization, mixing many influences—but that other civilizations, including Western Europe, were also syncretic. Interestingly, discussions of social and economic features did not loom large: the debate focused on culture and on sympathetic or unsympathetic evaluations.

new regimes attempted significant land reform, most commercial production stayed in the hands of great estate owners; nonetheless, there was a good deal of confusion because of unrest and the disruption of trade ties with Spain. The ending of slavery in places like Mexico and Venezuela removed a key source of cheap labor that was not quickly replaced, while taxes rose to support growing armies. Furthermore, boundaries in several countries were drawn without regard to earlier economic patterns. Thus Bolivia and Peru, centers of the great silver mines, were cut off from the rich agricultural plains of Argentina. More serious still was the decline in production of precious metals, particularly in the Andes region, which reduced one of Latin America's chief exports. At the same time, independence opened Latin American markets to industrially produced cloth and tools from the West, especially Great Britain, which flooded out many local suppliers. Poverty among urban workers increased, while rural manufacturing was nearly wiped out.

By 1850, as we have seen, conditions often improved. There were exceptions, though—poverty increased in Mexico under Porfirio Díaz even as economic development advanced. Large estate owners, some of them foreign, tightened their grip on the Indian and mestizo labor force. But many Latin American countries developed a key cash crop or mineral specialty that allowed them to capture a growing export market. In Cuba and part of Central America, the product, sugar, was a familiar one. Brazil concentrated on coffee, and in 1889 the country produced 56 percent of the world's coffee; by 1904 the figure had risen to 76 percent. Argentina exported beef and wheat from vast ranches; Chile focused on copper and nitrates, Bolivia on tin. Mexico became a leading petroleum producer after 1900, spurred by U.S. investments and much foreign ownership. These concentrations on food and raw materials were highly vulnerable, however. Latin American production increased rapidly, but this risked flooding the market and thus lowering prices and total earnings. Brazil, for example, faced a devastating slump in coffee prices around 1900. Many countries also affected the environment by cleaning out forests and promoting crops like coffee that were not native to the region.

At the same time, demand for products manufactured in the West tended to grow rapidly. Upper-class Latin Americans, often winning new revenue from trade, mines, or estates, wanted European luxury items. They quite consciously backed the growth of export sectors as the basis for their style of life. Further, the railroads and ports that governments sought to promote required imports of equipment from the United States and Europe. Latin American nations accumulated rising foreign debts when their exports did not match their imports. Government indebtedness led to frequent Western intervention, which often averted bankruptcy but never attacked the basic economic imbalance.

Outright foreign economic control compounded the problem. Britain led in investments to Latin America in this period, but the United States and other Western nations were also heavily involved. Foreigners owned many of the most lucrative estates and industries. In Díaz's Mexico they bought a great deal of land; in Colombia and Chile they owned most railroads, banks, and mines. Western investments brought frequent pressures on Latin American governments to protect Western property. They deprived Latin America's struggling business class of a full range of opportunities, for top management remained in foreign hands. And they took much-needed profits out of the region altogether.

Finally, the economic development that did take place in the later 19th century, whether foreign-owned or not, created intense pressures on the lower classes. While Latin American dependence on the world economy was not new, it had previously coexisted with village agriculture. Into the 1880s many Indians and mestizos operated village farms adequate for local subsistence needs. They were able to work according to traditional rhythms and conduct frequent festivals, full of dance, song, and drink. This pattern yielded quickly to the growing commercialization of the Latin American economy in the last decades of the 19th century. In virtually every region, more land than ever before was gobbled up by large estates. Indians, accustomed to community ownership, were pressed to sell out to individual owners. In Mexico, for example, a law of 1894 ruled that land could be declared vacant and open to purchase if legal title to it could not be produced; but few Indians had such title, depending on traditional use rather than modern notions of property. In Colombia and elsewhere, governments, often in liberal hands and eager to promote economic growth, opened new territories to bidding, which in fact displaced many traditional villages not regarded as having property rights. Other peasant owners were simply defrauded by shrewd speculators, or encouraged to go into debt. Some of the new estates embraced thousands, even millions of acres; one Mexican estate was as large as West Virginia.

And the peasants, once displaced, encountered still further indignities. They had little choice but to work on the large estates, where they were paid low wages or, even more commonly, paid in kind and kept permanently in debt. Virtual serfdom spread, as workers were not allowed to leave the land until they had paid their debts, and not allowed to earn enough money to have a hope of making these payments. Furthermore, hard-driving commercial estate owners tried to spur greater work zeal. They clamped down on traditional festivals, regarded as dangerous wastes of time. This was a pattern not entirely different from the pressures earlier placed on European or U.S. industrial workers, for a real commercial revolution was underway. But Latin American peasants suffered far less freedom and far more poverty than most Western workers, for the economy, because of its weak position in the world markets, depended on massively exploited labor. Investment in new equipment, which might have provided an alternative to cheap labor, lagged. And while many estate and mine owners worked conscientiously to expand production, as opposed to the stereotype of idle drones living in luxury with no attention to management, the gap between the wealthy, mainly creole or foreign, owning classes and the impoverished masses grew ever wider.

Finally, many former peasants, forced off the land, sought refuge in the growing cities, where they faced competition for jobs from new immigrants from Europe. A large, often miserable propertyless class spread in the cities, pitting sprawling slums on the outskirts against the impressive upper-class districts nearer the center of town. Because industrialization was slow, there were relatively few factory jobs to absorb the newcomers. Aided by foreign capital and European immigrants, countries like Brazil did develop some industries in food processing, textile, and metallurgy. But the numbers of workers these industries employed were small, as Western competition continued to eat into available markets for manufactured goods. Hard-pressed governments had few resources to devote to welfare programs, so urban poverty and shantytowns grew unchecked.

The Latin American masses were not quiet under this new assault. Organization of urban trade unions was difficult, because of widespread misery and sheer confusion; government oppression also complicated any protest efforts. But peasant uprisings to seize land and escape the commercially driven work routines became common from the 1880s onward; indeed, they continue in many areas today. Peasant rebellions were not annual affairs, for peasants were usually repressed and could not be supported by legal organizations. But they also proved impossible to put down permanently. Countries like Mexico, Bolivia, and Colombia faced major revolts every 10 or 20 years. Rural banditry also increased in many regions, recruiting displaced peasants and winning quiet support from even larger numbers, who saw the bandits as expressing their discontent and hatred of landlords. Finally, rates of individual violence were high in many countries. Essentially frontier conditions persisted in many places, as the formal presence of the central government was sporadic at best. Hence many peasants took vengeance into their own hands. But high levels of violence also reflected the deep grievances of landless peasants whose cheap labor sustained Latin America's production for trade.

Latin America during the late 19th century thus generated a paradox of rapid change and continued vulnerability in the world markets. Many sectors of the economy were out

Mexican rebels on the march toward Xochamilcu, August 15,1914.

of Latin American hands. Emphasis on agriculture and mining continued, with only halting industrial development. Cities grew, but without a vigorous manufacturing base. Social structure remained oddly traditional, with great estate owners at the top of the heap, masses of peasants and propertyless workers at the bottom, and a small middle class in between. Slavery had been abolished, but poverty and near-serfdom replaced it not only for many blacks but also for Indians, mestizos, and many immigrants as well. Family structure remained rather traditional, with strong emphasis on the inferiority of women. Many lower-class women in fact entered the labor force, both on estates and in the cities, but officially and legally their place remained subordinate to men at virtually all social levels.

CONCLUSION: TENSION AND CREATIVITY

The tensions of Latin American society help explain the importance of strongman governments and the diverse roles of religion, through the late 19th century and beyond. One country, Mexico, was on the verge of revolution in 1900, driven by the unusually heavy hand of Porfirio Díaz and the extensive exploitation of Indian and mestizo labor. But most of Latin America would long avoid outright revolution, though not recurrent protest, as army, church, and sometimes foreign intervention combined to keep the lid on. Efforts by artists and intellectuals to voice the yearnings of the masses or to provide a spiritual identity distinct from Western values gained growing significance. Latin American civilization was formed under many unusual difficulties and under strong tutelage from the more powerful West, yet it managed to generate not simply an array of problems but also a unique flavor that blended diverse traditions with the creation of new countries and rapid economic change.

SUGGESTED READINGS

A useful source collection is B. Keen's *Readings in Latin American Civilization* (1955). For discussions reflecting recent scholarship, see T. Skidmore and P. Smith, *Modern Latin America* (1984); the book's only drawback is its concentration on single national or regional cases. See also David Bushnell and Neil Macauley, *The Emergence of Latin America in the Nineteenth Century* (1994), and Fernando Henrique Cardoso and Enzo Faletto, *Dependency and Development in Latin America* (1979), which disagree on the dependency emphasis. On political patterns, see Tulio Halperin Donhi, *The Aftermath of Revolution in Latin America* (1973), and Claudio Veliz, *The Centralist Tradition in Latin America* (1980). On key topics, see: E. Bradford Burns, *Poverty or Progress: Latin America in the Nineteenth Century* (1973); Herbert Klein, *Bolivia* (1982); June Nash and Helen Safa, eds., *Sex and Class in Latin America* (1980); and Charles Berquist, *Labor in Latin America* (1986).

Russia and Japan: Industrialization Outside the West

Focal Points

Among societies outside the West or the "frontier West," Japan and Russia alone launched industrial revolutions by the late 19th century in response to Western challenge. Why were they able to do so? What factors allowed Japan, unlike China, to adopt a process of rapid change? Both Russia and Japan needed to introduce other reforms besides new economic policies: What did they emphasize? In what sense did Japan "prepare" its industrialization more thoroughly than Russia? The early industrial revolution had many effects in Russia and Japan similar to those in Western Europe a bit earlier. Were there any marked differences? Did Japan become "less Japanese," Russia "less Russian" as they consciously imitated Western industrialization?

THE SPREAD OF INDUSTRIALIZATION

Both Russia and Japan escaped full Western economic dominance during the 19th century. Russia remained backward by Western standards, and its leaders grew painfully conscious of this fact. Even after 1900 its economy depended heavily on Western trade, technology, and capital; only revolution, in 1917, would seriously alter this situation. But Russia had displayed dynamism in previous centuries despite an economic lag, and this pattern persisted during the 19th century. Russia continued to expand, though it met Western and, at the end of the century, Japanese resistance at key points. The nation gained territory in central Asia and the Far East, and it achieved important influence over new, small states in southeastern Europe. Finally, the Russians began to sketch a reaction to the Western example of industrialization. Without becoming Western, Russia tried to alter its social pattern to conform to the requirements of an industrial society, and by 1890 it had launched the early phases of a real industrial revolution.

The response of Japan was even more striking. Continuing its policy of isolation until the 1850s, when Western pressure forced new contacts, the Japanese then produced a rapid transformation of basic political and social institutions, generating initial industrialization and a military reform that soon made Japan Asia's leading power. These events more clearly than ever before divided Japan from its Chinese neighbor, though in fact they still shared many cultural and artistic customs. For a time, indeed, the Japanese seemed bent on imitating everything Western, as the tradition of isolation made it difficult to sort out which Western habits were essential to economic and military strength and which were optional. But no more than Russia did Japan become Western; a key aspect of both Japanese and Russian development was an ability to industrialize without shaking off all distinctive features of their societies.

Japanese and Russian efforts form the first examples of what can be called "latecomer" industrial revolutions, in that they began after the West had a pronounced lead in the process. Latecomer industrialization involved certain factors that had not been necessary in the West. Capital was hard to come by for essential investment; neither Japan nor Russia had the West's advantage of prior colonial and merchant wealth. Unfamiliar technology must be mastered. There may be an inevitable tendency for government to take a greater role in latecomer industrializations than was true in the West, to amass scarce resources through taxation and to guide in the imitation of foreign techniques. At least this was clearly the case in both Russia and Japan, where, in any event, previous political structures made strong government seem logical. Latecomer industrialization may also impose greater strain on the people involved, because change is even more abrupt than it was in the West, where innovation caused tension enough as it was.

While sharing both the ability to respond strongly to Western example and some common features of the latecomer pattern, Russian and Japanese initiatives differed in crucial respects. Russian efforts to change, and failures to change rapidly enough, produced a revolutionary climate by 1905 when a first Russian revolution broke out. Japan avoided revolution in a literal sense, though in some ways revolutionary transformation was imposed from the top down after an intense internal struggle in the 1860s. At the same time Japan shifted traditional policies more radically than Russia did, not only in industrializing so rapidly but also in adopting an aggressive diplomatic stance quite foreign to its own precedents.

Neither Russia nor Japan was fully industrialized by 1914; both would continue to lag behind the West for some decades still. But the 19th-century breakthroughs were crucial in both countries. They ultimately had an influence even beyond national borders, in showing people in other parts of the world that Western economic tutelage was not the only way to produce change, and that a strong response could keep Western imperialism at bay.

RUSSIA

CONSERVATISM AS AN ALTERNATIVE TO THE WEST

The first half of the 19th century saw relatively little change in Russian culture and society. Russian leaders were indeed proud of their seeming immunity to the revolts and tensions that plagued Western Europe in the same period. After the defeat of Napoleon's armies, the Russian state viewed itself as one of the guardians of conservative order in Europe. Its acquisition of new territory in Poland at the Congress of Vienna, in 1815, furthered its longstanding interest in expansion. The Russian tsar Alexander I flirted with liberal ideas, and a few reforms were introduced, notably to improve the training of Russian bureaucrats. But neither the authoritarian state nor the tight system of Russian serfdom was seriously altered.

In December 1825, a minor revolt broke out, led by Western-minded army officers who wanted to see their country change. The Decembrist revolt was easily put down, but it inspired the new tsar, Nicholas I, to more outright conservatism. Repression of political opponents increased, as the secret police expanded. The press and schools were tightly supervised. What political criticism survived did so mainly in exile, in places like Paris and London, and with little impact on Russia itself. In 1830–1831, Nicholas I brutally put down a nationalist uprising in Poland, led by Catholics and liberal aristocrats who chafed under foreign rule. He also intervened in the revolutions of 1848, sending troops to Hungary in 1849 to help the Habsburg monarchy restore their government. Russia itself remained untouched by the revolt and agitation that spread virtually throughout Western Europe.

But while Russia seemed calm, it was in fact falling further behind the technological and economic levels of the West. Russia responded to Western industrialization initially by a further tightening of labor obligations of the serfs, so that the great grain-growing estates would have more to export. Individual factories opened using Western equipment, but there was no significant change in overall manufacturing or transportation mechanisms. Russia remained a profoundly agricultural society based on essentially unfree labor. Russian aristocrats, conscious of the West's greater dynamism, papered over differences by their enthusiastic embrace of European cultural styles, keeping up to date on the latest in costume, dance, or painting; but this important current did not close the economic and social gap between the two societies.

This gap was dramatically driven home by an apparently minor war in the Crimea, in the mid-1850s. Russian leaders had continued to peck away at Ottoman holdings in central Asia, maintaining what was by now a traditional foreign policy interest. However, British and French power in the Middle East constituted a new opposition force. When Nicholas provoked war with the Ottomans in 1853, the Western countries came to the sultan's aid. Essentially because of industrialization, which provided superior equipment and relatively rapid transport, the Western forces, far from home, prevailed over the Russian army in its own backyard. Here was a severe blow for a regime that prided itself on military dynamism.

The Crimean War resulted in the great event in 19th century Russian history, the emancipation of the serfs. Some aristocratic landlords were no longer sure that serfdom provided the most profitable system of labor in any event. Many Russian leaders were also concerned by the periodic peasant uprisings, against their lack of land and freedom, that continued to punctuate Russian history even after the collapse of the great Pugachev rebellion. Some upper-class Russians were persuaded by ideals of liberty and humanitarianism, finding serfdom wrong in principle. But above all, Russian leaders, including the new tsar Alexander II, wanted to rid Russia of a social system that seemed to be holding it back in relation to the West. If Russia were to develop a more dynamic economy, it needed workers that were free to move to cities and factories. It needed to encourage better methods even in agriculture, which the easy reliance on servile labor prevented. It needed, in sum, a partial revolution from above.

THE BEGINNINGS OF INDUSTRIALIZATION

The decision to emancipate the serfs came at roughly the same time as, in the United States, and shortly before, in Brazil, the decision to free slaves. Some of the motives, including humanitarianism and a desire to convert more fully to a free labor market, were also similar. No more than slavery did rigorous serfdom suit the economic needs of a society that could hold its own in modern world trade.

In some ways the emancipation of the serfs in 1861 was more generous than the liberation of slaves in the Americas. While aristocrats retained part of the land, including the most fertile holdings, the serfs got most of it—in contrast to slaves who received their freedom but nothing else. But Russian emancipation was careful to preserve essential aristocratic power and above all the tight grip of the tsarist state. The serfs obtained no new political rights at a national level. They were still tied to their villages until they could pay for the land they were given—the redemption money going to the aristocrats. Many peasants, as a result, could still not move freely or even sell their land, though some became more mobile. High redemption payments, in addition to state taxes, kept most Russian peasants miserably poor. Emancipation did bring change; it helped create a larger urban labor force. But it did not spur a revolution in agricultural productivity, as most peasants continued to use traditional methods on their small plots. And it did not bring contentment; indeed, peasant uprisings became more rather than less common, as hopes for a brighter future now seemed dashed by the limits of change.

Alexander did, to be sure, introduce further reforms during the 1860s and 1870s. He created local political councils, the *zemstvos*, that had a voice in regulating roads, schools, and other conditions. The zemstvos gave some Russians, particularly middle-class people like doctors and lawyers, new political experience; but they had no influence on national policy, where the tsar resolutely maintained his own power and that of the extensive bureaucracy. Alexander liberalized legal codes and created new courts. Reformers modernized the army, through encouragement of promotion by merit and other organizational changes. Recruitment was extended, and many peasants learned new skills, including literacy, through their military service.

These adjustments, like emancipation itself, were important. They imitated some Western principles; the new law codes, for example, provided milder punishment for crimes and enforced equality before the law. But they were not designed to create a Western society: they did not attack the fundamental power of the aristocracy and they did not modify political authoritarianism. The reforms were sufficient to spur the beginnings of Russian industrialization. They were not sufficient to provide a stable social base for this economic upheaval. Political as well as peasant unrest increased and provoked a return to more repressive measures.

From the 1870s onward, Russia began to construct an extensive railway network. It served as a vital link in the giant country—the establishment of the trans-Siberian railroad, connecting European Russia with the Pacific, was the crowning achievement of this drive, largely completed in the 1880s. Railroad facilities were also necessary to integrate Russia's wealth in coal and iron and to bring these resources in turn to markets—for Russia's river system, running south to north, was not particularly useful in this regard. Moreover, rails aided Russia's drive to export grain, essential for earning capital to purchase Western machinery. The rail system, finally, helped spur a modern coal and metallurgical industry, for while some key equipment had to be purchased from the West, the government stimulated native industry as much as possible. By the 1880s, when Russia's railroad network had almost quintupled compared to 1860, modern factories had sprung up in Moscow, St. Petersburg, and several Polish cities, and an urban working class was growing apace.

Russian industrialization was not unopposed, however. Quite apart from impoverished factory workers, who soon proved susceptible to revolutionary doctrines, some Russian leaders worried about the unsettling impact of this Western force. But industrialization appealed to the widespread desire to catch up with the West. It allowed further Russian territorial expansion in central Asia and northern China, for rails enabled Russia's massive armies to be moved more quickly and established technological superiority over many Asian states. Furthermore, Russian industrialization flowed in part from the authoritarian position of the state. Railroad development was a state-run operation. Many factories were also state-run, and the government oversaw some of the industrialization effort.

Under Count Witte, minister of finance from 1892 to 1903 and an ardent economic modernizer, the government enacted high tariffs to protect new Russian industry, improved its banking system, and encouraged Western investors to build great factories with advanced technology. As Witte put it, "The inflow of foreign capital is . . . the only way by which our industry will be able to supply our country quickly with abundant and cheap products." By 1900, approximately half of Russian industry was foreign-owned and much of it foreign-operated, with British, German, and French industrialists taking the lead. Witte and others were confident that government controls could keep the foreigners in line, rather than converting Russia into a new imperialist playground, and in the main they seemed correct. By 1900, Russia had surged to fourth rank in the world in steel production, and was second to the United States in petroleum production and refining. Russian textile manufacture was also impressive. Long-standing Russian economic backwardness was beginning to yield.

This was still, however, an industrial revolution in its early stages. Russia's world position was a function more of its great size and population, along with rich natural resources, than of really thorough mechanization. Agriculture remained backward, as peasants had neither the means nor the motive to change their ways. Literacy was gaining and peasant habits did begin to change—for example, thanks to urban contacts courtship loosened, with more sexual overtones—but agricultural methods lagged. This in turn retarded the growth of cities and made periodic famine a recurrent threat. Many Russian factories were vast—the largest, on average, in the world—and an urban artisanry also gained ground in fields like printing. But the urban labor force, though expanding rapidly, was still a minority, and many workers had yet to convert to new work values. Nor did a powerful business class arise in Russia. Government controls and foreign investment produced industrialization without a surging middle class. Some Russian entrepreneurs showed impressive dynamism, and the number of business and professional people increased; but Russian industrialization did not engender the kind of assertive, self-confident middle class that had arisen in the West. Industrialization was, in sum, still tentative, and it was definitely proceeding along distinctive lines.

THE FOUNDATIONS OF REVOLUTION

The nation's early industrialization increased the already fearsome tensions within the society. Peasant discontent, though not a constant force, continued to rise. Famines regularly provoked uprisings. Peasants, who deeply resented aristocratic estates and the redemption payments and taxes that burdened them, were also pressed by rapidly growing population levels, which augmented land hunger. Along with the peasantry, many educated Russians, including some aristocrats, clamored for revolutionary change. Their goals and motives varied, but in general they wanted political freedoms while maintaining a Russian culture different from that of the West, which they saw as hopelessly plutocratic and materialist. Upper-class radicals claimed that a spirit of community lay deep in the Russian soul, which could serve as the basis for an egalitarian society free from the injustice of the capitalist West. Many Russian radicals were anarchists who sought the abolition of all formal government. While anarchism was not unknown in the West, it took on particular force in Russia in opposition to unyielding tsarist autocracy. Many anarchists turned to extremely violent methods, forming the first large terrorist movement in the modern world. Terrorism, in the form of assassinations and bombings, seemed an essential approach given the lack of other political outlets. It appeared that anarchist-terrorist tactics often focused more on destruction than on coherent political goals for the future. As the anarchist leader Bakunin put it:

> We have only one plan—general destruction. We want a national revolution of the peasants. We refuse to take any part in the working out of schemes to better the conditions of life; we regard as fruitless solely theoretical work. We consider destruction to be such an enormous and difficult task that we must devote all our powers to it, and we do not wish to deceive ourselves with the dream that we will have enough strength and knowledge for creation.

Not surprisingly, the recurrent waves of terrorism merely confirmed the tsarist regime in its resolve to avoid further political change, in what became a vicious circle in late-19th-century Russian politics.

By the late 1870s, Alexander II pulled back from his reform interest, fearing that change was getting out of hand. Censorship of newspapers and political meetings tightened; many dissidents were arrested and sent to Siberia. Alexander himself was assassinated by a terrorist bomb in 1881, and his successors, while escalating the effort to industrialize, continued to oppose further political reform. New measures of repression were also directed against minority nationalities, as a conservative nationalism, hostile to internal minorities and Western influence alike, swelled in praise of Russian values. The Poles and other groups were carefully supervised, and persecution of the large Jewish minority was stepped up, resulting in many executions and seizures of property; as a consequence, many Russian Jews emigrated. In general, moreover, the late-19th-century tsars sponsored a vigorous drive to impose Russian culture and language on the minority peoples. They thus tried to Christianize many Jewish children by force, while forbidding Poles and other minorities from using their own language for public purposes. In response, many minority nationalist movements spread on an underground basis, joining the anarchists in their energetic, if illegal, resistance to the tsarist regime.

One final political current arose by the 1890s. A number of radical leaders, drawn from the same educated circles as the anarchists, were attracted to the Marxist doctrines that were being disseminated in the West. Largely underground or in exile, Marxist groups formed, committed to a tightly organized proletarian revolution. While the Marxist movement remained small, its ideas took hold among some urban industrial workers, who chafed under the harsh conditions of the early factories and the illegality of ordinary trade union activity.

By 1900, the contradictory currents in Russian society may have made revolution inevitable. While the forces demanding change were not united, and while extensive police work and military repression kept most uprisings in hand, the combination of pressures may have been too powerful to resist. Peasants had little concern for the more formal political ideas; indeed, anarchist efforts to reach out to the people in previous decades had been largely ignored. Marxists and anarchists cordially disliked each other, for indeed both their methods and their goals were different. The small middle class, interested in some political voice but not eager for full-scale social upheaval, constituted yet another piece on the complex Russian chessboard. Revolution was to come in 1905, after Russia

Shooting of strikers in St. Petersburg, January, 1905—this bloodshed helped launch the Revolution of 1905.

had suffered yet another disastrous and surprising military defeat, this time at the hands of Japan, which opposed further Russian expansion in northern China and Korea. Defeat unleashed massive general strikes by urban workers and a tumultuous series of peasant insurrections. In response, the tsarist regime loosened the postemancipation rural system, allowing peasants greater freedom to buy and sell land and operate independently of redemption payments and village controls. Yet a halting pledge to appease middle-class sentiment by creating a national parliament, the Duma, was soon dashed by renewed political repression; the Duma became a hollow institution, satisfying no one. And no gains were offered to the Marxists at all. The prospect of further revolution loomed, and then became reality when Russia plunged into yet another conflict—World War I—hoping that battle would bring new territory and distraction from internal stress. The gamble failed, and in 1917 one of the great revolutions in world history took place.

THE CULTURE OF EASTERN EUROPE

Many smaller East European countries followed patterns similar to those of Russia during the later 19th century. New nations such as Romania, Bulgaria, and Serbia, free from Ottoman control, liberated the serfs, but amid restrictions that retained the bulk of the land for the aristocracy. Parliaments were established on superficially Western lines, but they had little power and were based on very limited voting rights. Most of the smaller East European nations industrialized less extensively than Russia and remained even more dependent, as agricultural producers, on Western markets.

Despite economic problems and political tensions, however, Eastern Europe, including Russia, enjoyed an impressive cultural surge, a final ingredient in the complex developments that accompanied reactions to Western industrialization. Many Western artistic styles were appropriated. Russian and other East European novelists and essayists wrote in the Romantic vein, glorifying national folkways; the Russian novel enjoyed unprecedented vigor in the hands of writers such as Tolstoy, Turgenev, and Dostoyevsky. Composers like Tchaikovsky brought Romanticism to music. Modern art currents in the West also found echo, as abstract painting and atonal music took shape in the hands of Russian practitioners soon after 1900. East European intellectuals also participated in the scientific developments of the later 19th century. The important experiments on conditioned reflexes conducted by a Russian physiologist, Ivan Pavlov, advanced the understanding of unconscious responses in human beings.

In many ways, then, Eastern Europe seemed to be drawing closer to the West in cultural activity, continuing a pattern visible since the time of Peter the Great. Combined with growing industrialization and some political impulses borrowed from the West, including Marxism, it seemed possible that, despite its political peculiarities, Russia might produce a version of Western civilization, just as it had moved into the Western diplomatic orbit in many respects.

But East European culture remained ambivalent about the West. While some intellectuals were ardent admirers of Western culture, others used partially Western styles to comment on the distinctiveness of the Russian or Slavic spirit. Many novelists joined political conservatives in finding a unique soul in their people, which, they felt, should be

Searching passersby in Riga during the Revolution of 1905.

exalted and protected against Western influence. Romanticism, in its East European manifestation, encouraged a vigorous set of cultural and political nationalisms, bent on capturing the glories of Russian, or Ukrainian, or Serbian peoples. A Pan-Slavic movement arose also—particularly in Russia, which claimed leadership of Slavic Europe—that argued for Slavic unity against the more materialistic and individualistic West.

Furthermore, the masses in Eastern Europe, mainly peasant, remained firmly attached to older traditions, including the Orthodox religion, different from those of the West and from those of the partially Westernized upper classes. Popular culture changed through the impact of growing literacy, rising urbanization, and military service, but it did not amalgamate with the popular culture of the West. Indeed, popular resentment against growing Western influence, including the power of foreign capitalists, would form yet another revolutionary ingredient during and after World War I.

By 1900, then, Russia and much of the rest of Eastern Europe represented a distinctive amalgam of tradition and change. Principles of authoritarian rule remained virtually unaltered, but they were now joined with diverse political opposition bent in the main on sweeping revolution rather than on purely liberal reforms. The tradition of territorial expansionism, though checked by resistance from the West and Japan, still ran strong. Pan-Slavic sentiments indeed encouraged new Russian influence in southeastern Europe. Massive social change had resulted from emancipation and early industrialization, but East European society continued to be more agricultural and in many ways more traditionalist than its Western counterpart. Finally, a larger ambivalence toward Western values persisted. East European intellectuals contributed creatively to general European artistic and scientific work, but a desire to define distinctive features, to resist full Westernization, remained lively in many quarters, both elite and popular. Eastern Europe was, in sum, developing its own pattern of change as it entered the industrial age. This pattern would soon embrace a distinctive kind of revolution as well.

JAPAN

Even more than Russia, Japan faced new pressure from the West during the 1850s, though it took the form of a demand for more open trade rather than outright war. After a tense debate during the 1850s and 1860s, Japan's response was more direct than Russia's and, on the whole, more immediately successful. Despite the long history of isolation, Japanese society was better adapted than Russia's to the challenge of industrial change. Market forms were more extensive, reaching into peasant agriculture; levels of literacy were higher. Japan had nevertheless to rework many of its institutions during the final decades of the 19th century, and the process produced significant strain. The result, by 1900, was different both from purely Western patterns and from the more obvious tensions of Russian society.

On the surface, Japan experienced little change during the first half of the 19th century. The Tokugawa shogunate remained intact, though there were signs that it was becoming less effective. The shogunate ran the country through a combination of central bureaucracy and alliances with the regional daimyos. It also encouraged some business interests and provided a central banking system. Japanese culture still relied heavily on Confucianism, and participation in Confucian schools grew rapidly. Traditional artistic and dramatic styles remained lively. The interest in Western science that had developed among a small number of scholars continued, through 18th-century contacts with the Dutch trading outpost in the port of Nagasaki, but no technological breakthroughs occurred. The Japanese boasted a productive agriculture and considerable rural manufacturing, but there were signs of economic stagnation, particularly in a growing number of peasant riots against poor conditions. Nevertheless, there is no reason to believe that Japan was on the verge of significant change before change was thrust upon it.

THE OPENING OF TRADE

In 1853 the American commodore Matthew Perry arrived with a fleet in Edo Bay, near Tokyo, insisting through threats of bombardment that Americans be allowed to trade. In 1854 he returned, and won the right to station an American consul in Japan; two ports were opened to commerce. Britain, Russia, and Holland quickly won similar rights. As in China, this meant that Westerners living in Japan would be governed by their own representatives, not by Japanese law. Other privileges soon followed, along with a few military skirmishes. Leading Western nations simply insisted on their need and right to trade, as part of the expanding world economy, while also seeking fishing rights in Japanese waters. For several decades they limited Japan's ability to decide on its own tariffs. Russian pres-

Commodore Perry's "Black Ship" as seen by the Japanese, 1854.

sure was a problem as well, as the nation's eastward expansion had already produced a few small clashes over control of islands in the North Pacific.

Some Japanese had already grown impatient with strict isolation. More important was the now-obvious fact that Japan could not compete with Western navies, and so had to yield. But many Japanese leaders, including conservatives who feared Western influence, wanted to strengthen their government in order to control their nation's future. Their interest caused them to bypass the shogun and appeal directly to the emperor for support. Long secluded as a religious figure, the emperor now began to gain power.

In the 1860s a political crisis came into the open, involving a clash between many samurai and the shogunate. The crisis was spiced by attacks on foreigners, including one murder of a British official, matched by Western naval bombardments of feudal forts. Virtual civil war broke out in 1866 as the samurai eagerly armed themselves with American Civil War surplus weapons, causing Japan's aristocrats to come to terms with the potency of Western armaments. When the samurai defeated a shogunate force, a number of Japanese finally were shocked out of their traditional reliance on their own superiority, with one author arguing that the nation was, compared to the West with its technology, science, and humane laws, only half-civilized.

This multifaceted crisis came to an end in 1868, with the proclamation of rule by a new emperor named Mutsuhito, whose regime was soon called "Meiji," or "Enlightened Rule." Backed by some samurai leaders, the new emperor managed to put down the troops of the shogunate and gradually built up support, setting up his capital in Edo, now named Tokyo. The crisis period had been shocking enough to allow further changes in Japan's basic political structure—changes that went much deeper at the political level than those introduced by Russia from 1861 onward. With the chief ministers actually taking the major initiative, the imperial government sponsored three decades of rapid change, designed to make Japan competitive with the West and so save national independence in what was, for Japan, a radically new and perilous environment.

The key to the Japanese response was heightened governmental centralization. Meiji leaders abolished feudalism, as the regional lords surrendered their land rights to the government. Ministries in the central government now directed national policy in a surprisingly quick political adjustment. And the ministers in the Meiji period were committed to further reform, as a government-sponsored reshaping of Japanese society was underway. Such reshaping, however, did not call into question the Japanese belief not only in their independence but also in the basic superiority of their culture. An early Japanese visitor to the White House wrote a self-satisfied poem that caught part of the national mood:

> We suffered the barbarians to look upon the glory of our Eastern Empire of Japan.

INDUSTRIALIZATION IN RESPONSE TO THE WEST

The Japanese combination of rapid adaptation and firm belief in the validity of their own values and institutions may explain the distinctive Japanese response in matching Western pressure without outright revolution and without full-scale Westernization. The Japanese leaders carefully blended economic political change with existing institutions and values.

Reform interests, in the Meiji period, focused on several targets. A new army was set up, modeled on the German system. It was based on universal conscription of young males. The training of officers improved, as new men replaced the older feudal generals. Military armament was brought up to Western standards, and a navy was formed initially with the aid of Western advisors. The government also quickly introduced Western public health measures, which promoted population growth.

Mass education spread rapidly from 1872 onward, for women as well as for men. Elite students at the university level often emphasized science, many of them studying technical subjects abroad. The rapid assimilation of a scientific outlook was a major new ingredient in Japanese culture. Other cultural changes ranged farther afield: Fearful of embarrassment in Western eyes—a factor of growing importance in world history—the Japanese government even tried to outlaw homosexuality around 1900 and to increase differences in dress between boys and girls.

Reform also meant further political change. A new constitution took effect in 1890, again based on the German model. A two-house parliament, elected by men of property, served under the supreme emperor. The parliament did not develop extensive powers, as the emperor named his own ministers and controlled basic policy. But several political parties arose to compete for votes. The Japanese political style now combined centralized imperial rule with limited representative institutions; the combination gave great power to a new oligarchy of wealthy businessmen and aristocrats, who influenced the emperor and also pulled strings within parliament. This rule by elite echoed earlier Japanese reliance on cooperation rather than on competition in politics, as well as a tradition of considerable deference to the authority of the upper classes. Here was a clear case of blending Japanese values with Western-style institutions.

Above all, reform meant industrialization, with the government taking a far more active role than its Russian counterpart. New banks were created by the government to fund growing trade and to provide capital for industry. State-built railroads spread across the

The first Japanese Parliament meets, 1890.

country, and the islands were connected by rapid steamers. While Japan still relied heavily on home or small-shop production, particularly of goods like silk cloth that were widely exported, factory industry expanded steadily. Finally, the market emphasis in agriculture increased, as new methods were introduced to raise output to feed the growing cities.

Japanese state initiative not only built transportation and banking systems but also led to government operation of mines, shipyards, and metallurgical plants. Scarce capital and the unfamiliarity of new technology seemed to compel state direction, which also served to supervise the many foreign advisors the Japanese required. Japan established a ministry of industry in 1870, and it quickly became one of the key government agencies, setting overall economic policy as well as operating specific sectors. But private initiative played a role as well. In textiles, private businessmen, many of them from older merchant families, ran the leading companies. In other industries, government concerns, tax-financed, were later sold to private interests, to the profit of the latter. Close collaboration between government agencies and private firms, especially big business concerns, early formed a hallmark of the new Japanese economy.

While Japanese big business developed rapidly, early industrialization also depended on massive exploitation of workers, particularly women workers. Tens of thousands of women were sold for labor service by fathers or husbands in the overpopulated Japanese countryside. They worked particularly in the silk industry, developed by the state on a labor-intensive basis to capture vital export earnings as Japan passed China in producing this luxury commodity.

CULTURAL AND SOCIAL-ECONOMIC EFFECTS OF INDUSTRIALIZATION

As earlier in the West, industrialization altered social structure. Only a handful of aristocrats and people from the samurai warrior class entered the ranks of successful businessmen. A new elite was formed that embraced leading entrepreneurs for the first time, and while old merchant families contributed to this group, talented people from diverse backgrounds, including former peasants, now rose to the top. Among the masses, the rise of a huge, propertyless class of urban workers was a new development. Both peasants and workers endured low wages and high taxes, as Japanese leaders used cheap labor to aid in competition with Western enterprise and to amass the capital needed for further investment. And while the new elite did not cultivate the luxurious life style of Western business magnates, being content with lower profit rates, it did insist on retaining power. Unions and lower-class political parties, though they began to emerge by 1900, made only slow headway, and a militant socialist movement was outlawed without difficulty.

Many Japanese copied Western fashions as part of the effort to become modern. Western-style haircuts replaced the samurai shaved head with a top knot—another example of the fascinating pattern of Westernizing of hair in world history. Western standards of hygiene spread, and the Japanese became enthusiastic toothbrushers and consumers of patent medicines. Japan also adopted the Western calendar and the metric system. Few Japanese converted to Christianity, however, and despite fads for Western popular culture, the Japanese managed to preserve an emphasis on their own values. What the Japanese wanted and got from the West involved practical techniques; they planned to infuse these with a distinctively Japanese spirit.

Thus, in education, an initial surge of interest in Western schooling in the 1870s, which included the use of hundreds of European and American teachers, yielded in the 1880s to a reassertion of Japanese group loyalty and attacks on excessive individualism. New exposure to science changed culture, but the growing stress on nationalism provided new focus for traditional beliefs in Japanese cohesion and distinctiveness.

Japanese family life retained many traditional emphases, as against Western customs. To be sure, unprecedented population growth forced increasing numbers of people off the land, which disrupted families and caused the unusual reliance on women's work in industry. But the Japanese were eager to maintain the traditional inferiority of women in the home. A new law promoted monogamy, but in practice mistresses were still widely accepted in the upper classes. The position of Western women seemed repellent. Japanese government visitors to the United States were appalled by what they saw as the bossy ways of women: "The way women are treated here is like the way parents are respected in our country." Standards of Japanese courtesy also contrasted with the more open and boisterous behavior of Westerners—particularly Americans. "Obscenity is inherent in the customs of this country," noted another samurai visitor to the United States. Other basic features of Japanese life, including diet, were maintained in the face of Western influence. Japanese religious values were also distinctive. Buddhism lost some ground, though it remained important, and Confucianism was attacked through the new emphasis on science in the schools; but Shintoism, which appealed to the rising nationalist concern with Japan's distinctive mission and the religious functions of the emperor, won new interest.

By 1900 Japan's industrial success did not bring the country to Western levels, and the Japanese remained intensely fearful for their independence. Economic change, and the tensions as well as the power it generated, did however produce a shift in Japanese foreign policy. With only one previous exception, the Japanese had never before been interested in territorial expansion, but by the 1890s, they joined the ranks of imperialist powers. Partly this shift was an imitation of Western models, and at the same time it was an effort to prevent Western encroachment. Imperialism also relieved some strains within Japanese society, giving displaced samurai a chance to exercise their military talents elsewhere and providing symbols of nationalist achievement for the populace as a whole. The Japanese economy also required access to markets and raw materials. Because Japan was poor in many basic materials, including coal and oil for energy, the pressure for expansion was particularly great.

Japan's quick victory over China, in the quarrel for influence over Korea in 1894–1895, was a first step. Japan convincingly demonstrated its new superiority over all other Asian powers. Humiliated by Western insistence that it abandon the Liaotung peninsula, the Japanese planned a war with Russia as a means of striking out against the nearest European state. A 1902 alliance with Britain was an important sign of Japan's arrival as an equal nation in the Western-dominated world diplomatic system. The Japanese were also eager to dent Russia's growing strength in East Asia, after the completion of the trans-Siberian railroad. Disputes over Russian influence in Manchuria and Japanese influence in Korea led to the Russo-Japanese War in 1904, which Japan won handily on the basis of its superior navy. In 1910, Japan annexed Korea outright; it was now not only a modern industrial power, but a new imperialist force as well.

THE STRAIN OF MODERNIZATION

Japan's success by 1900 was amazing. Its victories over China and then Russia surprised virtually every observer outside of Japan. There is no question that Japan's rapid transformation, like its more recent success in becoming one of the most advanced industrial societies in the world, constitutes a unique achievement. Furthermore, the Japanese—unlike Russia or major parts of the West—prepared the groundwork for industrialization without serious threat of popular revolution.

Yet this achievement, even blended as it was with substantial continuities from earlier Japanese culture and political styles, had its costs. Many Japanese conservatives resented the passion that some Japanese displayed for Western fashions. Their concern helped ensure that Japanese women, initially the subject of some reform interest, would be mainly confined to family roles. Nevertheless, disputes between generations, with the old clinging to traditional standards, the young more interested in Western dress and Western dances, were commonplace and very troubling in a society that stressed the importance of parental authority. Social tensions added to the strain, as expectations rose more rapidly than standards of living. Crowded conditions in the growing cities produced misery at least as great as in earlier Western slums. Rising divorce rates—Japan had the highest in the world by 1900—showed another kind of strain.

Some tension translated into politics, even with the narrow voting system. Political parties in Japan's parliament, called the "Diet," sometimes clashed with the emperor's ministers over rights to determine policy. The government frequently had to dissolve the Diet and call for new elections, seeking a more workable parliamentary majority.

Another kind of friction emerged in intellectual life. Many Japanese scholars copied Western philosophies and literary styles. But in addition to an interest in more traditional forms, intellectuals expressed a deep pessimism about the loss of identity in a changing

Yet, in 1900, it was the world's diversity that remained most striking, as it blended longstanding differences in cultural and political traditions with the newer variations produced by responses to Western imperialism and industrial example. Some of the divisions taking shape between industrializers including "early latecomers," such as Japan, and more dependent economies, would have continuing influence in world history into the late 20th century. Other divisions, between an India open to forced Western influence and a more traditionalist China, would be complicated or superseded by later developments. What was becoming clear was the new set of divisions among civilizations, based no longer on evolving tradition alone, but on response to new change and challenge.

SUGGESTED READINGS

A. Gerschenkron, *Economic Backwardness in Historical Perspective: A Book of Essays* (1962), helps define the conditions of latecomer industrialization. Russian reforms and economic change are discussed in W. Blackwell, *The Industrialization of Russia*, 2nd ed. (1982) and Jerome Blum, *Lord and Peasant in Russia from the Ninth to the Nineteenth Century* (1961). On social and cultural developments, see: Victoria Bonnel, ed., *The Russian Worker; Life and Labor under the Tsarist Regime* (1983); Barbara Engel, *Mothers and Daughters: Women of the Intelligentsia in Nineteenth Century Russia* (1983); and Jeffrey Brooks, *When Russia Learned to Read: Literacy and Popular Culture* (1987). On another vital area of Eastern Europe, see L. Stavrianos, *The Balkans, 1815–1914* (1963).

Japan in the 19th century is viewed from a modernization perspective in R. Dore, ed., *Aspects of Social Change in Modern Japan* (1967). For a comparative view, see Peter N. Stearns, *Starting School: The Rise of Modern Education in France, the United States, and Japan* (1997). See also: W. W. Lockwood, *The Economic Development of Japan: Growth and Structural Change 1868–1938* (1954); J. C. Abegglen, *The Japanese Factory: Aspects of Its Social Organization*, rev. ed. (1985); Hugh Patrick, ed., *Japanese Industrialization and Its Social Consequences* (1973); Andrew Gordon, *The Evolution of Labor Relations in Japan* (1985); R. H. Myers and M. R. Beattie, eds., *The Japanese Colonial Empire 1895–1945* (1984); and E. O. Reischauser, *Japan, the Story of a Nation* (1981).

CHAPTER 25

World War I and the End of an Era

Focal Point

One of the devastating wars of all time broke out in Europe in 1914. World War I had international significance and international causes. It marked the beginning of the end of Western Europe's world supremacy. But its causes also reflected other major changes, in Europe and elsewhere, that also indicated significant shifts in the framework of world history.

The period in world history that opened after 1750 clearly came to a close in the first two decades of the 20th century. The period had featured Western industrialization and imperialism and the varied and important efforts of other societies to react. Events soon after 1900 did not yet add up to the coherent set of trends, but they clearly signaled an end to what some historians have called the "long 19th century."

Item: Women obtained the vote in several Scandinavian countries plus Australia, and feminist agitation heated up in other parts of Western society.

Item: Australia became fully independent in 1900, a symbol of the changing role of the European frontier societies in world history.

Item: A Chinese revolution in 1911 toppled the imperial system for the first time since the collapse of the Han dynasty. China was in the throes of massive change.

Item: A Mexican revolution began in 1910 that called into question some of the political and social arrangements that had been common in 19th-century Latin America.

Item: Japan's victory over Russia and the Russian revolution of 1905 signaled dramatic new power alignments and the potential for turmoil in one of the major empires.

Item: The outbreak of World War I in 1914 launched a conflict that would have massive effects in Europe and the Middle East, with important spillover in East Asia and the Pacific, Africa, South Asia, and North America. The war pitted Britain, France, and Russia against Germany and the Habsburg monarchy—the world's most heavily armed nations came to blows through rival alliance systems. Other areas joined as colonies of the European powers or independently through hopes of territorial gains or other advantages. By the time the war ended in 1918 the 19th-century world order had been severely disrupted, though many Western leaders, eager to return to what they called normalcy, refused to recognize this fact.

The causes of World War I hardly summed up all the main trends that had emerged by the end of the 19th century, but they captured a fair number. The specific trigger for the war lay within the small nations of southeastern Europe, recently independent from Ottoman control. Ottoman weakness had created a vacuum of power in this region that continues to this day. The new Balkan states, all highly nationalistic, frequently quarreled among themselves, conducting two regional wars before 1914. Russia and the Habsburg Monarchy vied for influence in the area, hoping to distract from internal tensions. Russia sponsored Slavic nationalism, while the Habsburgs, with large and restive Slavic minorities, tried to beat down the same force. In 1914 a Serbian nationalist assassinated a member of the Habsburg royal family. Austria threatened war, but Russia backed Serbia. Then the larger European alliance system came into play: Germany feared to abandon Austria lest it face Russia and France alone. France and, more reluctantly, Britain decided they had to support Russia. Rigid diplomacy and fervent nationalism in all the European great powers parlayed a regional crisis into full-scale war. Europe's alliance system, combined with growing military rivalry and massive armaments, thus trapped the major powers into decisions that led inevitably to war.

Larger issues were at play, as the causes of war revealed massive fault lines in Western society. Huge weapons industries had grown up in all the European powers, partly because of imperialist rivalries, partly to ensure sales to influential industrialists. Arms races—particularly navy-building competitions and particularly between Britain and Germany—enhanced anxiety and made it more difficult to compromise when disputes broke out. Russia, Germany, and France all had rigid strategic plans that encouraged prompt military action—in hopes, which proved completely illusory, of delivering quick knockout blows to the enemy.

Imperialism itself had created a growing sense in Europe that aggressive expansionism was normal state policy. But by 1914 the opportunities for further colonies were essentially exhausted, and the fervor that had gone into empire building now turned back on Europe itself. Politicians had become accustomed to pointing to nationalist triumphs as a means of wooing voters, and the habits persisted. Russia and Austria-Hungary, keenly aware that they had fallen behind in imperialist races, had particular reasons to hope for triumphs that would divert public opinion.

European political and military leaders also worried about broader social tensions within their societies. Labor unrest was mounting, joined in some cases by feminist agitations and other repressed groups such as, in Britain's case, the Irish who increasingly pushed for independence. Many officials worried that internal difficulties would erode national power—that it was safest to have war now, while strength was still high. Others argued that a good war would unify the population, reducing the strength of socialist dissent. Ordinary people, bored or oppressed by industrial life, saw war as an attractive option—unaware of how devastating industrial warfare would actually be. Boys in various

Women help their men carry heavy rucksacks to the station during Germany's troop mobilization. Their rifles are decorated with flowers.

social classes had been raised on a diet of toy soldiers and aggressive sports—war could seem a glorious prospect in societies in which the importance of masculinity was asserted but not always easily expressed. Enthusiasm for war, in sum, drew on a number of tensions and anxieties created by industrial society.

Europe's decision for war also reflected its position in the world, strengths and weaknesses alike. Europeans were feeling at least vaguely threatened by the rise of societies outside their borders. Japan's industrial and military surge, plus stirrings in China, made some European nationalists talk of a new "Yellow peril" that might displace Western supremacy. United States economic rivalry was keenly felt. British observers, greeting the new century in 1900, had wondered if their days of easy empire were numbered, given new rivals and the sheer numbers of the colonial peoples. Oddly, given Britain's strength, but revealingly, they looked forward to the new century with real dread. These anxieties might, of course, have prompted a new European protective unity, but national divisions ran too deep for this. Instead, countries concerned about their future turned to the familiar, nationalist military response. In essence, Europeans worried about their world position but at the same time assumed an assured dominance that made it seem safe to engage in internal conflict. This assurance would lead, among other things, to a rapid impulse to extend European warfare to the colonies themselves and to use colonial troops on the European front. The result was a genuinely world war, and one that would redefine world alignments.

But war in an industrial age, and in the changing world context, had itself changed. While many Europeans entered this conflict gaily, assuming a quick and glorious end, World War I brought unprecedented dislocation and a host of unforeseen consequences. A new period in world history was baptised in blood, as the most powerful civilization tore itself apart.

CONCLUSION

Even more than the fall of Constantinople to the Turks in 1453, World War I constituted an event that reshaped world history. Along with other developments, such as the upheaval in East Asia, it furthered a realignment of power in the world. The war also promoted other shifts, such as changes in gender relations in Western society, that had been taking shape more gradually. The Western powers would seek to put the world back in its prewar framework after the great conflict ended, but their success was both fleeting and superficial. A new age was brewing.

SUGGESTED READING

On causation, see James Joll, *Origins of World War I* (1980), and K. Robbins, *The First World War* (1984). For a wider view, see Eric Hobsbawm, *The Age of Extremes: A History of the World,1914–1991* (1996), and G. Barraclough, *An Introduction to Contemporary History* (1968).

PART VI

The Contemporary World

INTRODUCTION: THE 20TH CENTURY—
TOWARD AN INDUSTRIAL WORLD

The dramatic, often violent events that unfolded between 1900 and 1918, headed by World War I itself, suggest that the 20th century opened a new phase in world history, with turmoil marking the transition. Several larger themes, setting the 20th century off from the previous period, point to the same conclusion.

The virtually unchallenged rise of the West, which along with the related development of a genuine world economy formed the central theme in world history from 1450 to around 1900, ended in the 20th century. The change was not immediately clear, and much of the first half of the century marked the ending of the old order rather than the visible shaping of the new. But three trends combined to end the West's continued dominance. First, Russia gradually emerged not merely as a power capable of affecting wider European affairs, but as a genuine world rival of Western leaders. Second, parts of eastern Asia, particularly Japan, became industrial equals to the West, undergoing much more rapid economic transformation than the West itself experienced after 1900. Finally, the age of Western imperialism ended with a wave of decolonization that established independent nations throughout the Middle East, southern Asia, Africa, and the islands of the Pacific and the Caribbean.

Quite simply, developments in the 20th century reversed several basic trends in world history, most of which had been operating since the 15th century:

• The West's clear military supremacy, initially established through naval gunnery and then amplified by industrial armaments, began to fade. Not only the military strength of powers like the Soviet Union and, for a time, Japan, but also new methods of warfare, particularly guerrilla tactics developed in places like Vietnam and Algeria, made military operations more difficult for Western armies. New wealth allowed many nations to acquire modern armaments sufficient to deter easy Western invasions.

- The West's near-monopoly on world trade yielded. Several areas generated more rapid economic growth rates, allowing them to catch up with the West. Even many poorer regions developed dynamic industrial sectors that made them competitive and that also reduced their dependence on the West for manufactured goods.
- Decolonization obviously reversed the long period of growing territorial acquisition by the West. Growing Western weakness and a desire to concentrate on rebuilding one's own society combined with growing demands for independence that echoed around the world. Here, tensions between the world wars set the stage for the rapid establishment of new nations between 1946 and the mid–1970s.

The diminishing of Western power was not the same, to be sure, as outright Western decline. The expanding strength of the United States helped qualify any notion of Western setback. So did new signs of economic and political vigor in Europe, particularly after 1945. Throughout the century, some observers have claimed to see symptoms of the kind of decay in the West that had earlier felled the Roman Empire or led to the more subtle deterioration of Arab civilization. While these forewarnings might turn out to be justified, they remained speculative. What was demonstrable was that the balance among societies began to alter and that Western dominance of the world, never absolute in any event, lessened.

Western culture continued to exercise worldwide influence, which further complicates the assessment of the West's relative decline. Western intellectual standards in science and modern art still define many fields, though researchers and artists from many societies now participate in these fields. In modern architecture, for example, practitioners from Japan, Latin America, and elsewhere now gained world-class status, but major styles still reflected their Western origins. The West, including the United States and Europe, also set international standards in popular culture, from sports through music, costume, and film. One of the key issues in 20th-century world history involved the reactions of different societies to Hollywood movies, fast foods, or Anglo-American rock music. Changes in the cultural balance around the world, in other words, lagged behind the rebalancing of power, though new religious currents by the 1970s signaled attempts by several societies to counteract Western influence in this area too.

Issues of power balance were not the only items on the new agenda of the 20th century. The 20th century also saw an unprecedented buildup of the world's population. By 1970 there were more people living than had ever reached adulthood in all the previous history of the human species. World population nearly tripled in the first three quarters of the century. Improved border controls by newly efficient governments and international organizations helped stop the historic pattern of devastating plagues. Swamp drainage, insect control, and basic sanitary measures reduced other traditional killers. While dire hunger persisted, advances in agriculture enabled greater numbers of people to be fed adequately. Falling death rates, though at varying levels in different regions, not only increased population outright but allowed more people to reach adulthood and have children of their own. So although per capita birth rates did not rise, overall birth rates did. The result was a veritable torrent of people, whose numbers easily compensated for the devastation of 20th century war, with hundreds of millions to spare.

Massive population growth helped account for a number of other key developments across the world. Urbanization proceeded rapidly in most civilizations. Individual cities in Asia and Latin America easily outstripped the Western giants in size. The growth of Tokyo, or Shanghai, or Mexico City involved huge movements of people. New migrations also occurred across the boundaries of nation and civilization. The West began to receive millions of immigrants from other societies—particularly southern Asia and the Middle East, Africa, and Latin America. The world population explosion also helps explain the frequent unrest of urban and rural masses in many 20th-century societies.

The nature of war and diplomacy changed in the 20th century. Imperialism had already established a world diplomacy, though of a one-sided sort; in the 20th century, particularly after 1945, international diplomacy became a normal practice. Alliances were routinely formed, and broken, across civilization boundaries. Wars intensified in scope. They involved greatly heightened powers of governments, as many states learned to mobilize entire economies and to inflame national opinion as part of the military effort. Above all, wars became more violent. New technologies facilitated the killing of more people than ever before. World War I saw the introduction of tanks, submarines, long-range artillery, aerial bombing, and poison gas; World War II brought more massive aerial and naval clashes and the dawn of nuclear and missile warfare. After both world wars, diplomats and ordinary people alike operated amid an atmosphere of fear and uncertainty engendered by steady advances in weaponry.

The pace of many human endeavors quickened in the 20th century. Air travel shrunk the globe even further than steam shipping had. Telephones, radios and, later, satellite and computer communications allowed more rapid transmission of greater volumes of information across greater distances than ever before. Multinational companies, operating on all inhabited continents, became capable of transporting goods and people with unprecedented swiftness. Popular culture, particularly but not exclusively in the industrialized societies, picked up the theme of speed. Olympic Games promoted competition in races of all sorts. People ate faster; by the 1980s most Japanese schoolchildren could no longer be bothered with chopsticks because the utensils made eating too slow, while fast-food restaurants cropped up in most major cities. Although speed was a factor above all in transportation and communication, it also affected the way people thought, and the tensions they imposed on themselves.

Finally, two major trends swept across many different societies in the 20th century, creating parallelisms, though not full homogeneity, in regions otherwise as different as Germany and Korea. Political change constituted the first common theme. Almost all nations had different political systems, by 1994, from those that had been in operation in 1900. Some regions had gone through several different political systems, in fact. This widespread pattern meant that many societies had to develop new beliefs and defenses of political legitimacy, while governments took on important new functions. Even the United States, which kept its basic system, redefined the role of the state from the 1930s onward. The second change involved culture: many people believed in different ideas, by the 1990s, from what their counterparts had been attached to in 1900. In some areas, traditional religions were challenged, while in other regions religious conversion topped the cultural agenda. As in politics, the point was not a common pattern but rather a common participation in change.

The 20th century thus contained most of the standard ingredients involved in the opening of a new world history period. The power balance among civilizations shifted from what had prevailed in the previous centuries—hence the relative decline of the West and the rise of new dynamism in places like Japan. Contacts among civilizations intensified, thanks to new technologies, new cultural diffusion as in the exchange of film and television, and new international organizations such as multinational businesses. The world became even smaller than it had been in the century of Western industrialization. Finally, a number of common themes spread around the world, inducing revisions of established political and cultural forms, the impact of unprecedented population growth, and the altered nature of war and diplomacy. Not since the 15th century had so many facets of the framework of world history altered direction.

In addition to these changes, of course, were a host of developments in individual civilizations. Russia, and China, and, more briefly Germany pioneered new forms of government controls. Experimentation in modern art and sleek architectural styles spread from the West to many parts of the world. The list of innovative trends and shattered traditions is long. They add up, in the view of many observers, to what one historian has termed "a world different, in almost all its basic preconditions," from the world of the late 19th century.

Identifying major breaks in world history, and not just the history of a single civilization, is a tricky business. We have emphasized long periods: the birth of agricultural society; the elaboration of key classical civilizations; the expansion of civilization and the impact of the great religions; and the rise of the West and the development of a new global economy. We cannot be absolutely sure, living in what is at best the beginning of a new period, that a definitive new era has dawned, and we certainly cannot be sure of all its major characteristics. A mere 100 years is, by world history standards—and even allowing for a faster rate of change—a rather brief span of time by which to judge. But if the 20th century does constitute a break in world history, as events and themes suggest, it is possible to speculate about the underlying dynamic that is opening up. The 20th century marked the start of the industrialization of the world. The 19th century had seen the first industrial revolutions, to be sure, and their results were brought to the world by Western merchants and imperialists. But the 20th century saw full industrialization achieved in some areas outside Europe and North America, particularly in Eastern Europe and the "Pacific Rim," including Japan, and the beginnings of gradual industrialization elsewhere—notably in China, Southeast Asia, India, and parts of Latin America. The world was by no means completely industrialized by the 1990s, of course, and in some ways economic disparities among some major civilizations increased. But the strivings for economic modernization and the adjustments to its impact now form a theme that literally encompasses the world.

Global industrialization, understood as a common process rather than a uniform economic system, underlies the precise trends that can be identified, on an international basis, as distinguishing 20th-century patterns. It was the industrialization of Russia and Japan that most clearly ended the undisputed rise of the West in world affairs. Offshoots of mechanization, in new sanitation procedures and agricultural techniques, led to world population growth, even though this same growth retarded actual industrialization in some parts of the world. Industry lay behind the fearsome technologies of contemporary war, and of course it set the stage for the new theme of speed. Political changes resulted in part from growing industrialization, as new government functions both preceded and followed economic shifts; the more traditional regimes, for the most part failing to keep pace, had to be replaced. Cultural changes, including new secular loyalties, followed from the spread of more industrial economies. Traditional social structures often shifted as well, as aristocracies largely disappeared and peasantries declined, to be replaced by new kinds of managers and a growing urban working class.

Industrial growth also redefined the kind of global economy that had come to life in the early modern period and then intensified during the 19th century. The West no longer monopolized the top spot in the world economy as Japan claimed a share. And while some regions were still exploited for their raw materials and cheap labor, a larger number of nations gained a middle position in world trade during the second half of the 20th century. Places like Brazil, China, and India could not rival the world leaders, but they had a vigorous industrial sector and some control over their economic destiny. International trade and technological exchange became more important than ever before; societies that attempted a new isolation usually suffered after a short time. But the nature of the world economy was more complex, with a wider variety of roles, than in the simpler days of the 19th century when the West led the way and almost every other region danced to its tune.

Not all was new. Many developments, including even massive population growth, built on earlier trends. Modern war was foreshadowed by the American Civil War and by the sophisticated weaponry of the later 19th century. One can understand the 20th century as the beginning of a transition to a new stage of world history without denying that important events, particularly during the 19th century, had paved the way. For example, the revival of traditional antagonisms between Christians and Muslims in central Asia and in the Balkans in the 1990s reminded the world of how many issues continue from the past.

Furthermore, the major civilizations responded to the challenges of the 20th century in different ways, in large part because of their distinctive traditions. Some developments, to be sure, became in fact international. It was possible to find examples of the same building styles, the same costumes, the same soft drinks, the same sports in most parts of the world. But along with closer international links came varied reactions, depending on prior experience. Thus while monarchy exited, several different political forms took its place. While the desire to industrialize spread, the economic system a given society would adopt, the kind of cultural change it would embrace, or the way it would define the roles of different family members, all varied widely. The world, though growing smaller, was not necessarily becoming more homogeneous; as a result, 20th-century history must be interpreted as a combination of sweeping trends and particular reactions based on tradition. Each civilization changed, without question; even the West went through an important transformation of its earlier industrial order. But it is vital to see new and old distinctions among civilizations, as well as shared problems and responses.

THEMES AND SUBPERIODS

Looking at the 20th century as the beginning of a new period in world history means asking some common questions about each major civilization. How did each area participate in cultural change and how did it react to Western influences in popular culture? How did change in each area relate to the redefined patterns of international trade and to what extent did the area gain greater control over its own economy? What impact did the major wars have, or the surge of world population? Did the area develop a new political style, and in response to what forces? These questions must be asked and answered both in terms of the new forces of the 20th century and in terms of prior traditions and institutions. How did responses to the common issues reflect the particular characteristics of each civilization, in relation to its own long history?

The 20th century as a whole, and the histories of most of the major civilizations, must also be divided into three major subperiods, each relating to the unfolding of the new global framework. The period from 1914 to 1945 was clearly transitional. Western Europe and, to an extent, the United States suffered the agonies of war and economic dislocation, but Japan and Russia, while heavily affected by war, solidified their industrial economies. Central governments strengthened in Latin America, while the nationalist challenge to imperialism surged forward in Asia, the Middle East, and Africa. From a Western standpoint these were dreadful decades, but from other vantage points these were decades full of new promise.

From 1945 onward, new structures were built, as imperialism beat its retreat. New nations arose, while Japan and its neighbors in the Pacific Rim advanced economically. The "industrialization of the world," though very uneven, clearly moved ahead. But these developments occurred under the shadow of the great cold war conflict between the United States and the Soviet Union. Political and economic systems varied greatly depending on cold war alignments.

Finally, beginning in the 1970s, the cold war loosened, then came to an end with the collapse of the Soviet system in 1989–1991. New diplomatic issues came to the fore, including a host of regional troublespots. Four other major trends shaped world developments at this point. First, industrial growth in virtually every society heightened the levels of global competition, while multinational companies set up operations wherever they could find suitably trained but cheap labor (and, often, relaxed environmental regulations). New economic problems and new growth areas resulted. Second, almost all societies decided to reduce the economic role of government in the interests of faster economic growth. The results varied, in part because the roles of government already differed, but on the whole the policy shift seemed to spur production while creating new gaps between rich and poor within most societies. And the decision itself constituted unprecedented, if not necessarily permanent, international agreement on basic economic goals and means. Third, a new enthusiasm for democratic political forms spread almost everywhere—though there were a few revealing exceptions. Never before had this political structure spread so widely, as many societies tried to replace authoritarianism or communism. Finally, religions revived in many areas, often in quite novel forms, setting up new cultural tensions within and among world societies between secular and religious styles and commitments. These trends promised to carry boldly into the next century.

World Events	Western Civilization	Soviet Union and Eastern Europe	East Asia
	1905 Einstein's theory of relativity formulated.	**1905** Revolution in Russia.	
1914–1918 World War I.	**1910** First use of assembly line production.		**1911** Revolution led by Sun Yat-sen.
1917 Russian Revolution.	**1918–1919** End of German empire, Habsburg empire.	**1917** Revolution in Russia. **October** Bolshevik takeover.	**1912** Fall of Chinese empire.
1919 Formation of Communist International.	**1919–1939** Period of U.S. isolationism.		**1916** Yuan Shi-h'ai named China's president.
1919 Paris Peace Conference (Versailles); founding of League of Nations.			**1919** Former German islands in Pacific taken by Japan.
			1919 ff. Growing regional warlord power in China.
	1920s Rise of fascism.	**1921** Lenin's New Economic Policy promulgated.	**1921** Formation of Chinese communist movement.
	1923 Fascist regime in Italy.	**1923** New constitution.	
	1920–1923 Rapid inflation.	**1927** Stalin in full power.	**1927** Communists expelled by Kuomintang.
		1928 Beginning of collectivization of agriculture, five-year plans.	
1929–1939 Worldwide economic depression.	**1929** Depression.		
			1934 "Long March" led by Mao Zedong.

India and Southeast Asia	Middle East	Latin America	Sub-Saharan Africa
1914–1918 Participation of Indian troops with Britain in World War I.		**1910–1917** Mexican revolution.	**1914–1918** Use of African troops in World War I; British takeover of German colonies.
1919 British colonial reforms; limited representative government.	**1915 ff.** Rise of Arab nationalism, encouraged during World War I.	**1917** New constitution; nationalization of mineral rights.	**1919** First meeting of Pan-African Congress; rise of African nationalism.
	1917 Promulgation of Balfour declaration, promising Jewish homeland in Palestine.		
1920 Beginning of Gandhi's nonviolent movement.	**1920** Treaty of Sèvres, ending Ottoman empire.	**1920** Obregón president; rise of National Revolutionary party.	**1921 ff.** Sporadic religious and nationalist riots against European rule.
	1920 ff. Growth of Jewish settlement in Palestine.		**1924** Color Bar bill backed by Afrikaner Nationalist party in South Africa, limiting black-white social contacts.
	1922 Partial independence granted to Egypt by Britain.		
	1923 ff. Independent Turkey created by Atatürk; beginning of modernization drive.		
	1923 ff. Rise of independent Persia under Shah Riza Khan.	**1929 ff.** Depression; rise of economic nationalism.	
	1935 Name changed to Iran.		

World Events	Western Civilization	Soviet Union and Eastern Europe	East Asia
	1933–1939 U.S. New Deal.		**1931** Japanese invasion of Machuria.
	1933–1944 Nazi regime in Germany.		**1932** End of political party government in Japan; rise of miltary rule.
	1938 Munich agreement; effort at British, French compromise with Hitler.		**1935** Further advance of Japan.
	1939 German-Soviet alliance.	**1937–1938** Great Purge conducted by Stalin.	**1937** New Japanese attack on China.
1939–1945 World War II.	**1940–1944** Holocaust, slaughter of 6 million Jews.	**1939** Signing of Soviet-German pact.	
1945 Atomic bomb dropped on Japan.	**1940 ff.** Rise of women in labor force.	**1941** German invasion of Russia.	**1941** Pearl Harbor attacked.
1945 United Nations set up.	**1945–1948** Postwar reconstruction; new democratic regimes in France, Italy, West Germany; rise of welfare state.	**1943** Red army pushes west.	**1942–1945** Momentum against Japan gained by U.S.
1947 ff. Cold war begun between United States and Soviet Union.		**1945–1948** Soviet takeover of Eastern Europe.	**1945** Atom bomb dropped on Nagasaki and Hiroshima by U.S.; surrender of Japan; beginning of U.S. occupation.
1948 ff. Decolonization; rise of new nations.	**1948–1949** Berlin airlift.		**1945 ff.** Communist-Kuomintang war in China.
	1949 Formation of NATO.		**1949** Communist victory.
			1950 Start of Chiang Kai-shek regime in Taiwan.
			1949 Korean War; U.S. intervention.
			1950 Chinese intervention.

India and Southeast Asia	Middle East	Latin America	Sub-Saharan Africa
1930–1931 Rioting in Indochina; rise of communist movement under Ho Chi Minh.		**1930** Military coup in Brazil; Vargas caudillo to 1945.	
1934 Philippine self-government increased by U.S.		**1933** Power in Cuba seized by caudillo.	
1935 New British constitution for India.		**1934 ff.** U.S. "good neighbor" policies begun.	
1935 Nationalist victory in Siam; nation renamed Thailand.	**1936** Syria promised independence by France.	**1934–1940** Cardenas president of Mexico; formation of Pemex.	**1936** Exclusion of blacks from South African voting.
1937 Nationalist petition in Indonesia.			
1940 ff. Japanese invasion of Southeast Asia.	**1945** Syria and Lebanon fully independent.	**1945** Juan Péron president of Argentina.	
1946 Hindu-Muslim clash in India.	**1948** State of Israel declared.		
1946 Philippines independent.			
1947 India and Pakistan independent.			
1948 Sri Lanka and Burma independent.			**1948** Full control of South African government gained by Afrikaners' independence from Britain and extension of apartheid.
1949 Indonesia independent.			**1953** Strikes by black workers barred by law.
			1959 Enactment of Bantu Self-Government law, setting up 10 homelands as the only legal black residences.

World Events	Western Civilization	Soviet Union and Eastern Europe	East Asia
	1950–1973 Growing economic prosperity.	**1951** Atom bomb developed by Soviets.	**1950 ff.** Rapid economic advance in Japan.
1955 First meeting of non-aligned nations.		**1953** Death of Stalin.	
1957 Sputnik, first artificial satellite, launched by Soviet Union, beginning the "space age."		**1955** Formation of Warsaw pact.	
		1956 Stalinism attacked by Krushchev.	
		1956 Hungarian revolution and its suppression.	
	1958 Establishment of French Fifth Republic.		
	1958 Founding of European Economic Community (Common Market).		
		1961 Berlin wall erected.	**1960s** Mao's Cultural Revolution.
		1962 Cuban missile crisis.	
	1968 Student protests, in U.S. and Western Europe.	**1968** Revolt in Czechoslovakia and its repression.	
			1969 Russian–Chinese border fighting.

India and Southeast Asia	Middle East	Latin America	Sub-Saharan Africa
	1950–1962 Completion of independence of Arab states.		**1952–1959** Mau Mau terrorism against white landowners, Kenya.
1954 End of French War against Vietnamese nationalists and communists; independence and division of Vietnam.	**1952** Egyptian revolution, fall of monarchy. **1956** Egyptian seizure of Suez Canal.	**1953** Reformist regime in Guatemala unseated by U.S. **1955** Péron overthrown by military coup.	
1955 First meeting of nonaligned nations, under India's leadership.	**1956, 1967, 1973** Israeli–Arab wars.	**1966, 1976** Other Argentine military coups. **1959–1960** Castro's revolution in Cuba. **1960 ff.** Independence achieved by most West Indies territories.	**1957–1980** Independence to most of black Africa. **1957** Ghana independent. **1958** French colonies semi-independent, soon fully so. **1959** Riots leading to Congo independence (Zaire).
	1962 Algeria independent.	**1960 ff.** Rise of liberation theology in Latin American church. **1961** Failure of U.S. "Bay of Pigs" invasion.	**1965** Southern Rhodesia declared independent under white rule.
1963 Beginning of authoritarian rule under Marcos in Philippines; military coup in Indonesia. **1964 ff.** Growing U.S. participation in North–South Vietnam war.		**1964** Military coup in Brazil.	**1974–1975** Angola and Mozambique independent from Portugal. **1980** Rhodesia renamed Zimbabwe under black government. **1960–1963** Civil war in Zaire. **1967–1970** Nigerian civil war.

World Events	Western Civilization	Soviet Union and Eastern Europe	East Asia
	1970s Introduction of microchip computer.		**1971** Partial Chinese–U.S. reconciliation.
1973–1979 Increase in world energy prices promoted by OPEC. **1978 ff.** Widespread trend to more market economies, reduction of state role. **1989** End of Cold War. **1989 ff.** Growing U.N. role in intervention in regional conflicts. **1988–1993** Widespread economic recession, rising unemployment: U.S., Europe, Japan. **1990 ff.** Increased United Nations peacekeeping and relief efforts in Africa. Eastern Europe, Southeast Asia, Middle East. **1994** North American Free Trade Association.	**1979 ff.** New economic tensions. **1981** Reagan president in U.S. **1990** German Unification. **1992** End of economic restrictions within Common markets. **1992–1993** Negotiations in extending Common Market toward single currency, etc. **1993** Full economic unification of European Community (now European Union). Maestricht treaty agreement for more coordination. **1994 ff.** Entry of Finland, Austria, Sweden to European Union.	**1979** Uprisings in Poland and their suppression. **1985** Gorbachev to power and reform in Soviet Union. **1988–1989** Liberalization movements throughout Eastern Europe; new constitutions, economic reforms; nationalities agitation in Soviet Union. **1988** New Soviet Constitution; establishment of the Congress of People's deputies. **1989–1991** Collapse of Soviet Empire; new elections throughout much of Eastern Europe; Gorbachev selected as President. **1991** Collapse of Soviet Union, replaced by Russia and numerous European and central Asian republics; Yeltsin replaces Gorbachev. **1991–1996** Civil war in parts of former Yugoslavia. **1997** NATO invites Poland, Hungary, Czech Republic as members.	**1976** Death of Mao; more pragmatic regime in China. **1978** More market economy in China. **1980** End of U.S.–Taiwan treaty alliance; economic rise of Pacific Rim. **1984** British–Chinese agreement to return Hong Kong to China in 1997. **1988–1989** Growing student agitation for liberal political reform in South Korea; elected civilian government installed. **1989** Suppression of democratic protests in China. **1993** Split of Japanese Democrats fall from liberal Democratic Party; Liberal Democrats fall from power in Japan. **1997** Hong Kong reverts to China.

India and Southeast Asia	Middle East	Latin America	Sub-Saharan Africa
1971 Revolt in Pakistan; creation of independent Bangladesh. **1973** End of Vietnam War. **1975** Control by North Vietnamese of all Vietnam; movement into Laos, Cambodia. **1975–1977** Suspension of civil liberties in India; sterilization campaign.	**1970s** Rise of Muslim fundamentalism. **1977** Egypt-Israeli peace. **1978–1979** Iranian revolution.	**1970** Chilean election won by socialist coalition. **1973** Allende murdered in U.S.-backed military coup; beginning of repressive regime of Pinochet. **1978** Agreement by U.S. to turn over control of Panama Canal. **1979** Sandinista revolt in Nicaragua. **1980 ff.** Growing U.S. involvement against guerrilla insurgency in Central America, and against Sandinista regime.	**1980s** Growing problems of hunger in parts of Africa. **1989** DeKlerck charts a path of peaceful reform in South Africa.
1984 Assassination of Indira Gandhi by Sikh extremists; smooth transition of leadership to her son Rajiv. **1986** Fall of Marcos regime in the Philippines. **1990** Economic reforms in India.	**1980–1988** Iran-Iraq war. **1981** Assassination of President Sadat of Egypt. **1982** Invasion of Lebanon by Israel. **1985** Withdrawal of Israel from Lebanon; Lebanon in chaos. **1990** Iraqi invasion of Kuwait. **1991** Gulf war against Iraq. **1993–1994** New peace movement. Palestinian autonomy in Israel. Israel–Jordan Treaty.	**1980 ff.** New democratic current in Latin America. **1980 ff.** International debt crisis in many Latin American nations. **1982** Argentina and Great Britain clash over the Falkland Islands (Malvinas Islas). **1983** U.S. invades Grenada. **1989** Sandinistas lose election in Nicaragua. **1989** U.S. invades Panama, disposes General Noriega. **1990 ff.** Decline of insurgency in Central America; high economic growth rates in Brazil, Argentina, Mexico.	**1984 ff.** New wave of black protest against South African apartheid. **1990** Nelson Mandela released from prison. **1990 ff.** Dismantling of apartheid. **1990** Several democratic elections in Kenya, other nations. **1992** U.N. intervention in Somalia famine. **1993** Agreement on democratic elections in South Africa. **1994** Election of Nelson Mandela as South Africa's president. **1994 ff.** Democratic regimes in several African states. **1997** Insurgent army establishes new regime in Congo (Zaire).
1998 Nuclear weapons tests in India and Pakistan.		**1997** Multiparty elections in Mexico.	

The West in the 20th Century

Focal Points

The West suffered greatly during World War I and the years between the World Wars, though some areas such as the United States were less deeply affected than others. New currents such as Nazism reflected and furthered the West's crisis. How can these new movements be explained? How much did they change the West? After World War II the West in many respects rebounded, though it did not capture its previous world dominance. What older institutions and values did the West re-emphasize? What were the main innovations in politics, the economy, and social structure, that made the West different by the 1990s from what it had been in the late 1940s? Was there still a definable Western culture?

STRENGTH AND RELATIVE DECLINE

While one of the themes of 20th-century world history is the relative decline of the West, particularly Europe, Western civilization has remained a standard-setter in many ways. By the late 1980s it still remained the wealthiest society in the world. The artistic and popular cultural forms it has generated have had far more influence on other civilizations than those of any other single society. Western nations still set much of the tone for world diplomacy. One sign of the West's continued importance has been its role as target for people in many parts of the world who dislike not only Western power but the threat it continues to pose to traditional values.

PATTERNS OF WESTERN HISTORY: 1914–1945

World War I, the explosion that effectively opened the new century, had international repercussions. Britain and France used many troops from their colonies. Some fighting occurred against German holdings in Africa. The Ottoman Empire's alliance with Germany produced conflict in the Middle East, which, among other things, encouraged Arab nationalism while further weakening the Ottoman state; many nations, including Italy, hoped for big colonial gains in the Middle East after the hostilities ended. Finally, Japan entered the war on the side of Britain and France and seized a number of German territories in the Pacific.

But the bulk of the fighting occurred in Europe, including European Russia. Germany invaded large parts of Russia, fueling the growing discontent that finally brought the 1917 revolution, which took Russia out of the war. Combat on the Western front, located mainly in France, was still more bitter. New weapons, including more effective artillery and tanks, led to the construction of defensive trenches, from which neither side could advance without huge casualties. Occasional offensive efforts cost tens of thousands of lives each day. The sheer loss of life and the frustration of nearly four years of virtual stalemate had a devastating material and psychological impact on the European combatants. Finally, in 1918, the exhausted allies managed to invade the still-more-exhausted Germany. The German emperor abdicated (as did the Habsburg ruler), and the war was over.

Picking up the pieces was virtually impossible, however. More than 10 million people had been killed in Europe. Vast amounts of property had been destroyed, and the European economy suffered a shattering blow through loss of investments abroad and huge debts accumulated internally to fund the wasteful war effort. A peace conference was held at Versailles, its work divided between desires for revenge against Germany and the idealism represented by President Wilson of the United States. Idealism led to the establishment of the League of Nations, designed to promote international harmony in the future, and the creation of a series of new states in central and eastern Europe, from the territory of Russia, the Habsburg Monarchy, and Germany. Poland resurfaced, along with other new Slavic states and an independent Hungary. The new states were weak, however, and created a new source of tensions in European diplomacy for the future. The League of Nations, though not insignificant in world affairs during the next 15 years, proved ineffective as well. At the same time, revenge motives caused the imposition of huge reparation payments and loss of territory on Germany, generating further resentments. Even the victorious allies were unsatisfied: France still feared its German neighbor, the United States pulled back from European entanglements into an unrealistic isolationism—not even joining the League of Nations—and Italy bemoaned its lack of success in acquiring vast new territory.

World War I and Versailles set the stage for the next two, messy decades of Western history. Diplomatic tensions eased somewhat during the 1920s, as Germany made some moves to accommodate to its reduced position; but fears and resentments still ran high. European and U.S. internal politics were largely ineffectual as a series of mediocre leaders gained the helms of state. Germany, now a republic, suffered at the hands of a number of groups who opposed democracy. Communist movements, linked to the Soviet regime that now ruled Russia, emerged to the left of socialist parties in many countries, serving as small but frightening revolutionary forces. The liberal middle sector of Western politics weakened, as many erstwhile liberals became more conservative in their desire to prevent major social reform. The absence of a strong center made effective government difficult, even in Britain, where the parliamentary tradition was particularly strong.

New political tensions might have been manageable had postwar economic trends not proved so disastrous. Many nations suffered from massive inflation during much of the 1920s, the result of wartime debts and postwar dislocations. Prosperity returned toward

The World of Western Dominance, 1914

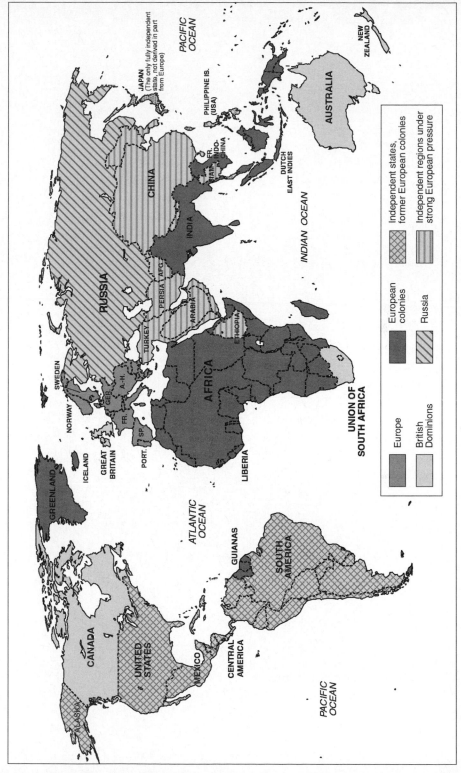

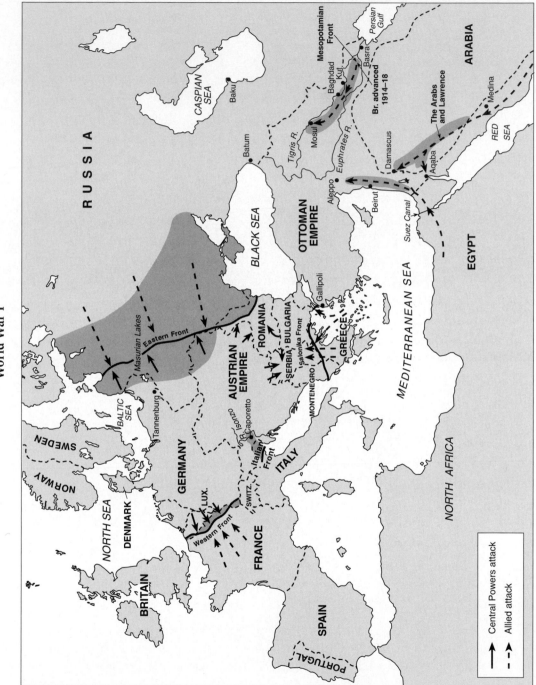

World War I

RUSSIA

CASPIAN SEA

Baku

BLACK SEA

Batum

OTTOMAN EMPIRE

Tigris R.

Euphrates R.

Mosul

Baghdad
Kut

Basra

Persian Gulf

Mesopotamian Front

Br. advanced 1914–18

ARABIA

Medina

RED SEA

The Arabs and Lawrence

Damascus

Aqaba

Aleppo

Beirut

Suez Canal

EGYPT

MEDITERRANEAN SEA

NORTH AFRICA

Gallipoli

GREECE

Salonika Front

MONTENEGRO

SERBIA

BULGARIA

ROMANIA

AUSTRIAN EMPIRE

Masurian Lakes

Eastern Front

BALTIC SEA

Tannenburg

GERMANY

Isonzo

Caporetto

Italian Front

ITALY

SWITZ.

LUX.

Western Front

FRANCE

SPAIN

PORTUGAL

SWEDEN

NORWAY

DENMARK

NORTH SEA

BRITAIN

Central Powers attack

Allied attack

the middle of the decade and the United States, in particular, enjoyed an industrial boom. But in 1929 a major depression occurred, as banks failed first in the United States and then throughout the Western world. The great depression resulted from a number of factors. Purchasing power was too low among many peasants and workers to sustain increased industrial production. Many peasants and American farmers faced a rapid decline in agricultural prices, due to overproduction; mechanized agriculture outstripped demand for food in the Western world, and this limited farmers' ability to buy. Nonindustrial countries in Eastern Europe and many other parts of the world also saw prices for their raw materials tumble as their production increased faster than Western demand; this crisis also weakened markets for Western goods. High tariffs, imposed by many nations to protect their own economies, added to the difficulties of trade. In essence, Western productive capacity outran available markets. As a result, speculative investments finally proved hollow, causing the stock market crash and bank failures of 1929.

The ensuing depression was the worst in modern memory. Millions of workers lost their jobs. Wages tumbled, and insecurity spread even among those who were employed. Levels of production collapsed, as up to a third of the economic capacity of countries like Germany and the United States was idled by 1932. And while the worst of the depression was over by the mid–1930s, its traces remained strong throughout the decade.

Only a few Western governments responded constructively. Scandinavian states increased government spending, providing new levels of social insurance against illness and unemployment and foreshadowing the modern welfare state. In the United States, Franklin Roosevelt's New Deal, from 1933 onward, enacted a number of social insurance measures and used government spending to stimulate the economy. The New Deal did not cure the American depression, but it alleviated the worst effects and provided new hope that forestalled major political pressure against the established order. Britain and France, however, reacted weakly to the economic catastrophe. Both countries continued to be plagued by inept leadership. They were also torn between socialist and conservative forces, and their allies on the political extremes; effective action seemed impossible.

The depression led directly to a fascist regime in Germany in 1933. Fascism was a product of World War I; the movement's advocates, many of them former veterans, attacked the weakness of parliamentary democracy and the corruption and class conflict of Western capitalism. They proposed a strong state ruled by a powerful leader, who would revive the nation's forces through vigorous foreign and military policy. Fascists vaguely promised social reforms to alleviate class antagonism, and their attacks on trade unions and socialist parties pleased landlords and business groups. A first fascist regime arose in Italy in 1923, and fascist parties complicated the political process in a number of other nations during the 1920s. But it was the advent of the National Socialist, or Nazi, regime in Germany, under Adolf Hitler, that made this new political movement a major force in world history.

Hitler appealed to a country bitter about its defeat in war and unusually hard hit by economic disorder. He promised many groups a return to more traditional ways; thus many artisans voted for Hitler in the belief that preindustrial economic institutions like the guilds would be revived. The middle class, including big business leaders, were attracted to Hitler's commitment to a firm stance against socialism and communism. Although Hitler never won a majority popular vote in a free election, his party did attain the largest single vote total by 1932. By this time the effects of the depression were compounded by the weak, divided response of Germany's parliamentary leadership, in a country that had never fully accepted the validity of liberal political forms.

Once in power, Hitler quickly set about constructing a totalitarian state—that is, a new kind of government that would exercise massive, direct control over virtually all the activities of its subjects. Hitler eliminated all opposition parties; he purged the bureaucracy and military, installing loyal Nazis in many posts. His secret police, the Gestapo, arrested hundreds of thousands of political opponents. Trade unions were replaced by government-sponsored bodies that tried to appease workers with low pay by offering full employment and various welfare benefits. Government economic planning helped restore production levels, with particular emphasis on manufacture of arrangements. Hitler cemented his regime by constant, well-staged propaganda bombardments, strident nationalism, and an incessant attack on Germany's Jewish minority. Hitler's hatred of Jews ran deep; he blamed them for various personal misfortunes and also for movements like socialism and excessive capitalism that in his view had weakened the German spirit. Obviously, anti-Semitism served as a catchall for a host of diverse dissatisfactions. Anti-Semitism also served Hitler's cause by providing a scapegoat that could rouse national passions and distract the population from other problems. Measures against Jews became more and more severe, as Jews were forced to wear special emblems, their property was attacked and seized, and increasing numbers were sent to concentration camps. After 1940, Hitler's policy insanely turned to the literal elimination of European Jewry; 6 million Jews were killed in the concentration camps of Germany and conquered territories; and other groups like Gypsies and homosexuals were targeted as well.

Hitler's policies were based on preparation for war. He wanted not only to recoup Germany's World War I losses but to create a land empire that would extend across much

A Nazi party Congress in Nuremburg, Germany. The Führer is saluted by his "storm troopers," in a demonstration of the Nazi use of mass orchestrations.

of Europe, particularly toward the east into the territory of what he saw as the inferior Slavic peoples. Progressively Hitler violated the provisions of the Treaty of Versailles, which had limited German rearmament. In 1936 he intervened in a civil war in Spain, on the side of fascist forces. Within two years he annexed Austria and seized part, then all, of Czechoslovakia. To all these steps the other European powers responded only weakly. France and Britain were too divided to pursue a resolute foreign policy. They negotiated with Hitler at Munich in 1938, offering him part of Czechoslovakia in hopes that this bone would satisfy his appetite; but their feeble attempt at appeasement merely inspired Hitler to further demands. The United States remained isolationist; the Soviet Union was worried but too isolated from potential Western allies, who feared its communism, to pose an effective counterweight.

WORLD WAR II

So Hitler moved forward, forming an alliance with the Soviet Union in 1939 that allowed both powers to attack Poland. This act finally convinced Britain and France that they could no longer sit idly by, and war was declared in September 1939. Hitler was far better prepared for conflict than were his opponents, and during the first three years of the war his forces, in alliance with Italy, swept over much of Western Europe. By 1942, Germany held France, Norway, the Low Countries, and the small Balkan states. But an invasion of Russia in 1941, following the collapse of the brief alliance between Russia and Germany, resulted in Germany's armies being bogged down as Napoleon's had been 130 years before. Furthermore, the United States, goaded by the Japanese attack on Pearl Harbor, entered the war in December 1941 on Britain's side. Three years of bitter fighting in Europe, the Pacific, and elsewhere followed. The Russian armies gradually recovered, with some assistance in the form of armaments from the United States, and pressed inexorably toward Germany's eastern borders. American and British forces, aided by resistance movements against Nazi occupation, drove Germany first from North Africa, then gradually from Italy. In 1944 a massive invasion moved across the English Channel into France, and within a year the allies entered Germany from the West. Hitler committed suicide, and the European war drew to a close.

Like its predecessor, World War II caused massive loss of life. Russia and Germany were hardest hit, along with the Jewish population of central and Eastern Europe. Economic devastation was even greater than before. Hitler had drained the occupied countries of labor and productive goods, as part of his frenzied war effort. Massive bombing had destroyed many cities and factories, as well as transportation networks. For several years after the war, Western Europe was the scene of grinding poverty, massive movements of dislocated people, and seeming hopelessness.

The war also redesigned the European map more fundamentally than World War I had done. Russian dominance extended through virtually all of Eastern Europe. Only two countries in Eastern Europe preserved any real independence: Greece, which was aided by Britain and the United States to maintain a noncommunist government, and Yugoslavia, which set up a communist regime independent of Soviet control. Germany was divided. Initially the Soviet Union, France, Britain, and the United States each occupied a zone of Germany. But the three Western powers gradually allowed their zones to be united in an

World War II: European and North African Theaters

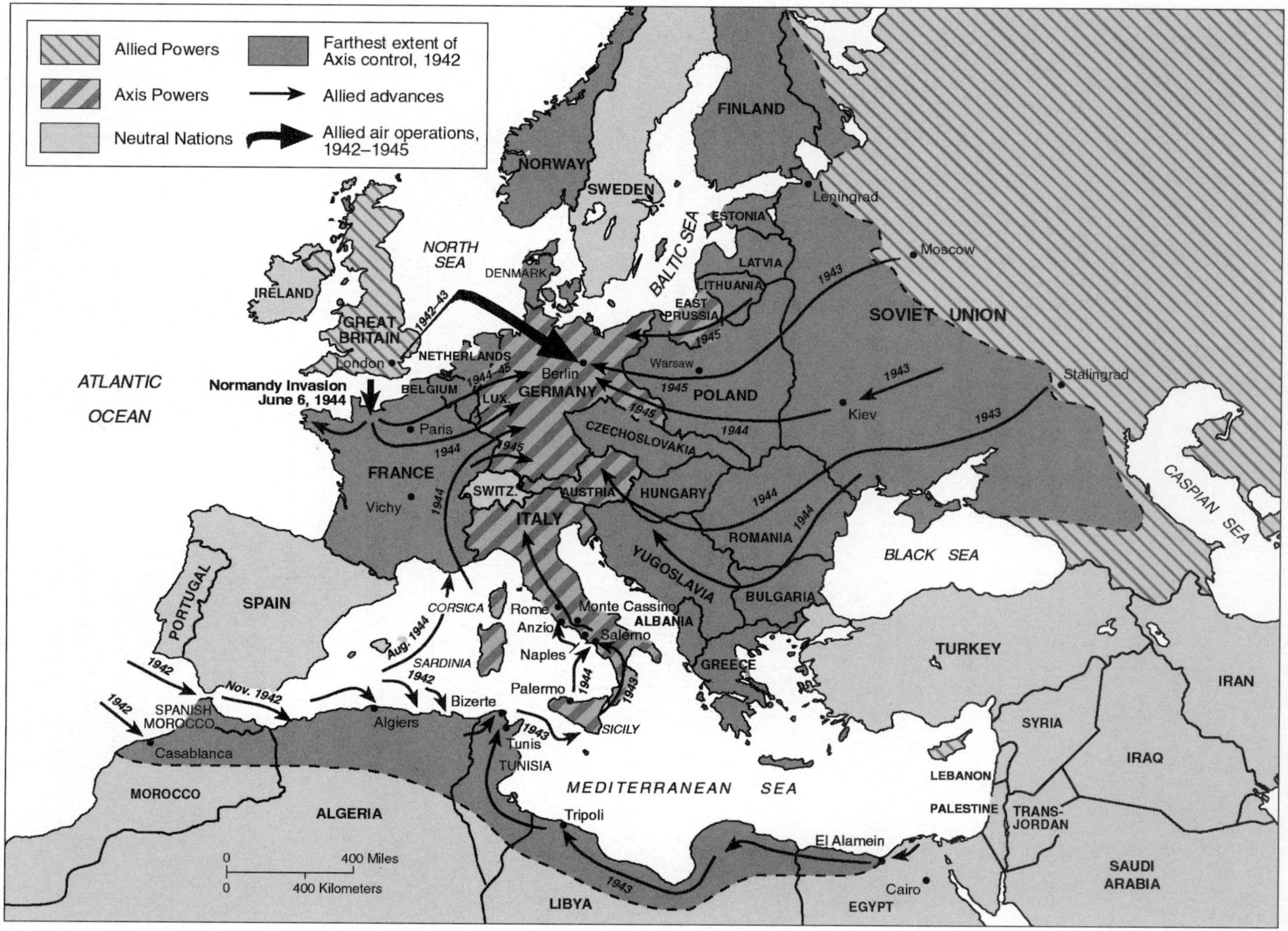

Legend:

Farthest extent of Axis control, 1942

→ Allied advances

⮌ Allied air operations, 1942–1945

Allied Powers

Axis Powers

Neutral Nations

independent Federal Republic, while the Soviet zone converted into a communist state heavily dependent on Russian military support.

The new boundaries of Europe ushered in a prolonged competition between the Soviet Union and the United States, each with a network of European allies and dependencies. A "cold war" was defined in 1947, pitting the two postwar giants against each other. Russia, with its virtual empire extending into central Europe, saw the United States construct an alliance system among the leading Western states and retain a substantial military presence of its own to guard against possible Soviet attack. Here, within Europe's own boundaries, was the cruel result of half a century of disarray and violent internal struggle.

PATTERNS OF WESTERN HISTORY: 1950 TO THE PRESENT

To many observers, by 1950, the future of the Western world, or at least its traditional European base, seemed unrelievedly bleak. If World War I had caused two decades of virtually unqualified confusion, could the consequences of a second blow be anything but worse? Yet in fact the West seemed to recover both economic and political vigor in the decades after 1950; and while the results were far from problem-free, they were certainly more constructive than the record of the interwar years.

Postwar Europe did not regain its previous diplomatic position. The dominance of the superpowers, the Soviet Union and the United States, continued. The United States formed the North Atlantic Treaty Organization (NATO) with most other Western governments in 1949, to oppose the Soviet threat; creation of the alliance ensured American preponderance over Western Europe in dealing with the Soviet Union. At the same time, weakened by world war and pressed by surging nationalist movements throughout the world, Western Europe lost most of its colonies, sometimes as a result of bitter struggle. India, Southeast Asia, and then Africa all gained independence. Although many Europeans resented this sign of decline, attempts to reassert some shadow of earlier authority largely failed. In 1956, for example, Britain and France tried to seize control of the Suez Canal from newly independent Egypt, only to be forced to pull back as a result of Egyptian resistance and United States and Soviet pressure. Yet, even aside from the great power of the United States as a representative of generally Western values, the West did not suffer perpetual diplomatic decline. Decolonization was largely accepted by the people of Western Europe, who did not attempt to hold out at the expense of political stability and economic growth at home. West European cultural and economic influence in many former colonies remained considerable. With time, leading European powers also gained a more independent voice vis-à-vis the United States. Though not military equals, individual states such as France were able to oppose American policies at key points.

There should be no mistake: the world's diplomatic framework decisively changed, and in many ways transformation worked to the West's disadvantage. The balance of power within the West shifted to the United States. When the age of imperialism ended, the West's direct voice in Asia and Africa was dramatically lessened. The cold war rivalry between the United States and the Soviet Union meant that even the West's leading power could not set the tone for world affairs, but rather faced a roughly equal competitor. By 1951, when the Soviet Union developed the atomic bomb, it became clear that the centuries of Western military superiority over all other civilizations had ended, and that Eastern Europe now shared this claim to strength. The fearsome power of modern weapons and the intense East-West rivalry left many Westerners concerned that a new war could destroy their own civilization and that of most other parts of the world. At times, diplomatic processes seem to have escaped human control.

Yet the Western world itself remained free from war after 1945. Early cold war tensions, particularly over the new divisions of Germany, brought war scares. In 1948–1949 the Soviet Union blocked off the city of West Berlin, a western enclave within East Germany, and only a massive American airlift relieved the pressure on supplies. Colonial wars also involved the West. France lost a bitter war to retain its Indochinese possessions and then faced a long, ultimately unsuccessful struggle to keep Algeria. Finally, in 1949 the United States, with wider world interests now than Western Europe, became involved in a war in Korea and then, in the 1960s in a long and disheartening struggle in Vietnam, both against communist forces. These regional wars were important, of course, but the fact remains that even major threats of war within the West now receded, as at least for a time the West became one of the world's more internally peaceful civilizations.

A key ingredient of the West's new diplomatic environment involved explicit West European initiatives to set its own diplomatic house in order after 1945, with some American encouragement. Eager to prevent further nationalist wars, and also anxious to promote economic development, leading West European nations joined hands in economic cooperation. Initial moves to coordinate industrial policies led in 1958 to the formation of the European Economic Community, which provided substantial interchange across national boundaries. Although the Common Market, as it is called, ultimately broadened to include Britain, Ireland, Denmark, Greece, Spain, and Portugal, as well as the initial membership of West Germany, France, Italy, and the Low Countries, it did not become a single government. But it did develop common policies and a common bureaucracy to oversee economic relations and, to an extent, to coordinate other policies. Nationalist tensions receded to a lower point than ever before in modern European history. In 1993 the European Community created full tariff unity and planned further integration possibly involving a single currency and exchangeable citizenship rights.

More striking still were new economic and political trends. Particularly during the 1950s and 1960s, the doldrums of the interwar decades were reversed. Political tensions declined, while economic growth soared. Western society avoided major depressions, though there were years of slackening prosperity; most Western nations enjoyed a growth rate ranging from 2 percent to 8 percent per year. The West easily retained its lead over most other civilizations in terms of per capita prosperity, and indeed the gap between its wealth and that of many agricultural societies widened. Only Japan caught up in this regard. Within the West, mass affluence, attested by widespread ownership of cars, refrigerators, and the now-ubiquitous television set, reached unprecedented levels. The United States, whose population had achieved affluence earlier, found its prosperity rivaled by dynamic European countries such as West Germany and France.

Western economic development was spurred by widespread transformation of leadership after World War II. In Western Europe, men and women who had fought in resistance movements against Nazism vowed to avoid the errors of the past and to create a new society. The influence of the older aristocracy was further reduced. Training for West Europe's elite now broadened to recruit more talented people from worker and peasant families, as scholarship support for higher education increased. University education itself was revamped to focus on more technical subjects. A new generation of managers, with a new spirit and educational background, brought new dynamism to the West in various fields.

During the crucial years immediately after 1945, Western society also forged new political institutions. Carefully wrought democratic constitutions were developed in West Germany and Italy, providing more stable parliamentary institutions than ever before. France revived its parliamentary system after the years of Nazi occupation; in 1958 government instability in the face of the paralyzing colonial war in Algeria prompted the nationalist leader Charles de Gaulle to engineer a new constitution, providing for a strong but democratically elected presidency overseeing parliament. Spain, Portugal, and Greece installed new democratic systems in the 1970s. Democracy and relative political stability were encouraged by the virtual destruction of the radical right in politics, discredited by Nazi excesses and defeat in war. Most Western countries had a strong conservative party fully committed to the democratic system. On the left, while significant communist movements remained in a few countries, reformist socialist parties, also committed to the democratic process and to extensive personal liberties, won wide support outside North America. The communist minority itself declined by the 1980s. The new political spectrum thus provided a multiparty system, with leadership characteristically alternating between major parties, depending on the performance of the economy; but the spectrum was bounded by the commitment of most groups to the basic political process. Even communist parties in Western Europe relied mainly on election efforts, abandoning attempts at revolutionary agitation.

The political system was altered, finally, by the elaboration of more extensive welfare institutions. In France and Italy, coalition governments combining conservatives, socialists, and communists enacted new welfare programs between 1945 and 1948. These programs provided state-sponsored medical insurance, payments to large families, and greater regulation of working conditions. France and other countries also created more formal state economic planning, to guide in postwar recovery and then further industrial development. Between 1945 and 1951, Great Britain extended its welfare state under the leadership of the Labor party. The British welfare state featured an unusually elaborate program of socialized medicine, with the government paying most medical bills from tax revenues; it also entailed government housing programs and other measures. Most other Western nations extended their welfare and economic planning activities; Canada, for example, enacted a state-funded medical insurance program. Even the United States, which had a more restricted array of welfare programs than most other Western countries, initiated the Great Society measures of the 1960s, providing medical insurance for the indigent and elderly, expanding the social security system, and passing a number of laws to protect the rights of minorities and women.

The pattern of economic growth and political stability that took shape in the postwar West was disrupted in the late 1960s by a series of student protests, joined in the United States by civil rights demonstrations and rioting among urban blacks. Campus unrest at major American universities focused on the war in Vietnam, which many students regarded as futile and immoral. Young people in Europe and the United States also targeted the materialism of their societies, seeking more idealistic goals and greater justice. Student uprisings in France in 1968 created a near-revolution. By the early 1970s, new rights for students and other reforms, combined with police repression, ended the most intense student protests. But some ongoing political concerns, including feminism and environmental protection, entered the arena during the 1970s partly as an aftermath of the student explosion; and in some Western European countries a terrorist movement, focusing on political and business leaders, caused anxiety as well. Economic growth also slowed during the 1970s, partly because of rising energy costs; in the late 1970s and early 1980s, the Western world faced its greatest economic recession since the postwar recovery. New leadership sprang up within the British Conservative party and the United States Republican party, seeking to reduce the costs and coverage of the welfare state to spur new economic growth. Other political currents arose in other Western countries, including new rightist parties and "Green" environmentalist movements.

Key problems intensified in the 1990s. Global economic competition hit the West hard. In Europe, the result was substantial unemployment, up to 12 percent or more, as goods requiring less skilled labor now came from elsewhere. The United States faced similar pressures but created a larger number of low-paying jobs; here, the new trend involved growing inequalities in income, greater than in any other industrial society. All Western nations, amid economic pressure, had to reconsider welfare state expenditures, and most cut back; again, the United States, with a smaller system in the first place, reduced protections for the poor most systematically. Various political changes accompanied these developments: more zealous conservatism showed particularly in the United States. Liberal and socialist movements in Western Europe as well as in North America developed a more moderate stance, less wedded to welfare traditions. A few new protest currents surfaced: a racist, neofascist movement in France called the National Front, a surge of paramilitary groups in the United States on the far right.

Compared to the frenzy of the 1920s and 1930s, Western society after 1950 has been relatively free from traumatic events. Decolonization created tension; United States involvement in world diplomacy had produced a host of new concerns; the student movement of the late 1960s was an assertion that all was not well in the affluent society. Cushioned by the rapid rise in wealth, however, the Western world remained considerably freer from major upheavals than did most other civilizations in the postwar decades. Indeed, boredom itself became an issue, as observers worried that the welfare state created too much security, that political consensus proved so embracing that many people no longer bothered to vote. In Western Europe, periodic terrorism reflected the discontent of a small minority with the calm of the existing system, while in the United States, declining voter participation raised questions about the vigor of the political process. Had Western society achieved a new harmony, or were the postwar decades a period of deceiving tranquility before a new storm?

WESTERN POLITICAL INSTITUTIONS IN THE 20TH CENTURY

Two somewhat contradictory themes ran through the political development of Western society after 1900. On the one hand, the power of the state increased; on the other hand, a commitment to democratic and liberal values remained strong and, after 1945, gained ground.

HISTORY DEBATE

Convergence

The Western world split apart during the 1930s, between fascist and democratic systems. After 1945, however, European nations became more similar than ever (though not identical)—a phenomenon called *convergence*. Industrial growth picked up countries like Italy. The results of World War II eliminated some German peculiarities, such as a rabidly conservative aristocracy. The spread of democracy was obviously a convergent development. So were key social trends, like an aging population and new roles for women. Nationalism declined. Growing West European unity both reflected and furthered the convergence phenomenon.

Convergence also reduced some key differences between Europe and the United States. On the West European side, the elimination of the traditional peasantry and the final demise of the aristocracy, along with rapid economic growth, made social and economic structures more similar on the two sides of the North Atlantic. A prosperous Europe also opened to some of the consumer culture of the United States, providing a growing (if occasionally critical) market for American TV shows, fast foods, even a Euro-Disney. Because of new immigration, Europe also developed some racial tensions similar to those in the United States, though usually less severe. On the American side, the New Deal and World War II had created a stronger government, more like its European counterparts, though the United States did not develop quite such a full-service welfare state. Although American popular culture predominated, European contributions like the miniskirt and the Beatles moved easily across the Atlantic in the other direction.

Differences remained. The United States participated with Europe in more open sexuality, but the nation was more prudish; topless beaches, the norm in Europe, did not move west. American moralism also showed in an unusually intense antismoking crusade. The largest new distinction involved obvious differences in military policy. The United States, the world's greatest power, rapidly increased its peacetime army and its armaments expenditures—spending rose 300 percent in the 1950s alone. American policy, as a result, was more determined by military pressures than was true in Europe, which often boasted of pioneering in a civilian society. Correspondingly, Europe depended on American military protection while its own global military capacity steadily diminished.

Different reactions to the economic pressures of the 1990s also seemed to contradict trans-Atlantic convergence. Western Europe was more reluctant to dismantle the welfare state or to accept growing gaps between rich and poor, though it participated in both trends. Convergence might not be permanent.

The rising power of the state showed in both world wars. Governments in democratic nations such as Britain and the United States increased their regulation of economic activities, introducing rationing and allocation of labor. Governments mounted massive propaganda campaigns to win the passionate loyalty of citizens to the military effort; enemies were pictured as the epitome of evil; newspapers were censored and the new media of radio and motion pictures were used to further intense patriotism. The powers of wartime government helped inspire the totalitarian dictatorships of Nazi Germany (and also communist Russia). Nazism demonstrated that under stress, a major Western society could abandon liberal values in favor of a government dedicated to the destruction of all competing sources of power and to the manipulation of individual citizens through mass education and propaganda. Authoritarian governments in some other states, such as fascist Italy and, after 1936, a semi-fascist Spain, also used new police and propaganda powers to repress opposition.

More generally, the rise of the welfare state throughout most of the West after 1945 represented a major extension of government power. Government expansion under the New Deal greatly increased the importance of the American state, which was then extended by the growth of military spending from World War II until the end of the cold war. Throughout the West, governments assumed the responsibility for providing some coverage of health care costs, adequate working conditions, and protection against dire poverty. The United States, more fully committed to older liberal values that relied on individual initiative and opportunity, stood slightly apart in this movement, but even here, by the 1970s, 21 percent of total tax income went for social welfare payments. Expanding

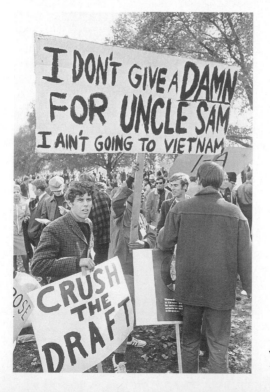

Youth antiwar protest: Washington, D.C., 1967.

welfare functions and growing involvement in economic planning obviously broadened the role of the state in individual lives. Taxes increased, and so did regulation of how employers could hire and fire, what crops farmers could plant, where poor people could live. Government bureaucracies expanded steadily.

The rise of the state has been balanced, however, outside of the period of the fascist regimes, by continued devotion to a multiparty democracy and substantial freedoms of speech, press, religion, and assembly. The West has developed a mixed system, in which important governmental authority has combined with private enterprise. In the economy, for example, state planning has left the operation of most businesses in private hands. West European countries did nationalize some economic sectors, such as railroads and mines. The nationalization movement took place primarily in the period of recovery after World War II, but a French socialist regime extended nationalization again in the early 1980s. Even here, however, most businesses have operated through private decision-making within frameworks partly established by government.

The extension of liberal, democratic systems after 1945 showed the continuing strength of parliamentary institutions in Western political culture. West Germany established a far more solid democracy than it had managed in the 1920s. Political debate has centered on significant disagreements between conservatives and socialists about the extent of the welfare state or about diplomatic policy; but it has not called the regime into question. While conservatives dominated German politics through most of the 1950s and 1960s, and again in the 1980s and early 1990s, socialist leadership took power peacefully at a number of points. The 1989 collapse of the Soviet empire brought about German unification in 1991, partly because of extensive East German demands for democracy. By the mid–1980s the Western world was more fully characterized by a single political system—liberal democracy—than at any time since the decline of feudalism. From Australia and New Zealand through North America to Western Europe, a tension between multiparty rivalry and personal freedom on the one hand, and powerful state planning, taxation, and welfare devices on the other, has constituted the core of modern politics. Alternative political themes such as fascism and even Marxism have declined.

The rise of strong-state democracy was accompanied by the decline of classic diplomatic and military issues in Europe. Old antagonisms between France and Germany or Britain and the continent declined. So did commitments to imperialism. While West European governments participated in the Cold War, military issues and expenditures receded. United States military concerns, however, increased, as did American diplomatic influence in European affairs—even after the Cold War had ended, the United States continued to take a lead in new issues such as the strife in the former Yugoslavia. Tensions between the United States and Western Europe occurred at times, particularly during surges of French nationalism or unusual American high-handedness, but they were rarely acute—never reaching the pitch of the older nationalist rivalries within the West.

CONTEMPORARY WESTERN CULTURE

Western culture continued to display great vitality during the 20th century, though at times it seemed to lack coherence. Artists and composers stressed stylistic innovation, as against older traditions and even the efforts of the previous generation. Scientific work flourished, as the West remained the center of most fundamental inquiry in the theoretical sciences. But complex discoveries, such as the principle of relativity in physics, qualified older ideas that nature can be captured in a few sweeping scientific laws. And the sheer specialization of scientific research removed much of it from ready public understanding. Because no unifying assumptions represent the essence of formal intellectual activity in the contemporary West, neutral terms like "modern" or "postmodern" are used even in the artistic field. Disciplines that once provided an intellectual overview, such as philosophy, declined in the 20th century or were transformed into specialized research fields; many philosophers, for example, turned to the scientific study of language, rather than writing basic statements about the nature of life and of the universe. And while work in theology continued, among both Catholic and Protestant thinkers, it no longer commanded center stage in intellectual life. No emphasis was placed on an integrated approach, no agreement was reached on what constitutes an essential understanding of human endeavor.

The dynamism of scientific research has formed the clearest central thread in Western culture after 1900. Growing science faculties commanded greatest prestige in the expanding universities; individual scientists made striking discoveries, while a veritable army of researchers cranked out more specific findings than scientists had ever before produced; and the wider public continued to maintain a faith that science held the keys to understanding nature and society and to improving technology and human life. Finally, while scientific discoveries have varied widely, a belief in a central scientific method persists: form a rational hypothesis, test through experiment or observation, and emerge with a generalization that will show regularities in physical behaviors and thus provide human reason with a means of systematizing and even predicting such behaviors. No other approach to understanding in Western culture has had such power or widespread adherence.

The first scientific breakthrough of the 20th century took shape with the discovery of the behavior of atomic particles. Experiments with X-rays and uranium produced the knowledge of electrons and the nucleus of the atom. At about the same time, by 1905, the work of Albert Einstein in Berlin transformed the old idea, central to Newtonian physics, of physical matter as a solid essence that behaved in absolutely uniform ways. According to Einstein's theory of relativity, space and time are not absolutes but are always relative to the observer measuring them. Einstein used time as a fourth dimension to explain behaviors of light and planetary motion that had been misstated in Newtonian physics. Radiation and other electronic activity are not regular, but occur in discontinuous waves. Increasingly complex mathematics, involving the abstract language of differential equations, was essential in understanding the actual behavior both of planetary bodies and of particles within the atom. By the 1930s, physicists began to experiment with bombarding basic matter with neutrons, particles that carry no electric charge; this work was to culminate during World War II in the development of the atomic bomb. Research in physics continued after World War II with a combination of increasingly sophisticated observation, made possible by improved telescopes and then lasers and space satellites, and the complex mathematical theories facilitated by the theory of relativity. Astronomers made substantial progress in identifying additional galaxies and other phenomena in space; the debate also continued about the nature of matter.

Breakthroughs in biology have primarily involved genetics. The identification, in the 1860s, of principles of the inheritance of characteristics received wide attention only after

1900. By the 1920s, researchers who used the increasingly familiar fruit fly had exact rules for genetic transmission. Discovery in the 1940s by British and American scientists of the structure of the basic genetic unit, the famous "double helix" pattern of deoxyribonucleic acid (DNA), advanced the understanding of how genetic information is transmitted and how it can be altered.

Biologists also produced major improvements in health care. New drugs, beginning with penicillin in 1928, revolutionized the treatment of common diseases, while immunization virtually eliminated scourges such as diphtheria. Discovery of hormonal behavior, leading in the 1920s to the science of endocrinology, also had widespread medical applicability. Genetics itself, by the 1970s, gave rise to a host of industries that utilized scientific principles to produce new medicines, seeds, and pesticides.

But the new science has also had some troubling features, even apart from its use in the weapons of destruction or its sheer complexity. The physical world is no longer considered to be neatly regulated, as it had been by Newtonian physics. Genetics made it clear that evolution proceeded by a series of random accidents, not through any consistent pattern. Use of the rational, scientific method thus has not produced the kind of simple world view that it had a century or so before, and the resultant uncertainties have influenced some artists in their attempts to convey an irrational, relativist universe. Yet, for most people in the West the belief in progress, defined both as better technology and as rational penetration of nature, largely persists.

The rational method, broadly conceived, also advanced in the social sciences from 1900 onward. The German sociologist Max Weber worked to characterize general features of institutions such as bureaucracies, for analysis and comparison. Many sociologists promulgated theories of human society, or aspects of it such as the behavior of elites, on the assumption that rationally conceived models captured the essential reality of human affairs. In economics, quantitative models of economic cycles or business behavior have increasingly gained ground. Work by the British economist John Keynes, stressing the importance of government spending to compensate for loss of purchasing power during a depression, played a great role in the policies of the American New Deal and efforts by European planners to control the economic cycles after World War II.

Like the sciences, the social sciences became increasingly diverse and specialized. Also like the sciences, many social scientists sought practical applications for their work. Psychologists became involved, for example, not only in dealing with mental illness but in trying to promote greater work efficiency. Governments called on economic forecasting. Social science thus added to the impression of an explosion of rationally generated and useful knowledge, even when research pointed to deterministic or irrational aspects of human affairs. Most leading social scientists continued to emphasize the quest for consistency in human and social behavior. After World War II the increasing use of mathematical models and laboratory experiments in the social sciences enhanced this emphasis.

Most 20th-century artists, concerned with capturing the world through impressions rather than through reason or the confinements of literal reality, worked against the grain of science and social science. Painting became increasingly nonrepresentational. The cubist movement, headed by Pablo Picasso, rendered familiar objects as geometrical shapes; and after cubism, modern art moved even further from normal perception, stressing purely geometrical design or wild swirls of color. The focus was on mood, the individual reaction of viewers to the individual reality of the artist. Musical composition involved

This example of the cubist style is by Pablo Picasso, the leading figure in 20th-century modern art, born in Spain and working primarily in France. The painting, *Violin and Grapes,* (Ceret et Sorgues) Spring-Summer 1912. Oil on canvas, 20 × 24 (50.6 × 61 cm). (The Museum of Modern Art, New York. Mrs. David M. Levy Bequest. Photograph © 1998 The Museum of Modern Art)

the use of dissonance and experimentation with new scales; after World War II, a growing interest in electronic instrumentation added to this diversity. Because writers are, in fact, constrained by words, their stylistic innovation was generally less extensive. But in poetry the use of unfamiliar forms, ungrammatical constructions, and sweeping imagery continued the movement of the later 19th century. Playwrights experimented with new types of staging and unconfined dramas, often seeking to involve the audience in direct participation. In literature the novel remained dominant, but it turned toward the exploration of moods and personalities, rather than the portrayal of objective events or clear story lines. A vast gulf grew between the scientific approach and the artistic framework as to how reality can be captured and, to an extent, what constitutes reality.

Many people ignored the leading modern artists and writers, in favor of more commercial artistic productions and popular stories. The gap that had opened earlier, between avant-garde art and public taste, generally continued. Some politicians, including Adolf Hitler, campaigned against what they saw as the decadence and immorality of modern art, urging a return to more traditional styles. And certainly art did not hold its own against the growing prestige of science.

Yet the artistic vision was not simply a preoccupation of artists themselves. Designs and sculptures based on abstract art began to grace public places from the 1920s onward; furnishings and films also reflected the modernist themes. Most revealing of a blend between art, modern technology, and public taste was the development of a characteristic 20th-century architectural style, the "modern" or "international" style. Use of new materials, such as reinforced concrete and massive sheets of glass, allowed the abandonment of much that was traditional in architecture. Need for new kinds of buildings, particularly for office use, and the growing cost of urban space also encouraged the introduction of new forms such as the skyscraper, pioneered in the United States. In general, the modern style of architecture sought to develop individually distinct buildings—sharing the goal of modern art to defy conventional taste and cultivate the unique—while conveying a sense of space and freedom from natural constraints. Soaring structures, free-floating columns, new combinations of angles and curves were features that described leading Western buildings from 1900 onward. Following World War II, when reconstruction in Europe and the expansion of new centers in the U.S. west and southwest provided massive opportunities for building, the face of urban space in Western society was greatly transformed.

There were a few unifying themes between the artistic and the scientific approaches. A constant quest for the new was one feature, as artists sought new styles, scientists new discoveries. Furthermore, Western culture in the 20th century, both in art and in science, became increasingly secular. Individual artists, writers, and scientists might proclaim religious faith, but the churches long since lost control over basic style or content. In Western Europe, despite an important reform movement within the Catholic church that cut down traditional ceremonies in favor of more direct contact between priest and worshippers, religion played a minor role in both formal and popular culture. Regular church attendance tended to be of interest only to a minority—5 percent of the British population, for example, by the 1970s. In the United States, religion maintained a greater hold, and both church attendance and popular belief remained at much higher levels than elsewhere in Western society. The United States also saw, both in the 1920s and again after World War II, a greater variety of popular revival movements and attempts to use religion to maintain or restore traditional values. Here was clear indication that, for some individuals, neither the artistic nor the scientific approach to understanding was fully satisfactory—and this became yet another ingredient in the cultural diversity and tension of Western society.

Western culture was not a monopoly of European civilization in the 20th century. Western art forms, particularly in architecture, spread widely, because of their practicality and their currency in what remained a highly influential society. The achievements of Western science, at least those related to technology and medicine, often had to be taken into account by societies seeking their own industrial development. Western arts and sciences were, by the same token, greatly enriched by many practitioners from other cultures—by Japanese artists, for example, or Indian medical researchers and computer scientists. Elements of Western culture thus became international, and we will have to trace their interweaving into a number of other civilizations. Yet no other culture, not even the Japanese, created quite the same balance between an overwhelming interest in science and a frenzied concern for stylistic innovation and individual expression in the arts.

ECONOMY AND SOCIETY

During the 20th century, rapid transformation characterized the economy and social organization of Western civilization. By the latter part of the century, some of the changes seemed almost as fundamental as those that had ushered in the industrial revolution two centuries before. The recurrent shifts in technology, economic organization, and social structure in Western industrial society had significant effects on the rest of the world as well, making it hard for industrializing nations to "catch up" to Western levels.

To begin with, economic change involved new products. During the first decades of the century, synthetic textile fibers, such as rayon and nylon, introduced variety into the clothing industry. Radios and, by the 1930s, early television brought instant entertainment and news into homes across the land (see Table 26.1). The automobile, though invented before 1900, increasingly became a consumer staple, first in the United States and then, after World War II, in Western Europe.

Economic change involved, in addition, new forms of organization. The growing role of the state in formal planning was one aspect of this. In the private sector corporate business became increasingly common, furnishing giant companies with extensive funds for widespread investment. Older family enterprises declined further. By the 1920s and again after World War II, many corporations established an international base of operations. U.S. firms took the lead here, for the extensive American market provided both capital and experience in dealing with large markets. But a number of European-based firms became multinational as well. They had marketing and supply offices, and production subsidiaries, on several continents. In domestic markets and to an extent internationally, concentration of ownership among small numbers of corporations was the rule. A multitude of aspiring automobile producers before World War I thus settled into a handful of big producers in most Western countries between the wars, and further concentration, including international operations, occurred after World War II. As one result, the Ford Motor Company manufactured cars in Britain and Germany, while German and French automakers stepped up operations in the United States, Mexico, and Brazil.

Agriculture experienced an organizational revolution of its own, particularly after World War II. In Western Europe, peasant farming gave way to cooperative links for purchases and sales; most small landholders acquired new market skills as well as modern

TABLE 26.1 *Television Ownership in 1957 and 1965*

Country	1957	1965
France	683,000	6,489,000
Germany	798,586	11,379,000
Italy	367,000	6,044,542
Netherlands	239,000	2,113,000
Sweden	75,817	2,110,584

Sources: The Europa Year Book 1959 (London, 1959) and *The Europa Year Book 1967*, vol. I (London, 1967).

equipment, making them more like rural business executives than peasants. In the United States, Canada, and Australia, great concentrations of land operation, called agribusiness, arose after 1950, as purely family farms became increasingly marginal. Organizational change plus improved machinery, seeds, and fertilizers steadily raised agricultural productivity in the Western world, though some worried about a decline in the actual quality of foods and also about growing environmental damage from the chemical spraying and other measures designed to maximize production.

Refinements in organization also affected the structure of work. Early in the 20th century, U.S. firms took the lead in developing ways to speed up the pace of manufacturing by defining and supervising worker tasks more closely. By 1910, early forms of the assembly line system were in effect, pioneered at Henry Ford's automobile plant. Such operations had workers doing repetitive tasks with a minimum of motion and thought, becoming as much like the machines they worked with as was humanly possible. After World War II, assembly line procedures were modified by the use of more automated equipment, with machines themselves—including, by the early 1980s, robots—performing some of the most routine functions.

Economic change meant, as it had since industrialization began, new technologies. Growing use of the internal combustion engine in manufacturing and transport, and growing use of petroleum instead of coal for fuel, marked important steps early in the century. Coal mining, long a staple of Western industrialization, declined, and some regions, particularly Western Europe, became dependent on fuel imports where their own oil holdings were small. Faster and more mechanized equipment steadily increased manufacturing productivity. Early in the century the production of machines was revolutionized by the use of automatic riveters, drills, and other equipment that provided the technological basis for an assembly line operation in what had been a craft industry. Production of chemicals and the ubiquitous plastics required automated procedures for transporting, mixing, and molding ingredients. After World War II a technological revolution took shape in communications and information storage as well, with the introduction of computers; in the 1970s the development of the microchip made computers smaller and more flexible, and increased the speed and volume of information flow, while displacing conventional storage operations such as manual filing.

The economic advance of Western society was not, of course, without setbacks. During the decade of the depression, many wondered if the economy could ever recover its former vitality. The two world wars caused immense loss and dislocation. The economic slowdowns of the late 1970s and the early 1980s, with rising rates of unemployment and fierce foreign competition particularly from East Asia, raised anxieties anew. In the 1990s global competition produced high unemployment in Western Europe while income inequality increased in the United States. Furthermore, not all Western nations fared equally well in the economic development process; previous leaders such as Great Britain fell behind. Australia and Canada produced large quantities of foods and minerals for export, which made them unusually dependent on the prosperity of more fully industrial centers like Japan or the United States, though they maintained considerable industry of their own.

Nevertheless, for the century as a whole the theme of continued economic vitality and change remains valid. Western society was quick to recover from wartime destruction, for example, bouncing back rapidly from the bombings of World War II, a sign that basic industrial capacity and know-how provided considerable resilience once they were firmly established.

Yet another area in which economic change had an impact was the class structure of Western society. Basic division between middle class and working class continued. But the middle class was defined increasingly by its managerial skills and education, rather than by property ownership; and the working class became less distinctive as its affluence increased. In the United States, indeed, the majority of workers identified themselves as middle class, on the basis of earnings. Furthermore, increased mobility, particularly in the decades after World War II, blurred class lines somewhat. Using new educational opportunities, a number of people from working-class backgrounds entered corporate upper management and the top levels of government service, though they still formed a minority. Interestingly, social mobility in Western Europe soon matched that of the newer nations of the Western world, such as the United States, despite a more explicit class structure.

The greatest change in social structure, however, was the rise of workers in the service sector of the economy. The percentage of farmers, already small, dropped further. But by the 1920s the number of factory workers began to stabilize as well, as production increased mainly through continuing mechanization. By the 1950s, it was clear that service work—that is, dealing with people and paper rather than producing goods—was the wave of the future. Restaurant workers, health-care workers from hospital janitors to doctors, teachers, recreation workers—all rapidly expanded in number, as did the secretaries and salespeople needed in a bureaucratized, consumer-oriented economy. By the 1970s over half of all workers in Western society were in the service sector.

Finally, again particularly after 1945, a new wave of unskilled workers entered the labor force, many of them immigrants. Western Europe drew hundreds of thousands of workers from the Middle East, North Africa, the West Indies, and Asia; immigration to the United States reached higher levels than ever before, drawing mainly from East Asia and Latin America. Not all the newcomers were unskilled, but many filled the ranks of agricultural laborers, maintenance workers, fast-food attendants, and other slots where pay was low and rates of unemployment often high. Many urban blacks in the United States also fit into this growing category, which often seemed tragically isolated from the prosperity and security of most sectors of Western society.

Like social structure, family life changed considerably in the 20th century without being totally transformed. Birth rates remained relatively low. Western society experienced an increase in birth rates from the late 1940s until the early 1960s—the famous baby boom. The boom was caused by growing prosperity, after many families had delayed births during the depression, and in some cases in response to government aid to families. But even the baby boom, while it severely pressed schools, day-care facilities, and so on, produced relatively modest birth rates. And after 1963 the baby boom ended, with birth rates again dropping rapidly. Further decreases in death rates for most age groups, due to improved medicine and new interest in exercise and fitness, have maintained the basic population pattern of the later 19th century: low birth rates and low death rates adding up to a stable or slightly rising population and a growing sector of older people. The increase in numbers of the elderly, while a significant burden on social security systems, has had only limited impact on families, as most older people in the Western world now live apart from younger relatives—a major change in residential patterns that began in the 1920s.

Western family life continued to emphasize the importance of intense emotional ties, between spouses and between parents and children, along with a new emphasis on sexual satisfaction before and during marriage. The role of the family in recreational activities increased. The annual family vacation became a standard experience as work time was shortened. After 1945, the advent of television made the home an attractive place to spend leisure hours.

But while family functions and family demography displayed striking continuities with the past, though with some interesting new twists, the roles of family members were revolutionized by new patterns of women's work. During World War I, with many men away in battle, women entered the labor force in vast numbers. This movement was largely cut off in the 1920s. But in World War II, women returned to the factories and offices, and after the war they tended to remain there. Increasing numbers of women in Western Europe and North America, now approximately as well educated as men, with relatively few children to care for, and in a society where earnings bring satisfaction and power, sought identity and income through work. At the same time the rise of service occupations deemed suitable for women facilitated the movement of women into the labor force, while increased expectations—a desire for better housing or travel or education—encouraged women to work. In all Western countries women's participation in the labor force rose steadily, reaching roughly 45 percent of the total by the late 1970s. Women of all social classes were now working, and they were doing so after marriage and even during active motherhood. Their earnings lagged behind those of men, and in response to this, an active feminist movement seeking fuller equality sprang up by the 1960s. But the change in work patterns easily reversed the earlier trends of Western industrial society, in which women had been encouraged to concentrate on family life.

Women's work fostered greater equality in family decision-making. But while the authoritarian position of husbands declined, new roles for women brought great confusion as well, for all parties concerned. Household work was not always equally shared by men, even when women found their family time decreased. Child care was another key issue. Increasing numbers of children, particularly in Western Europe, were raised in part in day-care centers, one of the new functions of the welfare state. But worry persisted about the quality of children's upbringing, as older values of maternal nurturing changed less rapidly than mothers' activities did. Many working mothers thus professed to believe that mothers, at least of young children, should not work.

Tensions of this sort easily fed concern about the family itself, a theme already raised during the industrial revolution. Many people complained about changes in family roles, claiming that children were receiving too little adult supervision and spending too much time in front of television sets. Certainly, the Western family became more unstable. Divorce rates rose during most decades of the 20th century, with the United States leading the way. By the 1970s, one marriage in two in the United States, and one in three in Great Britain, ended in divorce. The fact that changing laws made divorce easier to obtain was merely a symptom of a growing tension between individual fulfillment and continued interest in family ties. The family has survived in the West, and in many ways adapted to new functions. One of the reasons for rising divorce rates has indeed been the high expectations Western people have about the family, as they seek love, sexual pleasure, and freedom from dispute. But there is no question that the family often failed, and that its contradictions occasioned great anxiety in the 20th-century West.

Along with social structure and family, pleasure seeking became an important theme of Western society in the 20th century, most obviously during the 1920s and again in the affluent era following World War II. With growing prosperity and shorter working hours—by the 1940s most people worked an eight-hour day—leisure interests exploded. Mass media, including popular novels as well as movies, radio, and television, brought escapist entertainment to the millions. Professional sports commanded growing attention, particularly soccer in Western Europe and football and baseball in the United States. Sex also won more open public interest than was the case during the 19th century. Birth control remained an essential consideration, but it was provided increasingly by artificial devices, not abstinence. And a society concerned with pleasure and with consumption of goods found sex a vital condiment. More revealing fashions, particularly for women; more open use of sexual themes in films and on television; and manuals devoted to teaching methods of greater sexual pleasure all marked this new chapter in Western history. Whether people actually gained greater sexual pleasure than before is open to question, but there was no doubt of their interest. Sex or sexual allusions became a vital part of having fun and of selling products. To some observers, indeed, sports and sex seem to take the place that religion had once held in popular Western culture.

The changes in Western society during the 20th century—including technological advances as well as setbacks like the depression—caused considerable social tension. Burgeoning unionization and rising rates of strikes into the early 1950s expressed class conflict, as workers reacted to automation and the power of their middle-class bosses. But with growing affluence and the rise of the service sector, where unionizing came harder,

Modern leisure: bathers at Coney Island beach and amusement park; New York, 1952.

strikes and unions receded somewhat. Other protest movements, including the student risings in the 1960s and feminism, reflected social change, including discontents within the family. Overall, however, collective protest did not surge forward in the West. But there were also more individualized signs of distress. Rates of violent crime went up in Western society after World War II, initially because of the dislocation of war itself but then as a result of new conflicts among youth and also among racial minorities. The United States had the highest per capita crime rates, but Western Europe faced an upward trend as well. Growing use of drugs was also seen as a reaction to boredom and lack of meaning in Western life.

For Western society, like Western politics and art, seemed enmeshed in a fundamental contradiction in the 20th century. On the one hand, the society encouraged individualism. Children were raised to think of themselves as individuals, to rise above their parents' achievements if possible, to adjust to new work opportunities. Leisure interests appealed to individual pleasure seeking. But individualism was severely curtailed by the growing bureaucratization of society. Most jobs involved routine activities, controlled by an elaborate supervisory apparatus; individual initiative counted for little, not only in factories but in offices of giant corporations. Leisure, appealing to individual self-expression in one sense, generally meant mass, commercially manipulated outlets for all but a handful of venturesome souls. By the 1950s television watching had become far and away the leading interest of Western peoples, and most television fare was deliberately standardized. Individualism also came in conflict with a continued devotion to family bonds, as we have seen. Ironically, individualism and its outlets often made collective protest against bureaucratization and routine extremely difficult.

To critics, inside Western society and without, late–20th-century Western society seemed badly confused. Poverty and job boredom coexisted with affluence and continued appeals to the essential value of work. Youth protest—including defiant costumes and pulsating rock music—family instability, and crime might be signs of a fatally flawed society. Rising rates of suicide and an increasing incidence of mental illness were other troubling symptoms. At the least, Western society continued to display the strains of change. People displaced by change or troubled by defiance of older values, as well as people caught up in new styles but disappointed by their results, showed the tensions of adjusting to a society still in rapid flux.

CONCLUSION: A POSTINDUSTRIAL AGE?

Many people in Western society came to believe that they were facing greater changes than ever before, whether for better or for worse. By the late 1960s a new concept of a "postindustrial" society took shape both in Western Europe and in North America. The idea was that Western society was leading in a transformation as fundamental as the industrial revolution had been. The rise of a service economy, according to this argument, promised as many shifts as the rise of an industrial economy had done. Control of knowledge, rather than control of goods, would be the key to the postindustrial social structure. Technology would allow expansion of factory production with a shrinking labor force, and attention would shift to the generation and control of information. The advent of new technology, particularly the computer, supported the postindustrial concept, by applying to knowledge transmission the same potential technological revolution that the steam engine had brought to manufacturing.

Changes in the role of women paralleled the postindustrial concept, and some observers began to talk of a postindustrial family in which two equal spouses would pool their earnings in a high-consumption life style. Postindustrial cities would increasingly become entertainment centers, as most work could now be decentralized in suburbs, linked by the omnipresent computer. Postindustrial politics were less clearly defined, though some commentators noted that the old party structure might loosen as new, service-sector voters sought issues more appropriate to their interests. The rise of environmental and feminist concerns that cut across older political alignments might thus prove an opening wedge to an unpredictable political future for the West.

The postindustrial society was not an established fact, of course, even by the late 1990s. Important continuities with earlier social forms, including political values and cultural directions, suggest that new technologies might modify rather than revolutionize Western industrial society. It is clear, however, that Western society has taken on important new characteristics, ranging from age brackets to occupational structure, that differentiate it from the initial industrial patterns generated in the 19th century. And this fact, even if more modest than the visions of some of the postindustrial forecasters, raises a vital question for the West and the world: How would a rapidly changing, advanced industrial society fit in a world that has yet fully to industrialize? How could the concerns of an affluent, urban, fad-conscious Westerner coexist with the values of the world's peasant majority?

SUGGESTED READINGS

Important overviews of recent European history are: Walter Laqueur, *Europe Since Hitler* (1982); D. A. Low, *Eclipse of Empire* (1991); Helen Wallace et al., *Policy-Making in the European Community* (1983); Alfred Grosser, *The Western Alliance* (1982); and R. Paxton, *Europe in the 20th Century*, 2nd ed. (1985). Some excellent national interpretations provide vital coverage of events since 1945 in key areas of Europe. See A. F. Havighurst, *Twentieth-Century Britain* (1982), and John Ardagh, *France in the 1980s* (1982). Volker Berghahn, *Modern Germany: Society, Economy and Politics in the 20th Century* (1983), is also useful. On post-World War II social and economic trends, see: C. Kindleberger, *Europe's Postwar Growth* (1967); V. Bogdanor and R. Skidelsky, eds., *The Age of Affluence* (1970); R. Dahrendorf, ed., *Europe's Economy in Crisis* (1982); and Peter Stearns and Herrick Chapman, *European Society in Upheaval*, 3rd ed. (1991). On the welfare state, see Stephen Cohen, *Modern Capitalist Planning: The French Model* (1977), and E. S. Einhorn and J. Logue, *Welfare States in Hard Times* (1982). On the relevant Commonwealth nations, see: Charles Doran, *Forgotten Partnership: U.S.-Canada Relations Today* (1983); S. M. Lipset, *American Exceptionalism: A Double Edged Sword* (1995) compares Canada and the United States; Edward McWhinney, *Canada and the Constitution, 1979–1982* (1982); and Stephen Graubard, ed., *Australia: Terra Incognita?* (1985). On the United States in the cold war decades, see: Walter LaFeber, *America, Russia and the Cold War, 1945–1980*, 4th ed. (1980); Thomas Patterson, *On Every Front: The Making of the Cold War* (1979); David Oshinsky, *A Conspiracy So Immense: The World of Joe McCarthy* (1983); Richard Polenberg, *One Nation Divisible: Class, Race and Ethnicity in the United States Since 1938* (1980); Harvard Sitkoff, *The Struggle for Black Equality, 1954–1980* (1981); and William Chafe, *The American Woman: Her Changing Social, Economic and Political Roles* (1972).

CHAPTER 27

Eastern European Civilization

Focal Points

The Russian revolution and its aftermath dominate Eastern European history in the 20th century. What caused the revolution? What were the principal changes it brought to Russia? What were the results of Russian power over the rest of Eastern Europe after World War II? How did communist society relate to earlier traditions in Eastern Europe? What changes resembled trends occurring within Western Europe and the United States? Why did the Soviet system fall apart in the 1980s and early 1990s? Based on current conditions and prior history, what is the future of this region likely to be?

NEW POWER FOR A NEW RUSSIA

During the 20th century, Russia, while experiencing many of the events that also rocked the West, developed a distinctive kind of industrial society under a communist system. This society reflected earlier Russian traditions and the massive innovations produced by the revolution of 1917. Until the 1940s, the smaller nations of Eastern Europe stood apart from this system, but as the Soviet Union extended its military influence, they too were brought under a communist economic and political framework. The result was considerable unity but also significant tensions in East European civilization as a whole. Then in the late 1980s the whole communist system split apart, within Russia as well as its empire.

The fundamental transformation in Russian society in the 20th century came through the completion of industrialization and the creation of a new social structure, freed from traditional aristocratic control and supported by mass education. The communist regime installed in 1917 was an instrument of change. Revolution itself resulted from the conflicts of a society in which population pressure, new political aspirations, and the early stages of Russian industrialization challenged older social and political forms without reforming them. As in France in the 18th century and China and other countries in the 20th century, massive revolution was essential in responding to the initial forces of change and in opening the way for further shifts. But the Russian Revolution did not alter every facet of society—no revolution does. The new Soviet political system, though vastly different from tsarist times, preserved the authoritarian tradition in Russian life, including many specific institutions such as the secret police. An expansionist foreign policy continued as well, though shaped by the results of two world wars. Russia's expansionism, combined with its new industrial strength, catapulted the country into superpower position, along with the United States, after 1945. Russia also preserved its longstanding ambivalence regarding Western culture, at once seeking to imitate features of the West and trying to avoid its contagion in the name of distinctive East European values. Thus, though science and a secular outlook gained ground in Russia, bringing it closer to modern Western culture in many respects, deliberate efforts to avoid Western artistic and popular cultural styles created divisions between the two civilizations. The events of 1989–1991 reopened the relationship to the West, redefining yet again the question of Russia's identity.

THE RUSSIAN REVOLUTION

The trigger to Russia's 1917 revolution was its suffering during World War I. Russian forces encountered many defeats, particularly at the hands of the better-equipped German armies, and civilian conditions deteriorated dreadfully as the country sought to sustain the war effort. Food shortages and high prices spurred massive discontent. But the basic problems ran deeper. The government had refused to provide meaningful political rights, as the parliament (Duma) remained a hollow shell. The tsar Nicholas II was both unintelligent and stubborn, and surrounded himself with corrupt advisors who weakened the regime's reputation. Urban workers formed the clearest revolutionary class, as they were subjected to harsh conditions in the early industrial factories that intensified the dissatisfactions they had inherited from their peasant background. But middle-class liberals and the peasantry had grievances of their own, and a variety of revolutionary movements and factions, though mostly operating illegally, were eager to channel any and all discontent. In essence, Russia constituted a traditional rural society being hurried into the industrial age at a dizzying pace, with an unresponsive political system—the formula for 20th-century revolution.

In March 1917, strikes and food riots broke out in Russia's capital, and they quickly assumed revolutionary proportions, calling not just for material aid but for a new political regime. A council of workers, called a "soviet," took over the city government and arrested the tsar's ministers. The tsar abdicated, thus ending the long period of imperial control. For eight months a liberal provisional government struggled to rule the country. But liberalism was not deeply rooted in Russia, if only because of the small middle class, and the regime also made the mistake of trying to continue the war effort. Nor were liberals ready to grant massive land reforms, for they respected existing private property and thus disappointed the peasantry. So a second revolution took place in November (October, by the Russian calendar), which soon brought the radical wing of the Communist party—the Bolsheviks—and their dynamic leader—Vladimir Ilyich Ulyanov, known as Lenin—to power.

The Bolsheviks formed one of the smaller revolutionary forces in Russia, but they had the advantage of tight organization and a coherent plan of action. They also had, in Lenin, one of the great revolutionary organizers of all time. Though in exile during most of the early years of the 20th century, Lenin had hammered out a distinctive version of

Marxist theory, arguing that a country like Russia, even though not fully industrialized, could have a working-class revolution on the basis of a well-organized vanguard of the proletariat. This vanguard would operate in the proletariat's name, initially as a dictatorial force. Revolution was further possible, according to Lenin, because international capitalism had extended so widely in the world: here was a powerful statement in the age of imperialism, facilitating Marxist movements not just against native capitalism, but against Western domination as well. Lenin built a cadre of trained, professional revolutionaries under his leadership. He dominated other Marxists, many of whom believed that Russia must first pass through a middle-class phase; and he outmaneuvered other radical groups as well. His organization became known as the Bolsheviks, or "majority," even though they were in fact outnumbered. His most formidable opponent was the Social Revolutionary party, which had anarchist roots and won wide appeal among the peasantry by arguing for the primary importance of land reform. During the early months of the revolution, Lenin also worked for peasant support, pressing for state control of all the land, and he gained growing influence among urban workers by backing their spontaneous revolutionary councils, the soviets. Above all, Lenin surpassed his rivals by calling for radical revolution immediately, rather than taking the cautious approach that most others advocated. As popular discontent persisted, with urban strikes and rural riots, Lenin's firm position won growing prestige. By October, Lenin had a majority in the leading urban soviets. On November 7, Bolshevik leaders coordinated a seizure of power throughout the capital city, and a national Congress of Soviets set up a Council of People's Commissars, headed by Lenin, to govern the state.

Bitter struggles remained after the Bolshevik seizure of power, however. Popular elections produced a majority for the Social Revolutionary group, but Lenin pressed this party to dissolve, concluding that "the people voted for a party which no longer existed." The assembly was shut down, and the Bolshevik-dominated Congress of Soviets took its place; Russia was to have no Western-style, multiparty system. A greater problem was posed by massive resistance in various parts of the country. The Bolsheviks had only a vague notion of what to do after power was obtained. They ended the war effort, signing a humiliating peace treaty with Germany that cost considerable territory. And they redistributed land to the peasantry. Gradually, they also nationalized basic industry under the Council of People's Commissars. But tsarist generals fought the new regime in many regions, backed at points by troops from Japan, France, Britain, and the United States, all appalled at the radical regime that ruled Russia. Civil war raged for three years, until the communists managed to construct a powerful Red army of their own and win widespread popular support against foreign intervention. Internal opposition, including competing revolutionary leaders, was gradually crushed, with numerous executions. Lenin also found it necessary to curry popular favor by issuing a New Economic Policy in 1921, which promised greater freedom for small businesses and peasant agriculture than the Bolsheviks had intended. Under this temporary policy, food production began to recover after years of widespread famine, and the regime gained time to prepare the more permanent policies of the communist system.

By 1923, the Bolshevik revolution was an accomplished fact. A new constitution set up a federal system of socialist republics, which gave minority nationalities some sense of freedom while preserving the dominance of ethnic Russians. The new nation was known as the Union of Soviet Socialist Republics, but firm Communist party control over the

Parade of the Red army, Moscow, soon after the revolution.

state governments, and centralization of all basic decisions in the new capital of Moscow (moved from St. Petersburg—now named Leningrad—to provide a more Russian, less Western tone to the revolutionary state), formed the basis of an authoritarian rule more effective than the tsarist regime had ever been. The revolutionaries also began to concentrate more exclusively on Russian affairs, after a brief period in which great hopes had been pinned on promoting communist revolution in other European states. The Bolsheviks maintained a Communist International office (Comintern) to support and guide communist parties elsewhere, but their main focus was on building their own state.

The Russian revolution was one of the most important transformations in human history. Building on widespread if diverse popular discontent and a firm belief in centralized leadership, the Bolsheviks beat back foreign intervention and avoided even a partial restoration of the "old regime," as had occurred in France after Napoleon. While the Bolsheviks utilized features of the tsarist system, including the authoritarian principles, they managed to create a new political, economic, and cultural structure without serious internal challenge after the initial chaotic years.

PATTERNS OF SOVIET HISTORY AFTER 1923

Lenin died in 1924, and after a few years of jockeying, Joseph Stalin succeeded him as undisputed leader of the Soviet state. Stalin, with his base in the Communist party, which now clearly dominated the new government, was a man of working-class background, with limited education and scant interest in theoretical Marxism, but he had a relentless drive to power. Under his rule Russia was to develop its own version of a socialist society—"socialism in one country," as Stalin put it, as opposed to the vision of worldwide revolution that had inspired many earlier leaders. By the time Stalin had fully eliminated potential rivals in 1927, Russia had advanced only slightly toward a socialist system, though its revolutionary momentum had not ended. Much of the land was in the hands of wealthy peasants, or kulaks, who seemed attuned to a profit-based market agriculture; even in industry, state-run enterprises and planning had only limited effect. Stalin devoted himself to a double task: to make the Soviet Union a fully industrial society, and to do so under the full control of the state, rather than private initiative. In essence, Stalin wanted modernization, but with a revolutionary, noncapitalist twist.

A massive program for collective agriculture began in 1928. Collectivization meant large, state-run farms, rather than individual holdings as in the West. Communist party agitators pressed peasants to join in collectives. The vast majority of kulaks refused, but through threats and mass executions and deportations to Siberia, they were forced to submit. Agricultural production fell drastically as a result, and though it gradually recovered during the later 1930s, the Soviet Union was saddled with the persistent problem of lack of peasant motivation. While collective farms allowed peasants small plots of their own, and job security, they created an atmosphere of factory-like discipline and rigid planning from above that left many peasants reluctant participants.

The collective farm system did, however, facilitate control of the peasantry so that rural profits could be reduced, in favor of providing capital for industrialization, and excess workers could be forced into the ranks of urban labor. If Stalin's handling of agriculture had serious flaws, his approach to industry was in many ways miraculously successful. A system of five-year plans under the state planning commission began to construct massive state-run factories in metallurgy, mining, and electric power, to make Russia an industrial country without foreign capital or more than minor foreign advice. The focus was on heavy industry, which built on Russia's great natural resources and also served to prepare for possible war with Hitler's Germany. This unbalanced allocation, which slighted consumer goods, was to remain characteristic of the Soviet version of an industrial society. Further, Stalin's ambitious hope to replace market forces with government decisions led to many allocation bottlenecks plus wasteful use of resources and labor, as production and supply quotas for individual factories were set in Moscow. But there was no question that rapid industrial growth occurred. During the first two five-year plans, to 1937—that is, during the same period when the West was mired in the depression—Russian output of machinery and metal products grew 14-fold. Russia had become the world's third industrial power, behind only Germany and the United States. Russia's long history of backwardness seemed to have ended.

Along with forced industrialization, Stalin continued to maintain the police powers of the state. Opponents and even imagined opponents were executed. During the great purge of high party leaders in 1937–1938, hundreds of people were intimidated into confessing imaginary crimes against the state, and most of them were executed. Party congresses and meetings of the executive committee, or Politburo, became mere rubber stamps, and a zealous internal police, renamed the MVD in 1934, perpetuated an atmosphere of terror in Russian society.

Ironically, Stalin's purges had weakened the nation's ability to respond to the rising threat of Hitler, the self-proclaimed leader of anticommunism. Along with understandable suspicion of the will and motives of the Western powers, this internal weakness encouraged Stalin to sign his pact with Hitler in 1939. The alliance bought some time for greater war preparation and also enabled Russian troops to attack eastern Poland and Finland in an effort to regain territories lost in World War I. Here was the first sign of a revival of Russia's long interest in conquest, which would be intensified by the results of World War II.

The war itself was devastating for the Soviet Union. Deep German invasions, though ultimately unsuccessful, brought massive death and hardship. Russia's new industrial base, hastily relocated to the Ural Mountains and beyond, proved vital in providing the material needed for war, along with some U.S. and British aid, but the effort was extremely costly. Great cities such as Leningrad and Stalingrad were besieged by the Germans for months, with huge loss of life. The war heightened Russia's age-old fear of invasion and foreign interference, already enhanced by World War I and Western intervention during the revolution. But as the Red army pressed westward after 1943, finally penetrating to the Elbe River in Germany, there was new opportunity for aggrandizement as well. Russia was able to regain its former western boundaries, at the expense of nations like Poland; some small states, set up by the Treaty of Versailles, were swallowed entirely. Larger East European states were allowed to remain intact, but their regimes were quickly brought under the control of Communist parties backed by the Soviet occupation forces.

Most of the small nations of Eastern Europe had encountered serious problems between the world wars. They were mostly new, the product of particularistic nationalisms honored by the Versailles treaty and carved from the western parts of the Russian empire plus the now-defunct Habsburg realm. Only in Czechoslovakia did a democratic, parliamentary regime win durable success. Most states, after a brief democratic experience, had turned to authoritarian rule under a monarch or army general. Land reform had been ignored in favor of continued aristocratic dominance. Bickering over boundaries had added to severe economic distress; industrialization lagged, and agricultural productivity actually declined. Then came the Nazi attack that easily overwhelmed the smaller, more backward armies of states like Poland. And this was followed, between 1944 and 1948, by effective Russian control. Through a combination of sheer military might and collaboration with local communist movements, opposition parties were crushed and an essentially Soviet political system installed in Poland, Hungary, Romania, Bulgaria, Czechoslovakia, and East Germany, in an unprecedented westward extension of Russian power. Only Yugoslavia and, later, Albania, with strong communist movements of their own and separate from Russian backing, and Greece escaped the new Soviet empire. Elsewhere, Russian-style agricultural collectivization and state-run industrialization began to take shape along with a single-party communist government. Ultimately the Soviet Union forged the Warsaw Pact alliance of military cooperation, to confront NATO in the West.

While the extension of Soviet control to the rest of Eastern Europe was the most dramatic diplomatic result of World War II, there were other significant developments as well. Russian participation in the late phases of the war against Japan brought an opportunity to seize some islands in the northern Pacific. Russia established a protectorate over the communist regime of North Korea, to match the American protectorate in South Korea. Russian aid to the victorious Communist party in China brought new influence in that country for a time, and in the 1970s Russia was to gain a new ally in communist Vietnam, which among other things provided naval bases for the Russian fleet. Russia's growing military and economic strength gave the postwar Soviet Union new leverage in the Middle East, Africa, and even parts of Latin America. The Soviet Union's superpower status was confirmed by its development of the atomic and hydrogen bombs and by its deployment of missiles and naval forces to match the rapid expansion of U.S. arsenals. Russia had become a world power.

Internally, the Stalinist system remained intact during the first postwar years. The regime was supported by the growing cold war with the United States, which convinced many Russians that firm authority was essential to counter the new foreign threat. But Stalin died in 1953, and from that time onward no single leader gained comparable power. Choice of single leaders by ruling committees balanced various interest groups in the Soviet hierarchy—the army, the secret police, the Communist party apparatus. The Soviet government had become in many ways quite conservative, with entrenched bureaucratic interests alert to defend their prerogatives, and no ruler could produce sweeping change. But in 1956 a new Russian leader, Nikita Khrushchev, attacked Stalin's dictatorial policies, blasting the late dictator's crimes against opponents. The de-Stalinization

Soviet and East European Boundaries by 1948

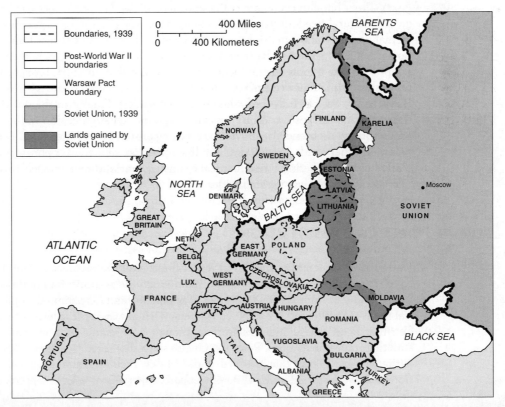

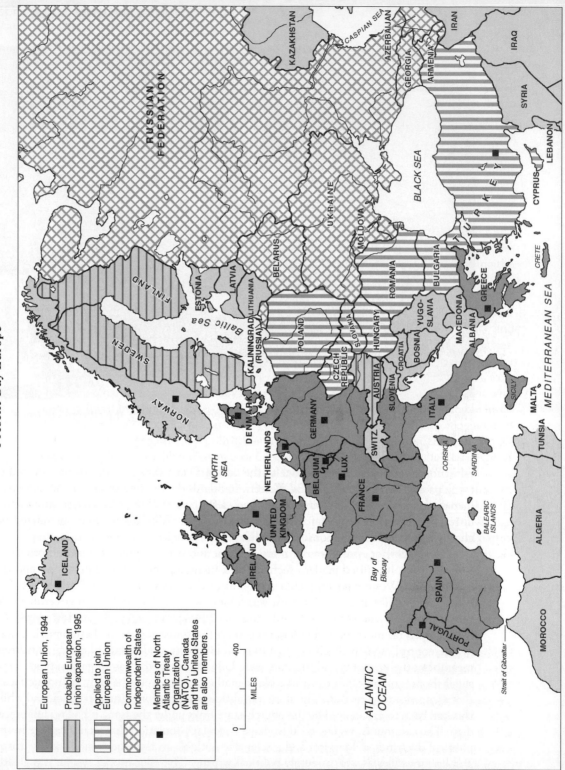

Present-Day Europe

Legend:
- European Union, 1994
- Probable European Union expansion, 1995
- Applied to join European Union
- Commonwealth of Independent States

■ Members of North Atlantic Treaty Organization (NATO). Canada and the United States are also members.

0   400
MILES

extended, bringing rapid gains in literacy and considerable access to higher education for talented students; this system, too, was designed to promote the state's vision of a loyal and productive citizenry.

Soviet leaders also constructed an elaborate state-sponsored welfare system. Able-bodied citizens, men and women alike, were required to work; the Soviets admitted no unemployment, though extensive underemployment often existed. But the state operated medical facilities, day-care centers, and youth organizations, and provided payments to the disabled and elderly. Many of these programs were administered by Communist party organizations, including the loyal trade unions that were not permitted to strike but that did mobilize many group recreational activities. Athletic clubs and beach resorts in southern Russia were among the state-run operations that cemented the welfare system. Far more literally than the welfare apparatus developed in the West, the Soviet version embraced its citizens from cradle to grave.

Networks of political police and police informers attempted to ensure loyalty to the state, continuing and extending the tsarist tradition. All major operations, from youth groups to collective farms, were monitored by Communist party members. Foreigners visiting Russia and Russian groups traveling abroad were carefully supervised. Groups and individuals suspected of dissidence were intimidated, often arrested. In the Stalinist era, in addition to the widely publicized purge trials and executions, millions of suspected opponents were sent to forced labor camps in Siberia. Under de-Stalinization, intimidation

In Memoriam to Y. Gagarin. Yuri Gagarin was a leading early cosmonaut. This painting is by A. Shmarinov, member of the USSR Academy of Arts, 1971.

was moderated somewhat. Some opponents of the regime were allowed to go into exile, others were sent to psychiatric clinics; outright political executions became rare, but an atmosphere of considerable fear remained.

Along with policing came extensive positive efforts at persuasion and propaganda. Press and other media were strictly state-controlled, giving carefully filtered versions of the news. Massive banners, pictures of leaders, and patriotic parades stimulated devotion and a sense of identification with the regime. The Soviets introduced a new set of holidays, commemorating the revolution and other anniversaries, including the international workers' day, May 1. Under Stalin, efforts to instill Marxist loyalty to the cause of the proletariat were blended with more traditional nationalism against foreign enemies, a powerful brew that unquestionably created a high level of emotional commitment among many Russian people.

The construction of the Soviet state was in many ways a remarkable achievement. The tsarist precedent helped, but tsarist and church officials were cast aside during the revolution, while a host of new functions were undertaken. The Soviets tapped vast reservoirs of popular talent and enthusiasm to construct their new bureaucracy. At the same time, this very creation became increasingly unwieldy. After important new access to political power for able workers and peasants in the 1920s, recruitment to the party and the bureaucracy increasingly came within the ranks of bureaucratic families, which favored their own. The Communist party itself was effectively run by a top committee, the Political Bureau, or Politburo, consisting of 20 people who were the real rulers of the country. Decisions were taken at the top, often in secret, and then transmitted to lower levels for execution; little reverse initiative, with proposals coming from lower bureaucratic agencies, was encouraged. Just as the new bureaucracy replaced the tsarist aristocracy in ruling the country, so it raised some of the same problems as a power elite often more concerned with self-perpetuation than with innovation.

SOVIET CULTURE

As in politics, Russian culture in the 20th century exhibited a fascinating blend of new elements, products of the revolution and industrialization, and more traditional themes.

Soviet leaders from the beginning viewed key features of traditional Russian culture as enemies to be attacked. Religion headed the list. While the new regime did not attempt to abolish the Orthodox church outright, it greatly limited the church's outreach. Thus the church could not give religious instruction to anyone under 18, while state schools vigorously preached that religion is mere superstition. The Soviet regime also limited freedom of religion for the Jewish minority, often holding Jews up as enemies of the state in what was in fact a manipulation of traditional Russian anti-Semitism. The larger Muslim minority was given greater latitude, on condition of careful loyalty to the regime.

The Soviet state also opposed the strong Western cultural orientation of the 19th-century tsarist elite, which had never widely touched the masses in any event. Modern Western styles of art and literature were attacked as decadent. Earlier styles, appropriated as Russian, were maintained. Thus Russian orchestras performed a wide variety of classical music, and the Russian ballet, though rigid and conservative by 20th-century Western

Parade of athletes and workers: Red Square, Moscow, May 1, 1981. May Day was a major civic celebration in the USSR and for workers' movement in many other countries.

norms, commanded wide attention. Soviet culture emphasized a style of "socialist realism" in the arts, bent on glorifying heroic workers, soldiers, and peasants. A vigorous strand of modern art in prerevolutionary Russia was repressed under Stalin, in favor of grandiose, neoclassical paintings and sculpture. Russian architecture emphasized functional, classical lines, with a pronounced taste for the monumental, though historical buildings were carefully preserved.

Russian literature remained diverse and creative, despite official controls sponsored by the communist-dominated Writers' Union. Leading Russian authors wrote movingly of the travails of the civil war and World War II, maintaining the earlier tradition of sympathy with the Russian people, great patriotism, and a concern for the Russian soul.

The most creative Soviet artists, and particularly the writers, often tread a fine line between conveying some of the sufferings of the Russian people in the 20th century and courting official disapproval. Their freedom also varied depending on leadership mood; thus censorship eased after Stalin, and then tightened somewhat though not to previous levels. Yet even authors critical of aspects of the Soviet regime maintained distinctive Russian values. Aleksandr Solzhenitsyn, for example, was exiled to the West because of publication of his history of Siberian prison camps, *Gulag Archipelago*, but found the West

Socialist realism: *In a Designing Office.* Notice bust of Stalin at left of painting.

too materialistic and individualistic for his taste. Though barred from his homeland until 1993, he continued to seek some alternative both to communist policy and to Westernization, with more than a hint of a continuing belief in the durable solidarity and faith of the Russian common people.

Along with interest in the arts, Soviet culture placed great emphasis on science and social science. Social scientific work, heavily colored by Marxist theory, nonetheless produced important analyses of current trends and of history. Scientific research was even more heavily funded, and Soviet scientists generated a number of fundamental discoveries in physics, chemistry, and mathematics. At times scientists themselves felt the heavy hand of official disapproval. Biologists and psychiatrists, particularly, were urged to reject Western theories that called human rationality and social progress into question. Thus Freudianism was banned, and biologists who overemphasized the uncontrollability of genetic evolution were jailed. But Russian scientists overall enjoyed considerable freedom as well as great prestige. As in the West, their work was linked with advances in technology and weaponry.

Shaped by substantial state control, 20th-century Soviet culture was neither traditional nor Western. Considerable ambivalence about the West remained, as Russian leaders shared Western enthusiasm for science while trying to reshape artistic styles and popular beliefs.

ECONOMY AND SOCIETY

The Soviet Union became a fully industrial society between the 1920s and the 1950s. Rapid growth of manufacturing and the rise of city populations to over 50 percent of the total were measures of this development. Most of the rest of Eastern Europe was also fully industrialized by the 1950s. East European modernization, however, had a number of distinctive features. State control of virtually all economic sectors was one key element: no other industrialized society gave so little leeway to private initiative. The unusual imbalance between heavy industrial goods and consumer items was another distinctive aspect. The Soviet Union lagged in the priorities it placed on consumer goods—not only Western staples like automobiles, but also housing construction and simple items such as bathtub plugs. Consumer-goods industries were poorly funded and did not achieve the advanced technological level that characterized the heavy manufacturing sector. The Soviet need to amass capital for development, in a traditionally poor society, contributed to the inattention to consumer goods; so did the need to create a massive armaments industry to rival that of the United States, in a society still poorer overall. Living standards improved greatly, and extensive welfare services provided security for some groups that was lacking in the West; but complaints about poor consumer products and long lines to obtain desired goods remained a feature of Soviet life. East European industrialization also paid little regard to the environment. Chemical pollution and exhaustion of waterways endangered large stretches of the region; some estimates held that as much as 40 percent of Russian agricultural land became endangered, while over 20 percent of Soviet citizens lived in areas of "ecological disaster."

The communist system throughout Eastern Europe also failed to resolve problems with agriculture. Capital that might have gone into farming equipment was often diverted to armaments and heavy industry. The arduous climate of northern Europe and Asia was a factor as well, dooming a number of attempts to spread grain production to Siberia, for example. But it seemed clear that the East European peasantry continued to find the constraints and lack of individual incentive in collectivized agriculture a deterrent to maximum effort. Thus Eastern Europe had to retain a larger percentage of its labor force in agriculture than was true of the industrial West and still encountered problems with food supply and quality.

Despite the importance of distinctive political and economic characteristics, Eastern European society echoed a number of the themes of contemporary Western social history—simply because of the shared fact of industrial life. Work rhythms, for example, became roughly similar. Industrialization in Russia brought massive efforts to speed the pace of work and introduce regularized supervision. Incentive systems designed to encourage able workers resembled those used in Western factories. In the 1930s the Soviets adopted a practice of rewarding heroes of labor—workers who exceeded production quotas—with extra benefits and prestige. Along with similar work habits came similar leisure activities. For decades, sports provided excitement for the peoples of Eastern Europe, as did mass media such as film and television. Family vacations to the beaches of the Black Sea were cherished.

Russian social structure also grew closer to that of the West, despite the continued importance of the rural population and despite the impact of Marxist theory. The aristocracy ended. Particularly interesting was an increasing division of urban society along class lines, between workers and a better-educated, managerial middle class. Wealth divisions were not as great as in the West, to be sure, but the perquisites of managers and professional people—particularly if they were Communist party members—set them off from the standard of living of the masses.

Finally, the Russian family reacted to some of the same pressures of industrialization that the Western family experienced. Massive movement of people to the cities and crowded housing focused the nuclear family unit, as ties to a wider network of relatives loosened. The birth rate dropped. Official Soviet policy on birth rates varied for a time, but the basic pressures became similar to those in the West: falling infant death rates, with improved diets and medical care, plus growing periods of schooling and some increase in consumer expectations, made large families less desirable than before. Wartime dislocations contributed to birth rate decline at points as well. By the 1970s the Russian growth rate was about the same as that of the West. Also as in the West, some minority groups—particularly Muslims in southern Russia—maintained higher birth rates than the Russian majority.

Patterns of child-rearing showed some similarities to those in the West, as parents, especially in the managerial middle class, devoted more attention to promoting their children's education and ensuring good jobs for them in the future. At the same time children were more strictly disciplined than in the West, both at home and in school, with an emphasis on authority that might have political implications as well. Russian families were never afforded the domestic idealization of women that had prevailed in the West during industrialization. Most married women worked, an essential feature of an economy struggling to industrialize and offering relatively low wages to individual workers. As in the peasant past, women performed many heavy physical tasks. They also dominated some professions, such as medicine, though these were far lower in status than their male-dominated counterparts in the West. Russian propagandists took some pride in the constructive role of women and their official equality, but there were signs that many women suffered burdens from demanding jobs with little help from their husbands at home.

By the 1970s, many Russians seemed satisfied with their political and social system. Police repression remained, but Stalinist excesses had been reduced. Pride in Russian space and athletic achievements was coupled with realization of the improvements in living standards and opportunity that had grown with the Soviet system. Many Russians also noted weaknesses in the West that enhanced their attachment to their own institutions: family instability, greed, and crime seemed lesser problems in the Soviet context, and only partly because the regime concealed accurate statistics. Except for the unpopular war in Afghanistan, Russian foreign policy had remained fairly prudent; American diplomacy might appear more unpredictable and warlike. In 1962, for example, the Soviets pulled back their missiles from Cuba, rather than risk outright conflict with the United States. Furthermore, of course, the Soviet system had partially isolated much of Eastern Europe, allowing only limited trade outside the communist system and only carefully regulated cultural contacts. The imagery of an "iron curtain" enclosing this civilization was not entirely an exaggeration.

THE EXPLOSION OF THE 1980s

Despite its many achievements, Soviet society began to come unglued by the early 1980s, opening a dramatic new chapter in East European and Central Asian history. The initial cause of this extraordinary upheaval lay in deteriorating economic performance, intensified by the costs of military rivalry with the United States. The Soviet economic system, after a strong growth rate in the 1950s and 1960s, stopped functioning well by the late 1970s. Industrial production began to stagnate and even drop, as a result of rigid central planning, health problems, and poor worker morale. Growing inadequacy of housing and common goods resulted, further worsening motivation. As economic growth stopped, yet cold war military competition continued, the percentage of resources allocated to military production escalated toward a third of all national income. This reduced funds available for other investments or for consumer needs. Disease rates, infant mortality, and alcoholism all increased. Younger leaders began to recognize, at first only privately, that the system was near collapse.

Yet the Soviet system was not changeless, despite its heavy bureaucratization. In 1985, after a succession of leaders whose age or health precluded major initiatives, the Soviet Union brought a new, younger official to the fore. Mikhail Gorbachev quickly renewed some of the earlier attacks on Stalinist rigidity and replaced some of the old-line party bureaucrats. He conveyed a new and more Western style, dressing in fashionable clothes (and accompanied by his wife, Raisa, who did the same), holding relatively open press conferences, and even allowing the Soviet media to engage in active debate and report on problems as well as successes. Gorbachev also urged a reduction in nuclear armament, and in 1987 he negotiated a new agreement with the United States that limited medium-range missiles in Europe. He ended the war in Afghanistan, and brought Soviet troops home.

Gorbachev proclaimed a policy of *glasnost,* or "openness," which implied new freedom to comment and criticize. He pressed particularly for a reduction in bureaucratic inefficiency and unproductive labor in the Soviet economy, sketching more decentralized decision-making and the use of some market incentives to stimulate greater output. In many ways Gorbachev's policies constituted a return to a characteristic Russian ambivalence about the West as he reduced Soviet isolation while continuing to criticize aspects of Western political and social structure. Gorbachev clearly hoped to use some Western management techniques and was open to certain Western cultural styles, without, however, intending to abandon basic controls of the communist state. Western analysts wondered if the Soviet economy could improve worker motivations without embracing a Western-style consumerism or whether computers could be more widely introduced without allowing freedom of information exchange.

Gorbachev also sought to open the Soviet Union to fuller participation in the world economy, recognizing that isolation in a separate empire had restricted access to new technology and limited motivation to change. While the new leadership did not rush to make foreign trade or investment too easy—considerable suspicion persisted—the economic initiatives brought symbolic changes, such as the opening of a McDonald's restaurant in Moscow, and a whole array of new contacts with foreigners for various Soviet citizens.

The keynote of the reform program was *perestroika,* or economic restructuring, which Gorbachev translated into more leeway for private ownership and decentralized control in industry and agriculture. Farmers, for example, were given the chance to lease land for fifty years, with rights of inheritance, while industrial concerns were authorized to buy from either private or state operations. Foreign investment was newly encouraged. Gorbachev urged more self-help among the Russians, including a reduction in drinking, arguing that he wanted to "rid public opinion of . . . faith in a 'good Tsar,' the all powerful center, the notion that someone can bring about order and organize perestroika from on high." Politically, he encouraged a new constitution in 1988, giving considerable power to a new parliament, the Congress of People's Deputies, and abolishing the communist monopoly of elections. Important opposition groups developed both inside and outside the party, pressing Gorbachev between opposing factions—liberals wanting faster reforms versus conservative hard liners. Gorbachev himself was elected to a new, powerful Presidency of the Soviet Union in 1990.

DISMANTLING THE SOVIET EMPIRE

Gorbachev's new approach, including his desire for better relations with Western powers, prompted more definitive results outside the Soviet Union than within, as the smaller states of Eastern Europe uniformly pressed for greater independence and internal reforms. Bulgaria moved for economic liberalization in 1987 but was held back by the Soviets; pressure resumed in 1989 as the party leader was ousted and free elections were arranged. Hungary changed leadership in 1988, and installed a noncommunist president. A new constitution and free elections were planned, as the Communist party renamed itself "socialist," and Hungary moved rapidly toward a free-market economy. Poland installed a noncommunist government in 1988, and again moved quickly to dismantle the state-run economy; prices rose rapidly as government subsidies were withdrawn. The Solidarity movement, born a decade before through a merger of noncommunist labor leaders and Catholic intellectuals, became the dominant political force. East Germany displaced its communist government in 1989, expelling key leaders and moving rapidly toward unification with West Germany, which occured in 1990—a dramatic sign of the collapse of postwar Soviet foreign policy. Czechoslovakia installed a new government in 1989, headed by a playwright, and again sought to introduce free elections and a more market-driven economy.

Although mass demonstrations played a key role in several of these political upheavals, only in Romania was there outright violence as an exceptionally authoritarian communist leader was swept out by force. As in Bulgaria, the Communist party retained considerable power, though under new leadership, and reforms moved less rapidly than in places like Hungary and Czechoslovakia. The same held true for Albania, where the unreconstructed Stalinist regime was dislodged and a more flexible communist leadership installed.

New divergences in the nature and extent of reform in Eastern Europe were exacerbated by clashes among nationalities—as in the Soviet Union itself, where Baltic nationalists and Asian Muslims both raised new demands. Change and uncertainty brought older attachments to the fore. Romanians and ethnic Hungarians clashed, while Bulgarians attacked a Turkish minority left over from the Ottoman period. In 1991 Yugoslavia, where the existing communist regime—though not Soviet-dominated—also came under attack, bloody civil war boiled up from nationalistic disputes as Slovenia, Croatia, and Bosnia-Herzegovina proclaimed independence and then Bosnia divided among warring Serb, Croat, and Muslim factions. Czechoslavakia divided peacefully between a Czech republic and Slovakia.

Amid many conflicts and uncertainties, the Soviet empire was dismantled. Gorbachev reversed postwar imperialism completely, stating "Any nation has the right to decide its fate by itself." In several cases, notably Hungary, Soviet troops were rapidly withdrawn, and generally it seemed unlikely that a change of heart, toward a repressive attempt to re-establish empire, would be possible.

RENEWED TURMOIL AFTER 1991

The uncertainties of the situation within the Soviet Union were confirmed in the summer of 1991, when an attempted coup was mounted by military and police elements. Massive popular demonstrations, however, asserted the strong democratic current that had developed in the Soviet Union since 1986. The contrast with earlier Soviet history and with the suppression of democracy in China two years before was striking. But Gorbachev's authority ironically weakened. The three Baltic states used the occasion to gain full independence, though economic links with the Soviet Union remained. Other minority republics proclaimed independence as well, but Gorbachev struggled to win agreement on continued economic union and some form of political coordination. By the end of 1991 leaders of the major republics, including Russia's Boris Yeltsin, proclaimed the end of the Soviet Union, projecting a commonwealth of the leading republics in its stead, including the economically crucial Ukraine.

Amid the disputes, Gorbachev fell from power, doomed by his attempts to salvage a presidency that depended on some sort of survival for a greater Soviet Union. His leadership role was taken over by Boris Yeltsin, who as president of Russia and an early renouncer of communism now emerged as the leading, though quickly beleaguered, political figure.

The resulting Commonwealth of Independent States won tentative agreement from most of the now-independent republics. But tensions immediately surfaced about economic coordination amid rapid dismantling of state controls; about control of the military, where Russia—still by far the largest unit—sought predominance, including nuclear control, amid challenges from the Ukraine and from Kazakhstan (the two other republics with nuclear weaponry on their soil); and about relationships between the European-dominated republics, including Russia, and the cluster of central Asian states. Unity in the former Soviet Union had largely ended, though Russia retained economic influence in Central Asia and close ties with some new Slavic states like Belarus.

The fate of economic reform was also uncertain, as Russian leaders hesitated to convert to a full market system lest transitional disruption further antagonize the population. Here again, more radical plans emerged at the end of 1991, calling for removal of most government price controls. Economic conditions improved by the late 1990s; food supplies, for example, were plentiful. But inefficient state-run factories persisted. Government revenues dropped. New gaps between rich business groups and workers and retirees created important tensions.

Political directions were also complicated. Russian leaders outlawed the communist party, for its leadership of the failed coup, but an alternative party system emerged only slowly. Soviet citizens took delight in tearing down the old emblems of the Revolution, including massive Socialist-Realist statues of Lenin. Even old tsarist flags and uniforms were trotted out for display. But effective new emblems had yet to be generated. Nonetheless, in some republics, including central Asia, party leadership retained considerable vigor, and political strife in several now-independent republics allowed the Russian army to regain some role. In Russia itself, Yeltsin quarreled bitterly with the parliament dominated by former Communists, dissolving it by force in 1993. Communist politicians retained a strong following, while a vigorous, militaristic nationalist movement won some support.

CONCLUSION: UNCERTAIN FUTURES IN EASTERN EUROPE

Inevitably, Soviet and East European history in the late 1990s is dominated by the surprising events of the most recent period, and by huge uncertainties about their consequences. The stirring events made clear that much less had changed in this region during the 20th century than had been recognized—even by Soviet citizens themselves. Soviet law had long trumpeted women's equality, and indeed Soviet women played vital roles in the labor force; but inequality in household chores continued while unavailability of reliable birth control devices—a result of shoddy consumer goods production—forced a high rate of abortions. Soviet constitutions had featured a system of federated republics, but in fact central government control and Russian ethnic dominance spurred minority nationalism, causing nationalist hostilities to burn brightly. Indeed nationalism, in Russia and among newly independent East European nations, threatened to divide the region profoundly. Religion also remained a vital force despite decades of secularization. Catholicism in the smaller nations and in the western republics of the former Soviet Union, and Judaism, and Islam in central Asia provided important loyalties.

Revolution and a totalitarian state had exerted only a limited impact despite theories of absolute control and undeniable police terror in key periods. The same system had done less to diminish a traditional attraction to Western values and standards than might have been imagined. Several East European states indeed rushed to proclaim a Western-style devotion to individual liberty as well as a market economy. In 1997 NATO granted membership to Poland, the Czech Republic, and Hungary, pulling them farther into a Western orbit as the old border lands moved to the institutions and culture of the West. In Russia itself, while nationalist loyalties and economic lags might limit openness to Westernization, in the long run it seemed unlikely that isolation could be resumed—a sign both of older East European interest in the West and the new intensity of international contacts.

Amid a host of questions about the future, once the Soviet mantle had been withdrawn, several key issues dominated analysis of the new Eastern Europe and central Asia. The first involved sheer stability. Conversion to a market economy and a democratic political system was bound to be difficult. Many experts thought Poland, Hungary, and the Czech Republic had an excellent chance to pull it off, because of a relatively advanced industrial structure and unusually great contacts with Western cultural and political values. Prospects for southeastern Europe and Russia itself were less clear, and efforts to move toward market structures and to abandon former Communist leadership were characteristically less rapid. Ethnic and religious battles seemed to promise more literal instability in the former Yugoslavia, in central Asia, and possibly other parts of the Balkans.

The second issue involved an estimate about traditionalist revivals. As communism fell in this region, many people turned back to older loyalties, like religion or ethnic nationalism, because they had no other beliefs to follow. Would these more traditionalist impulses persist, or would a more Western-style, semisecular mentality develop? Though predictions were inherently best guesses, history offered some guidelines. It was vital to realize that the revolution of 1917, extended to the rest of Eastern Europe after 1945, would not be entirely undone. No one seriously called for a return of the peasantry and aristocracy or an end to industrialization or mass literacy. Despite dramatic changes, there was no revolutionary overturn of the past system; most of the new leaders in politics and business came from the Communist apparatus, carefully renouncing their past. Specific features of the revolution attached to the communist system came under bitter attack, but not the more fundamental restructuring. This might facilitate democracy, compared to its fate in places like Poland between the wars. At the same time history also warned against facile assumptions that this region would easily assimilate with Western society after some adjustment period. Russians, for example, maintained their attachment to a more extensive welfare system, while attacking unattractive features of Western individualism like high crime rates and youth unrest. Many resented profiteering, on grounds of more egalitarian beliefs than were common in the West. Many disdained the new influx of "junk food," sold for high prices.

Finally, the relationship not just to the West but to the wider world focused important questions. The Soviet empire, though somewhat closed to outside contact, had organized politics and economics in a huge part of Europe and Asia, building on the previous expansion of the tsars. Much of this was now undone. The empire had also played a vigorous role in world affairs, providing political guidance and economic and military aid to every continent. Economic failure eclipsed this role, at least for the moment. But what world role would Russia and its neighbors now play? In the immediate aftermath of collapse, particularly after 1991, Russian leaders carefully supported most Western diplomatic initiatives. Was this likely to persist, given different traditions and interests? Would Russia, still industrial and still a territorial giant, renew contact with its longstanding, if variously defined, sense of mission? These are questions not yet answered, as Russia's new role unfolds.

Suggested Readings

Recent Soviet history is treated in: Martin McCauley, *The Soviet Union, 1917–1991* (1993); Richard Barnet, *The Giants: Russia and America* (1977); A. Rubinstein, *Soviet Foreign Policy Since World War II* (1981); Alec Nove, *The Soviet Economic System* (1980); Stephen Cohen et al., eds., *The Soviet Union Since Stalin* (1980); and Ben Eklof, *Gorbachev and the Reform Period* (1988). On the Russian revolution, see B. Wolfe, *Three Who Made a Revolution* (1955); D. Footman, *Civil War in Russia* (1962); and T. Skocpol, *States and Social Revolutions* (1979), a major interpretive effort.

Other areas of Eastern Europe are treated in: Joseph Held, *The Columbia History of Eastern Europe in the 20th Century* (1992); F. Fetjo, *History of the People's Democracies: Eastern Europe Since Stalin* (1971); J. Tampke, *The People's Republics of Eastern Europe* (1983); Timothy Ash, *The Polish Revolution: Solidarity* (1984); H. G. Skilling, *Czechoslovakia: Interrupted Revolution* (1976), on the 1968 uprising; and B. Kovrig, *Communism in Hungary from Kun to Kadar* (1979).

On the early signs of explosion in Eastern Europe, see K. Dawisha, *Eastern Europe, Gorbachev and Reform: The Great Challenge* (1988). Bohdan Nahaylo and Victor Swoboda, *Soviet Disunion: A History of the Nationalities Problem in the USSR* (1990), provides important background. On women's experiences, see Barbara Engel and Christine Worobec, eds., *Russia's Women: Accommodation, Resistance, Transformation* (1990).

placed, the issue of what to do next was far less quickly resolved. For China was not ready for a spring into modern life Western-style. Sun Yat-sen's movement had attracted student support because of its optimistic belief that China could regain its full independence and become politically like the West with no difficulty. But the Chinese had never had direct experience with voting or with representative bodies. The decline of the imperial institutions made it difficult simply to govern the country, much less reform it. The revolutionaries set up a military general, Yaun Shi-h'ai, as president of the new republic, to conciliate the army and prevent foreign, particularly Japanese, intervention. The choice also reflected the fact that Sun Yat-sen and his colleagues had no government experience, and they proved to be indifferent administrators. But the new president was no reformer; although he briefly tolerated an elected parliament, he worked to consolidate his own power as a possible future emperor. He was not capable of improving government efficiency, as tax revenues dwindled and Western influence expanded. In fact, China by 1916 was collapsing into a series of regional governments, headed by competing warlords, each with his own local army. Sun Yat-sen and his associates tried to counter the growing chaos by forming a political party of their own, the Kuomintang, but they gained influence only in part of China, mainly around the city of Canton. Thus the 1911 revolution had destroyed key traditional institutions, but it had not created adequate substitutes. For this reason revolution simmered through the next decades, producing a defective new regime until after World War II.

There was, briefly, a more hopeful interlude. During the later 1920s, the Kuomintang armies were able to subdue a number of the warlords. The regime also induced the major Western powers to renounce their claims on Chinese territories; the Western-controlled treaty ports thus returned to Chinese hands, with the exception of Portuguese Macao and British Hong Kong. Revolutionary leaders became more skeptical of Western political models and capitalist economics, and the values behind them, and the idea of a Chinese version of modern society gained ground. The new leader of the Kuomintang, Chiang Kai-shek, granted a constitution that established authoritarian rule but was designed to lead to democracy. New laws also attacked traditional limits on women in Chinese society, including the practice of footbinding; and growing numbers of students attended modernized universities, some run by Christian missionaries, where Western-style science and social science were taught. But this period of renewal was short-lived. Chiang Kai-shek did not effectively rule the whole country, and the warlords soon revived. Chiang's own government became increasingly opportunistic, making deals with warlords and business leaders rather than focusing on political reform, and the hopes for full democracy became increasingly frustrated. Furthermore, the Kuomintang faced another internal opponent in a strong communist movement, inspired by Marxism and the Russian Revolution. Driven out of the Kuomintang itself, the communists staged the heroic "Long March" to the distant Shensi province in the northwest, where they held out under the leadership of Mao Zedung.

It was in this confusion that Japan's path fatefully crossed China's once again, as Japan's industrial strength continued to grow. As in the Soviet Union, the 1920s–1930s constituted a vital second stage in the Japanese industrialization process. Heavy industry expanded rapidly, as the Japanese developed their own machinery production and spread electrification widely. With a growing skilled male labor force, the Japanese also reconsidered earlier industrial policies. Many workers were given security of employment in return

East Asia in the 20th Century

Focal Points

In the 20th century, East Asia divided between societies experiencing revolution and the establishment of communist regimes and those that maintained democracy or authoritarianism. The process of revolution was immensely disruptive in China and later in Vietnam, but it brought huge changes in economy, society, and culture. What were the main stages of revolution and change? What earlier traditions were particularly attacked? Noncommunist East Asia, headed by Japan but ultimately including other parts of the dynamic Pacific Rim, emphasized rapid industrial growth, though involvement in World War II created important new developments as well. Why was the Pacific Rim so successful economically? East Asia remained divided in the 1990s, but new Chinese and Vietnamese policies and some common cultural features beneath the surface of formal politics began to call growing attention to the region as a whole.

THE CLASHING REGIONS OF EAST ASIA

In the 19th century, East Asia had been divided by the differing responses of Japan and China to Western pressures. These divisions continued in the 20th century. Japan maintained an aggressive foreign policy that helped launch World War II and then became one of the most accomplished economic actors on the world stage. China, in contrast, continued to struggle to industrialize. The giant nation was wracked by two revolutions, the second bringing a communist regime that resembled Soviet Russia in important ways.

Yet East Asia has maintained something of its own character. Japan, though an advanced industrial nation and a democracy, continued to differ from the West in many ways. China, though ultimately a communist society, showed marked variations from the Soviet model. It selected from the Soviet example, somewhat as Japan had earlier picked and chosen from the West. There were some signs, also, that characteristics of East Asia would propel much of the region, and not just Japan, into the ranks of fully industrialized nations by the early 21st century. Certainly the rapid economic flowering of South Korea, Hong Kong, and Taiwan, and the possibility that China itself might make the turn to full industrialization, has raised new discussion of East Asian "advantages" in the process of latecomer modernization. Finally, even amid diversity East Asian nations continue to interact. Japan's invasion of China in the 1930s colored the development of both nations. New economic exchanges by the 1970s again focused some attention on the links within this historic region.

East Asia in the 20th century thus split between the Chinese communist pattern, shared to an extent by Vietnam, and Japan's rapid industrialization joined after the 1950s by other parts of the Pacific Rim, including much of southeast Asia. Both parts of East Asia continued to utilize older traditions of strong government and Confucian values, blending them with new ingredients—and in China's case, outright revolution—and gaining increasing impact in the world at large.

PATTERNS OF EAST ASIAN HISTORY

A Clash of Cultures: Revolution and War

During the first two decades of the 20th century, Japan continued its policies of rapid industrialization and imperialist expansion. Exploitation of Korea developed rapidly from 1910 onward. Japan's participation in World War I involved little major fighting but provided a chance to gain former German island colonies in the Pacific. At the same time, Japan was not given high status in the Versailles Peace Conference, which Japanese leaders found humiliating; pressure built for a more aggressive stance that would compel the Western powers to recognize Japan's greatness. Internal stresses were also accumulating in Japanese society. A growing radical-socialist movement picked up working-class grievances, though it was successfully outlawed. Intellectuals continued the discussion of Japan's identity.

But as important tensions swirled in Japan, it was in China that more dramatic events occurred in the century's first decades. Growing Western penetration of the empire, combined with the government's sluggish response and the wave of students eager to see major reform, brought about a revolutionary climate. A new republican movement sought to replace the age-old empire. Headed by Dr. Sun Yat-sen (see p. 552), the educated son of a poor family who had spent time both in British-controlled Hong Kong and in Hawaii, the republicans believed that China should imitate Western principles of nationalism and democracy while introducing socialist policies to protect the people's welfare. Sun Yat-sen was no blind admirer of Western values; his emphasis on socialism was designed to guard against the excesses of capitalism and individualism. But he and his student followers were advocating a radical departure from Chinese political traditions.

In 1908, the death of the dowager empress brought government promises of a written constitution and an examination of other aspects of Western government. But these vague assurances were not enough to prevent widespread student rioting, which led to outright revolution in 1911. Sun Yat-sen hurried back from a trip abroad to head the provisional government, as the empire was ended in 1912.

The revolution demonstrated the weakness of the imperial regime, victim of the long decline characteristic of earlier Chinese dynasties but heightened by the inability to counter growing Western imperialism. However, while the old regime was easily dis-

Sun Yat-sen (1867–1925) was a vital figure in 20th-century Chinese history, who helped solidify the revolution that toppled the traditional imperial government. Dr. Sun failed, however, to create a fully successful alternative, becoming one of those fascinating leaders in world history whose reach exceeds their grasp. Sun Yat-sen was born into a poor family near Canton, but he acquired an education at the point when students were experiencing new influences from the West and becoming resistant amid Chinese traditions. Because of his opposition to the conservative imperial regime, Dr. Sun spent much time abroad, particularly in the United States, and he was thoroughly familiar with Western political thought. His writings proclaimed goals of nationalism, democracy, and ultimately socialism for a China that would be new but not a victim of some of the social ills that plagued the West. These writings made him a hero of Chinese students educated abroad. When revolution broke out in 1911, Dr. Sun rushed back to China from the United States and became provisional president. His insistence helped ensure that no compromise with the imperial regime would be struck, and the boy-emperor resigned in 1912. Sun Yat-sen could not control the presidency, however, which passed to a military general. Dr. Sun formed a Nationalist (Kuomintang) party to compete with military bosses as part of an effort to organize a parliamentary state. But his efforts to include communists and conservatives in his new movement failed with his death in 1925. China remained deeply divided for another two decades. Was Sun Yat-sen the best kind of leader to try to create a new state in China? What were the main barriers to trying to fulfill the task he set for himself?

for hard work and loyalty to the firm, while the government itself increasingly combined emperor worship with nationalism in order to prevent social unrest. Political stability, however, proved elusive.

After a period of moderate politics, during the 1920s, in which Japan seemed to accept a multiparty political system, even allowing nonaristocrats to serve as prime ministers for the first time, Japan pulled away from liberalism after 1930. The nation suffered severely from the early stages of the depression, as international trade plummeted. Dependent on exports to earn money to pay for food and fuel, Japan saw unemployment rise steadily when Western depression reduced its available markets. The silk industry, long an export staple, suffered as Western synthetics like nylon cut into sales—a sign of Japan's continuing industrial vulnerability. Furthermore, population growth contributed to the pressure, as 65 million inhabitants were crowded into territory about half the size of the state of Texas, with a million a year being added through the combination of high birth rates and falling death rates.

Economic chaos, though short-lived, allowed Japan's military leaders, allied with conservative business and agricultural interests, to regain the upper hand in politics. This group rebelled against the cautious liberalism of the reigning politicians, using assassination and the threat of mass unrest as weapons. Japan's powerful but fearful oligarchy turned to an essentially fascist approach, foreign, in its violence and intimidation methods, to Japan's political tradition. This transformation reflected not only the crisis of the depression but also the strains that rapid industrialization had placed on Japanese society—strains that did not produce outright revolution, but did lead the ruling oligarchy to its militaristic lines of defense. Parliamentary rule became increasingly hollow, as military leaders manipulated the politicians or, like General Hideki Tojo, held office directly. And with this authoritarianism came renewed interest in foreign expansion, as the Japanese sought an assured sphere of influence in eastern Asia to deal with the nation's overproduction and overpopulation. The more aggressive foreign policy aided, and was aided by, Japan's quick rebound to renewed industrial growth.

In 1931 the Japanese launched an undeclared war on China, seizing the province of Manchuria and turning it into a satellite state. This was the first of the acts of aggression in the interwar period that led toward World War II; Chinese leaders were unable to gain Western support, beyond moral condemnations of Japan, and this failure helped teach other rulers, such as Hitler, that aggression paid good dividends. Chiang Kai-shek hoped to satisfy the Japanese by agreeing to the loss of Manchuria, but in fact the Japanese soon resumed their advance, extending control over additional provinces in 1935 and then in 1937 mounting a new war against China, which effectively continued until Japan's World War II defeat in 1945. Thus China, already internally divided, faced 15 years of invasion and occupation. Vast stretches of the country were seized, many resources diverted to Japanese war industries, and millions of people killed or uprooted. Chiang's regime was driven from the great cities, but he was able to maintain control of many rural provinces. Both the warlords and the communists joined in opposition to the Japanese, the communists gaining prestige and important military experience through their resistance role.

Stalemated in China, Japan used the outbreak of war in Europe as an occasion to turn its attention to other parts of Asia. It seized Indochina from France's troops and then allied with Germany and Italy in a pledge of mutual military assistance. This alliance, along with continued expansion in Southeast Asia as the Japanese attacked Malaya and Burma, put the Japanese on a collision course with the United States, which as a Pacific power itself was unwilling to allow Japan to become a predominant force in the Far East. U.S. holdings in Hawaii and the Philippines, the fruit of earlier imperialism, convinced Japanese leaders that a clash was inevitable. Negotiations with the United States broke down with American insistence that Japan renounce all gains acquired since 1931. It was in this setting that the Japanese attacked Pearl Harbor on December 7, 1941, and then in the following months seized American possessions in the eastern Pacific, including the Philippine islands. Only toward the end of 1942 did the United States begin to turn the tide, using its greater numbers and superior level of industrialization. Scattered islands were reconquered, followed in 1944 by the Philippines, while massive air raids began an onslaught on Japan itself. Meanwhile American, British, and Chinese forces continued to tie down a considerable Japanese army on the Asian mainland. Finally, in 1945, the United States dropped atomic bombs on the cities of Nagasaki and Hiroshima, forcing a full surrender of Japan and a period of American occupation.

RETURN TO STABILITY IN JAPAN

The end of World War II separated the paths of Japan and China once again. Japan's imperialist surge ended, seemingly for good. It had been an anomaly in Japanese history in any event, and American-imposed changes in government personnel and limitations on military activity further reduced the potential for military adventurism. Victims of the only actual use of atomic weapons, many Japanese advocated an antimilitarist stance, while official Japanese policy accepted American protection against possible Soviet aggression rather than mounting a significant defense capacity directly. Internal politics were restructured as well, as American occupation forces helped produce a more liberal constitution, which enhanced the power of parliament, reduced the emperor from religious figure to figurehead, and provided important safeguards for freedom of speech and press. Universal suffrage, first granted in the moderate period of the 1920s, was restored, and a number of political parties contested the major elections. In fact, a single party, the Liberal Democrats, held the reins of government throughout most of the postwar decades, but the existence of political criticism and potential opposition affected its policies. Japan produced a new era of political stability, in which major concentration turned to economic development, as the Japanese soon entered the ranks of the world's most technologically sophisticated nations.

UPHEAVAL AND LATER REVOLUTION IN CHINA

With Japan's defeat, China emerged as the leading power in the Far East. Chiang Kai-shek was welcomed as a postwar leader, particularly by his U.S. allies; the Chinese were treated as a great power, along with Britain, France, the United States, and the Soviet Union, in forming the new United Nations—the first time an Asian nation had been accorded this kind of status in Western-dominated diplomacy. But the honeymoon was short-lived. Chiang was unable to assert a firm hold on China, for communist opposition began to mount.

Hiroshima, 1945, after the first atomic bomb was dropped.

The communist struggle with the Kuomintang went back to the aftermath of China's first modern revolution. Inspired by the revolutionary atmosphere and also the example of Russia's Bolshevik success, a communist movement formed among students in Beijing between 1919 and 1921; the movement quickly came under the leadership of Mao Zedung, a librarian who was from a wealthy peasant family. Communists and Kuomintang collaborated for a time, both interested in establishing a revolutionary regime and opposing the warlords. But the goals of the two groups were quite different, and Chiang Kai-shek expelled the communists in 1927, summarily executing anyone found with red dye on his neck, the color left from having worn the emblematic communist scarf. Recurrent battles continued, for while the communists were weakened, they were not eliminated. Then a renewed military effort in 1934 brought the historic Long March, in which Mao led his followers to a remote northwestern province, where they built a strong reform movement among the peasantry and an independent power base. World War II gave the communists a chance to display their solid organization and guerrilla fighting techniques, and they also gained important new territory in their resistance effort against Japan.

By the war's end the communists claimed to control over 70 million Chinese, with an army of almost a million. The Kuomintang, in contrast, had been exhausted in its war effort, as the Japanese had taken over the coastal cities where the movement had its power base. Economic problems and internal divisions and corruption further weakened

World War II: Pacific Theater

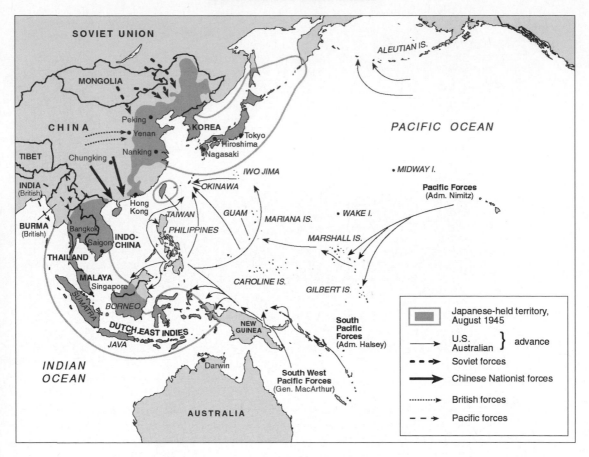

the Kuomintang, which could not prevent communist guerrilla attacks and sabotage that undermined support for the existing regime. The communists offered not only successful military strategies but a much clearer program of land reform to China's peasant majority than did the Kuomintang, which increasingly seemed little more than a Western-dominated militarist group, its heritage from Sun Yat-sen mere rhetoric. Soviet aid to the communists also helped, while American support for the Kuomintang actually enhanced the government's organizational confusion. While Stalin had no love for the Chinese communists, and Mao had long since diverged from the Russian model in his concern for peasant issues, a temporary reunion provided a final ingredient in communist success.

Civil war between the communists and Chiang's armies broke out in 1945, and the Kuomintang lost ground steadily. Indeed, the speed of communist success surprised everyone, including the communists themselves. By 1949 the communists were in full control of Mainland China. By 1950 Chiang had been driven to the island of Taiwan, which the communists could not capture because they had no navy. There, Chiang and his army imposed an authoritarian regime, while still plotting an eventual return to the mainland. But in fact the mainland belonged to Mao and the communists.

Communist victory, in turn, meant a second revolution in modern Chinese history—or a culmination of almost half a century of revolutionary pressure. The new rulers executed at least 800,000 political opponents and arrested many more. Their goal was to destroy all traces of China's old ruling groups—educated bureaucrats, landlords, and capitalists alike. In their place the communists constructed a strong centralized state dedicated to economic modernization and social change. Five-year plans were issued, based on the Soviet model, to encourage heavy industry. Agriculture was collectivized, with peasant communes replacing traditional villages. With property seized from the landlords, the revolution in the countryside reached major proportions. The government strictly controlled education and information, mounting a major attack on the various religions of China.

In its early years Mao's regime maintained its close alliance with Soviet Russia. This alliance, plus a desire to assert China's traditional power in Asia, prompted the communist regime to resist U.S. advances in the Korean War. Divided between a communist north and noncommunist south after World War II, Korea had become a battleground in 1950 when the communists invaded the south. The United States came to the aid of its southern protectorate and then crossed into North Korea. This move brought massive Chinese intervention, which ultimately forced American retreat and a restoration of the previous Korean regimes and boundaries. China thus served notice that no outside power could claim East Asian dominance, in contrast to the humiliating decades of Western and Japanese imperialism. But this same new strength soon caused a rift between Chinese and Russian communists. Mao began to attack post-Stalinist Soviet policy as a violation of true Marxism. Russian aid and advisors to the new Chinese regime were withdrawn, and tensions along the Soviet-Chinese border increased. While ideological differences colored the new disagreement, it became clear that territorial disputes entered in as well: the Chinese had not forgotten earlier Russian seizure of some northern lands, while Russian rulers were keenly aware of the potential pressure of China's massive population on their sparsely peopled Asian republics. By the 1960s the two giants of the communist world had become virtual enemies.

The rift with Russia prompted Chairman Mao to experiment with a different path to communism during the 1960s. Instead of five-year plans for heavy industry, Mao began to emphasize small-scale workshops in which intensive labor would substitute for advanced technology. Peasant communes stressed the need for a new Chinese personality, with common dining halls and massive propaganda attacking the evils of traditional family ties and Confucian hierarchical values. Finally, schools were transformed into pure agencies of Maoist propaganda, and technical and scientific study was abandoned. Many teachers and other intellectuals were ordered to the countryside to do agricultural work. During the 1960s China seemed engulfed by this new revolutionary fervor, as Mao sought to solidify his power, to defy the Soviet model, and, above all, to attack many of the traditions of Chinese society, in order to produce a modern nation that was also free from the trappings of Western modernization or the bureaucratic conservatism of the Soviet Union. During this period of Cultural Revolution, bands of youths were organized to attack any vestige of traditional hierarchy in schools, family, and even the army. As one manifesto

Peasants thrashing rice on an agricultural commune near Beijing.

proclaimed, "We are bent on striking down not only the reactionaries in our school, but the reactionaries all over the world. Revolutionaries take it as their task to transform the world."

The cultural revolution in China began to yield, however, by the late 1960s. Disruption of the schools and the attempt at backyard industry had worsened the Chinese economy. Pressure from the Soviet Union, including outright border fighting in 1969, prompted Mao to seek a partial reconciliation with the United States, which occurred in 1971. More moderate communist leaders also regained influence, and on Mao's death, in 1976, assumed control. Under the leadership of Deng Xiaoping, the communist regime, though maintaining tight political authority, began to devote itself to intensive but rather conventional modernization efforts, stressing technical education and industrial development. In fact an important student movement for democracy in 1989 was put down in favor of continued authoritarianism.

EAST ASIA TOWARD THE END OF THE CENTURY

The major events of East Asian history in the 20th century can seem bewildering in their complexity. Japan moved from imperialism to modernization, from authoritarianism to democracy and a concentration on economic advance. China endured two revolutionary periods punctuated by Japanese invasion, and then, under the communists, three distinct periods: Russian-style consolidation, radical experimentation during the

Election workers count the vote: Mao Zedung poster helps inspire during elections to the National Peoples Congress.

Cultural Revolution, and then more pragmatic modernization since the late 1970s. Clearly, East Asian nations were groping for appropriate political forms during much of the 20th century. Stability in Japan since World War II, and considerable stability in China since the end of the Cultural Revolution, may suggest that such a goal finally has been achieved.

East Asia was also adjusting to new power alignments. Along with the period of conflict between Japan and China, the region was engaged in limiting Western influence and preventing major new Soviet gains. China's expulsion of special Western treaty rights, Japan's attack on Western-held territories, and China's Korean intervention all worked to this end, albeit in different ways. While Soviet and American influence in East Asia remained considerable, there was little question by the 1970s that the region had regained substantial freedom of action. Internal conflicts subsided as well, so that since the end of the Korean War a period of effective peace took hold within the region. Tensions continued, to be sure: the regimes of North and South Korea faced each other across a precarious border; the Chinese People's Republic officially claimed sovereignty over a now-separate regime on Taiwan; and China encountered tensions with Vietnam to the south. But compared to many other parts of the contemporary world, the region became fairly trouble-free—as it had so often been in earlier periods of history. Relative stability and a reduction in the turmoil that had marked the earlier decades of the century have given the major regimes of East Asia a chance to define their characters.

JAPAN, INCORPORATED

Twentieth-century Japan, for all its transformations in political regime and foreign policy, displayed two consistent traits: an ability to combine adaptation to selected Western imports and technologies with a distinctive cultural identity, and a dynamism that brought the nation to world prominence first as a military force and then as one of the economic giants of the final decades of the century. The two traits were interrelated. Japan's skill in borrowing without loss of identity, and its ability to utilize traditional characteristics such as strong group cohesion, had much to do with military and economic success. Such was Japan's impact that by the 1970s, along with continued Japanese interest in Western ways, came an almost obsessive Western eagerness to learn Japanese secrets, including traditional social traits that seemed so strikingly useful in an advanced industrial age. Western business and labor leaders began to make pilgrimages to Japan with some of the same zeal that Japanese students had displayed in their visits to Western nations during the previous century.

Japanese politics, certainly, blended modern democratic forms with traditional elite ties. As in the Meiji era and to an extent during the authoritarian period of the 1930s, postwar politics were dominated by civil servants and business leaders. Through democratic suffrage prevailed and a number of political parties showed strength, the fact was that postwar Japan experienced no shifts in party leadership. Opposition groups were less important than factional jockeying within the Liberal Democratic party. Few major policy shifts occurred after World War II. Only in 1993, amid growing evidence of business payoffs, did the Liberal Democrats split and lose their parliamentary majority, opening the

Contemporary Tokyo.

possibility of more innovative politics. At least until this point, unusual stability in party dominance, which made Japan less similar to Western political patterns in fact than the constitutional structure would suggest, related to the other distinctive feature of the contemporary Japanese state: an unusual alliance with business interests toward the promotion of economic development and the expansion of exports. Government economic planning remained extensive, and business leaders willingly acquiesced to government production guidelines and other regulations; there was no sense of division of interests between public and private spheres, as still prevailed to an extent in the West. Small wonder that the coordination of economic policies produced the half-admiring, half-derisory Western label of "Japan, Incorporated."

Close business and political interaction resulted in part from the needs of a wartime economy and then postwar reconstruction. It was supported by Japan's precarious resource position, as the nation needed to import petroleum and most other vital raw materials, and so depended on active exports, which in turn the government helped promote. But the interaction also followed from a long cultural tradition in which group cohesion was seen as the logical basis of society's functioning, a cohesion that easily blurred what Westerners saw as the lines between private enterprise and state action. Government initiative also played a key role in ending Japan's rapid population increase. Once imperialist expansion ended, Japanese leaders realized that population must stabilize, and they used government, in the late 1940s and 1950s, to organize an active campaign toward birth control and legalized abortion, which indeed reversed a century-long trend of demographic expansion. Unlike the West, where government policy had little to do with population trends and sometimes ran counter to such trends, Japan's more integrated political-social system allowed concrete action in a vital aspect of family behavior, which in turn encouraged more orderly economic growth and an improvement in living standards.

Important segments of Japanese culture were also bent to the task of economic development. The extensive school system built up during the Meiji period was further expanded. Japanese children were encouraged to achieve academic success, with demanding examinations for entry into the university defining much of the youth of ambitious men and women. Higher education, in turn, placed heavy emphasis on technical and scientific subjects, though research and teaching in the social sciences gained ground as well. Contemporary Japanese culture thus placed a premium on rational inquiry, reflected in growing creativity in science and technological innovation. Growing university enrollments, based on examination performance, recruited on the basis of educational merit, creating one of the most open social systems in the world.

Japanese culture also preserved important traditional elements, however, providing aesthetic and spiritual satisfactions amid rapid economic change. Japanese films and novels recalled earlier history, including the age of the samurai warriors; they also stressed group loyalties, as opposed to individuality or strong assertions of will. Interest in rituals, including tea ceremonies and traditional costumes for recreation, remained significant themes as well. Japanese artists participated actively in the "international style" developed in the West, but they typically infused it with earlier Japanese motifs such as stylized nature painting. Japanese architects, also working in the modern style, incorporated traditional themes as well. Finally, both Buddhism and Shintoism, despite a largely secular culture, sustained religious forces in Japanese life. Overall, Japan during the 20th century produced a blend of new cultural interests, many of which originated in the West, and older approaches, which allowed Japan in turn to make distinctive contributions to international artistic and scientific movements.

But, particularly after World War II, it was through rapid economic growth that Japan made its clearest mark. Industrial development had continued at a steady pace through the 1920s, and again in the late 1930s, as Japan built upon its efforts during the Meiji era and produced a fully industrialized society. Then from the 1950s onward, the Japanese moved into the orbit of advanced industrial nations, easily surpassing the level of technological development current in Eastern Europe and challenging Western nations for world leadership. Beginning in the middle of the century, economic growth rates were among the highest in the world. By the 1970s Japan became the world's chief producer and exporter of automobiles and many kinds of electronic equipment.

Japan's economic success rested on several factors. Wages remained lower than those common in the West, though living standards improved rapidly, particularly by the 1960s. The collaboration of business and government was supplemented by the large corporate combines, called *zaibatsu*, that emerged by the 1920s as a means of reducing competition within Japan itself. Business concentration took place in the West as well, but the mutual arrangements among large Japanese concerns, backed by government planning, went further still. The Japanese also cultivated an unusual degree of worker loyalty and diligence. While some labor unrest occurred both in the 1920s and after World War II, strike rates were low by Western standards and Japanese workers were noted for their careful workmanship and productivity. In the big companies, workers were assured of job security; they could not be fired. They were often consulted on possible technical improvements. At the same time, businesses sponsored group exercises and other collective activities that contributed to morale. Japanese managers also showed less interest than their Western counterparts in high profits, while emphasizing group decision-making and loyalty over individual ambition within a corporate hierarchy.

The Japanese approach to labor relations had some serious political and social costs, however. Many workers were forced to join company unions, as Japan's ruling oligarchy continued to find ways to undermine protest. Pressure to maintain high productivity was intense, and some workers who could not toe the line were forced to retire. Workers themselves were divided between those with job security and a large number, about 60 percent of the manufacturing labor force, including most working women, who faced more unstable market pressures. The *zaibatsu* system, effective in economic coordination, also helped suppress political competition, though less completely and arbitrarily than in the 1930s. But at least into the early 1990s the Japanese pattern, in the eyes of many Westerners and many Japanese themselves, was a powerful economic instrument, creating unprecedented productivity and economic growth and a rising margin of exports over imports that steadily increased Japan's role in the world economy. Economic growth slowed in the 1990s, partly because of the new global competition, but the nation remained a world powerhouse.

An additional element in Japanese economic success was the application of distinctive social relations to an advanced industrial technology. By Western standards the Japanese seemed durably nonindividualistic, loyal to group endeavors and not very concerned with personal reward or private expressions of discontent. Continued use of elaborate ceremonies of politeness, plus heavy emphasis in the schools on the importance of patriotism, helped explain this unique national psychology. So did Japanese methods of child rearing. Children were encouraged to conform to group standards, among other things by the use of shame for nonconformity—an approach the West had largely abandoned in child rearing by the early 19th century. Japanese social solidarity showed even in the nation's legal practices. Lawyers were uncommon in 20th-century Japan, for it was assumed that people could make firm arrangements on the basis of mutual agreement and that individuals had no reason to use the courts to protest the activities of neighbors or business or government leaders.

Not surprisingly, Japanese family customs and important aspects of personal behavior developed in ways different from the contemporary West. Male authority remained preeminent in 20th-century Japan. Relatively few women worked after marriage, and women's wages lagged well behind male levels—about 40 percent compared to the 70 percent common in the West. Women's role in the family, particularly in shaping young children, was heavily stressed. Japanese family structure stabilized after the high incidence of divorce around 1900, but it emphasized the domestic functions of women. Though a few individual Japanese feminists emerged, there was no movement comparable to that in Western society demanding new rights for women. Yet Western influence showed, for example, in growing approval of romantic love. In intimate life as in culture, Japan blended diverse ingredients. In the area of personal behavior, Japanese psychiatrists reported a distinctive pattern of mental illness. Problems of loneliness and alienation were far less great than in the West, as the Japanese remained highly dependent, emotionally, on group activities. Conversely, in situations where individuals encountered competition alone, as in university entrance tests, stress levels were much higher than in analogous Western experiences. The Japanese also had their particular ways to relieve tension. Bouts of drunkenness were more readily tolerated than in the West, as a time when normal codes of conduct could be suspended. Businessmen had recourse to the traditional geisha houses, for female-supplied cosseting, as a normal and approved activity.

Japanese popular culture was not static. Western influences entered this area too. During the 1920s Western styles of dress, sports, and music gained acceptance in the cities. Fashionable residents of Tokyo were even called "maden boi" and "modan garu" (modern boy or girl). The U.S. presence after World War II brought a growing fascination with the sport of baseball, and a number of professional teams were set up. In the early 1980s, a new passion for television game shows, adapted from their American progenitors, took hold, though the Japanese typically altered the characteristic form to provide more elaborate humiliation (or shame) for game show losers. Romantic soap operas hit Japan with *Tokyo Love Story*, in 1989, quickly the most-watched TV show in the nation's history. In popular as in formal culture, Western domination caused some concern among conservatives, who worried that vital traditions—like the use of chopsticks—might be lost for good. But to Western eyes the Japanese ability to assimilate imported culture within a distinctive context seemed far more striking.

As noted, Japan was not without its problems amid economic success. Many nations both in the West and in Asia resented Japanese competition, often seen as unfair because the Japanese were slow to open their own markets to outside goods. Japanese dependence on imported oil and other products made the nation vulnerable to events in distant areas, such as the oil-producing Middle East. Pollution became an increasing problem with industrial growth and the rapid expansion of cities; traffic police, for example, often had to wear protective masks simply to breathe. New regulations after the 1970s did reduce pollution problems and helped generate growing environmental industries. Competition from other parts of Asia increased. Some Japanese experts, worried that the nation's economic vigor would prove fragile, wrote articles with such titles as "The Short, Happy Life of Japan as a Superpower," and growing unemployment plus sluggish production rates caused new concern by 1995.

THE COASTAL COUNTRIES OF EAST AND SOUTHEAST ASIA: THE PACIFIC RIM

A number of other East Asian nations developed an extensive industrial economy from the 1950s onward, though none could rival the advanced forms of Japan. South Korea, Taiwan, the British colony in Hong Kong, and, further to the south, the city-state of Singapore (whose population is largely Chinese) produced rapid economic growth. By the 1980s Malaysia, Thailand, and Indonesia began to join in. Most of these nations were long ruled by authoritarian regimes; political opposition was downplayed. Governments and business leaders collaborated to develop new factory industries, with emphasis both on consumer goods and metallurgy. Growing exports earned revenues needed for the import of raw materials and advanced Western or Japanese technology.

As in Japan, the Pacific Rim states stressed national and group loyalties and limited what they saw as excessive individualism, including undue consumerism, which they considered to be wasteful and a threat to economic growth. Korean leaders emphasized traditional Confucian morality as part of this effort. The intent, as in Japan, was to change traditional values and social structures sufficiently to modernize the economy, but to preserve enough of these same values to avoid Westernization. The success of these nations suggested that East Asia, led by but not confined to Japan, was becoming the world's second industrial civilization, along with the West, as the region easily outstripped Eastern Europe. The prospect was made all the more probable by the region's ability to maintain the world's highest rates of economic growth during the 1970s and early 1980s. Greater openness to democracy was an important additional development in much of the Pacific Rim by the 1990s, but so was a new problem of financial instability in 1998.

CHINA UNDER COMMUNISM

China, the mother country of East Asian civilization, did not participate fully in the initial East Asian economic surge. The political system remained resolutely authoritarian. Once again, East Asia was a divided region, in politics and in economic patterns, as the fits and starts of the communist regime in China abundantly demonstrated.

Communism took hold in China for a number of reasons. Historical accident played a role: the distraction of the Kuomintang by Japanese invasion prevented concerted attack on the communist forces and allowed the latter to consolidate their provincial power base. The inspired leadership of Mao Zedung was a vital ingredient; as in Lenin's Russia, communist revolution depended heavily on individual talent. Mao converted to communism during his student years, in 1918, seeing it as a means of challenging Western economic dominance while also facilitating fundamental changes within China itself. The all-encompassing belief system that Marxism provided played a role here as in the West and Soviet Russia. But Mao adapted Marxism to Chinese circumstances early on, particularly in his emphasis on the power of the Chinese peasantry. He argued in 1927 that "the force of the peasantry is like that of the raging winds and driving rain. . . . The peasantry will tear apart all nets which bind it and hasten along the road to liberation." By promising land reform and conciliating peasants during the revolutionary struggle, Mao's forces gained vital support in their war against the better-armed Kuomintang.

But while communism was a new force in Chinese history, with the goal of genuine revolution and not simply the seizure of power, it coincided with traditional features of Chinese society—as had been the case in the Soviet Union. The Chinese legacy of a strong state, with an elaborate bureaucracy, lent itself readily to a communist system, in which state power was further extended and in which government bureaucrats, though recruited from new sources and held to a new political faith, regulated large sectors of the economy and even family life. Mao's success, after the earlier failure of more liberal politics during the 1920s, was in this sense no accident. From the late 1940s onward, communist officials prevented political opposition, monopolized the sources of information and propaganda, and abandoned all pretense of establishing a Western-style parliamentary regime. The Communist party ruled the new People's Republic of China, and the party itself was dominated by Mao's direction. While the communist state was more efficient in its use of police and its active promotion of political loyalty than the empire had been, the ordinary Chinese might be excused for noting some similarities as well. Indeed, Communist leaders themselves soon found that they had re-created an extensive bureaucratic apparatus that posed some of the same barriers to change that the old Confucian bureaucracy had done. By the 1970s appeals to bureaucrats to recognize the importance of new technologies and management methods became standard, as the Chinese continued to seek a reconciliation between strong state authority and economic vigor.

For Mao's state and that of his more pragmatic successors was bent on transformation outside the political arena. China had been changing even before the communist revolution. During the 1920s the port cities continued to expand, and factory industry took root. Modernized patterns of work and education gave new voice to young people, weakening the ancestor-venerating tradition of Confucianism. The importance of student groups expressed this shift. The position of women began to change, as women in the cities acquired formal education and practices such as footbinding declined. More and more marriages were based on mutual affection rather than economic arrangements alone. Educational reforms brought even greater shifts in outlook, as science began to play a more significant role; many educated Chinese, at home and abroad, contributed actively to scientific and technological research.

Mao sought to extend and formalize the pattern of cultural and social change. He attacked Confucian values head-on. Harmony, ceremony, and ancestor worship were fetters on the liberation of China's masses, in his view. He encouraged the new importance of

installed in South Korea, Taiwan, and the Philippines, and in the face of their own massive student rebellion of 1989, Chinese leaders maintained the importance of an authoritarian regime. Russia's troubles in combining political and economic reform further convinced them that toleration of dissent was a mistake. The regime eagerly moved forward toward a more market-based economy, with profit incentives and private initiative along with state planning. Chinese exports soared in order to pay for new equipment and expertise from abroad. But it insisted—as China had so often done in the past—on its own political formula. Assimilation of the former British colony of Hong Kong, from 1997 onward, gave China another dose of ardent capitalism, but also another set of issues about freedom of expression.

CONCLUSION: EAST ASIA AND THE WORLD

As the communist revolution spread across China, while Japan adapted to a more democratic political structure after World War II, the differences among East Asian societies seemed overwhelming. Even by the 1990s, the variations in levels of economic development and political forms constituted major distinctions not only between Japan and China, but among the smaller nations as well. Japan represented, along with the leading Western industrial states, a key participant in annual "free world" economic conferences, because of shared political concerns as well as world market interests. Countries like South Korea and Taiwan were less industrialized, though growing rapidly; they also faced periodic protest against their authoritarian political structures, which liberalized somewhat at the end of the 1980s, while China and Vietnam, still partially isolated, tried to combine economic reforms with maintenance of its communist system.

Yet, with time, some enduring common features among East Asian societies have reemerged. An emphasis on strong social cohesion is one such element. China's Communist regime seeks tight social solidarity, while Japanese values stress group ties from family through nation. From a common Confucian past, albeit much altered by recent events, East Asian nations also preserve an interest in ceremony and emotional restraint. They share a desire to develop or maintain industrial dynamism without becoming carbon copies either of Western or of Russian society.

For both China and Japan, though open to more international influences than ever before in their history, have continued to stand somewhat apart from other civilizations. Visitors to Japan report a polite but distant reception, as the Japanese continue to mark the distinctiveness and superiority of their culture, to which foreigners can rarely if ever gain full admission. China, though embarking on renewed contacts with the West after the vigorous attack on all foreign influences that was part of the Cultural Revolution, continues to monitor outsiders closely, making it clear that amicability and selective imitation should not expose the Chinese people to wholesale tolerance of foreign ways. East Asia, more influential in the wider world by the later 20th century than at any previous point in history, has maintained its traditional ability to see this world through its own lens.

SUGGESTED READINGS

For an overview on China, see I. Hsu, *The Rise of Modern China*, 2nd ed. (1975). For an excellent interpretive study, using a modernization model, see G. Rozman, ed., *The Modernization of China* (1981); see also Wolfgang Franke, *A Century of Chinese Revolution* (1970). On the Chinese revolutions, J. Spence, *The Gate of Heavenly Peace: The Chinese and their Revolution 1895–1980* (1982), is invaluable; on the communist revolution specifically, Edward Snow, *Red Star Over China* (1968), is quite readable. Consult also, as a source, A. Freemantle, ed., *Mao-Tse Tung: An Anthology of His Writings* (1962). On more recent developments, I. Hsu, *China Without Mao: The Search for a New Order* (1983) is worthwhile.

On Japan, an excellent cultural interpretation is E. O. Reischauer, *The Japanese* (1988). See also P. Duus, *The Rise of Modern Japan* (1976) and M. Howe, *Modern Japan: A Historical Survey* (1986). See also H. Patrick and H. Rosovsky, *Asia's New Giant: How the Japanese Economy Works* (1976). An important specific topic is covered in R. Story, *The Double Patriots: A Story of Japanese Nationalism* (1973). Japanese economic success and its significance is treated in Ezra Vogel, *Japan as Number One: Lessons for Americans* (1980). On the Pacific Rim, see Philip West et al., eds., *Pacific Rim and the Western World: Strategic, Economic and Cultural Perspectives* (1987); see also G. Rozman, ed., *East Asian Region: Confucian Heritage and Its Modern Adaptation* (1991); and Bruce Cuming, *Korea's Place in the Sun: A Modern History* (1997).

CHAPTER 29

India and Southeast Asia

Focal Points

The first half of the 20th century in India, and to a large extent in Southeast Asia, was dominated by the struggle against colonialism and the rise of nationalism. Why did the colonial powers finally yield? What were the goals of nationalists beyond national independence, and how did some of them disagree? India was noteworthy among the new nations for its ability to maintain democracy; what facilitated this political form? It also experienced important economic changes, as food production increased and new manufacturing sectors emerged. Amid change, what balance did Indians strike between traditional cultures and newer beliefs? What happened to some of the historical ingredients of Indian society such as the caste system? Compared to China, was India helped or hindered by the fact that it did not undergo a real revolution?

INDIA AND SOUTHEAST ASIA FROM WORLD WAR I TO INDEPENDENCE

During the first half of the 20th century, nationalist pressures built steadily on the Indian subcontinent and in Southeast Asia. Dislocations produced by World War II prompted the ending of European controls. In a few cases—most notably Vietnam—continued struggle was needed well after World War II to achieve independence, but in most instances, including India, decolonization occurred quickly and without much further conflict with the former imperialist powers. Thus the history of India and Southeast Asia since the late 1940s is characterized by the formation of newly independent nations and the establishment of their distinct political styles. India became the world's largest democracy, building on older political traditions as well as the legacy of British rule and nationalist struggle. Other nations on the Indian subcontinent and in Southeast Asia were more authoritarian in political structure, while Vietnam became communist. The earlier pattern of political division thus persisted in Southeast Asia, though in new forms. Problems of economic development also loomed large. Again there was great diversity; a few new nations, such as Bangladesh, proved to be among the world's poorest. But in

India itself, significant economic change took place, while parts of Southeast Asia pulled into the dynamic orbit of the Pacific Rim.

THE RISE OF NATIONALISM

India provided a key example of the growing struggle for independence after 1914, just as it would help lead the movement of new nations after World War II. Rising nationalism in much of Southeast Asia proved somewhat similar to patterns in India. Throughout southern Asia, indeed, the issue of national freedom moved to the top of the agenda during the years between the world wars. Problems in Europe weakened the hold of the imperialist nations, though they remained militarily dominant until the 1940s. Many Europeans became increasingly open to the idea that their colonies should work toward ultimate freedom. New currents in India and Southeast Asia provided an even greater impetus to nationalism. The example of the Russian Revolution and the Leninist idea that a massive social revolution was possible as part of the struggle against the empire also converted some Indian and Southeast Asian leaders. Outside Vietnam, where nationalism and Marxism were closely linked, Marxism had less impact in southern Asia than in China, but it was a significant element nonetheless.

More important still was a new wave of peasant unrest in various parts of southern Asia. Peasant agitation resulted from growing population pressure combined with the more efficient tax collection and commercial agriculture that were part of imperialist rule. Peasants had their own idea of social justice, which included the more tolerant leadership of village headmen and greater access to land; they were rarely directly concerned with national independence, but their goals were compatible with liberation movements in that they resented the economic and administrative measures brought by outside rule.

But it was nationalism itself, gaining new vigor and adherence, that focused the political history of southern Asia during the first half of the 20th century. Copied from Europe initially, nationalism took on, if anything, greater importance in India and Southeast Asia, where it meant freedom from foreign domination and a chance to come to terms with the modern world while preserving vital features of traditional civilization. In India, nationalism promised a kind of unity that the country had almost never known and a self-expression that had not been possible for many centuries. The Indian patriot Chittaranjan Das, writing early in the century, put the nationalist case as follows:

> What is the ideal which we must set before us? The first and foremost is the ideal of nationalism. Now what is nationalism? It is, I conceive, a process through which a nation expresses itself and finds itself, not in isolation from other nations, not in opposition to other nations, but as part of a great scheme by which, in seeking its own expression and therefore its own identity, it materially assists the self-expression and self-realization of other nations as well: Diversity is as real as unity. . . . I contend that each nationality constitutes a particular stream of the great unity, but no nation can fulfill itself unless and until it becomes itself and at the same time realizes its identity with Humanity.

The idealistic fervor of southern Asian nationalism, and especially the nationalism that took root in India, provided real force on its own, quite apart from specific issues and grievances.

Indian nationalism was given direct impetus by the events of World War I. Three million Indian soldiers fought in British armies during the war. At the same time, taxes and food shortages at home created discontent, bringing new strength to the Indian National Congress and an alliance between the Hindu leadership of the Congress party and the nation's Muslim League. This united front called for self-government within the British Empire. Britain did indeed set up new provincial legislative councils, providing voting rights for 6 million of the nation's 250 million people; the councils had jurisdiction over such areas as education and public health. But this 1919 measure was obviously halfhearted, indicating London's continued suspicion of India's ability to rule itself. The central government remained firmly in British hands, with advisory councils elected by only a million Indian voters. The British followed a classic pattern of offering enough reform to encourage new expectations—along with the excitement caused by World War I and the principles of national self-determination discussed at Versailles—but not enough to satisfy. At the same time the British tightened police measures against those they viewed as troublemakers. The new repression brought a wave of rioting across the subcontinent. Police nervousness even prompted clashes at Hindu religious festivals; in one such confrontation 379 celebrants, all unarmed, were killed by British-led troops. Police brutality here, and in major labor strikes, heightened Indian nationalism and helped unite upper-caste leaders with large numbers of workers and peasants.

Popular agitation continued in the 1920s. An influenza epidemic and crop failures that killed 5 million people led to a wave of rural uprisings against landlords and moneylenders. Some urban protest developed as well, with strikes among textile and railroad workers; Marxist doctrines made some headway. This diverse discontent was grist for the nationalists' mill, as it served to press the British. Middle-class nationalists themselves discussed a boycott of British goods, to protest India's economic dependence.

THE NONVIOLENT STRATEGIES OF GANDHI

In this context of growing agitation, the emergence in 1920 of Mohandas Gandhi (see p. 575) as the leader and master tactician of the nationalist forces was a key development. Gandhi became an almost universally respected symbol of India's political awakening, the most important political figure in Indian history since the Mauryan and Gupta dynasties in the classical period. Gandhi had been born into a merchant family that also wielded great political influence in a small princely state north of Bombay, under British rule but shielded from the most direct Western pressure. His family had been devout Hindus, keenly persuaded of the importance of group loyalties. Gandhi himself studied law in Britain, and practiced for a time in South Africa, where he became keenly aware of the desperate plight of many Indians whom the British had imported as indentured laborers and who, like Gandhi himself, were often victims of brutal discrimination in public. Gandhi's reaction was not just one of indignation, but a deep search for a strategy by which the weak could overcome imperialist strength. His conclusion, drawn from his version of Hindu tradition plus other religious reading, was collective nonviolence in resistance to injustice. He organized a campaign of peaceful marches to protest discrimination in South Africa, including nonviolent resistance to police attacks and arrest, which was successful in removing some of the most overt limitations on Indians in that colony.

Then, in 1915, Gandhi returned to India, and after a few years of reflection and experimentation with different tactics, he seized the opportunity to mount a campaign of nonviolent resistance provided by growing popular and nationalist unrest. Gandhi's great gift was to unite educated nationalist leaders with the rural masses, who saw in Gandhi an incarnation of deep spiritual values and whose Hinduism accorded with the emphasis on nonviolence. Gandhi told the Indian masses, who had long left the fighting to the warrior castes, that they too could be courageous:

> Wherein is courage required—in blowing others to pieces from behind a cannon, or with a smiling face to approach a cannon and be blown to pieces? Who is the true warrior—he who keeps death always as a bosom-friend, or he who controls the death of others? Believe me that a man devoid of courage and manhood can never be a passive resister.

Under Gandhi's leadership, the Congress movement became a mass political force for the first time, giving Indians a far greater taste of political participation than Britain's timid legislative experiments allowed. Gandhi served also as a significant figure in a revived and revised Hinduism, in which ethical principles were stressed over both ceremonialism and the caste system.

Gandhi was also a master of tactics. His simple, holy style of life, which included renunciation of sex, brought him the title Mahatma, or "saintly one." He could attack castes, and so please the masses and the Muslims, while also wooing Brahmin religious leaders by praising tradition. He could talk both to striking workers and moderate reformers. Above all, his stress on nonviolence confounded British authorities, who found it difficult to respond with all-out repression. Gandhi was frequently arrested, but his sentences roused so much mass furor—heightened by well-publicized refusals to eat during imprisonment—that he ultimately had to be released. While Gandhi was not able to prevent periodic violence against British officials, he did direct most attention to peaceful mass disruption, refusals to pay taxes, and other tactics that were hard to counter. "We must voluntarily put up with the losses and inconveniences that arise from having to withdraw our support from a government that is ruling against our will." In this spirit, Gandhi and his followers boycotted elections, blocked trains by lying down on the tracks, and surrounded government buildings with thousands of quiet demonstrators so that officials had to walk over bodies to get to work.

By the 1930s the British realized that they had to offer further reforms. But a series of conferences with Indian leaders convinced the British that there was no way to please Hindus and Muslims, radicals and princes. Indeed, many Muslim leaders were increasingly antagonized, despite Gandhi's efforts at reconciliation, by the development of an Indian nationalism based largely on Hindu symbols and customs, and began talking of the need for their own nation, a "Pakistan," or "land of the pure," instead of a unified India. Britain also played its own role in encouraging Hindu-Muslim divisions, in spite of considerable Muslim support of Congress party goals. In this setting the British issued a new constitution, in 1935, that provided for a federal system of 11 provinces, each with an elected assembly and ministers responsible to it, with a British-appointed governor to oversee. At the center a two-house parliament would have some real power, though British officials remained in charge of defense and foreign affairs. The vote was extended to 35 million people.

Although disappointed at the lack of full self-government, the Congress party ran in the new elections and won majorities in most states. Gandhi himself advocated service in the new governments as long as the British did not unduly interfere, while more radical

Mohandas Gandhi (1889–1948) was unquestionably the leading figure in India's independence movement, and one of the more striking individuals in 20th-century world history. Trained in part in England, Gandhi later turned to modifications of Hindu tradition in setting up his nonviolent mass protests against British rule. He also projected an Indian alternative to modern society as it had developed in the West. Gandhi's tactics worked, though his goals were less completely realized. How much did he shape and reflect a distinctive Indian experience, and would India's independence have occurred differently without his guidance?

leaders, including Jawaharlal Nehru, wanted continued resistance. But all leaders agreed on the need for ultimate independence, and when Britain remained vague after 1940, they refused to cooperate in the government's World War II effort. Gandhi, Nehru, and other leaders were arrested as Japanese attack threatened, and Britain ruled through military control until the war's end.

NATIONALISM IN SOUTHEAST ASIA

A similar national awakening developed in Southeast Asia during the 1920s and 1930s, though without such a compelling figure as Gandhi. In French-ruled Indochina, an advisory council was permitted, but, as in India, such halfway reforms proved insufficient. Rioting broke out in major cities in 1930–1931; although it was put down by force, nationalist agitation continued. Serious peasant outbreaks occurred as well, caused more by economic hunger, as the market for agricultural exports collapsed during the depression, than by nationalism. A significant Marxist movement also took shape under the leadership of Ho Chi Minh, who became an enthusiastic convert to Marxism while working as a waiter in Paris, finding it a faith that could sustain him in a long battle for national freedom. But amid the new unrest the French determined to hang onto power. A similar pattern prevailed in Indonesia. Dutch rulers granted local leaders half the seats in a national assembly, but when nationalist and socialist unrest spread against the limited reforms, the government responded by jailing the leaders—which stimulated further agitation. In 1937 the nationalists petitioned the Dutch crown for dominion status within ten years.

Nationalism and peasant unrest against lack of land and high taxes created new ferment in Burma and Siam, where British influence predominated. In Siam, nationalist sentiment prompted a successful attack on Western control of tariff policy and special legal rights for foreigners. The nationalists celebrated their achievement by renaming their nation Thailand, or "land of the free." Finally, nationalists pressed U.S. control over the Philippines, where a popularly elected legislature already had real powers. While Americans talked of ultimate independence, they also discriminated against native Filipinos, whom they tended to treat with the same racism that they expressed toward blacks at home. Thus Filipino nationalism persisted, and it too was enhanced by the economic problems brought by the depression, as United States resistance to Filipino exports grew amid the crisis. In 1934 the U.S. Congress increased Philippine rights to self-government and promised outright independence for 1944.

Southeast Asian nationalism generally was stimulated by the results of World War II. Japanese control of the Philippines, Indochina, and other areas was often harsher than Western imperialism, but it demonstrated that the West was vulnerable and to this extent spurred hopes for ultimate freedom. When Tokyo surrendered, in 1945, many Westerners prepared to return to the Southeast Asian plantations and social clubs as if nothing had happened, but in fact a new era had begun in the whole region. Imperialism, difficult in the 1930s, had become impossible.

DECOLONIZATION AFTER THE WAR

Thus it was not surprising that the current of decolonization, which would soon sweep the world, bore its first postwar fruit in southern Asia. With nationalist resistance already well established in places like India, most European powers, now exhausted, were unwilling to take the trouble and risk of trying to hang on any further—even assuming that they could have done so successfully. The new Labor party in Britain was positively eager to leave India after 1945, for the costs of government had become too great to bear. A crucial issue remained the split between Hindu and Muslim, which to the sorrow of leaders like Gandhi occasioned bitter rioting as independence neared, but the deepest conflict was resolved in 1947 by the creation of two states, a Muslim Pakistan and a predominantly Hindu India. Religion-based nationalism triumphed over the larger territorial nationalism of the Congress tradition, though this tradition persisted in India along with frequent religious and ethnic challenges.

Britain extended its decolonization policy by granting freedom to Sri Lanka (formerly Ceylon) and Burma in 1948. Malaysia also won independence after the British suc-

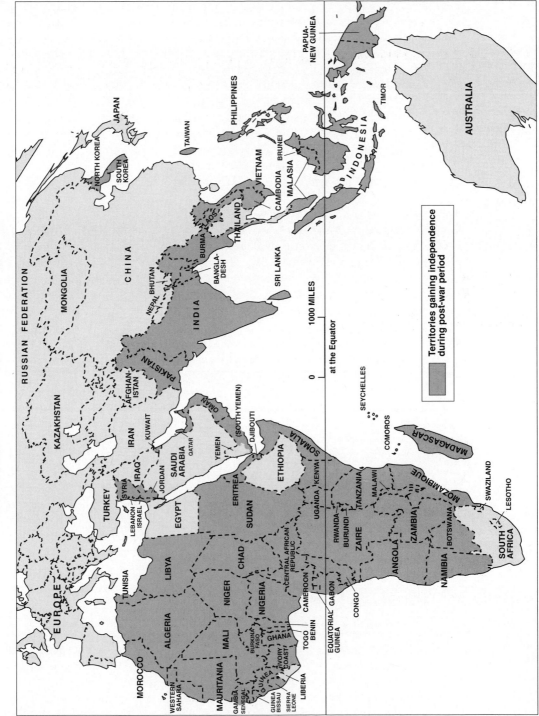

Decolonization in Africa and Asia After World War II

Territories gaining independence during post-war period

577

cessfully suppressed a communist guerrilla movement. The United States redeemed its earlier pledge by freeing the Philippines in 1946, while retaining substantial military bases on lease. Dutch retreat from Indonesia was somewhat less graceful, as there was an attempt to reconquer the territory after the end of World War II; but the effort failed, and an independent Indonesia was recognized in 1949.

Only in Indochina was national independence seriously delayed after World War II. The French, particularly eager to reassert their military strength after their disastrous loss to Hitler's armies in 1940, were unwilling to recognize the strength of the nationalist movement. They were abetted by the United States, which was hostile to communism, especially after the success of the Chinese revolution, and eager not to "lose" another Asian region to their cold war enemy. Ho Chi Minh, however, proved to be a stubborn opponent, successfully organizing a guerrilla warfare that depended on widespread peasant support and that was impossible to suppress by conventional tactics. A series of defeats of French troops led to a peace settlement in 1954, which brought division between a communist North Vietnam and a noncommunist South Vietnam. The French also withdrew from Laos and Cambodia. North Vietnam soon began to press its southern neighbor, with aid from the Soviet Union and China. As South Vietnam faced guerrilla attacks, it turned to the United States for aid. American participation in the conflict escalated in 1964, after North Vietnamese ships allegedly attacked American vessels, and over the next ten years more than 2 million U.S. soldiers were sent to fight in Vietnam. Despite massive American bombing raids, however, communist guerrilla forces gained ground, and the fighting also spread to Laos and Cambodia. Opposition to the war effort within the United States helped prompt peace talks, begun in 1969, which finally resulted in an end to the war in 1973. With U.S. forces withdrawn, and amid accusations from both sides about treaty violations, North Vietnam increased its troop levels in the South, and by 1975 it had gained full control of this region. A united, communist Vietnam then proceeded to impose military control over Laos and Cambodia, though these nations later regained a shaky independence.

The rise of a communist regional state in Southeast Asia was an extremely important development. The bitter warfare that had led up to this state played a significant role first in French and then in United States politics. More important, the same warfare brought massive devastation and loss of life to the region itself, creating durable scars and severe problems of economic reconstruction. The military experience and the communist regime separated this part of Southeast Asia from the bulk of the new nations, where independence had come earlier and with far less trauma.

SOUTHEAST ASIA AFTER INDEPENDENCE

The rise of nationalism during the first half of the 20th century had provided most of southern Asia with such a compelling cause that the problems that independence itself would bring were often obscured. The focus was on freedom from outside control. Leaders were less clear about what would be constructed when and if the Westerners left. Most nationalists assumed a democratic, parliamentary structure—to this extent, they copied Western values. But there was profound division among religious groups, as in India, and between educated leaders and the peasant masses. This could make democracy difficult. Nationalists were also typically vague about economic and social issues. Gandhi, for example, had little interest in economic development in the sense of industrialization. He was not opposed to factory production but insisted on preventing its dehumanizing effects on workers; at times, he seemed to prefer a stress on enhancing peasant agriculture and home-based manufacturing. But other Indian leaders called for an aggressive drive toward economic modernization. Peasants, though often drawn to the nationalist cause, were far more interested in land and protection from world market fluctuations than in purely political reforms or in economic modernization. Urban workers, poorly paid and badly housed amid the conditions of early factories, also pressed for greater social justice. Dealing with the various pressures, while also establishing the institutions of government, was an arduous task after the excitement of attaining national freedom.

The new or revived nations of Southeast Asia illustrated the range of possibilities and problems that followed from decolonization. Southeast Asian civilization had always been diverse. Traditional variations continued to be important, as differing religious and ethnic backgrounds determined distinctive policies. But now new distinctions arose as well, as in the split between communist Vietnam and the noncommunist—sometimes anticommunist—policies of the other states of the region. With encouragement from the United States, a number of Southeast Asian governments formed a loose alliance to coordinate resistance to Chinese and Vietnamese communist influence and to discuss common economic interests; but this grouping was not a significant unifying force amid the region's fascinating cultural and political diversity.

Most Southeast Asian nations attempted to set up democratic parliamentary institutions after attaining independence, but most found these institutions impossible to maintain. Lack of political experience among the peasant masses, divisions within the population that prompted frequent rioting, and, often, the ambition of individual nationalist leaders tended to turn governments toward more authoritarian policies. In the Philippines, for example, a parliamentary system modeled on that of the United States lasted until 1963, when President Ferdinand Marcos seized full power, which he would retain, amid considerable corruption and political violence, for over two decades. The Philippine government faced attacks from communist guerrillas, which were mostly controlled. It largely avoided any effort at land reform; a wealthy elite dominated the country, sharing power with the military. The gap between rich and poor was substantial, and there was little progress toward economic development. The government nevertheless received substantial U.S. aid and support, from postwar reconstruction onward, in part because of American concern for maintaining its military bases on the islands. Only in 1986 was the Marcos regime toppled, after trying to rig a new election, and replaced by a reformist regime that installed more genuine democracy.

In Malaysia and the monarchy of Thailand, parliamentary institutions functioned somewhat more effectively than in the Philippines, and repression of political opposition was less complete. By the 1970s, Thailand faced considerable pressure from the powerful Vietnamese armies on its northern border. Malaysia had earlier beaten down a communist guerrilla movement run mainly by the ethnic Chinese minority on the peninsula. Tension between native Malays and the Chinese minority continued to produce friction, however. It also made impossible a brief union with the city-state of Singapore, dominated by the

Chinese; Singapore split off under a strong-willed leader bent on rapid economic growth and tight control of the city's population.

Burma, like Thailand a largely Buddhist nation still, opted for considerable isolation soon after independence, hoping to avoid contamination both from the West and from the communist nations. A series of generals ran the country, whose culture remained highly traditional, one of the only nations in the world that kept so fully apart from broader international currents. Only a few hints of greater openness occurred in the late 1990s, as the country adopted the new name, Myanmar.

Indonesia gained independence under the leadership of Achmed Sukarno, who soon established authoritarian rule in part as a means of unifying a diverse population. A strong communist movement influenced Sukarno, but an outright communist uprising in 1963 was put down and the army seized power, killing at least half a million communists and radicals. The military also attacked the ethnic Chinese minority, who were resented for their hold over merchant activity in the cities. Sukarno was forced out of power, and the army generals ruled with no pretense of democracy. Firmly Muslim, the new government supported Islamic law and customs, though without the rigor of some other nations in the Islamic orbit. The authoritarian regime did, however, attack several minority nationalities as it retained its hold against the democratization current into the late 1990s.

In Vietnam—first the North, after 1954, and then the larger nation after 1975—a political and social system developed with many similarities to that of China under Mao Zedung. Private businesses were seized, and land was taken from the large landowners and turned over to government-controlled communes. Vietnamese society was colored by the heavy toll of prolonged war, including the military outlays needed for the conquest of Cambodia against considerable resistance. The Vietnamese regime relied heavily on Soviet support, as relations with China soured. China had never welcomed a strong Vietnam and objected strenuously to the attack on Cambodia. Border tensions, including one brief war, further encouraged the strong military tone of the Vietnamese version of communism. Economic development remained meager into the later 1980s, because of wartime dislocations and continuing military costs. By the 1990s Vietnam followed China's policy of greater openness to the outside world and a more market-oriented economy, still combined with a strong communist state.

Except for Vietnam, and the Philippines until 1986, most Southeast Asian governments tried to combine an interest in social reform, including aid to the peasantry, with considerable private enterprise. A number of nations experienced noteworthy economic growth. More productive crops were developed in the 1960s as part of the Green Revolution, which brought the aid of Western science to bear on the food problems of agricultural countries, thus allowing most Southeast Asian nations to feed themselves; particularly important were new strains of rice, which grew faster and had higher yields than those grown formerly. The Green Revolution favored wealthy farmers who could afford expensive seeds and fertilizers, but it did help many nations regain self-sufficiency in food production. Even so, economic advance was modified by considerable population growth. Most Southeast Asian nations continued to depend heavily on raw materials and cash crop exports to the industrialized nations of the West or Japan, and this dependence brought the usual problems of low and uncertain incomes on the world market. Except in dynamic Singapore, full industrialization had yet to come.

INDIA AND PAKISTAN

India presented an unusual mixture of strengths and weaknesses as it attained independence in 1947. It lacked a consistently successful political tradition, having far more often been divided and/or ruled through outside conquest than by self-government. It embraced a wide array of regions, religions, and languages. Despite some pockets of modern industry, it possessed a largely agricultural economy pressed by a rapidly growing population. On the other hand, India had an unusually well established nationalist movement, which had a recognized and experienced leadership. Because of roughly two centuries of British rule, it also had been exposed to Western political ideas and institutions, including an effective civil service system.

The birth pains of the new nation were a severe disappointment to Gandhi and other nationalist leaders. Growing Muslim insistence on a separate nation met vigorous Hindu opposition, as Congress-style nationalism ultimately failed to override religious divisions, but massive violence during 1946 convinced both sides that unity was indeed out of the question. The nation of Pakistan formed two regions, the heartland being the northwestern portion of the subcontinent nearest the Middle East, where Islam had strongest roots, with a second area in the northeast. Even partition was insufficient to prevent further religious antagonisms. In the weeks after independence, Hindus and Muslims battled each other, causing at least 100,000 deaths and forcing 3 million people to flee their homes to seek sanctuary with co-religionists in one of the two new nations. Gandhi and the Congress party were powerless to stop this hatred, and when Gandhi started a fast to protest Hindu persecution of Muslims and to restore "best friendship" between the two peoples, he was shot by a Hindu fanatic. Tensions with a Muslim minority continued to affect India, and relations between the nations of India and Pakistan were characteristically hostile, with each eyeing the other warily and devoting hard-won tax revenues to military expenditures designed to keep the other at bay.

Pakistan followed a political pattern rather similar to that of the Southeast Asian nations. It adopted an authoritarian form of government in 1958, under military leadership. Even with this, the nation proved unable to maintain unity among its two main provinces, as East Pakistan constantly complained of neglect. In 1971 a revolt in the east produced the new nation of Bangladesh, the eighth most populous country in the world and one of the poorest. Pakistan itself, though less crowded, faced serious problems of economic development. Land reform was slighted in favor of supporting the regional elite. In the 1970s in an appeal to religious tradition, Pakistan's military government adopted increasingly rigorous Islamic laws. The nation also faced tensions with the Soviet Union as a result of the invasion of Afghanistan, and this too was a burden despite U.S. aid. More democratic elections occurred in the 1990s, but political stability was fragile and the army kept a watchful eye.

Rioting in India.

India, which controlled the majority of the territory and population on the subcontinent despite the 1947 partition, developed a distinctive political and cultural pattern that combined tradition and change. Most striking was its ability to maintain democracy; indeed, India has been one of the few newly independent nations to preserve this political form with any consistency since World War II. Equally important was India's resolve to combine serious social reform with economic development and esteem for many aspects of Hindu culture.

Politically, India retained a federal system, which reflected the nation's regional diversity and the pattern set under British rule. Individual states had considerable power, though there were disputes with the central government at various points. The nation was ruled by the nationalist Congress party with only two exceptions—in the late 1970s, when a coalition of conservative groups took office briefly, and again through the 1990s. But multiparty competition was free and fierce, and freedoms of the press and of association were not normally limited. Control of many state governments, indeed, passed to parties other than the Congress group, including the Communist party. Congress party leaders themselves, though mainly drawn from the political elite, learned to campaign effectively among the masses, combining the prestige of high status with genuine popular appeal.

There were some questions about Indian democracy, to be sure. Congress party dominance prevented a great deal of experience with partisan shifts at the central government level. As in the Japanese Liberal Democratic party, more political maneuvering took place among factions within the dominant group than among different parties. India also experienced few leadership changes at the top. The first prime minister, the nationalist Jawaharlal Nehru, held power for 17 years. He was succeeded by his daughter, Indira Gandhi (no relation to Mahatma Gandhi). Though Indira Gandhi was initially selected by Congress party stalwarts for her presumed manipulability, she proved to be a tough-minded leader who was very conscious of her power. Indeed it was under her rule that liberal rights were suspended, from 1975 to 1977, as she tried to clamp down on a number of opposition groups and arrested many political critics. These policies led, however, to the Congress party's defeat in 1977, which suggested that curtailment of democracy in India

The Partition of South Asia: The Formation of India, Pakistan, Bangladesh, and Sri Lanka

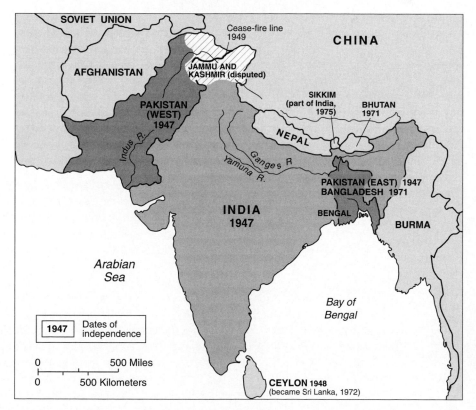

was costly. New elections in 1980 restored Indira Gandhi to power, but there was no attempt to revive authoritarian rule. Regional disunity, however, remained a serious problem. Gandhi faced growing opposition from the minority Sikh religion, which wanted greater autonomy for the Sikh-dominated state of Punjab. This led in the early 1980s to renewed religious rioting, this time between Hindu and Sikh, and Indira Gandhi's assassination by Sikh militants. Her successor was her son Rajiv, which raised concern about a new dynasty ruling India; but again, the formal institutions of a liberal democracy continued to function, doubtless solidified by some popular faith in the ruling family. Rajiv's assassination by southern Tamil separatists ended his family's reign, but a new political coalition took over smoothly. India had produced four decades of strong political performance, suggesting that its democratic forms responded to traditions and needs alike and had become part of the nation's political heritage.

India also took a lead in establishing a distinctive diplomatic policy. The new nation remained friendly with its former British rulers, and indeed participated actively in Commonwealth meetings to discuss mutual concerns with Britain, Canada, Australia, New Zealand, and the growing number of other former British colonies. At the same time, Nehru and his successors were firmly resolved to avoid entrapment in alliances that were irrelevant to India's needs. The government thus assumed the initiative in organizing interested non-Western nations in a nonaligned, or "third force," bloc that would seek to deal both with the West and the Soviet Union while shunning military pacts with either side. The first meeting of this neutral group took place in 1955, and although the cohesion of the grouping oscillated, India persevered in seeking good relations with both the United States and the Soviet Union, often lecturing the great powers on the evils of their competition. India itself faced diplomatic problems, particularly with Pakistan and, at times in the 1960s, with China as well. But the nation avoided extensive involvement in issues outside its regional concerns, save at the level of a sometimes moralizing rhetoric.

Congress party leaders from Nehru onward were eager to remake their nation without losing its identity; independence and political power were not enough. Their vision differed somewhat from that of Mahatma Gandhi's in that they were more concerned with economic modernization and less disdainful of factories and sophisticated commerce; but Gandhi, too, had sought some changes in India's old order. Key targets in early legislation were the caste system and traditional gender relations, as India sought to institute equality under the law. The nation's constitution granted equality to women, including the right to vote, and allowed women to seek divorce and to marry outside their caste. The caste system itself was outlawed. The government tried to encourage former untouchables to participate more fully in Indian society, by establishing quotas for "ex-untouchables" in the universities and in government jobs. But India's attack on these ancient social traditions was of necessity less forceful than China's war on ancestor worship and other family practices, for outright coercion or the formation of radical new institutions such as communes would have been incompatible with democratic forms. India had no revolution. So in fact strong remnants of the caste system remained in India, though not enforced by law. Most government leaders were drawn from the traditionally higher castes, as were most of the growing numbers of university-trained professionals and managers. At the family level, the authority of men continued strong, particularly among the rural majority. Practices such as arranged marriages, often with the partners plighted during their teens and not even necessarily meeting before their wedding, continued to be widespread at all social levels.

In economic policy, India's leadership professed a nondoctrinaire socialism. This meant, in practice, considerable economic planning toward allocation of scarce resources; it meant government operation of key services such as airlines and railroads. But substantial private enterprise remained as well. Government welfare services focused mainly on basic hygiene, as the nation's poverty prevented a more elaborate social security system. The government also encouraged widespread peasant landownership, breaking up some former estates and helping to clear new land toward this end. This policy, along with progressive taxation, reduced the economic power of the old princely aristocracy.

A key concern, even in the heady early days of independence, was economic development. Congress party leaders had long wanted fuller economic equality for India, as against Western dominance. Furthermore, steady population growth virtually compelled attention to the issue of economic growth. Government planning and private enterprise, plus some foreign economic aid, promoted substantial growth during the 1950s; the national income expanded by 42 percent. But the nation's population grew from 360 million to 439 million during the same decade, which wiped out half of the economic gain. During the 1960s, per capita income stagnated, and India was forced to import food to prevent starvation. This prompted greater concern for improved agricultural production. The government helped sponsor Green Revolution research on better seeds; it also promoted fuller use of fertilizers and pesticides. These measures brought impressive results; despite continued population growth, the nation remained self-sufficient in agriculture from 1970 onward.

The government also attacked the population problem directly. Under Nehru, official measures were halfhearted, but with a growth rate of 2.4 percent per year, it became increasingly clear that no serious improvement in living standards for the impoverished masses could occur without birth control. Indira Gandhi's government stepped up propaganda efforts, with slogans such as "A Happy Family Is a Small Family," and medical personnel provided free birth control devices and procedures, including vasectomies for men. But the campaign butted against massive popular resistance. Men and women alike feared to tamper with God's ways. Men worried that an operation such as a vasectomy would destroy their "male power," making them as docile as castrated animals. They also continued to value a large family as a sign of good fortune, seeking particularly a sufficient number of sons to ensure protection in parental old age. Popular resistance to birth control helped prompt Indira Gandhi's suspension of liberties in 1975 as the government launched an effort to force poor men with large families to undergo vasectomies. This campaign stopped, however, in 1977, as the government returned to intense propaganda and widespread medical services. India's birth rate did begin to slow in the later 1970s, as people became more aware of family planning as an alternative to the starkest poverty, but birth rates remained substantial.

Despite population pressure, which diverted extensive resources to increasing agricultural production and which unquestionably maintained massive poverty in the countryside and crowded cities alike, India managed to resume its pattern of economic growth in the 1970s. Modern industrial technologies were applied to metallurgy and chemical production, creating islands of advanced factory industry in a still-agricultural nation. India produced cars, and tried to limit imports. With ready technological interchange with the West as well as with Soviet Russia, India for a time in the early 1980s surpassed the technological level of China. Modern factories as well as rising agricultural productivity accounted for a 4-percent annual growth rate in the years after 1975. India has remained vulnerable in the world economy, and its export performance has lagged despite important industrial sales in the Indian Ocean region. The nation's growth record fell well behind that of the Pacific Rim, particularly after the mid–1980s. But despite widely publicized problems, it has engaged in serious economic change. Efforts to cut back state controls to spur growth occurred in the 1990s, while training in computer science expanded.

Indian cultural life showed a predictable balance between new themes and old, but with a bias here toward the more traditional. India's leaders encouraged a rapid expansion of education, which gradually cut into widespread illiteracy. By the 1970s literacy rates had doubled over the 1947 figure to 30 percent. At the elite level, scientific training spread widely, and Indian researchers participated actively, both in India and in foreign laboratories, in advances in physics, biology, medicine, and computer science. The Indian government even mounted its own space program. Cultural change was also encouraged, though particularly among the elite, by the continued reliance on the English language, which maintained openness to developments in Western culture. Congress party leaders had hoped to promote Hindi as a new national language, but regional resistance was so great that English remained the only language with countrywide currency in government, the universities, and the press. A number of leading writers also relied primarily on English. Because Indian universities produced more trained professionals than the society required, a large number of doctors and lawyers emigrated to Britain or North America, giving India further ties to the West, though at some economic cost.

At the popular level, however, traditional cultural forms predominated, albeit sometimes in new guises. An active film industry produced innumerable stories of adventure and romance, couched in the terms of traditional popular literature. Few foreign movies penetrated beyond elite levels, while at the same time Indian films themselves almost never reached beyond the country's borders. Along with films, literature in the various traditional languages remained active, as did traditional artistic styles. Indian painters and sculptors did not participate widely in modern or "international" artistic developments, preferring to continue to work mainly in older modes. Artistic imagery, both old and new remained a vital part of Indian popular life, as did religion. Devotion to Hindu ritual and belief was widespread among the majority, and the reverence for holy men continued high.

Part of India's distinctiveness rested on the ongoing divisions between elite and popular culture. The elite, drawn mainly from higher castes, showed themselves responsive to new educational opportunities as well as to the new outlets for political and managerial leadership. In this group both men and women played a meaningful role, for here India's attack on gender divisions had considerable result. Women graduated from universities in growing numbers and held important government and professional positions. The elite did not become Western. Traditional patterns such as arranged marriages continued among this group, as did distinctive religious and cultural interests. But there was significant change in elite values, including the substantial contact with Western (particularly English-language) cultural and scientific products. Popular culture was quite a different

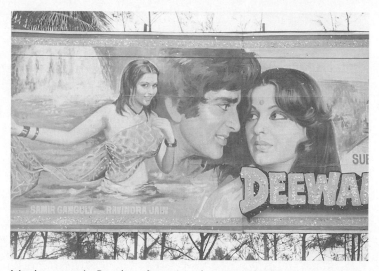

Movie poster in Bombay, featuring the actor Shashi Kapoor in the film *Deewangee*.

matter, which helps explain the widespread resistance to government-sponsored measures such as birth control in the name of religion and family. India's masses did change, as a minority entered jobs in modern factories and a larger number altered some of their methods in agriculture. But change here definitely took place amid vigorous devotion to a host of earlier values. Distinctive religious and cultural interests showed even in basic outlook, as Indians preserved a greater place for imagination in their child-rearing practices putting less stock than did Westerners (or East Asians) on careful lessons in the distinction between pretend and "reality."

India's divisions were regional and religious as well as social. Lacking a highly centralized culture, India had long experienced religious diversity. Despite Mahatma Gandhi's hopes to use nationalism to transcend these differences, and despite a long tradition of considerable tolerance, relations among Hindus, Muslims, and Sikhs grew more tense by the 1990s. Cultural change, including the partial secularism of the elite, challenged toleration, leading to many clashes that threatened the stability of the government. A Hindu fundamentalist movement arose, calling on the government to promote Hinduism at the expense of other religions—a fascinating, perhaps ominous development, all the more interesting in that use of the state was not in fact a Hindu tradition. Fundamentalist political power increased in the 1990s, and Hindu nationalists won control of the government, increasing military spending and nuclear development.

CONCLUSION: INDIA AND CHINA

Because India established an independent democracy just as China underwent its communist revolution, comparisons between the two Asian giants became commonplace. Which path would produce greater political success? Which path would prove most compatible with economic development? American observers initially pinned their faith on India, convinced that democracy and real modernization must ultimately go hand in hand. But as India's democracy proved incapable of stemming population growth—and as India insisted on neutrality rather than alliance with the West, to the annoyance of many Americans—opinion veered, and China often seemed the better bet. Indian traditions, including religiosity and dreaminess as well as spectacular fertility, now seemed less suited than forceful Chinese methods to the necessary reforms. As China became friendlier to the United States in well-publicized moves, enthusiasm for China's development prospects increased.

By the late 1990s, neither China nor India has managed to achieve a full industrial revolution in the style of Japan. At the same time, both have produced significant economic change. Both have health rates and per capita income rates significantly above those in the poorest agricultural nations, with China, however, now in the lead. Both have seemingly vigorous governments, albeit with quite different institutions, styles, and problems. Comparison is complicated, to be sure, by ignorance of some Chinese developments, as official control of information remains extensive. But it seems certain that, building on government tradition and communist zeal, China has become more effective than India at reducing the rates of population growth. Most experts assume that India will indeed pass China as the world's most populous country by the year 2000. On the other hand, India has pressed forward more consistently in technological development and promotion of higher education, and it has more regular contacts with the outside world. Each nation, then, uses both distinctive traditions and distinctive current political forms to produce its own balance sheet of strengths and weaknesses. Ongoing differences between India and China recall different traditions set in the classical period, particularly in terms of political values and institutions but also attitudes toward the outside world. Later developments also explain: India's complex experience as a colony compared to the Western treatment of China, the fact that China had a revolution and India did not, perhaps even the different creative styles of Gandhi and Mao as seminal 20th-century leaders. If China ultimately gained the edge in economic growth, it may have suffered more in terms of cultural instability and dislocation.

SUGGESTED READINGS

India's recent political history is covered in J. Brown, *Modern India: The Origins of an Asian Democracy* (1985), and S. Wolpert, *New Oxford History of India* (1983). On specific topics, see: J. Brown, *Gandhi's Rise to Power: Indian Politics, 1915–1922* (1978); F. Frankel, *India's Political Economy 1947–1977* (1981); V. B. Singh, ed., *Economic History of India 1857–1956* (1965); K. M. Panikkar, *The Foundation of New India* (1963); V. P. Menon, *The Transfer of Power in India* (1957); and A. de Souza, *Women in Contemporary India and South Asia* (1980).

A provocative general study of Asian politics, with particular reference to southern Asia, is L. W. Pye, *Asian Power and Politics: The Cultural Dimensions of Authority* (1985), which argues for the difficulty of using Western concepts to grasp the Asian state. Eric Wolf, in *Peasants* (1966) and *Peasant Wars of the Twentieth Century* (1970), offers considerable South Asian coverage on a general subject.

On Southeast Asia, D. G. E. Hall, *A History of South-East Asia* (1981), is a good survey; see also R. N. Kearney, *Politics and Modernization in South and Southeast Asia* (1974). Useful works on the Vietnam conflict are: E. J. Hammer, *Struggle for Indochina* (1954); C. Cooper, *The Lost Crusade: America in Vietnam* (1972); and J. Zasloff and M. Brown, *Communist Indochina and U.S. Foreign Policy: Forging New Relations* (1978). An important study on recent Southeast Asian history, with larger theoretical implications, is James Scott, *The Moral Economy of the Peasant: Rebellion and Subsistence in Southeast Asia* (1976).

Excellent source reading on 20th-century India is provided by various English-language novelists, who write directly of Indian life, though using Western literary conventions as well as language. A well-known example is Rabindranath Tagore. More strictly contemporary authors are Kamale Markhndaya, Shanta Ramarao (on women), T. Shizasankara Pillai (on the south), and R. K. Narayan (on peasants). Also relevant, is the novelist and essayist V. S. Naipaul, who is of Indian extraction though raised in the West Indies and writing as an outsider.

CHAPTER 30

Middle Eastern Civilization in the 20th Century

Focal Points

The Middle East has been a center of recurrent international conflict in the 20th century. Struggles against European colonialism yielded after the 1940s to frequent regional wars. What have been the main ingredients of conflict? The Middle East has also seen many changes, some of them similar to those in other parts of the world: new political regimes sought stability, various leaders promoted economic development, new values developed among many nationalists. Why did the Middle East, in the main, accept neither democratic politics nor communism? Amid important departures from tradition, Islam remained a potent force, and it could motivate a reaction against certain kinds of change. What kinds of divisions over appropriate goals emerged in the Muslim nations? Were Islamic fundamentalists hostile to all signs of change?

CHANGES AND TENSIONS

Several major themes are interwoven in the most recent historical stage of the oldest civilization area in the world. Political unity in the Middle East, already tenuous in the 19th century, ended completely after World War I. A few subsequent efforts to revive larger units, usually under the banners of Arab nationalism or Muslim brotherhood, failed. As new nations were carved out of the former territory of the Ottoman Empire, semi-imperialist controls by various European states along with the independence of several regional states between the wars yielded after World War II to outright independence for the entire region. Divisions among Middle Eastern nations were compounded by a diversity of political forms. Monarchies arose in a few cases—virtually the only recent instances in which monarchy remained a serious political force in the 20th century. Strongman regimes were even more characteristic. Some Middle Eastern states worked vigorously to modify age-old traditions, including the force of Islam, while others sought to preserve older values above all.

Partly because of political divisions, the Middle East became the world's leading trouble spot after World War II. This status was not entirely new; already in the 19th century, the weakness and instability of the Ottoman Empire had drawn conflict. The oil wealth discovered in the Middle East in the 20th century gave the region new importance in the world economy, but it also attracted greed; this intensified the potential for outside interference in Middle Eastern affairs, along with the region's proximity both to the West and to the Soviet Union. Further, the creation of a new Jewish state after World War II produced a seemingly unresolvable tension that provoked internal warfare within the region and a series of great-power interventions from the leading actors in the cold war.

Finally, the Middle East generated an unusually complex pattern of reform efforts and counter-reactions. A new regime in Turkey, installed in the wake of the collapse of the Ottoman Empire, provided the first of many secularization attempts that would succeed in producing some industrialization and agricultural development, as well as new systems of education and new relationships both in society at large and within the family. But change came painfully in the Middle East, and a number of Islamic leaders, in the name of traditional ideals, helped mobilize reactions against the new trends. Thus the Middle East produced a more bitter and overt clash between reformist and conservative forces than did any other civilization in the contemporary world. Friction was often heightened by disputes over political form and rivalries among the new nations, adding greatly to the intricacy, and often the tragedy, of recent Middle Eastern history.

PATTERNS OF CONTEMPORARY MIDDLE EASTERN HISTORY

The Ottoman Empire's participation on the German side in World War I opened the most recent chapter of Middle Eastern history. Britain and France worked to undermine Ottoman rule as part of their own war effort; they encouraged Arab nationalism, against Turkish control, and the British also vaguely pledged Jewish leaders a new homeland in Palestine. Wartime promises plus the ringing ideals of President Wilson at the Versailles Peace Conference prompted many Arab leaders to hope for outright freedom. Instead, they encountered victorious Western allies bent on extending imperialism to their region; not only Britain and France but also Italy and Greece were eager for new territory as the spoils of war. Thus Middle Eastern nationalism was at once stimulated and frustrated, a dangerous combination.

REPLACING THE OTTOMAN EMPIRE

One point was clear, however: the Ottoman Empire could no longer be supported. Arab leaders, united in their hatred of the Turks, agreed on this point with European imperialists, who hoped to carve up the region for their own purposes. Arab uprisings were led by the chief magistrate of Mecca, Hussein Ibn Ali. Then at the war's end, French and British forces moved into the Middle East, the French taking over Syria and Lebanon, the British occupying Palestine, Jordan, and Iraq. Efforts to conquer Turkey itself failed, however. A Young Turk military leader, Mustafa Kemal, organized a Turkish resistance movement,

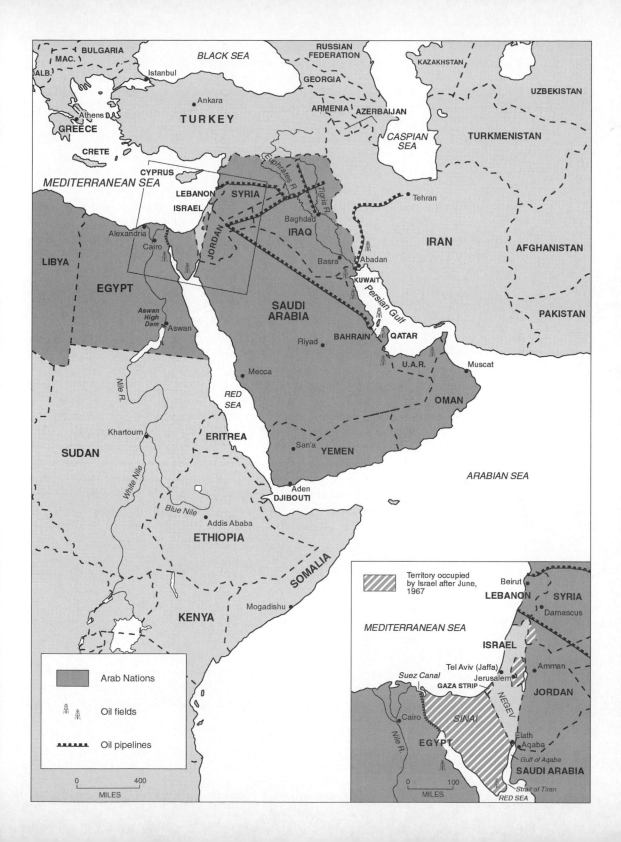

MAC.

BULGARIA

BLACK SEA

RUSSIAN
FEDERATION

KAZAKHSTAN

ALB.

Istanbul

GEORGIA

Ankara

ARMENIA

AZERBAIJAN

UZBEKISTAN

GREECE

Athens

TURKEY

CASPIAN
SEA

TURKMENISTAN

CRETE

CYPRUS

MEDITERRANEAN SEA

LEBANON

SYRIA

Euphrates R.

Tehran

Tigris R.

ISRAEL

Baghdad

JORDAN

IRAQ

IRAN

AFGHANISTAN

Alexandria

Cairo

Basra

Abadan

KUWAIT

Persian Gulf

PAKISTAN

LIBYA

EGYPT

SAUDI
ARABIA

BAHRAIN

QATAR

Aswan
High
Dam

Aswan

Riyad

U.A.R.

Muscat

Mecca

OMAN

Nile R.

RED
SEA

Khartoum

ERITREA

San'a

YEMEN

ARABIAN SEA

SUDAN

White Nile

Aden

DJIBOUTI

Blue Nile

Addis Ababa

ETHIOPIA

SOMALIA

Mogadishu

KENYA

	Territory occupied by Israel after June, 1967

Beirut

LEBANON

SYRIA

MEDITERRANEAN SEA

Damascus

ISRAEL

Tel Aviv (Jaffa)

Amman

Suez Canal

Jerusalem

GAZA STRIP

NEGEV

JORDAN

Cairo

SINAI

Nile R.

Elath

Aqaba

EGYPT

Gulf of Aqaba

SAUDI ARABIA

0   100

MILES

Strait of Tiran

RED SEA

	Arab Nations
	Oil fields
	Oil pipelines

0   400

MILES

beating back Greek and Western invasion forces even though the sultan had agreed, in the 1920 Treaty of Sèvres, to the end of the empire. Kemal's success brought new negotiations with the European powers and produced a 1923 treaty that created Turkey as a new, separate nation. This treaty not only ensured Turkish independence but guaranteed the nation's continued strategic importance in European and Russian diplomacy because of its strategic geographic position.

Buoyed by his military and diplomatic success, Kemal unseated the sultan and proclaimed a secular republic in the new Turkey. Like Muhammed Ali in Egypt a century before, Kemal intended to lead the modernization of an Islamic nation, to achieve parity with the European states on their own terms. He carefully fostered a new Turkish nationalism separate from religious faith. He moved the country's capital from Istanbul to Ankara, in the Turkish heartland. Profoundly influenced by Western political ideas, Kemal introduced parliamentary institutions and a new voting system. But his version of democracy was tightly controlled, with a single party—the People's party—preventing any legal opposition. Like other notable Westernizers—including Peter the Great—Kemal believed that authoritarianism was an essential precondition of change, for the people had to be forced to accept reforms. Kemal, who took the name Atatürk, or "father of the Turks," vigorously attacked the hold of Islam. He abolished the religious caliphate and made the state secular. Civil marriage was required, and a secular school system was established. The regime outlawed many Muslim customs and symbols, including polygamy and traditional costumes—Western dress was mandatory. Sunday rather than Friday was made the day of rest, and Muslim law was superseded by the laws of the state, which were modeled after Western codes. Arabic script was replaced with a Latin alphabet for the Turkish language, judged easier to learn and thus more appropriate for modern education. Against Islamic tradition also, Atatürk granted women the right to vote and to receive education. A concerted effort to extend primary schools reduced illiteracy from 85 percent in 1914, to 42 percent in 1932.

Atatürk's regime also promoted industrialization. A number of factories were established under state guidance. Cities grew. Turkey vigorously pushed the training of engineers and other technical personnel, to make foreign experts unnecessary. At the same time, unions were forbidden to strike, in order to prevent barriers to economic growth. By 1939, a year after Atatürk's death, the economy had advanced enough so that foreign railroad companies could be bought out—a major blow against lingering economic imperialism.

Atatürk's hopes were not entirely fulfilled, however. His power base was secure; nationalism unquestionably gained ground; traditional culture yielded to new interests in science and in economic development. But the rural majority was not entirely won to the new regime, as Muslim objections to secularism persisted. Many crusading schoolteachers reported persistent traditionalism—in their view, superstitious belief—among their students and village leaders. Atatürk's successors had to allow for this deeply rooted religious faith, as they cut back the pace of reform. Furthermore, while Turkey became a new nation and successfully maintained its independence, bolstered by the largest, best-disciplined army in the region, it did not fully industrialize. Economic growth was slow, poverty widespread. Despite the genuine revolution in Turkish politics and culture, this was no Japanese-style leap forward in terms of economic change.

Turkey was the most dramatic case of new Middle Eastern politics after World War I, but it was not the only one. Persia, dominated before the war by British and Russian influence, proclaimed new independence as well, shaking off British efforts to maintain control. Persian nationalists selected an army officer, Riza Khan, soon known as shah, or king, as their new leader. The new ruler worked for economic change as well as independence, building rail lines and schools and creating a banking system. The government encouraged enough factory industry to provide for national needs in clothing and metals, reducing dependence on Western imports. The regime benefited from important oil revenues, developed by a British company under Persian license. In 1935, to signal the beginning of an era, the kingdom's name was changed to Iran. But the shah was deposed during World War II, in favor of his son, in part because of efforts to gain advantages from both sides in the war. Muslim opposition to modern trends, along with hostility to the luxurious life style and dictatorial methods of the shah himself, created far more tension than persisted in Turkey.

One policy that Iran explicitly introduced from the 1920s onward deserves particular note, because countries in other regions would soon move in the same direction: import substitution. At the end of the 19th century, Russia and Japan had moved toward full industrialization, hoping to catch up with the West. This approach required active exports, particularly in Japan; it was motivated by military as well as economic goals. Import substitution suggested a more modest approach: build enough factory industry to reduce dependence on Western goods in areas like textiles and basic machinery (later, automobiles would be added to this list). Success here would give the nation more economic independence, though it might not become a world economic power. Turkey followed this policy to a degree, as did India after 1947; Latin American nations did the same from the 1930s onward. Successful import substitution would have its own impact on the world economy, and of course it did not preclude a more active export stance later on.

ASSERTIONS OF ARAB NATIONALISM

While important new regimes arose in the northern Middle East, marked by commitment to reform and authoritarian rule, the bulk of the Middle East lay under European control during the 1920s and 1930s. North Africa, of course, was held as colonies by France, Britain, and Italy. The major areas of the Middle East proper, now taken over by France and Britain, were governed as League of Nations mandates, rather than as outright possessions, which implied some commitment to ultimate independence. Nevertheless, Arab indignation at this new foreign rule gave a further spur to nationalism. Riots and demonstrations forced Britain to recognize the technical independence of Egypt in 1922, and Iraq and Jordan soon followed, though in all these cases Britain continued to regulate economic and military affairs. France made fewer early concessions to nationalism in its territories. It split Lebanon off from Syria, encouraging division between Christians and Muslims in Lebanon as well. And while Lebanon achieved independence under French protection, and Syria won promise of the same in 1936, European influence remained strong. Indeed, in oil-rich territories such as Iraq, European and United States companies gobbled up ownership rights, which actually increased the Western stake in the region even as formal imperialism was declining.

Another key issue for Arab nationalists during the 1920s and 1930s was the growing Jewish presence in Palestine. Although Jews constituted a mere 11 percent of the total population of the region in 1914, Jewish emigration from Europe, encouraged by Zionist organizations and also by Hitler's anti-Semitic onslaught, increased the number of Jewish residents rapidly, to half a million by 1940. The Jewish population was still outnumbered by Palestinian Muslims and Christians, but Arab nationalists were alert to this threat to what they regarded as their land. They pressed Britain, as the mandate power in Palestine, to restrict immigration, but British policy in fact zigzagged, failing to content either Muslims or Jews. In the meantime Jewish organization of agriculture and industry in Palestine, around communal farms known as kibbutzim, gained ground steadily, greatly increasing traditional productivity and developing new export crops such as citrus fruits.

Arab nationalism thus had a number of targets, including the beginnings of a Jewish nation in Palestine as well as the trappings of European imperialism. But while nationalism became more intense, it was also a divisive force in the Middle East. Not only were nationalists distracted by the boundaries drawn among mandate territories, such as Lebanon and Syria, but they also disagreed about the future of the Middle East. Some, as in the new kingdom of Saudi Arabia, advocated traditional Muslim ways, while others talked of Western-style parliamentary democracy; still others, like the Iraqi Kamil Chadrichi, preached an Arab socialism. Few groups in the Middle East were outright Marxists, for Marxist hostility to nationalism and to religion, demonstrated by attacks on Islamic groups in the Soviet Union, was too severe even for most secular reformers. But no single non-Marxist formula for a Middle Eastern future emerged.

Then came World War II, which further weakened Western Europe's tenuous hold on the region. Turkey remained carefully independent during the conflict, bent on developing its own state without distraction. But much of the rest of the area was caught up in the hostilities, as German forces invaded North Africa and then faced defeat at the hands of the British-American alliance in 1942. More important was the sheer weakness of Britain and France after the war, which gave new hope to Arab leaders. France yielded to riots in 1945, abandoning all government powers in Syria and Lebanon. Britain followed suit, though it was delayed by attempts to find solutions to Arab–Jewish conflicts in Palestine. Riots and terrorist attacks by the two groups against each other and against the British marked the period 1945–1948. When the British pulled out, the Jews simply declared a new state of Israel (May 1948), beating off an attack by the surrounding Arab countries and conquering more territory. Almost a million Muslim refugees were expelled from Palestine, creating a legacy of great hostility between the Arabs and Israel and its political allies, including the United States.

Defeat at Jewish hands triggered a revolution in Egypt, where the army colonel Gamal Abdel Nasser drove out the corrupt, pro-Western king in 1952. The goal was a secular, reformist state under one-party leadership. Nasser, who for a time spearheaded Arab nationalism generally, seized the Suez Canal in 1956, provoking a British-French-Israeli attack that managed to invade Egypt but was forced back by United States and Russian pressure, as the two superpowers were bent on courting Arab favor. A fully independent Egypt, which proved its technical competence by running the Suez Canal efficiently, was a major new actor in the Middle East from this point onward. Nasser quickly demonstrated his reformist inclination internally by dividing the great estates along the Nile and giving land to the peasants, thus ending the longstanding manorial system.

Completion of Arab independence came between 1956 and 1962; the final North African colonies won their freedom as the states of Libya, Tunisia, Morocco, and Algeria. The key battle here focused on Algeria, a French holding since the mid–19th century and symbolic, to many French leaders, of France's battered claims to greatness in the world of power politics. Nationalist agitation led to outright civil war for almost a decade, as the minority of European settlers supported the French army effort against a pattern of guerrilla attacks and terrorism that proved impossible to suppress. Finally the French, rightly worried about the effects of the long, brutal struggle on their own internal political stability and national morality, pulled back, agreeing in 1962 to Algerian independence.

With independence achieved, through a welter of individual states, the most coherent thread in Middle Eastern affairs remained the dispute between the Arab states and Israel. Israel's immediate neighbors were most directly involved, but other Arab leaders found Israel a convenient target to generate popular enthusiasms at home, and a genuine affront to Arab and Muslim authority in the region. For its part, Israel created a strong military force, with far more modern armaments than the Arab states could boast and an aggressive outlook designed to avoid any further scapegoating of the Jewish people. Wars broke out between Israel and its neighbors in 1967 and in 1973, with the first war leading to substantial new Israeli-controlled territory, including the entire city of Jerusalem, regarded as a religious center by Muslims and Christians as well as Jews. Even apart from outright war, guerrilla attacks and terrorism were widely employed by Palestinian groups hostile to Israel, while Israel frequently retaliated with bombing missions against refugee camps suspected of harboring terrorists. In 1982 Israel invaded Lebanon in order to unseat Palestinian terrorists, producing literal anarchy in this nation as no group seemed capable of ensuring order. There were few bright spots in the seemingly unresolvable conflict over Israel. In 1977 the Egyptian president, Anwar Sadat, made a stunning gesture by visiting Israel and negotiating a peace. While this initiative reduced tension, it led to no overall settlement, since Israel refused to surrender most of the acquisitions it had gained in 1967 and many Arab nationalists refused to recognize Israel's right to exist. In 1993 Israeli agreements with the Palestinians in some autonomous regions, followed by a 1994 peace treaty with Jordan, opened hopes for wider dispute settlements. Tensions increased after 1996 with the victory of a more right-wing party in Israel.

In addition to the issue of Israel, questions of alignments with the world's superpowers focused Middle Eastern attention. Israel was a firm Western ally, receiving massive financial and military aid from the United States. Turkey, anxious about its Soviet neighbor to the north, was also in the Western camp as a member of NATO. Most other Middle Eastern nations, however, oscillated between alignments. Egypt's Nasser helped organize "neutral" nations in the world, along with India during the 1950s, as an alternative to alliance with either side in the cold war. And most Middle Eastern leaders would probably have preferred an essentially neutral course, so that they could concentrate on foreign and domestic objectives of their own. However, Western influence continued to loom large. Western nations were targets of attack as allies of Israel or remembered imperialists or capitalist exploiters. They were also valuable sources of arms, purchasers along

The Palestinian issue, 1979: Israeli soldier patrolling Arab village during a Palestinian general strike against Israeli-ordered expulsion of a mayor sympathetic to Palestinian independence.

with Japan of most of the oil produced in the region, and usefully hostile to Marxism. Most of the more conservative Arab states thus tended to develop relatively close ties with the West, while more secular regimes either alternated—like Egypt, which used Russian aid after the Suez war and later renounced it in favor of American support—or leaned toward heavy reliance on Russia, like Syria during the 1970s; or they tried to win support from both sides. In any event, competition between the cold war camps continued to weigh heavily on the Middle East, which could not resist substantial outside influence because of internal divisions and military and economic weakness. At the same time, great-power rivalry gave many states a chance to play the two sides off and thus gain room for independent maneuver.

Two other factors played a considerable role in Middle Eastern events after the end of outright imperialism: local rivalries and efforts at economic coordination. A number of newly independent states clashed over territory or policy. Egypt and Libya developed a rivalry; Morocco and Algeria disputed territory; in the early 1980s a particularly brutal and protracted war broke out between Iraq and Iran, over territory and also a fundamental policy dispute between a secular state in Iraq and the fervent religious revolutionaries who had seized the helm in Iran in 1978. Iraq's own expansionism led to invasion of Kuwait in 1990; a subsequent alliance among Saudi Arabia, Egypt, Syria, and the major

The Middle East Before and After World War I Settlements, 1914–1922

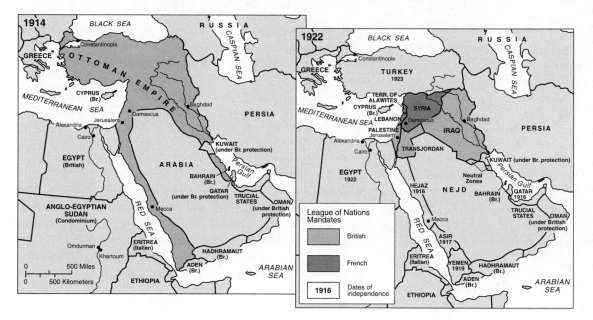

Western powers beat back the Iraqis while trying unsuccessfully to replace their strongman leader, Saddam Hussein.

　　Against this pattern of frequent fighting, a few institutions of greater scope provided partial balance. The Arab League existed to help reconcile quarrels in the name of a larger ideal of renewed Arab unity. Periodic efforts to unite different nations surfaced; Syria thus briefly merged with Egypt. While these attempts seldom had much substance, they served as a reminder that a higher political dream for the region persisted and might someday have greater impact. Finally, and more pragmatically, oil-producing Arab states, headed by Iran, Iraq, and Saudi Arabia, took the lead in forming OPEC (Organization of Petroleum Exporting Countries) in 1961, though there were important non–Middle Eastern participants as well. The formation of OPEC resulted from successful Arab and Iranian efforts to reduce the independence of Western oil companies operating in their region, as either nationalization or at least substantial government supervision took hold. OPEC nations also attempted to coordinate production levels and pricing policies, and during the 1970s had considerable success in raising the price of oil and therefore the earnings of member nations. Here, at least briefly, was an important alteration in the usual dependent posture of raw material suppliers in the world market. By the end of the 1970s, however, competition from other regions and even among OPEC members, plus Western conservation efforts, reduced OPEC's effectiveness in maintaining revenues. Nevertheless, OPEC, along with individual efforts by wealthy Arab states such as Saudi Arabia to provide economic support to petroleum-poor states like Jordan and Egypt, again demonstrated that narrow nationalist rivalries did not alone capture the complexities of Middle Eastern politics.

THE POLITICAL CULTURE OF THE MIDDLE EAST

THE NEW ROLE OF THE STATE

With growing nationalism and then independence, the states of the Middle East developed a number of similar functions. Most assumed new responsibility for providing systems of education; an economic infrastructure including roads, ports, and airlines; and some limited welfare programs. Most regulated foreign companies to some extent, and the region gained leverage against the West. Universities were created, teaching secular subjects along with or instead of Islamic faith. Even conservative regimes such as the Saudi Arabian monarchy spurred technical training. The new functions of government demonstrated the novelty of many of the forces impinging on this region during the 20th century. What was happening in the Middle East, as elsewhere in the world, was a common pattern of political modernization, defined simply as the extension of government functions to new areas, like mass education and economic planning, and the attempt to focus new loyalty on the state. This effort may seem obvious, but it was profoundly unsettling to some. Nationalism itself was a new loyalty, not an inevitable outgrowth of Middle Eastern tradition. Many Muslims believed that nationalism was irrelevant so long as pious Muslims controlled the government; thus, for example, it was unimportant that Arabs be ruled by an Arab government. By the same token, Middle Eastern nationalists had to tread very carefully in the area of religious devotion, insisting that nationalism did not contradict true belief and emphasizing a common interest in the glorious Muslim past, while urging some reforms in Islam itself. Definitions of nationalism also varied and clashed. Was a nation a region with boundaries set by Europeans after World War I? Should it embrace all Arabs? Should it be secular or Muslim?

Changes in government functions and the rise of nationalism did not mean Western-style political forms in the typical Middle Eastern states. Liberal democracy did not take hold in this region; here was another common point in the Middle Eastern political style. Along with China, the Middle East indeed proved to be the region more resistant to the spread of democracy in the 1980s and 1990s. The one consistent exception was Israel, where a parliament achieved great power and a multiparty system flourished. Even here, Israel's focus on military development and repression of its Palestinian minority at times clouded the nation's liberal vision, as did the power of extremist religious groups in winning government support for Orthodox Jewish practices.

Most Middle Eastern states either did not pretend to establish parliaments or, as in the more secular states, limited their effectiveness by preventing multiparty competition. Even Turkey, which periodically experimented with opposition parties and a fairly free press after World War II, often retreated into military regimes. A multiparty system did gain ground, producing a first woman prime minister in the 1990s. But then victory by a pro-Muslim party caused the military to intervene in 1997 and install secular politicians, though on the basis of a party coalition in parliament. Elsewhere, monarchy or strongman rule normally prevailed. Muslim political tradition provided scant basis for liberal political values, while the tensions within Middle Eastern society convinced many leaders that their power could not be preserved within a framework of political competition. Most countries, then, imposed restrictions on the press, used political police extensively, and relied heavily on military support in an essentially authoritarian political pattern.

Yet there was no single vision of how the state should operate. A key division opened between the monarchies—Morocco, Jordan, Saudi Arabia, Iran before 1978, and some smaller states on the Persian gulf—and the secular republics, where individual strongmen typically wielded power, often backed by a single political party. Most of the monarchs, while working for economic development, not only discouraged political opposition but tended to support the existing social hierarchy and conservative Muslim social values. Saudi Arabia was the most extreme example. The country sought to use oil revenues to develop a wider industrial base as well as new cities and extensive education, but it also enforced traditional Arab dress and social segregation of women, as well as substantial penalties for sexual misconduct or drinking or dietary habits that contravened Islamic law. The government forbade women to drive cars, even though many had learned to drive during visits to the West. Most republics, on the other hand, while just as hostile to political opposition as were the monarchies, sought to encourage not only industrial development and agricultural reform but a more secular outlook. They worked for new educational and job opportunities for women, while discouraging traditional dress. Like Atatürk's regime, they tried to limit Muslim habits—such as fasting during the day for the month of Ramadan—that would affect economic productivity. A number of the republics worked toward a policy of what was called Arab socialism, designed to produce a society different from the West and from the communist nations alike. Arab socialism meant regulations for business—particularly foreign-owned business—but not state control of the entire economy. It involved attempts to limit inequality, through heavier taxation on the rich and land reforms to benefit the peasantry. Arab socialism did not, however, represent a full-scale attack on religion or a devotion to elaborate political doctrine; it was an impulse more than a well-defined movement.

THE RISE OF FUNDAMENTALISM

Political and economic change produced an important backlash in Middle Eastern political and cultural life, which became increasingly vivid from the 1970s onward. Furthermore, failures of reform—in the continuation of massive poverty—created pressures to use religion for protest. The spiritual power and pervasive legal framework of Islam explain why many people, ordinary peasants as well as religious leaders, were tempted to use their Muslim faith as a rallying point against change or for different kinds of reform, and especially against any signs of Western cultural influence. Thus the Ayatollah Khomeini, ultimately the leader of Iran's 1978 revolution, reacted to educational change:

> Our universities must become Islamic. . . . They have served to impede the progress of the sons and daughters of this land; they have become propaganda arenas. Our young people may have succeeded in acquiring some knowledge, but they have not received an education, an Islamic education. . . . The universities do not impart an education that corresponds to the needs of the people and the country; instead they squander the energies of whole generations of our beloved youth, or oblige them to serve the foreigners.

Thus a new Islamic fundamentalism took shape, after 1970, that in essence sought a return to original Muslim political ideals of a state committed to religious values and enforcing these values as its first priority. This was not pure traditionalism; fundamentalists used novel methods and often displayed an intolerance that was not characteristic of Islam in the past. Most leaders were urban-educated. But there was a protest against change. Many Muslim scholars and other religious leaders, including the ulema scholars, raised important objections to trends in the Middle East (and also in neighboring Muslim societies such as Sudan, Afghanistan, and Pakistan). They viewed concentration on economic advance as evidence of improper priorities: adherence to religious duties should come first. Westernized costumes—particularly for women, and particularly in recreational areas and on beaches—and other imports, including films, were attacked as scandalous and immoral. The tendencies of more secular states to push education without a firm anchor in religion and to cooperate with Christian Westerners were condemned, while the Muslim purists also insisted on a more concentrated attack on the problem of Israel. In short, Muslim fundamentalists called for a restoration of many older values, including a reorientation of political functions.

Appeals for a return to traditional values have been a standard part of modern history in societies exposed to rapid change: they occurred in Christian societies in the 19th century, and they still crop up in some parts of the West, including the United States; they occurred, in different terms, in Japan. Hindu fundamentalism echoed similar themes in

An Iranian revolutionary trains women in military skills.

The Iranian Revolution, 1979: anti-American demonstration, with posters of Khomeini.

India. But the fundamentalist movement in Islam seems to have struck a deeper chord in the Middle East than analogous movements in other civilizations. Deeply committed Muslim groups emerged in most Middle Eastern states by the 1970s. Even in conservative Saudi Arabia they put pressure on the regime to carry out Muslim laws more faithfully. Thus, in some show trials, adulterers were stoned or beheaded. A group of fundamentalists was responsible for the assassination of President Anwar Sadat, in 1981, though Egyptian policy was not massively affected by the conservative current. Fundamentalist pressure in Pakistan prompted the military regime to introduce a new law code more in line with Muslim tradition, providing, among other things, harsher punishments for such crimes as sexual immorality. In the 1990s, fundamentalist pressure increased in Turkey, though the military tried to control it. Algerian military rulers faced an even tougher battle with a larger fundamentalist group, and there was much mutual violence. In general, Muslim fundamentalism added an important ingredient to the Middle Eastern mix, even where states largely resisted the pressure.

The greatest victory of the Muslim militants occurred in Iran. It was revealing that the most dramatic revolution in the 20th-century Middle East was religious in spirit, unlike all other contemporary revolutions in the world. The Iranian revolution has been called, in fact, the first real "third world revolution," in that it sought not a special national path to modernization using ideas such as Marxism first created in the West, like the communist revolutions in Russia and China, but a commitment to ideals of Islamic law. The revolutionaries were zealous Shi'ites, a majority in Iran though a minority in Islam overall. Shi'ites had long been bent on creating a purer religious state, against what they saw as the errors of the Sunnites, the majority group of Muslims. This aspect of the Iranian struggle renewed a conflict that had been going on for centuries within Islam.

The specific framework for the Iranian revolution involved a rapid reform program that had taken place in Iran, building on the efforts of the 1920s and 1930s, combined with brutal political repression. The shah's government, which with U.S. help had defeated a 1953 protest, had launched a crash program of modernization rather like that of Atatürk earlier in Turkey, but with the added fillip of substantial oil revenues and greater contact with the West. The regime supported education, including the training of many Iranians abroad, plus industrial and military development. These changes caused much discontent. The rural majority was neglected. Inflation ran high, for even with oil earnings the new projects were expensive. The shah's brutal repression of political opposition, through a powerful secret police, antagonized additional, liberal segments of Iranian opinion, as did extensive corruption. Other grievances rested with the Muslim faithful. Islamic leaders were appalled at the new surge of Western influence, visible in the 100,000 foreigners who helped run the economy. They protested the resort areas developed for foreigners' use, where use of liquor and skimpy bathing suits clashed with Muslim law.

Revolt broke out in 1978, forcing the exile of the shah early in the following year. The new leader was the aged holy man, the Ayatollah Khomeini, who had long campaigned against the "godless and materialistic" regime of the shah. The revolutionary government quickly suppressed other discontented groups, including liberals and communists. It banned Western music, bathing suits, and liquor, and set out to create a Shi'ite holy state. Traditional dress, including head coverings, was required of women. During the long war Iraq launched against Iran, leaders hoped to export its political principles to other Muslim states; the ayatollah talked of a new jihad, or holy war, that would bring the whole Middle East back to a literal version of the Islamic state. A high level of religious and revolutionary excitement continued in Iran through the mid–1980s. Fundamentalists, mainly Shi'ites, were also active in the troubled nation of Lebanon, after the 1982 Israeli invasion, and they stirred elsewhere; in Syria, for example, an insurgency was put down with considerable brutality.

Fundamentalist reaction to change in the Middle East thus formed an important current in the late 20th century. There was no way to determine its durability; certainly key states such as Iraq and Syria, as well as most North African regimes, managed to maintain their secular policies that were, in any event, not in full opposition to Islam. But fundamentalists put massive pressure on governments, as in Algeria, along with frequent terrorism. Even the Soviet Union worried about a potential fundamentalism current among its own Muslim minority; this was one reason for the invasion of Afghanistan, to guard against a fundamentalist regime in this neighboring state. Debates over Muslim policy resumed in the new Central Asian republics that followed the Soviet collapse. Finally, the incompleteness of industrialization and divisions of outlook, even in well-established secular states such as Turkey, suggested that, in part because of the continued commitment of many faithful to older ways, Islam and some aspects of a conventional reform program were not easily compatible. Again, Islam's spiritual hold, its emphasis on obedience to Allah, and its tradition of regulating social life in some detail, gave it an unusual role among world religions in the 20th century.

By the late 1990s, it was not clear how important Islamic resistance and innovation would prove to be. Certainly the continued strength of a fairly literal Muslim faith has added to the diversity of Middle Eastern politics in the later 20th century. It suggests, also, an ongoing complexity to the process of change in this vital region. For Islamic fundamentalism has by no means been triumphant. Its surge reflects the fact that substantial political and social change has already touched Middle Eastern civilization—for example, the gradual but steady urbanization, bringing over 65 percent of the population of major countries like Egypt into the cities, away from rural work and rural roots. If Westernization obviously cannot capture the patterns of the contemporary Middle East, in politics and culture alike, no more so does an image of unaltered traditionalism.

MIDDLE EASTERN CULTURE AND SOCIETY

One fully industrial country emerged in the Middle East after World War II: the state of Israel. The new nation, though severely pressed to defend its existence, benefited from extensive foreign aid, deep commitment on the part of many of its citizens, and experience in working an industrial economy. Most initial Israeli leaders were immigrants. Hundreds of thousands of European Jews migrated to the new nation after the Nazi Holocaust of World War II. Substantial immigration from the cities of the Middle East developed as well, as hostilities between Arabs and Jews disrupted earlier patterns of tolerance and the new Israeli state served as a beacon for the Jewish faithful. With immigration came population growth and the infusion of a multitude of skills in business and manufacturing. Israeli commitment to industrial output and market agriculture, including extensive projects of desert reclamation, produced a dynamic economy that easily placed Israel among the technologically advanced nations of the world. Although the new country faced economic problems, particularly because of heavy military expenditure, it had easily jumped the basic hurdles of 20th-century economic development. The country turned increasingly to consumerism by the 1990s, which caused concern among religious groups and secular nationalists alike.

In contrast, manufacturing, market agriculture, and levels of technology lagged in most other parts of the Middle East. Indeed, the gap in technological sophistication between Israel and its rivals was one of the bases of Israeli survival, as Israeli production of up-to-date armaments became a major industry. Variety among the Muslim states in economic conditions itself increased. The region embraces about 60 percent of the world's known petroleum reserves, but they are not evenly distributed. Nations with substantial oil production and small populations—among them some of the traditionally poorest desert states—suddenly surged to immense per capita wealth. The Persian Gulf state of Kuwait thus ranked in 1980 as the richest in the world in terms of average income. Saudi Arabia also rose to great wealth. Lavish new urban construction and extensive medical and educational services followed from oil revenues in these nations, particularly during the heyday of OPEC price manipulation. Regional manufacturing did gain ground, generating additional import substitution and a new minority of factory workers. But though the oil-rich states struggled to

HISTORY DEBATE

Fundamentalism

Many Western experts on the Middle East urge great care in interpreting fundamentalism. They note that fundamentalist hostility to the West, particularly the United States, makes sympathetic interpretation difficult. They especially urge that fundamentalism not be seen as a single movement. Not all fundamentalists oppose all change. Muslim tradition is perfectly compatible with commercial advance in any event. Most fundamentalists accept certain kinds of change, including new technologies and the importance of mass education (though they seek a strong religious element in this education and some careful regulations of girls' dress). Even the effort to implement the laws of the Sharia is new, for the attempt has never been carried so far. Further, fundamentalism picks up both traditionalist resistance to change *and* discontent amid modern problems like massive urban poverty.

Another big question involves the relationship between this strong, growing current in Islam and religious change elsewhere. Hindu attachments became more vigorous in the 1980s and 1990s, as we have seen. The collapse of the Soviet system gave some new push to Orthodox Christianity in Eastern Europe, while Protestant fundamentalists also worked for converts. Religious pressures also increased in Israel in the 1990s, particularly in the Orthodox Jewish stronghold of Jerusalem. Protestant fundamentalism, pushed by missionaries mainly from the United States, was the most rapidly growing new belief system in Latin America in the 1980s and 1990s. Islamic fundamentalism, in other words, played a special role in the Middle East and North Africa, plus adjacent territory in Pakistan and Central Asia. But it may be part of a wider international cultural current in the late 20th century, which means that its explanation must go beyond strictly Islamic bounds.

Other observers, however, stress some specifically Islamic ingredients. They note the relevance of the old Sunni-Shi'ite rift, and also Islam's extensive legalism, its host of rules and regulations, that make it harder to accept certain kinds of social and cultural change than is true for other religions. Islamic law applies to so many aspects of life, from the position of women to the daily schedule, that its mandates can clash with any modern reform drive. This provides a special basis for the more general temptation to defend tradition in the contemporary world. Interpreting fundamentalism, or any specific manifestation such as Islamic fundamentalism, clearly raises important challenges.

invest their earnings in industries that could sustain a better-balanced economy and provide wealth even when oil production declined, they encountered serious difficulties. Many, indeed, invested substantial funds abroad, especially in the West, because there simply were insufficient productive opportunities at home. Lack of other resources, continued limitations in technical training and interest, a pronounced gap between rich and poor that restricts consumer demand—these were some general factors that inhibited a translation of oil wealth into industrialization. Heavy military expenditures also played a role, for these investments involved purchases from abroad rather than stimulus to domestic production. When military expenditure turned into war, as in the Iran-Iraq conflict, the impact on economic conditions could be devastating.

Nations without oil wealth faced even more severe economic problems. Here, too, military expenditures and, in some cases, political instability limited economic development. Many countries were also burdened by substantial population growth. Lack of available land haunted many rural people, while opportunities in the cities did not keep pace with need, even as urbanization accelerated. Muslim beliefs slowed conversion to new birth control methods. A number of governments attempted massive projects to expand production. Egypt's President Nasser, for example, with substantial Soviet aid, orchestrated the construction of a huge dam at Aswan, on the Nile, designed to increase agricultural land through irrigation while providing low-cost electrical power for industry. The dam was also meant to symbolize Arab greatness and recall the glory days of ancient Egypt; thus Nasser described the dam as "more magnificent and seventeen times greater than the Pyramids." Unfortunately, the Aswan project, though successful, did not keep pace with Egypt's population growth. Both the urban masses and the peasant population of this key nation remained desperately poor.

New oil revenues, land reform, and some real growth in urban manufacturing did bring economic change to the Middle East, particularly after World War II. City populations outstripped rural populations in most countries as Middle Eastern urbanization levels exceeded those of India and China. Yet, outside of Israel, a breakthrough to some version of an industrial economy has yet to occur, and standards of living in the larger countries tend to stagnate. One result was considerable emigration in search of jobs, as many Turks and North Africans sought work in Western Europe, while other Arab peasants took unskilled jobs, often at low pay, in the oil-rich states.

Middle Eastern culture, like the economy, also balanced between tradition and change. Outside of Israel, few Middle Eastern artists participated in international styles. Most Muslim art continued to use traditional styles and themes, though "modern" architecture did find a place in the city development undertaken in countries like Saudi Arabia and prerevolutionary Iran. While some Western films were shown in the more secular nations, Muslim film-making remained largely separate from patterns developed in the West, partly of course for religious reasons. The Muslim world retained an active allegiance to traditional musical styles, relying, even for most popular music, on instruments and singing techniques different from those in the West. While important work has been done in art and literature—an Egyptian novelist won the Nobel prize for literature in 1994—and also in Muslim theology and law, there was little sense of a revival of creativity that would recall the brightest periods of Middle Eastern culture.

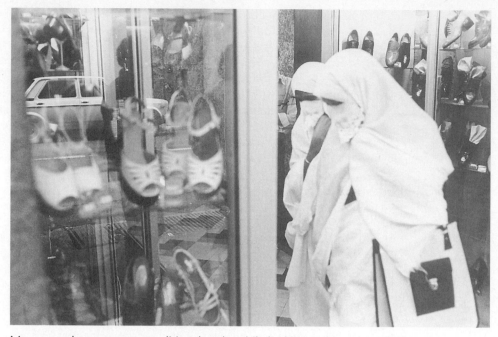

Moroccan shoppers wear traditional garb, while looking at Western-style shoes.

Most Middle Eastern governments encouraged growing interest in science. Nasser set up a Supreme Science Council in Egypt, arguing that

> we have to keep up with the new world and new discoveries. We suffered so much in the past because we were left behind by the ages of steam and electricity. What suffering awaits those who fail to keep up with the new dawn will certainly be much greater than whatever we have experienced in the past. . . . In this world of breathtaking discoveries, to be left behind is to forfeit one's right to existence.

While improved scientific training added an important dimension to Middle Eastern culture, it did not propel the region into the top ranks of scientific creativity; the Middle East remained heavily dependent on the West for basic scientific research. The dissemination of a scientific outlook to a larger population through the expanding school systems, along with growing literacy, established a basis for further change in the future, though it clashed at points with Islamic fundamentalism.

Society in the Middle East reflected the growth of cities and the policies of reform-minded governments. It also reflected population pressure and, in places, the impact of war. But there were important continuities with the past here as well. Many Middle Eastern villages have changed only slowly. Some new agricultural equipment was introduced, and contacts with urban markets expanded. But the pace of life and work remained recognizable in traditional terms. While throughout most of the region landlord dominance was reduced, the gap between peasant masses and local notables was an important fact of life.

A key tension in Middle Eastern society involved the position of women. In a major break with the past, increasing numbers of women gained access to formal education. In the more secular states, such as Turkey, Egypt, Algeria, or Syria, many women also cast aside traditional costumes, abandoning the veil and adopting Western dress. Many governments tried to encourage new work patterns among women, seeing them as a vital resource for fledgling industrial economies. Thus some women entered the ranks of factory and office workers. But the economic and social segregation of women remained severe. Work outside the home, and especially a commitment to professional jobs as doctors or lawyers, was widely disapproved, and few women could hope to support themselves without family resources. The gap between male and female school attendance remained greater than in any other civilization. Male dominance within the household was still pronounced, and the relatively high birth rate both caused and reflected the domestic emphasis of women's lives. Conservative states like Saudi Arabia enforced even more pronounced separation between the spheres of men and women, including the severe penalties for sexual infidelity among women and men. And the Iranian revolution showed that even reformist regimes like the shah's can yield to more traditional practices concerning women.

During the Iranian Revolution, a middle-class feminist demonstration.

Again, the result was not uniform. Countries like Turkey had large numbers of "Westernized" women, wearing cosmetics and European-style clothes, active in urban jobs including politics and possessed of a secular education. They shared the streets with women in traditional dress, enmeshed in Islamic culture and family life. In a few cases, they also faced attack from the assertions of the fundamentalist movement.

CONCLUSION: A TROUBLED REGION

Many more question marks dot the appraisal of trends and prospects in the Middle East than is the case for the other major Asian civilizations in the late 20th century. The region has produced no unity in political form. The existence of divisions and diversity is no novelty in Middle Eastern tradition, of course, as periods of chaos often punctuated efforts at unification in the past. But there is certainly no clear end in sight to some of the fundamental conflicts that describe political and military life in the region. Disputes between secular reformers and Muslim fundamentalists continue to constrain many national governments and divide behaviors among women. The precise blend of tradition and change that will continue to define a Middle Eastern civilization has yet to be found. The civilization remains unique and faces a number of problems of significance to other parts of the world as regional wars spill over into wider tensions.

Perhaps the troubles of the Middle East will prove transitory. Once before, when the Arab caliphate declined but before the full hold of the Turks was secure, the region passed through many decades of disarray. Regional political units refused to coordinate their policies. An outside force—the Kingdom of Jerusalem established by European crusaders—seized a holy territory but could not easily be dislodged. Out of frustration, terrorist groups—called the Assassins—arose. Yet this chaos did subside, as a new wave of Turkish invasions—the Ottomans—brought political unity and military strength, while preserving many features of Islamic civilization, including considerable tolerance and regional diversity. History may, in some basic ways, repeat itself; certainly this particular analogy is interesting. Yet analogies are never certain—Israel is no mere crusader state; economic development issues and basic disputes over politics complicate any earlier pattern—and this one, in any event, would take several more generations to work out. In the meantime, the Middle East, unquestionably dynamic in many ways, remains one of the world's trouble spots.

The collapse of the Soviet Union added to the complications facing Middle East politics, with the emergences of the new Muslim nations in nearby central Asia. These nations had their own problems: what kind of political system to set up, how to handle minorities like Armenian Christians in their region, and how to plan economic development in an area long used by Russia as a raw-materials center. They also had a new opportunity to reach out to their Muslim brethren. Iranian fundamentalists hoped to guide them back to their version of Islam. Diplomats from more secular Turkey tried to persuade them of the virtues of top-down reform. Questions about the eventual fate of Islam became no easier to answer, but gained even greater importance.

Suggested Readings

Several interesting sources are available on the Middle East in this period. See David Ben-Gurion, *Israel: Years of Challenge* (1963) and I. Khomeini, *Practical Laws of Islam* (1983) and *Islam and Revolution: Writings and Declarations of Iman Khomeini,* Hamid Alger, tr. (1981). Mahmud Makal, *Village in Anatolia* (1951), is an exceptionally interesting account of the tension between a modernizing Turkish schoolteacher and his village environment.

A useful overall survey is G. Lenczowski, *The Middle East and World Affairs,* 4th ed. (1980); see also Hain Faris, *Arab Nationalism* (1986); and Juan Coley, ed., *Comparing Muslim Societies* (1992). On specific national and diplomatic topics, J. C. Hurewitz, *A Diplomatic History of the Near and Middle East* (1956); W. Lacqueur, *Communism and Nationalism in the Middle East* (1956); N. Safran, *The United States and Israel* (1963); W. Lacqueur, *A History of Zionism* (1972); R. Cottam, *Nationalism in Iran,* rev. ed. (1979); K. Wheelock, *Nasser's New Egypt* (1960); E. B. Childers, *The Road to Suez* (1963); and Z. N. Zeine, *The Struggle for Arab Independence* (1960), are all useful works. See also E. Boserup, *Women's Role in Economic Development* (1974), which covers a vital aspect of Middle Eastern development (and also the patterns in other non-Western areas), though with a controversial theoretical framework. For the individual Muslim states, see Ira M. Lapidus, *A History of Islamic Societies* (1988).

Latin America in the 20th Century

Focal Points

Many Americans regard Latin America as a highly traditional area. In fact, the 20th century has created a number of rapid economic and political changes, though Latin America retains some of its distinctive cultural identity. Compared to 1900, Latin America in the 1990s is strikingly democratic: when and why did this political trend set in, and what political themes preceded the move toward democracy? Government responses to the depression of the 1930s form a particularly important, predemocratic turning point. Without becoming fully industrial, major regions of Latin America improved their position in the world economy. What are the main indications of economic change? How has Latin America balanced extremely rapid urbanization with some relatively stable family patterns? Has Latin American culture shifted as rapidly as the economic and political structure of the civilization?

THE LEADING THEMES

After 1900, Latin America maintained many of the characteristics it had developed during the 19th century. This society did not have to contend with the problems of outright new nationhood that preoccupied so many other parts of the world. Great-power intervention remained a concern, particularly because of the economic and military outreach of the United States in the Caribbean and Central America. Dealing with North American influence was not a novel issue, however, though it took some new twists, especially after World War II. Latin America also remained free from major warfare except for a 1932–1935 Chaco War between Bolivia and Paraguay. Nationalist rivalries existed and led to some conflict, but the region was far more peaceful, in terms of formal diplomacy, than most of its counterparts elsewhere in the world. These were no regional arms races, and military arsenals, although they expanded after World War II, were modest for the most part. Major internal violence, however, was directed against peasant protesters and

Indian minorities as landowners and caudillos, or military dictators, sought to maintain their power.

Yet after 1900 there were new themes and strains in Latin American society. The revolution in Mexico, early in the 20th century, reflected some of the same tensions that plagued China and Russia in the period, although the revolution yielded a distinctive result. Latin American politics were redefined by a growing role for central states, beginning in the 1930s. Popular unrest in Latin America rivaled that of other peasant societies, though it did not always lead to significant political reform until the early 1980s, when a new democratic trend gained ground. The 20th century, in sum, saw important new political contests and governmental forms.

A second area of change focused around economic problems. Issues of economic development inevitably took on new urgency, as growing numbers of Latin American governments, both democracies and caudillo-led authoritarian regimes, sought a more active economic role. Moreover, rising levels of population brought Latin America new problems as the region became one of the most rapidly growing areas of the world. A number of societies developed significant industrial sectors, breaking through the economic weakness that had characterized Latin America's place in the international economy in the past. New problems, but also new approaches, thus described economic patterns during this period.

Finally, the Latin nations continued to develop their distinctive cultural amalgam, blending styles generated in the West with a variety of ingredients created locally. Indeed, the 20th century proved to be a rich period in Latin American culture, with major innovations in painting, architecture, and literature. Even as economic and political tensions seized attention, the cultural and religious creativity suggests a civilization still actively expanding its range.

PATTERNS OF LATIN AMERICAN HISTORY: THE MEXICAN REVOLUTION, 1910–1920S

Revolution in Mexico, from 1910 to 1917, was the great event of the early 20th century in Latin America, though it directly affected only the one major nation. The Mexican conflict embraced some of the same peasant grievances that surfaced in Russia, as the peasantry was caught in the pressures of expanding market agriculture while lacking full access to the land. Discontented intellectuals also played a role, attacking a political regime seen as corrupt and inefficient—though in the Mexican case the regime lacked the deep roots of the Russian or Chinese empires. Resentment against foreign economic influence, visible in China and Russia, played an even more obvious part in Mexico. And while the Mexican revolution produced no single leader of the stature of Lenin or Sun Yat-sen, it had its share of dramatic figures and, at least in a strictly political sense, proved more successful than its Chinese counterpart of the same years.

The specific roots of the Mexican revolution went back to 1900, when a small group of intellectuals began to agitate against the authoritarian and corrupt regime of General Porfirio Díaz. The agitators sought democracy, a more liberal economic policy, and new restrictions on the church; the movement soon broadened to include social issues of con-

Latin America Today

CANADA

UNITED STATES OF AMERICA

ATLANTIC OCEAN

MEXICO

Gulf of Mexico

Mexico City

Havana

Nassau

BAHAMAS

HAITI (1804)

CUBA (1898)

DOMINICAN REP. (1844)

Santo Domingo

JAMAICA (1962)

Port-au-Prince

San Juan

PUERTO RICO (U.S.)

CARIBBEAN SEA

BARBADOS (1967)

Port of Spain

TRINIDAD & TOBAGO (1962)

CENTRAL AMERICA See Inset Below

PACIFIC OCEAN

Caracas

VENEZUELA (1811)

Bogotá

COLOMBIA (1821)

GUYANA (1966)

Georgetown

Paramaribo

Cayenne

FRENCH GUIANA

SURINAM (1975)

Equator

Quito

ECUADOR (1822)

GALÁPAGOS IS. *(Ecuador)*

Amazon R.

PERU (1821)

Lima

BRAZIL (1822)

Brazilia

0   1000   2000

MILES

BOLIVIA (1825)

La Paz

Sucre

Rio de Janeiro

PARAGUAY (1811)

Asunción

CHILE (1818)

URUGUAY (1828)

Buenos Aires

Montevideo

Santiago

ARGENTINA (1816)

La Plata R.

FALKLAND IS. (Br.)

CAPE HORN

CENTRAL AMERICA

GUATEMALA (1821)

Belmopan

BELIZE (1981)

Guatemala

HONDURAS (1821)

Tegucigalpa

Salvador

EL SALVADOR (1821)

NICARAGUA (1821)

Managua

San Jose

COSTA RICA (1821)

Panama Canal

Panama

PANAMA (1903)

JAMAICA (1962)

Kingston

CARIBBEAN SEA

PACIFIC OCEAN

Dates indicate year of independence

615

cern to urban workers and the peasantry. Landless rural laborers, receiving low wages for work on land that had once been theirs but that under Díaz had been seized by a small landlord class, were particularly restive. Their resentment focused on foreign owners; economic nationalism, or a desire to return control of economic life to Mexican hands against outsiders, especially U.S. investors, remained an important part of the revolutionary movement. Peasant leaders included Emiliano Zapata, whose motto was "Land and Liberty" and who saw revolution as the uprising of rural and urban workers against capitalist owners of all sorts. Bandit leaders were also active in some rural regions. Pancho Villa established something of a Robin Hood reputation, robbing the rich and befriending the poor. Revolution, in sum, drew on diverse groups with varied goals—as successful revolutions must always do.

Fighting broke out late in 1910. At first a moderate leader, Francisco Madero, came to the fore, arranging for elections of a new president after Díaz escaped the country. Madero thought too strictly in terms of political reform to content the working-class and peasant leaders, however, and the revolution soon escaped his control. Zapata, in particular, organized new revolts, which in turn terrified business interests, including many Americans; with U.S. backing, a military leader replaced Madero, executing him and many other rebel leaders. Revolutionary forces continued to operate, though, and in the south Zapata set up a regional government of his own. In 1916 a change in U.S. policy lent support to a more moderate leader, Venustiano Carranza, who seized power in that year. Carranza began to solidify key revolutionary gains. A new constitution, in 1917, proclaimed Mexican ownership of all mineral rights, thus reducing the role of foreign investment; land ownership was reserved for Mexicans, and many large estates were broken up, to the benefit of mestizo and Indian peasants. The power of the Catholic church, which had supported Díaz and then the repressive regime that attacked Madero, was also restricted.

Carranza's reform goals were limited in practice, however. He showed little interest in a liberal political government, preferring to hold power directly; and he did not in fact carry land reform too far. In 1920, revolutionaries pressed for new leadership; under the presidency of Álvaro Obregón, the long period of disorder drew to a close, and the results of revolution took clearer shape. Obregón confirmed Zapata's land redistribution in the south; Pancho Villa and his bandit forces were bought off by the gift of a cattle ranch. Obregón moved slowly with further changes, however, lest conservative opposition overturn the new regime. Fearing U.S. hostility, he even allowed existing foreign owners to retain their holdings. Instead of a full attack on the social system, comparable to that in the new Soviet Union, Obregón preferred to concentrate on selective reforms that would encourage economic development. He pushed forward a widespread system of primary education that taught Spanish, and Mexican nationalism, to many Indians for the first time. The government worked actively on public health measures, and also expanded cultivable lands through irrigation. But the regime did not try to seize control of the urban economy from business groups, nor did it remove the entire landlord class. And while the Catholic church found its political influence reduced, there was no effort to uproot it. Revolution in Mexico, in social terms, meant change but not upheaval.

Politically, the revolution during the 1920s ended the nation's long history of instability, creating a system that differed both from liberal democracy and from caudillismo. A single political party, the PNR (National Revolutionary Party), dominated political life, coopting opposition leaders and vigorously repressing dissent. Presidents, who were selected from within the party and thus faced election with assurance of victory, wielded huge powers; some grew rich on public funds, much as old-style caudillos had done. But the new system prevented any one person from ruling the country permanently, for the presidency had to change hands every six years, and so the worst excesses of caudillismo were avoided. Furthermore, the PNR did present itself for elections and remained responsive to many wider concerns. At times its rhetoric and slogans, which boasted of worker and peasant rights, outstripped its achievements. But there was no question that the power of the traditional ruling classes was now limited by the PNR's desire to retain popular loyalty, or that foreign influence in Mexican affairs had been dramatically reduced. The regime's successful balance between forces old and new was reflected in its durability, amid only occasional, usually minor, political attacks. Into the mid–1990s, as what was renamed the PNI began to allow freer elections, Mexico has known considerably more political stability and considerably more independence in policy than many other Latin American nations—particularly those close to the orbit of the United States.

PATTERNS OF LATIN AMERICAN HISTORY SINCE THE 1920S

Unlike many revolutions, Mexico's had little spillover to other areas. For one thing, its sometimes chaotic course reduced its appeal. Nor did the revolution produce a single doctrine, like Marxism, capable of rousing support elsewhere. U.S. opposition to political radicalism also helped limit the revolution's impact in Central America. Furthermore, while the revolution generated important reforms and encouraged a vigorous cultural movement, it did not propel Mexican economic development to new heights, nor did it lead to a full industrial revolution, again in contrast to the Soviet regime in Russia. Its social achievements were not great enough to draw discontented peasants elsewhere. For this reason also, the Mexican revolution failed to usher in a new period in Latin American history as a whole.

EFFECTS OF THE DEPRESSION: 1930–1950S

The worldwide economic depression of the 1930s had widespread, catastrophic effects on Latin America, which in turn triggered a new round of political turmoil. The value of Latin American exports decreased by a full two-thirds; the economy had depended on selling agricultural goods and minerals to the industrial nations of the West, which now simply could not afford to buy. As unsold goods piled up in warehouses, poverty increased. No sweeping revolutionary movement resulted, although popular rioting continued in many areas. But the results of the depression encouraged a desire to win fuller economic independence and to use government power to gain greater economic control. Various kinds of political regimes evinced this new, nationalistic concern.

The despair caused by the depression did encourage Marxist movements in several countries, including Chile and Brazil, but these were generally kept in check by firm military rule. A revolutionary movement in Peru produced a doctrine combining socialism, fierce anti-Americanism, and a stress on Indian cultural values; but while it promoted agitation, it did not seize power.

The tide of economic nationalism proved more successful. Unequal land distribution, illiteracy, and poor production methods spurred a number of governments to take remedial action. Many of the regimes proved willing to run some industries directly, and most saw the need to regulate foreign investment and require foreign firms to employ Latin American managers. Most important, state-sponsored programs of export substitution increased the industrial sector.

A series of populist leaders came to the fore in many countries, builiding multi-class alliances, including urban workers (whose importance was obviously growing).

In Mexico, a spirit of reform was rekindled by the election of Lázaro Cárdenas as president in 1934. Cárdenas seized foreign oil companies, setting up a state corporation, Pemex, to manage the industry. A series of land reforms broke up additional estates. Education spread, and with it an effort to integrate Indian culture more fully into national life. A state bank was organized to encourage industry; as a result, Mexican production increased more rapidly than that of any other Latin American country from 1940 to 1960, though immense poverty persisted.

In Brazil, weak political leadership and deteriorating economic conditions led to a military revolt, headed by Getúlio Vargas, which produced a reasonably mild caudillo-style dictatorship that lasted from 1930 to 1945. Vargas did away with elections and parliament, while regulating the press and operating a secret police that kept the opposition divided. Deeply committed to economic modernization, Vargas hoped to free Brazil from dependence on coffee exports. Under his administration the state constructed important steel mills, and the nation began to produce most of the industrial goods it required. The Amazon basin was opened to agricultural development. Cities expanded, their centers graced by modern office buildings and apartment houses. Brazil remained a largely agricultural nation, but one capable of considerable economic growth.

The government of Chile responded to the effects of the depression without dismantling its liberal, parliamentary system. A state Development Corporation was set up during the 1930s to provide funds and planning for industrial projects.

Other parts of Latin America reacted less forcefully to the economic and political stress of the 1930s. Poverty and static social and economic conditions were particularly vivid in the Andes nations of Peru, Bolivia, and Ecuador, with their large Indian populations. Here, as in a number of other countries, army-backed caudillos often ruled without great vision beyond the maintenance of power, amid recurrent rural unrest and frequent changes of regime.

Argentina was governed during the 1930s by a military and landholding elite. Only in 1943 did real change take place under the populist authoritarian Juan Péron (elected president in 1946). Even more than Brazil's Vargas, Péron appealed to the masses with a policy of benefit programs. His government crushed free trade unions and opposition parties, while directing the main branches of the economy. Foreign-owned companies were bought out, and the old landholders were weakened by state controls over the price of their goods. Péron promoted the general thrust of economic nationalism, but with a populist twist—an effort at frenzied mass appeal that suggested European fascism. The expense of Péron's massive welfare programs limited Argentina's real economic growth, even as popular loyalty to Péron remained high. A military coup in 1955 displaced the Argentine strongman, with an attempt to restore parliamentary democracy. But worried by the continued strength of Péronism and eager to ensure stability, the military took political control in 1966 and again in 1976, each time with vigorous police repression of opposition political forces.

REVOLUTION AND RESPONSE: 1950s–1990s

Despite important variations in political forms and economic development, by the late 1950s there was considerable optimism about Latin America's prospects. Leading countries, including Mexico, post-Vargas Brazil, and post-Péron Argentina, were firmly bent on economic development, some social reform, and some degree of political freedom, if not usually through a full-fledged, multiparty system. Despite Marxist currents, radical political efforts had little appeal. U.S. opposition to anything that smacked of communism

Mass demonstration for Peron in Buenos Aires, with a heroic statue.

combined here with the strength of conservative forces. A reform-minded regime in the Central American nation of Guatemala was unseated with U.S. aid in 1954, as the giant to the north briefly resumed the tradition of intervention of a half-century before. Yet the United States did not consistently oppose the nationalist policies that had emerged since the 1930s. A major social revolution in Bolivia in 1952–1953 produced significant agrarian reform. While United States business interests exercised great power in many countries, Washington also welcomed the economic growth of nations like Brazil and Mexico even though considerable government planning and investment were involved. "Good neighbor" policies initiated during the 1930s, during Franklin Roosevelt's administration, took some of the rougher edges off U.S.–Latin American relations, though a profound power disparity remained and much of the "good neighbor" rhetoric was purely cosmetic.

Hopes for a new level of stability were challenged by revolution in Cuba. Long virtually a U.S. protectorate, Cuba had suffered from weak political institutions. A strongman leader named Fulgencio Batista had ruled since 1933, amid great personal corruption. A pronounced gulf divided a rich minority from the impoverished masses, as in many Latin American nations, and while the Cuban economy was relatively prosperous, it depended dangerously on sugar exports to the United States. During the 1950s a guerrilla rebellion arose against the Batista regime, headed by the magnetic leader Fidel Castro. Castro's political goals were unclear, though he promised a "real" revolution; his attack on corruption and foreign influence, and his plea for land reform, constituted an important new revolutionary current, blending peasant grievances with explicit political concerns. Military victory came in 1959–1960. The new regime frightened away or expelled wealthy Cubans, while deteriorating relations with the United States followed from, and also encouraged, an increasingly communist tack in the Castro government. The Cuban Communist party, initially hesitant, embraced Castro fully. A U.S. effort in 1961 to topple Castro failed miserably, leaving the new regime free to build a society along modified Soviet lines. State ownership combined with worker committees in factories, while the great sugar estates were confiscated and turned into collective farms. The new regime promoted greater racial equality. The result was in many ways a more thoroughgoing revolution than had occurred in Mexico—and it also led, thanks to Castro's policies and rhetoric but also to U.S. response, to the importation of cold war tensions into Latin American politics. Revolution in Cuba came to mean a close alliance with the Soviet Union, and a leadership cult grew up around the vigorous personality of Castro.

The Cuban revolution did not have the unsettling effects on the rest of Latin America that its supporters had hoped or its opponents had feared. Many Latin American governments maintained good relations with the new regime, rather pleased at Cuba's success in defying the North American giant but not eager to install a communist system in their own nations. U.S. policy shifted, in reaction to its failure to dislodge Castro, toward more ample economic aid to other Latin American countries, though momentum in this effort dwindled by the 1970s. A radical regime arose in Peru in 1968, but the reform results were meager, and military coups soon snuffed out the civilian revolutionaries. Much later, in 1979, a radical uprising in Nicaragua unseated a U.S.-backed dictator, with assistance from Cuba. The new regime, like its Mexican and Cuban predecessors, gradually limited political opposition, and it also attacked an Indian minority group. It did promote land reform, seizing great estates (many of them owned by U.S. concerns), and enacted education and public health measures. It also encouraged guerrilla movements in other Central American nations, notably El Salvador. During the early 1980s the United States provided military aid and encouraged its own guerrilla activity in defense of more conservative regimes in the region. By the 1990s, peace had been largely restored on the basis of democratic elections and a merger of separate military forces.

The establishment of a communist system in Cuba encouraged a new round of authoritarianism in some other countries, as military and civilian leaders sought the fullest possible protection against any new subversion. Populist regimes also seemed to have failed by the 1960s in places like Argentina, while economic contractions increased internal disputes pitting workers against the middle classes and elites. The resulting series of military regimes, though they did not affect every country in the 1960s, became increasingly common. Fear of communism encouraged the military regimes in Argentina, beginning in 1966. In 1970 in Chile, a Marxist-led coalition of communists, socialists, and radicals won a free election. No carbon copy of Castroism, the new regime proceeded to a number of key reforms, including nationalization of U.S.-owned copper mines and divi-

Urbanization: Belo Horizante, Brazil, 1967. Then only 70 years old, the city had over a million inhabitants.

sion of the great landed estates. This in turn provoked reaction from the middle and upper classes, and the conservative resurgence won U.S. support. A military coup toppled the reformist government, amid considerable bloodshed, and a tight dictatorship was installed that lasted into the late 1980s.

The spread of democratic systems began to overtake the surge of conservative military dictatorships in the 1980s, starting with the new Argentine regime of 1982. At first the trend seemed merely a renewal of the oscillations long characteristic of Latin American politics. Free elections occurred in Brazil in 1984. A newly elected leader in Uruguay noted that "there are winds that blow in favor, winds that blow against. It is evident in this era the winds are favorable to democracy." Chile's authoritarian ruler yielded to democracy, as did the revolutionary party in Nicaragua. Mexico retained one-party dominance, but contested elections became more common and opposition groups controlled some state governments; elections in 1997 were freer than at any point since the revolution. Paraguay, one of the classic authoritarian states, adopted democracy in 1993. At least for the moment, Latin American leaders decided that democracy spared societies painful costs of repression and potentially dealt with issues of economic development and other pressures at least as effectively as authoritarian systems had managed in their time. The surge resembled the rise of liberalism in the late 19th century, but it was not only democratic but less authoritarian. Amid oscillations of regimes, Latin American political values unquestionably changed during the 20th century, even before the democratic surge. More groups gained political consciousness. In Mexico and many of the Andes nations, Indians obtained new rights and political involvement. Women received the vote for the first time in many countries—in Mexico in 1954. By the 1990s a significant minority of women served as elected officials. Extension of education and of the vote to propertyless males was another important, though not uninterrupted, tide in countries like Brazil.

Still more significant was the trend of growing commitment of Latin American governments to programs of economic development, though there had been some precedents for this interest in the 19th century. By the 1950s few caudillos remained who sought only personal power and the enrichment of themselves and their followers. Cuba's Batista was one such; so was the Nicaraguan leader deposed by revolution in 1979. Most authoritarian leaders, like Péron or Vargas, now adopted a new stance, extending the functions of government in important new directions, while the same held true for the Mexican regime and the expanding democratic systems at the end of the 20th century.

The new-style authoritarian leaders might be just as brutal toward political opponents as their more traditional predecessors had been, but they were increasingly likely to sponsor economic planning, to encourage new technologies, and to seek to regulate foreign investment in order to achieve greater economic nationalism. In most cases, their interest in development led to some concern for social reform, as authoritarian as well as liberal leaders moved to break up at least some of the vast landed estates and to provide some welfare protection for urban workers. Except for Cuba, no government-sponsored revolutionary social reform during the 20th century, but with rare exceptions governments did take on new functions, including the extension of education and public health and the outright operation of certain economic sectors. Here was a significant, evolutionary transformation of the Latin American political style under various constitutional arrangements. Authoritarian rulers might now appeal directly to popular support and engage in vigorous reforms unsettling to conservative interests.

The democratic current in the 1980s emphasized greater free enterprise. Governments sold off many state-run businesses, as the international emphasis on freer trade and capitalism strongly affected Latin America. Mexico, for example, reduced the government's role in the economy as part of its participation in the North American Free Trade Association (NAFTA) with the United States and Canada. Government activities remained extensive and in some areas, such as environmental regulation, they increased somewhat. Latin America did not return to the weak government structures that had predated the 1930s.

Partly because of more vigorous governmental efforts, leading Latin American nations also managed to win increasing independence from outside influence during the 20th century. The Mexican revolution, though it by no means eliminated foreign economic activity, unquestionably reduced U.S. ability to determine key political or diplomatic policies. Nationalization of some crucial foreign enterprises, inaugurated by the Mexican oil operation, was taken up by diverse governments in several Latin American countries. In the Caribbean islands many former colonies gained political freedom after the 1950s, leading to a number of new island nations formed from previously British and some Dutch holdings. In the late 1970s the United States arranged for the eventual transfer of control of the Panama Canal to the nation of Panama—another sign of the waning of the imperialism that had surged around 1900.

At the same time, Latin American independence was far from complete—again a sign of continuity amid change. Cuba exchanged U.S. influence for Soviet in its economy and diplomacy. France, the Netherlands, and the United States maintained some outright colonies still, though they upgraded their status, as in the case of the Commonwealth of Puerto Rico. Britain kept control of an island group claimed by Argentina and rather easily beat back a military attack there in 1982. The ability of the United States to intervene in Central America, reasserted in the 1980s, remained an important factor, though it was not clear that the intervention could be as straightforward, or as successful, as in the past. Most important, the continued economic power of the United States and Western Europe, in the still-dependent economies of Latin America, seriously qualified the general tendency toward greater national freedom and self-assertion.

LATIN AMERICAN CULTURE

In culture, even more clearly than in politics, the close interaction with Western values left a definite mark, as Latin Americans participated vigorously in Western-initiated artistic developments of the 20th century. Yet this was no simple extension of Western culture either, for a new artistic and literary vigor brought growing emphasis on distinctive styles and themes.

Most wealthy Latin Americans shared Western tastes in fashion, furnishings, and art. Throughout the 20th century a considerable market existed for Western imports of this sort, and some Latin American artists produced for this market as well. A number of Latin American composers made a mark in symphonic music after 1920, and major cities boasted orchestras performing a wide repertoire of Western-style music. Still more impressive was the region's contribution to modern architecture. Economic and political development encouraged new building in most Latin American cities, as hotels and office complexes sprang up in the sleek styles familiar in the West. Particularly breathtaking was the erection of an entire city, Brasília, constructed in the 1960s as Brazil's new capital; although criticized for its costliness, Brasília became a powerful symbol of modern architectural and urban-planning concepts.

Latin American initiatives in science lagged somewhat, as in the past. Major universities trained their students in science and technology, but the expense of research at the forefront, and traditions in a civilization that still placed greater emphasis on the artistic and spiritual aspects of culture, limited the importance of science in overall intellectual life, compared to several other contemporary civilizations.

In art and literature, Latin America contributed vigorous 20th-century styles, though with an ongoing link to Western patterns. The Mexican revolution spurred innovative developments in painting. Two great muralists, Clemente Orozco and Diego Rivera, created numerous and powerful epics of the struggle of the Mexican lower classes from colonial days to the 20th century. Their forceful human figures and stark colors emphasized the suffering and courage of agricultural and factory workers, women as well as men. Their choice of wall paintings, rather than conventional canvas, was a result of their so-

Diego Rivera mural. The subject is Mexico's Aztec past.

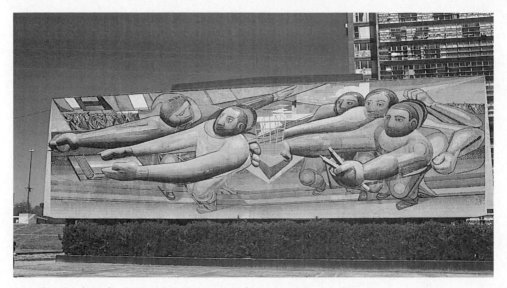

Mural to Students by Sequeiros; University of Mexico, Mexico City.

cial commitment, for their art decorated many public buildings and was not confined to museums or private collections. Both painters achieved international reputations. A number of other artists, from several countries, moved toward less representational styles after World War II, but an interest in forms and coloration derived from Latin America's Indian and black heritage remained.

Contributions to Latin American literature, though at times constrained by political repression, involved both poetry and the novel. Major writers emerged in Chile, Mexico, Brazil, and Argentina. The Mexican revolution spurred realistic novels that dramatized the plight of Indians and other laboring groups. Masterpieces of the Mexican revolutionary period include Mariano Azuela's *Los de agajo* (1916) and Martin Luis Guzmán's *El Aquila y la serpiente* (1928). The rise of Latin American fiction was symbolized by the receipt of three Nobel prizes for literature after World War II. Major writers took up many themes—history and anthropology, foreign domination including United States imperialism, and a strong current of fantasy that built on earlier poetic motifs. Both fantasy and stark realism, sometimes combined in the same novel, were intended to convey the special features of the Latin American experience; they added up to a different balance of subject matter from that characteristic of 20th-century European fiction. In addition to the use of Indian themes and the strong social awareness, Latin American literature often dealt with problems of identity—trying to define what their culture was amid strong European and North American influence. At the same time, Latin American and Western writers worked in similar styles as well as languages, and they shared much reading and criticism.

A final feature of Latin American culture, both formal and popular, was its dynamic Christianity. Though the political power and wealth of the Catholic church declined in some countries, such as Mexico, religion remained a much more pervasive force in Latin America than in Europe and North America. In terms of numbers of believers and pious devotion, Latin America indeed became the most significant Christian civilization by the mid–20th century, with 233 million listed Catholics—not all, to be sure, fervent believers—by 1985. But Latin American Catholicism was not simply a traditional force. From the 1960s onward, a new generation of priests and theologians produced increasing social commentary, urging Catholic involvement in the cause of social and political reform. Some Catholic leaders aided peasant guerrilla movements, while sympathetic bishops pressed governments for improved welfare programs, land reform, and popular political rights. Statements about the church's social responsibility became known as liberation theology. The new currents in Latin American Catholicism brought on clashes with some authoritarian governments and also criticism from the papacy, which by the 1980s was not enthusiastic about political activism. Catholic debate formed another important channel for Latin American culture and additional evidence of a new level of intellectual vigor. Catholicism was itself challenged, however, by popular religions that mixed Christian and African elements—particularly in Brazil—and by a surprising current of conversion to fundamentalist Protestantism, creating a vibrant new religious minority. The advance of Protestantism, particularly among poorer groups seeking cultural outlets, could be truly striking: by the late 1990s, 30 percent of the Guatemalan population was Protestant, and similar changes had occurred in Brazil. These developments complicated the society's cultural map but confirmed the unusual importance of religious expression in 20th-century Latin America.

ECONOMY AND SOCIETY

Latin America experienced rapid social and economic change, particularly after 1950, though important features continued from the past. In many countries the social division between rich and poor remained great; the wealthy minority controlled landed estates in many countries—in some cases 4 percent of the population owned 80 percent of the land—and also operated the leading commercial and manufacturing concerns. Many cities juxtaposed luxurious mansions and life styles with mass squalor. Widespread employment of female domestic servants remained a standard prerogative of upper-class households. Social reform efforts, even in revolutionary Mexico, rarely did more than dent the basic division, though some changes occurred. Regional disparities remained considerable as well. The Andes nations were particularly impoverished. Argentina maintained its position as a significant exporter of grains and meats, but the Argentine economy was often hampered by political problems and a level of government spending that encouraged paralyzing inflation.

Another troubling continuity involved Latin America's inability to free itself from reliance on vulnerable export items. Despite concerted policy attention and some diversification, the civilization continued to depend on imported Western technology, while exports consisted disproportionately of agricultural goods like coffee, sugar, raw materials, and oil, all vulnerable to low and fluctuating prices. Furthermore, most Latin American nations, because of their poor earnings position in the world economy, remained heavily indebted to Western banks. Ambitious development programs often merely increased the debt, which by the 1980s severely burdened both richer and poorer economies within the civilization. Even Cuba, which defied tradition in many ways, proved unable to escape economic dependency, as it relied for its export earnings on sales of sugar to Eastern Europe and million-dollar-a-day Russian aid. The Soviet collapse brought new problems to the island that highlighted the failure to industrialize.

Yet many areas of Latin America gained new economic strength. Agricultural production improved in many countries, as new techniques and seeds, including the innovations of the 1960s, the Green Revolution, were adopted. Tourism expanded, bringing foreign earnings and influences. Chile dramatically expanded its exports in commercial agriculture, gaining growing prosperity by the 1990s. Manufacturing output advanced, too, and the wealthier Latin American nations began to produce most of the industrial goods they required for normal consumption. Textile and metallurgical industries spread widely, and a few countries, headed by Brazil, began to export basic manufactured goods to other parts of the world, including the United States. Brazil also developed the world's fourth largest computer industry, specializing in less sophisticated computers than those from Japan or the United States, but ones that could function reliably in other less-developed nations.

To be sure, advancing mechanization still fell short of a full industrial revolution. It did not bring Latin America to the levels of economic development being achieved in the Pacific Rim. The high birth rate, averaging between 2 and 3 percent annually after World War II, limited gains in the standard of living. Catholic hostility toward birth control measures and the strong traditionalism of many Latin American families contributed to this growth in population, which in many countries literally consumed the gains in food and manufacturing production. One result of population pressure was the extraordinary rate of emigration, both legal and illegal, to the United States. Another result was a low-wage economy that induced many U.S., and some European and Japanese, firms to establish factories in Latin America for inexpensive exports to industrialized areas of the world.

Many Latin American countries, however, did make a turn to greater population control. Mexico, for example, underwent a demographic transition in the 1960s, resulting in markedly smaller families even though population expansion continued on the basis of earlier growth. Furthermore, the manufacturing gains—the evolution toward a more industrial society—brought measurable improvements in living standards for many people. Brazil's economic growth, at 6 percent per year during some decades, increased both the middle class and the urban working class. Many began to participate in new consumerism. By 1990, 22 percent of all Brazilians owned cars, 56 percent had televisions, and 63 percent had refrigerators. These gains, which were echoed in Mexico and elsewhere, surpassed levels in Eastern Europe or the Pacific Rim (apart from Japan). Not yet industrialized, Latin American economies were carving out a distinctive position among the major societies of the world.

Both population pressure and industrial gains furthered the rapid urbanization of Latin America from the 1930s onward. Here too, the society held an unusual place, becoming more urban than most of Asia and Africa though less so than the industrialized societies. City growth was itself distinctive, combining new manufacturing with huge swaths of dire poverty. The rural populations simply could not be accommodated in the countryside, particularly when the land was held in large estates. Cities provided some

Urban slums in Caracas, Venezuela. Migrants to the city stake out their unauthorized living spaces.

factory jobs to a privileged segment of the masses; to even more people they offered some hope of receiving occasional work plus charity or welfare.

In 1925 only 25 percent of Latin America's population was urbanized; by 1975, 60 percent lived in cities—in contrast to a mere 30 percent in China or India. Massive shantytowns arose in Mexico, Brazil, and elsewhere, as a largely unemployed population constructed houses out of cans and boxes. The world's largest city took shape in the Mexican capital, which had 3 million people in 1950 but an overwhelming 9 million by 1970, and 16 million by 1995 with projections of over 20 million by 2000. Excruciating problems of pollution as well as dire poverty followed from this extraordinary urban development.

Population pressure and urban problems inevitably added to earlier social grievances, notably the unequal distribution of land and the gap between rich and poor, to produce recurrent popular protest. Rural rioting occurred in many countries in the 20th century, even aside from the major revolutions. Peasant attacks on landlords paralyzed much of Colombia in 1947. Indian peasants formed guerrilla bands that controlled stretches of Bolivia and Peru in the 1970s and 1980s. A rural rebellion erupted in southern Mexico in 1994. Urban strikes and riots dotted the 20th-century landscape as well. And violence spilled over into other areas. Mass sports events often featured fights between partisan crowds. In countries like Mexico and Venezuela, murder rates were among the highest in the world.

Yet there were strengths in Latin American society as well as fearsome tensions. Family structure remained tight, characteristically under male domination. Popular festivals and religious celebrations featured traditional dances and music and provided joyful release to many groups. The ability of Latin Americans to preserve family institutions and cultural forms in the face of rapid population movement to the cities set some limits to the worst confusions of social transformation, though the same traditionalism enforced limitations on the conditions of women under the sway of *machismo* traditions and strong emphasis on sexuality. Amid problems common to many parts of the world—such as that of underemployment—Latin American popular culture retained some distinctive flavor.

CONCLUSION: TOWARD A GREATER WORLD ROLE?

Latin America has always occupied a somewhat ambiguous place in world history. The civilization first developed as a dependency of the West, a status still not fully shaken off. While Latin Americans participate fully, if not always influentially, in the world economy, they have generated neither dramatic cultural forms nor catastrophic military upheavals of international impact. Nationalism and literary preoccupation with issues of Latin American identity follow from a sense of being ignored or misunderstood in the wider world. The United States, which continues to play a powerful role in Latin American affairs, stands particularly charged with ignorance and neglect.

Yet the trends of Latin American history in the later 20th century argue for an increase in the civilization's visibility. Latin America constitutes a growing share of the world's population. Its economic advance, though often troubled, places it in the middle rank of developing nations. Its importance in world religious life is on the increase. Some observers would add that the civilization's potential for social upheaval remains unusually great, though the 20th-century experience thus far has suggested a balance between unrest and conservative continuities. The directions of Latin America's future are at least as unclear as those of other major civilizations. Brazil and a few other leaders may soon make the turn to a self-sustaining industrialization—but hopes of this sort have been disappointed before in our century. Democracy may solidify, but the civilization's history reminds us that it also may not. But the likelihood of a growing international impact in the future seems high, as the 20th century has brought new self-consciousness and millions of new people to a civilization increasingly proud of its achievement, if still resentful of its economic dependency.

SUGGESTED READINGS

General coverage of 20th-century Latin America is provided by Tulio Halperin-Donghi, *The Aftermath of Revolution in Latin America* (1973), and R. A. Humphreys, *Tradition and Revolt in Latin America* (1969); see also the Skidmore and Smith volume cited in Chapter 22. On economic dependency, see E. Bradford Burns, *Latin America: A Concise Interpretative History,* 4th ed. (1986). On revolution and other developments in Mexico, John M. Hart, *Revolutionary Mexico* (1987); R. D. Anderson, *Outcasts in Their Own Land: Mexican Industrial Workers 1906–1911* (1976); and Jan Bozant, *A Concise History of Mexico from Hidalgo to Cardenas, 1805–1940* (1975), are helpful. Other key countries are covered in:

H. S. Ferns, *Argentina* (1969); Robert Potash, *The Army and Politics in Argentina 1945–1962* (1980); and E. B. Burns, *A History of Brazil* (1970). On the Cuban revolution, consult Hugh Thomas, *Cuba: The Pursuit of Freedom* (1971), and Carmelo Mesa Lago, *Revolutionary Change in Cuba* (1971). For economic patterns, important works include Celso Furtado, *The Economic Development of Latin America* (1970), and N. Sanchez-Albornoz, *The Population of Latin America* (1974); on women, see June Hahner, *Women in Latin American History* (1976). On labor, see Charles Berquist, *Labor in Latin America* (1986).

Sub-Saharan Africa: From Colonies to New Nations

Focal Points

African history in the 20th century divides fairly neatly into three stages: the rise of nationalism amid ongoing European domination; the struggle for independence; and the particularly demanding issues of new nationhood during the past few decades. It is vitally important to understand the growing economic and cultural hold of colonialism during the first half of the century: How did the living patterns and beliefs of ordinary Africans change? What new problems did independence bring? What political forms were used to deal with these problems? Why did Africa's economic position in the world lag behind its political and cultural innovations? Africa was also the scene of cultural changes more diverse and complex than those of any other civilization in the century.

PATTERNS OF AFRICAN HISTORY IN THE 20TH CENTURY

Africa south of the Sahara had been fully swallowed by European imperialism only 20 years before the 20th century began. For several decades after 1900, when other areas of the world were rousing to new nationalisms, African history continued to be characterized by the operations of the colonial governments and Western Europe's increasing economic impact. But nationalism took root here as well, and after World War II it gained momentum. The result, occurring only slightly later than in most of Asia, was the independence of a number of new nations. From the 1960s onward, their efforts to establish the institutions and loyalties of nationhood represented the primary focus in the region. Problems of economic development, and in some areas recurrent famines and disease, complicated national politics. And the continued existence of a powerful, white-dominated South African nation long cast its shadow over the continent.

Even before independence was achieved, and certainly after its first results were digested, issues of cultural identity and social and economic transformation played a vital role in the patterns of Africa. Imperialist policies brought fuller contact with the world economy and encouraged some internal economic development along with great dislocation. One result was a marked resemblance to earlier characteristics of Latin America, the other society most fully touched by Western economic dominance and cultural and political influence. African civilization, to be sure, was by no means obliterated to the extent that American Indian cultures had been. But Africa displayed patterns of economic dependency comparable to colonial and 19th-century Latin America, including reliance on vulnerable cash crops and mineral exports; of tensions of new nationhood, including frequent reliance on authoritarian political forms; and even of considerable cultural innovation, the result of both Muslim and Christian missionary efforts that made this civilization, again like Latin America, the scene of high religious fervor and creativity.

Africans, on the other hand, were less closely linked to Western cultural styles than were Latin Americans, and they faced more acute problems of defining their identity amid new or outside influences. And Africa emerged from its brief colonial experience less developed—in terms of city size, literacy levels, amount of manufacturing and commercial agriculture—than any of the other major contemporary civilizations. Generating further change, particularly toward industrialization or a better-rounded economy, and adjusting to 20th-century trends such as population increase and urbanization, have posed acute challenges for contemporary Africans. Efforts to combine cultural and family traditions with modernization reflect a desire to maintain a distinctive African-ness and to cushion the impact of new political and economic styles.

EMERGING NATIONALISM

World War I triggered some new currents in colonial Africa. Scattered fighting took place in the German colonies in the south, which were then taken over by the British, with one possession, South West Africa, or what is now called Namibia, administered as part of South Africa. The French used large numbers of loyal African troops in their European campaigns. Discussion of national rights after World War I encouraged a rethinking of the future of the African colonies. European diplomats spoke of their holdings as "a sacred trust of civilization" to help educate peoples "not yet able to stand by themselves under the strenuous conditions of the modern world." This outlook produced new efforts to better the standard of living of the colonial peoples by building local schools, hospitals, libraries, and so on. Belgium, known for its harsh exploitation in the Congo, shifted its policies significantly. Colonial-run police forces tried to prevent tribal warfare, and attention was paid to improving agricultural techniques.

Western imperialism did not change its stripes entirely, however. Assumptions of African inferiority continued. Schools reached only a minority of Africans, and they often taught details of European history and culture that made little sense in the African context. Belgian officials in the Congo, for example, insisted that educated Africans learn Flemish as well as French, though the language had little wider utility, simply because this was the expectation back home and home was a pinnacle of civilization. Many schools were run by missionaries, including large numbers from the United States, who undertook an attack on religious traditions in the name of Christianity; and a Christian minority, both Catholic and Protestant, did develop in most colonies. Most colonial governments allowed Africans to enter only the lower levels of the bureaucracy and military. French policy encouraged an African elite to enroll in schools in France and to assimilate to

French culture, but there was little concern for the masses of Africans. Britain paid attention to a larger number, but reserved the upper ranks of administration for British officials. Few African soldiers could rise above the rank of sergeant. Thus 20th-century imperialism, though it involved new outlays for the colonies—Britain may have spent more in Africa during the 1920s and 1930s than it earned there—remained very much an imposition from the outside.

Imperialism also brought continued pressure for economic change. In largely British-ruled eastern Africa, where population levels were low and prior political forms relatively loose, a wealthy minority of white colonists set up estates on the rich agricultural lands of the plateaus, using African labor; other Africans preserved a hunting-and-gathering existence or worked as farmers on the less fertile lands. In western Africa, with more of its own commercial experience, African business entrepreneurs along with Europeans introduced cash crops, like peanuts and cocoa, for sale on the world market. Railroads and shipping lines also opened further access to raw materials. Belgium drew rubber, copper, and vital minerals from the Congo; British Rhodesia exported copper; South Africa mined gold and diamonds. Mining operations were owned and operated by Europeans, or by white South Africans, using poorly paid gangs of African labor. Thus the ties of Africa to the world economy became more extensive, but largely on terms that brought profits to the Europeans.

The impact of this burgeoning economic activity on Africans was mixed. Some businessmen drew substantial profits while becoming accustomed to the ways of international commerce. In the boom years of the 1920s, rich business leaders in British West Africa gained a heady life style: "Motor cars were purchased right and left, champagne flowed freely, and expensive cigars scented the air." This elite also participated in local elections,

African mission school run by Europeans. Probably from the Belgian Congo, 1920s.

for governing bodies that had limited voice over such issues as roads and public health. A far larger group of Africans were drawn into the emerging cities and the mining centers as laborers. Many traditions and family ties were disrupted by the move to the cities, particularly because women were often left behind. A tension began to develop, between older customs and the attractions of a partially Westernized urban life that would influence African culture from this point onward. Finally, large numbers of Africans remained generally isolated from the economic transformation, in scattered agricultural or hunting settlements rarely reached by Europeans.

In South Africa, a special pattern of European–African relations continued to develop. Here, white settlers, some of English origin but primarily Afrikaners of Dutch extraction, were more numerous than in any other African region. Clashes between the English and the patriotic Boers, the name given to the Dutch settlers, intensified the friction. The Afrikaners increasingly supported the Nationalist political party, which talked of leaving the British Empire and vowed to keep black Africans, the majority, in a subordinate place. The party slogan was "South Africa: A White Man's Land." During the 1920s the Nationalists sponsored the Color Bar bill to prevent blacks from holding skilled jobs. In 1936, blacks were excluded from voting in elections. White South Africans were gradually creating two separate societies, preventing any contact between whites and blacks save that between employer and unskilled laborer.

Nowhere, of course, did Africans have extensive political rights. What was unusual in South Africa is that representative institutions did exist but were reserved mainly for whites. In other colonies, voting rights, if any, were limited to an urban minority of Africans, and the bodies they elected had few powers and were dominated by whites.

African bitterness toward white rule broke out periodically. To promote black rights, a group ultimately named the African National Congress formed in South Africa as early as 1912. In 1921 in the Congo, a carpenter named Simon Kimbangu formed a religious movement with emotional rituals and revolutionary political doctrines, drawn in part from the Bible. His movement roused considerable mass support until Kimbangu was arrested and executed. In Kenya a government clerk, Harry Thuku, organized the East Africa Native Association to protest reduction in wages; his arrest, in 1922, on charges of sedition, led to a wave of riots.

Outright African nationalism developed only gradually. The experiences of the African elite, some trained at European universities, brought growing awareness of nationalist ideas. The Pan-African Congress met in Paris in 1919 to press for national independence, and similar meetings occurred periodically through 1945. Pan-African nationalism, bent not only on freedom from European control but on a glorification of the strengths and traditions of Africa and a hope for some new, unprecedented African unity, received powerful stimulus from the writings and political leadership of U.S. and West Indian black leaders in the 1920s and 1930s. Figures like the American Marcus Garvey, who sought new links with Africa as part of the freedom struggle of blacks in the United States, helped African nationalists, particularly in the British colonies, articulate their own strivings. But the limits to Western-style education in Africa meant that nationalist ideas spread slowly. To many Africans, the concept of nationhood was an abstraction, compared to the known loyalties of tribe and extended family. Even more than in the Middle East after 1918, most African colonies were arbitrary units, embracing many tribes and language groups with no precedent in Africa's earlier political history. Loyalty to these nations thus came hard. Nationalist leaders themselves debated inconclusively about whether they wanted a large African unity, tribal units, or nation-states based essentially on colonial boundaries. This was a seedtime for African nationalism, not, before 1945, a full flowering. Many individual leaders who would emerge after World War II gained their nationalist convictions during this period, however. For example, Jomo Kenyatta, educated at the London School of Economics and later in Moscow, began to write of the strengths of African traditions as against Western materialism and corruption. Kenyatta would later lead the nationalist movement in Kenya and become its first president. Leopold Senghor, a Catholic native of Senegal who lived in Paris, learned of the cultural traditions of Africa and also admired the achievements of blacks from the United States and the West Indies. He began to write of the beauties of *négritude,* or blackness, seen as a source of racial pride and confidence in black creativity, particularly in the arts.

The depression hit Africa hard. The region's growing dependence on sales to the West of low-price items like cocoa beans, and on Western companies that directly organized raw-materials production, was brought home vividly. Loss of jobs and wages increased unrest and spurred the nationalist movement as strikes and riots attacked the power and greed of European and U.S. companies.

World War II heightened nationalism still further. A number of black leaders in French colonies had supported the resistance movement against Nazi control of France. They felt real loyalty to France, but expected growing political rights in return. The rise of anticolonial movements in other parts of the world and the retreat of once-proud empires in Asia served as obvious inspiration in Africa. For their part, European administrations recognized the need to work harder for social and economic improvements in Africa. France thus poured more money into its African colonies between 1947 and 1957 than it had done in the whole previous half-century. British leaders began to talk of ultimate self-government, suggesting that the role of the colonies was now to train in nationhood. But the Europeans seemed to be in no hurry to admit that Africans were ready to take over. Their belief in African inferiority and their desire to hold onto this one vestige of imperialism, while the rest of the empire was crumbling, posed obvious barriers. In many colonies, particularly in British East Africa, the demands of the influential white-settler minority also retarded change: how could this group be protected if colonialism came to an end?

European hesitation was met by a new generation of nationalist leaders, most of them trained in European or North American universities; many had experience in trade unions or local governments. They thought in terms of independent nations built on the basis of existing colonies: ideas of African unity or a return to tribal organization now faded. The new leaders mounted mass rallies of urban Africans. Often arrested, they used their imprisonment to dramatize their cause. Many also battled traditional African leaders, including the tribal chiefs, to whom the nationalist idea remained foreign. Direct raids on European settlers, as in Kenya, added to the pressure from yet another source, as villagers and hunters protested the hold of whites on the best lands.

THE TRANSFORMATION TO INDEPENDENCE

Between 1957 and the mid–1970s, the colonial era drew to a close. The country named Ghana arose first, based on Britain's western Gold Coast colony; Kwame Nkrumah was its nationalist leader. A schoolteacher, he had studied for a decade in the United States, where he was deeply influenced both by European socialism and by American black nationalists who called for a rebellion against white domination. Returning to the Gold Coast in 1945, Nkrumah built a mass political movement among urban elements and commercial cocoa farmers with the slogan "Self-Government Now." Many of his followers saw independence as a key to a brighter future across the board, in which economic as well as political problems would be swept away by the searchlight of freedom. Nkrumah organized a series of riots and strikes, which brought him a jail sentence; he dominated local elections from 1951 onward. Britain conceded the inevitable, and Ghana, drawing its name though not its boundaries from the historic kingdom, won its freedom in 1957.

Other British colonies in West Africa gained independence soon after. France sought to prevent a complete rift with its colonies, after its bitter experiences in Indochina and then Algeria, by granting commonwealth status to its 13 sub-Saharan holdings in 1958. African leaders deeply attached to France supported this move, though Sékou Touré, a radical leader in the colony of Guinea, insisted on full independence immediately. The other nations gained national status in the early 1960s, though most of them retained close ties to France. Belgium lost the Congo to a series of riots in 1959—one of the only cases outside southern Africa where the granting of independence did not come peacefully. Britain's East African colonies also gained national freedom, despite the agitation of white settlers. Only in Southern Rhodesia did major delays arise, as the white minority broke away from Britain in 1965 and held out for over a decade against a guerrilla war

Native Nigerians rehearse a traditional dance to prepare for independence celebrations, 1960.

conducted by black nationalists, and against substantial diplomatic pressure from Britain and the United States. Here too independence won out, through the creation of a black-run government with assurances of white minority representation; in 1980 the new nation shook off its colonial name and took on another historic title—Zimbabwe. Finally, also in the 1970s, a change in political regime in Portugal, along with substantial guerrilla warfare and some backing from the Soviet Union and Cuba, led to independence for Angola and Mozambique. In the space of two decades, approximately 40 new nations had been born in sub-Saharan Africa.

THE CHALLENGES OF NEW NATIONHOOD

The ease with which most—though not all—former colonies had achieved their freedom was somewhat deceptive. Many Africans and Westerners alike expected great gains once the distraction of imperialism had ended. In fact, most African states found independence a greater challenge than the battle against European control had been. Though conditions varied widely in a civilization still quite diverse, most of the new nations were poor. Independence did not transform the economy or promote new power on the world market. In a few cases, as in the former Belgian Congo (renamed "Zaïre"), initial disorder disrupted trade patterns and caused a flight of Western managers and technicians that was only later repaired. Many new nations, like Nigeria, adopted policies of what they called "indigenization," or partial nationalization, which required that business and landed estates pass from European hands to majority African control within a decade or so. This approach, in seeking fuller national command over the economy, was understandable; indeed, it resembled the economic nationalist policies of Latin American countries in the earlier decades of the 20th century. But indigenization efforts had to be balanced against continued needs for Western technologies and capital. Nor could indigenization free most economies from the previous status of dependency. For many African workers, indigenization merely substituted African for European capitalists in a cash-crop or mining operation, as land was not widely redistributed and reliance on poorly paid labor remained extensive.

Leadership was also a problem in the new nations, along with agonizing economic issues. Some stirring nationalists proved inept or corrupt once in power—Ghana's Nkrumah was a case in point. Filling bureaucracies with competent staff was not easy when so few Africans had prior political experience. Here was one reason for frequent reliance on authoritarian rule, after brief attempts at parliamentary systems, as firm lines of control might compensate for political inexperience. The fact that army leaders had more organizational training—of the modern, bureaucratic type as opposed to the personalized, tribal sort—than most, and had national rather than local loyalties helps account for frequent periods of military control. But reliance on armies was no panacea. Many armies were run by generals who the year before had been sergeants; and while some quickly learned the lessons of complex management, others were inefficient.

Many of the new nations faced periods of civil war soon after independence. In this their experience resembled that of Latin America and the United States in the 19th century—but precedent was cold comfort. Divisions by tribe and language group made central administration difficult, in some ways more difficult than when the Europeans had

The New Africa

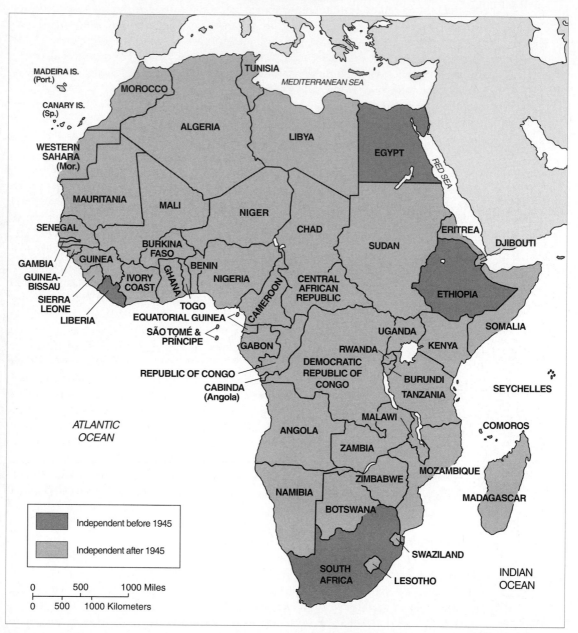

Independent before 1945

Independent after 1945

| 0 | 500 | 1000 Miles |
| 0 | 500 | 1000 Kilometers |

been in charge. Leadership could now be identified as belonging to one group, which tended to antagonize the others. The former British colony of Nigeria, in West Africa, dramatically illustrated a common problem. A large, populous nation, potentially one of Africa's wealthiest because of rich oil holdings as well as commercial farms, Nigeria was divided among three major language groupings. Each group had distinctive political and cultural traditions—some emphasized military values, others business success. Nigerians in the north were Muslim; southerners were Christian or polytheist. Independent Nigeria was thus initially organized as a federation of three regional governments, but internal warfare resulted nevertheless. A group of army officers, devoted to national unity, took control in 1965 and abolished the regions; but because most of the new leaders were from a single tribe, the Ibos, the result was a fierce attack from the Muslim north. The attempt by the Ibo region to form an independent state in 1967 led to three years of bloody warfare in which hundreds of thousands died of starvation. But national unity survived, as the central military leadership held on and then conciliated the defeated Ibos through economic aid and local autonomy.

Internal warfare also surfaced in Zaïre, though in this case regional conflicts were heightened by Western and Soviet interference. With backing from European business leaders and military forces, a pro-Western unity government was ultimately established. Warfare between majority and minority tribal groupings also plagued Zimbabwe after independence, though outright civil war was avoided. Another bloody clash between two tribes broke out in Rwanda in 1994. Tribal conflict and also hopes for political and economic reform were involved in an insurgent military movement in Zaïre in 1997, that displaced the aging dictator and restored the name Congo. In general, the problems of holding together nations that had no real tradition, that embodied a host of diverse, often antagonistic groupings, dominated African history after independence.

And there were other complications. Boundary disputes led to regional warfare in a few instances. Ethiopia and Somalia conducted a bitter territorial quarrel in the late 1970s. The Pan-African Congress met periodically to resolve disputes, often with considerable success, and the civilization was far freer from warfare than the neighboring Middle East. Cold war tensions also affected the new nations. Soviet backing for Angolan independence included the provision of Cuban troops. The Ethiopian-Somali dispute was envenomed by aid from both the Soviet Union and the United States, as first Somalia and then Ethiopia became Soviet allies. Most African nations tried with some success to stay clear of firm alignment to either cold war side, but great-power rivalries could be an undeniable distraction.

The issue of South Africa proved to be one of the most intractable problems of the late 20th century. White minority rule continued in this powerful country, long defying the movement toward black independence. South Africa boasted the only industrialized economy on the continent, built on unusual mineral wealth and rich agriculture; it also maintained the continent's strongest military force. Afrikaner power in South Africa, which had increased gradually during the first half of the 20th century after the Boer War, burst forth in outright victory in elections held in 1948. The National party ruled the country until 1994, separating itself from the British Commonwealth in 1961. The Afrikaners progressively fashioned a system called "apartheid," or separation, to keep the black majority in economic and political subjection. In most public places, blacks were not permitted to use white facilities; intermarriage was forbidden; blacks, even when working for white-owned firms, were required to live in segregated urban compounds; and many rural blacks were forced onto artificially created homelands, usually on the worst lands, where superficial self-government barely masked white control. Protests from a liberal white minority were silenced by police action and censorship, though moderate opposition activity was allowed to continue. Agitation from black groups, and also from

Protesting apartheid: demonstration at the funeral of a riot victim shot by South African police, 1985.

Indian and mixed-race minorities, surfaced periodically, only to be crushed amid widespread brutality.

Yet pressures from blacks for political rights and against an economic discrimination that confined them to unskilled, low-paying, and often dangerous jobs could not be prevented. Unrest developed particularly among black workers in the urban compounds; it was supported by sympathy from many parts of the world, which also prompted some superficial concessions in apartheid policy during the 1970s, though in 1984–1986 a new series of bloody riots led to the reimposition of martial law. Only at the end of the 1980s did a breakthrough begin, as a new white leader, de Klerck, negotiated with Nelson Mandela (see p. 642) of the African National Congress. Apartheid was legally dismantled and negotiations continued toward election-based universal suffrage with some protections for the white minority. Conditions remained uncertain, and violence between whites and blacks and among black groups continued high, but the long era of white domination ended. Mandela was elected president in the first elections based on universal suffrage, in 1994.

For most of sub-Saharan Africa, which kept rather separate from South Africa while denouncing apartheid, three themes dominated the decades after independence. First, national unity was successfully maintained. Administrations were extended over the new nations, school systems expanded, national loyalty preached through government-dominated organs of press and the ubiquitous transistor radio. In key cases, as we have seen, secessionist movements were defeated, and with a few exceptions pressure for full commitment to either side in the cold war was avoided.

Second, initial attempts to maintain democratic political structures were quickly abandoned. Despite Western expectations, though in part because of the limited political experience that had been possible during the colonial period, virtually all of the new nations dismantled parliamentary institutions, multiparty political systems, and guarantees of political freedom. In Ghana, Kwame Nkrumah soon jailed his political opponents and outlawed all parties save his own. His goal was a one-party state, capable of rousing the kind of loyalty that would hold the nation together and maintain his personal power. Nkrumah finally failed, victim in part of poor economic management that bankrupted the new nation, but he was replaced by military leadership. Most other African countries converted either to military rule or to one-party systems that brooked no legal opposition. One-party governments arose in Kenya and Tanzania and in most of the former French colonies. Military rule predominated in Zaïre, Ethiopia, Liberia, and elsewhere. During the 1950s and 1960s, Africa experienced at least 70 attempted military takeovers (20 of which succeeded), and the pattern continued in later decades. Nigeria's military government turned power over to an elected civilian government in 1979, but another military coup soon followed.

The third theme of postindependence African history involved determined efforts in many nations to promote economic change. Most of the new African leaders saw economic development as a vital expression of independence, an essential accompaniment to the national unity they worked hard and successfully to preserve. Such a goal proved far more compelling than Western-style liberalism, though its achievement remained elusive amid a particularly daunting set of economic and demographic barriers.

Early in the 1990s a resurgence of democracy began to emerge. While stable political regimes collapsed in some nations, like Somalia, Africa (including the now-democratic regime in South Africa) was influenced by international trends and pressures toward more open political regimes. By 1997 seventeen countries had installed freer elections with multiparty competition. The trend was still halting, but it suggested some interesting political potential for the future and the closeness of African ties with influences in the wider world. Tensions with the military persisted, however, partly because the end of the Cold War reduced foreign aid and the weapons supply that had been used to placate the armed forces. Military coups continued. Two major states, Nigeria and Kenya, saw democratic elections set aside by authoritarian leaders, while the successful military movement in the renamed Congo brought a leader whose promises of future elections were somewhat tentative. African definition of a stable political order that was not simply authoritarian, proved to be no easy task.

AFRICAN POLITICAL CULTURE

The almost uniform conversion of independent African states to authoritarian political structures in the later 20th century is not surprising. Latin America and many Asian nations have shown a similar pattern in response to new nationhood. African political traditions, which so often emphasized the divine power of kings and which more recently had been shaped by colonial administrations imposed from without and defended by police attacks on opposition, offered scant base for a more liberal political approach in the Western or Indian sense.

Nelson Mandela (b. 1918) became the major nationalist leader in South Africa during the 1960s and 1970s. Despite the unusual features of the South African racial situation, Mandela's career in many ways resembled that of other early African nationalist leaders. Mandela was the oldest son of a chief in a Bantu tribe (the Tembu) and was raised as a nationalist. Active earlier in the African National Congress youth league (the ANC, founded in 1912), he quickly became one of its most articulate spokespersons. Like nationalists before him he studied law, hoping to work toward elimination of apartheid discrimination. With other leaders he became more radical, supporting some terrorist activities in the early 1960s. This in turn brought repression; Mandela was arrested in 1962 (the picture above dates from shortly after his arrest) and found guilty of treason in a major trial in 1964. He stayed a prisoner until his release in 1990, despite increasing health problems. His dignity and statesmanlike interviews during the long imprisonment brought worldwide attention and support. Upon his release, he worked to forge unity among the native African population while pressing for political democracy and offering some pragmatic concessions to the white governing elite—a difficult combination, which Mandela worked hard to pull off. Nelson Mandela's extraordinary personal and symbolic qualities are clear, but his full place in history awaits the further unfolding of the South African drama. In 1993 Mandela led negotiations for the first democratic elections in South Africa's history, and shared in the Nobel Peace Prize. He became president as a result of the elections, in 1994, and moved vigorously for national reconciliation. South African politics remained amazingly stable under his leadership.

African leaders, many personally ambitious and almost all eager to defend the unity of their new countries as the top political priority, found it hard to countenance opposition that seemed a personal affront and often expressed regional or tribal loyalties that threatened the nation. Success in maintaining unity—and the new African nations fared better in this regard than the initial Latin American nations had done in the first half of the 19th century—seemed to require strong police effort. Authoritarian rule also came naturally to many military leaders, who represented one of the most solid national institutions in most new nations. Many ordinary Africans, particularly in the fast-growing cities, placed great faith in the more charismatic leaders. Rural Africans might be less involved, but their loyalties, more traditional, went to smaller units such as family, village, and tribe, not to a national opposition force. While a number of Africans defended liberal values, the extent of support for parliamentary politics that helped forge an oscillation between liberal and authoritarian forms in the Latin American tradition did not surface, at least in the first decades of independence. And so the authoritarian style went largely unchallenged until the 1990s, save for attacks by rival aspirants to authoritarian power.

But while authoritarian government in Africa meant characteristic attacks on opposition leaders, monopoly of the press and radio, and an emphasis on an internally strong army, other policies of authoritarian leaders varied widely. At one extreme was the brutal corruption of a number of leaders in Uganda, where at least two dictators used their armies to attack rival tribes and kill hundreds of thousands of civilians. This kind of brutality brought no stability, as rival claimants to power chased each other out of office with some frequency. Another authoritarian style involved emulation of the Soviet Russian example. Ethiopian Marxists, who took power after revolt toppled the nation's ancient monarchy, talked in terms of a totalitarian state that would represent workers and peasants. But the Soviet model was unusual in Africa. Few Africans found that doctrinaire Marxism described their political or economic conditions. Even in Ethiopia the active power of the government, in an impoverished agricultural economy and amid great regional strife, hardly permitted the political controls of the Soviet state. A few kingdoms bordering South Africa, in yet another pattern, maintained some of the trappings of divine kingship, with rulers enjoying lavish ceremonies. Though not officially a king, the ruler of the giant state of Zaïre took on divine kingship features, stressing ritual demonstrations of power and receipt of tribute, along with a strong army, but the actual administration was very loose.

A number of nations with one-party systems won impressive political stability. Kenya faced tensions between two main tribal groups, but the ruling party created considerable unity and produced able leaders who transferred power without creating strife. Kenya's capital city of Nairobi gained stature as the headquarters for several United Nations agencies and a meeting place for African organizations.

Several African nations pursued non-Marxist socialist policies, hoping to combine economic advance with social reform. In Tanzania, Julius Nyerere tried to build on African community traditions to create a distinctive form of rural socialism. The government supported village cooperation. Nyerere argued that "socialist societies in different parts of the world will differ in many respects . . . reflecting both the manner of their development, and their historical traditions." An African definition of socialism appealed to nationalist sentiment and reflected an unquestionable distaste, on the part of many

Africans, for the greed and competitiveness of Western capitalism. Nyerere's practical policies in Tanzania, however, were hampered by poor economic management, and the country did not develop rapidly. Zimbabwe, though late in winning independence, offered a more hopeful example. Robert Mugabe, the prime minister, though a Marxist in theory, devoted himself to a program of practical reforms, which would redistribute some land and offer some protection to manufacturing workers but which would not antagonize the white minority or repel foreign investors.

Several West African governments made scant reference to socialist ideas. Leaders in Nigeria supported private enterprise while also using government funds and planning to encourage further economic development. Great hope existed in the 1970s that government oil revenues could be channeled into industrial investment, though the decline of oil prices in the early 1980s threatened economic advance and brought widespread unemployment.

The strength of authoritarian rule in postindependence Africa raised questions about the solidity of the democratic trend that emerged in the 1990s. African states, despite economic planning and expansion of educational systems, had not uniformly cut into more localized politics, including tribal loyalties. This might lead to fragmentation, amid democracy, that established authorities like the army could not accept. In 1993, for example, the army deliberately set aside the results of elections in Nigeria, Africa's most populous country, dimming prospects for democracy of any sort. Yet democratic leadership gained new vigor, backed by the successful transitions, including South Africa.

AFRICAN CULTURE

Men and women who, as artists or writers, attempted to articulate African culture in the 20th century faced a vital contradiction. On the one hand, a widespread and fruitful awareness existed of traditions that should be maintained, as bridges between the civilization's past and its future and as alternatives to Western (or Marxist) styles. In this sense contemporary African culture served many of the same purposes as cultural traditions in the Middle East or in India. On the other hand, defense of African culture has often involved use of alien languages and forms of expression. For example, the novel, as a work of literature, did not grow out of the African heritage. Moreover, except for those who wrote in Arabic or Swahili, most novelists turned to Western languages—English, French, or Portuguese. They thus evinced some separation from the masses of Africans, many of whom remained illiterate, even as they tried to express and guide the values of the populace. Here was a source of friction inherent to some extent in any formal intellectual life, in a culture that had long been largely oral. Yet in Africa the newness of many cultural outlets, particularly the educational system and written literature, posed a vivid challenge to the preservation of vital traditions.

Indeed, one sign of the tension of intellectual life showed in characteristic education of the small minority that passed beyond the primary level. African secondary schools preached nationalism and taught African history; to this extent they departed from the habits of the older colonial schools. But the schools taught in Western languages, of necessity. They maintained a strong interest in European history and social science, as well as some Western science. Large numbers of British, American, and French schoolteachers

HISTORY DEBATE

Perspectives on Contemporary Africa

After the heady days of African independence, news from the continent often seemed dire. The 1990s brought some outstanding political breakthroughs, but also massive tribal violence in Rwanda and repression of democracy in other key states.

Not surprisingly, many observers tried to explain the subcontinent's problems through comparison. Some urged the parallels between Africa today and Europe before the 17th century: in both cases, solid political units were hard to form and internal divisions led to bitter wars. Was this a useful analogy? Did it do justice to specifically modern factors, like the more complex world economy, or indeed to Africa's own rich past? What trends would it suggest for the future? Other observers compared Africa's recurrent political turmoil to Latin America a century and a half ago, because in both cases colonial status yielded fairly suddenly to new nationhood. What conclusions would this comparison bring about prospects for the next century? Is it a better guide than the European comparison? Is new nationhood more complex in the late 20th century than it was in the early 19th, or essentially the same? Or should Africa simply be understood as a case in itself, where some political systems seemed capable of continued adjustment as the 20th century closed?

served the system, which was still linked to examination procedures in European countries. Zambia's standardized secondary tests, for instance, were prepared and graded in England. Despite the drawbacks, genuine progress resulted as the educated African leadership expanded; but the challenge to older cultural habits was far greater than in any other 20th-century civilization.

An important group of African writers emerged after 1920. Creating essays and poetry, but particularly the novel, these writers came to grips with a number of contemporary African issues. White South African writers, many critical of the policy of apartheid but deeply attached to their homeland, wrote of the tensions and forebodings of their society. Black writers typically stressed the virtues of African traditions, pointing out that their people had a rich heritage before the Europeans came. The Senegalese poet and political leader Leopold Senghor thus criticized Western scientific traditions that separate humankind from nature; he advocated, instead, an African tradition of intuition about nature through experience in it. The Angolan Agustinho Neto praised the power of African culture, again attacking many Western standards and describing a unique black personality. Jomo Kenyatta, glorifying tribal culture in Kenya, vaunted the position of women in African society over the discontentment of their Western counterparts. A

Modern African art showing traditional themes: Cameroon brass sculptures of two "juju men" wearing the costumes used at religious ceremonies. (The Granger Collection)

West Indian poet, popular in Africa, praised the new black consciousness of superiority over Western values:

> Hurrah for those who never invented anything hurrah for those who never explored anything hurrah for those who never conquered anything hurrah for joy hurrah for love hurrah for the pain of incarnate tears.

More soberly, Nigeria's leading novelist, Chinua Achebe, stated "the fundamental theme" of the rising group of African writers:

. . .the African people did not hear of culture for the first time from Europeans; . . . their societies were not mindless but frequently had a philosophy of great depth and volume and beauty, . . . they had poetry and above all, they had dignity. It is this dignity that many African peoples all but lost in the colonial period, and it is this that they must now regain. The worst thing that can happen to any people is the loss of their dignity and self-respect. The writer's duty is to help them regain it by showing what happened to them, what they lost.

But the new African novelists were not simply apostles of tradition and black pride. They also wrote of the anxieties that accompany modernization. Achebe's brilliant novels dealt with the corrosive effect of Western ideas, including Christianity, on powerful village characters. In his works he examined the stress of city life on popular traditions and expressed the disillusionment of many African intellectuals with corrupt and power-hungry rulers, worrying that the masses "had become even more cynical than their leaders and were apathetic into the bargain." African culture, with writers like Achebe, combined traditional values with new forms of expression to present powerful dramas of a changing society.

African artists and craftspeople preserved a thriving legacy, working in older stylistic conventions largely apart from the "modern art" styles of the West, which, ironically, had been partly inspired by African forms. Design and decoration in village houses retained their distinctive quality. Sculptors continued to create powerful figures for both religious and aesthetic purposes. African dance and music remained lively art forms, both at the popular level and in formal troupes sponsored by governments and touring internationally. African culture was not isolated however, and many craftsmen and musicians interacted with other styles. Some crafts, catering to tourism, pandered to Western ideas of what African art should be like.

The interactions that dominated 20th-century African culture showed clearly in the religious area. Africa remained a religious society, though in the cities secular values might compete. Islam, which gained many new converts in the north and center, maintained a trajectory as the most rapidly growing popular religion, winning about 40 percent of all Africans south of the Sahara. Africa's Christian minority, almost as large, grew rapidly as well. Black Protestant leaders played a leading role in moderate resistance to apartheid in South Africa. African Catholicism won a growing role in the Roman church, as the first African cardinal was named and the pope visited the continent for the first time in the 1970s. Catholicism in Africa expanded more rapidly than in any other area, as the number of African Catholics more than doubled from 29 million in 1965 to 66 million in 1985. Christian and Muslim gains meant that Africa experienced the kind of growth of monotheism and new spirituality that civilizations such as Western Europe had passed through after the classical age. The result, as in these earlier cases, was both exciting and unsettling. New converts often retained older beliefs in part, for syncretism was common. African Christianity characteristically combined conventional Christian doctrine with traditional values—including, in some areas, a desire for polygamy and a definite scorn for Catholic valuation of celibacy—and traditional rituals. At the same time, outright polytheistic beliefs retained some vitality, in both city and countryside. Traditional remedies were often used to treat disease, according to the quite logical principles of spirit-caused illness and its cure. Popular religious leaders, some of them women, helped rouse fervor in several regional 20th-century revolts, in which faith in divine guidance combined with this-worldly grievances against colonial rule or economic exploitation. A number of movements, focusing less on protest than on prayer-healing and an expectation of the millennium, blended traditional animist creeds with ideas taken from the Christian Bible. Overall, while religious diversity—and sometimes bitter conflict—continued, a general esteem for the religious orientation to life, society, and nature continued to characterize African culture.

The surge of literary creativity and the complex religious transformations were not the only cultural innovations in 20th-century Africa. Nationalist leaders obviously urged cultural change, away from purely traditional attachments; while attacking imperialism they usually argued for some importations from the West, including new kinds of science and medicine. Yet they also tried to highlight important African qualities, such as community and family solidity. In the cities, other Western cultural influences, including consumerism, constituted yet another force, adding to changes in belief and creating complicated combinations of old and new.

ECONOMY AND SOCIETY

Changes in African culture, and particularly the spread of education and Western-language literature, raised some questions about the relationship between culture and social change. Even as praise for traditional styles and values resounded, there were signs of unusually rapid disruption of many customary social forms. Writers like Achebe wondered whether the breakup of long-held beliefs had not weakened Africans' ability to find an anchor amid so much change. Other intellectuals, however, stressed the continuing validity of basic religious orientations and family attachments, contrasting African strength in this regard with what they saw as a demoralization of Western society.

Most of sub-Saharan Africa did not face, through the 20th century, the kinds of pressures for land redistribution that deeply affected Latin America and parts of Asia. White minorities opened large estates in East and South Africa; many of these were retained, after independence, in white or African hands, though some African governments were able to introduce limited land reform. In more populous West Africa, peasant small-holding remained the norm, except for the cash-crop estates that relied on low-wage labor.

Yet the persistence of village-based agriculture raised issues of its own. During the colonial decades, Western governments pressed African peasants to convert to cash crops like peanuts or cotton. Some farmers made some profits on such crops, but others had to minimize production of basic subsistence foods in favor of meeting commercial quotas. When, in addition, many village men were forced or induced to labor in distant mines, the result could be massive economic and social disruption. Portuguese Mozambique, for example, compelled women farmers to grow cotton on lands ill-suited to the purpose. Food production faltered, leading to malnutrition. And while a few village headmen made money on cotton sales, and bought bigger homes, bicycles, and even art reproductions, the bulk of the population suffered.

Commercial pressures often continued after independence in Africa, though some areas reverted to more localized agriculture. Major gains in agricultural production came slowly, as peasants lacked both capital and education to undertake new methods. Many governments were more concerned with creating public works and factories than with modernizing agriculture. Despite the clearance of new lands for farming, agricultural production lagged in many parts of Africa. Dependence on root crops in the drier lands meant that the gains of the Green Revolution were irrelevant. Agricultural stagnation plus population growth made key regions vulnerable to disasters of climate. In the early 1970s and again in the early 1980s and 1990s, drought conditions on the Sahara's southern rim and down the east coast caused widespread famine. More generally, agricultural lag promoted inadequate nutrition and helped explain widespread poverty, even when severe weather problems did not add to the burdens. Finally, reliance on cash crops like cocoa, cotton, or peanuts for export, while it brought profits to some African landowners and merchants, continued to distract from well-balanced agricultural production, leaving many nations divided between export farmers and a subsistence-minded peasantry wedded to largely traditional methods.

Development of the cash-crop system continued to tie many African countries closely to the Western-dominated world economy. This dependence did not disappear with decolonization. Despite their nationalism, many African countries remained firmly linked to the markets, shipping, and commercial know-how of their erstwhile European rulers. Despite a brief flurry of radical rebellion against Belgian business in Zaïre, for example, Belgian capital and expertise remained fundamental to the nation's economy, as the mineral wealth of the mines continued to be directed toward Western markets almost exclusively. No African country aside from South Africa created a large industrial base of its own. Government encouragement promoted factories for local food processing and clothing and tool production, in countries like Kenya. By the late 1990s, a few countries, including Botswana and Uganda, were reporting rapid manufacturing growth, leading some observers to wonder if Africa might finally begin to participate in the kind of industrial evolution that had taken root in Latin America and parts of the Middle East some decades before. Everywhere, however, reliance on the technologies and manufactured imports of the West remained substantial. Many African nations ran up huge debts because of the gap between export earnings and import needs.

Despite the limits of economic change, a new class of wealthy, urban Africans took shape both under colonialism and with independence. Merchants, the cash-crop landlords, and top government officials stood out from the African mass by their luxurious life style, as Africa joined other agricultural societies in a radical division between the wealthy and the masses. In Swahili-speaking East Africa, common people called the new elite "*wa Benzi*," meaning "those who ride in a Mercedes-Benz." In stark contrast, per capita annual income for the general population often stagnated; in mineral-rich Zaïre, for example, average income stood at $137 in 1976, and at $160 in 1985.

Furthermore, substantial population growth hit sub-Saharan Africa during the 20th century. Medical and public health measures promoted by colonial regimes and extended by independent African governments accounted for some of the gain. So did disruption of village community controls as a result of new market earnings from commercial agriculture or labor in the mines and cities. Population increase occurred despite the absence of a real agricultural revolution and the severe limits of climate and soil fertility in many regions. Indeed, population growth helped worsen agriculture in some cases, as land was overfarmed, its fertility declined—hence recurrent famines in key regions that, ironically, did not halt population growth.

From the 1970s onward the spread of AIDS in East Africa added to economic woes, as many children and young adults were afflicted—over 25 percent in some regions—thus curtailing the available active labor force. Rapid population growth continued, however, as Africa remained one of the regions in which new forms of birth control spread most slowly. This growth, new transportation facilities, and more modern government forms, along with some growth in commerce, spurred the rapid expansion of African cities, particularly after World War II. The entire African continent had only 8 percent of its population in cities in 1925, and only 13 percent in 1950; but by 1973 the percentage had soared to 23, and the trend gained momentum. Most urbanization did not depend on expansion of factories; it was based on trade, on political concentration, and, above all, on the absence of alternatives in the countryside, as population growth and cash-crop estates raised the number of propertyless poor. As in Latin America, urban populations crowded into hastily built slums, hoping for survival by means of occasional unskilled jobs, begging, or prostitution, or peddling in the omnipresent open markets of the African city.

African urbanization, unlike that in Latin America, involved considerable family disruption. Because far more men than women moved to the cities, a significant number of families, particularly in the countryside, were headed by women alone. Indeed, Africa resembled the West, by the 1970s, in the dissociation of a growing minority of men from family and the problems, economic and psychological, that occured when women raised children on their own. African traditions of extended-family aid modified these pressures to some extent, as relatives provided moral support and more tangible assistance to female-headed households. And, while their husbands were absent in urban or mining-village boarding houses, some women found their new independence challenging, as traditions of male domination faded. But issues of family disruption in Africa—a civilization proud of its close and supportive family ties—seemed inescapable as part of social change in the later 20th century. Changes in social structures and in personal values warred with older expectations, in one of the several urgent dramas of 20th-century Africa.

A weekly newspaper in Zambia featured a "Dear Josephine" column that mirrored the process of change, as urban Africans developed new and more individualized patterns in a society long characterized by strong family traditions and tightly knit communities. Africans wrote to ask if they could marry despite the fact that older brothers in their families remained unwed; tradition held that the eldest should marry first, but what should one do when one found the right girl? Or how was a city dweller to pay a bride-price in cattle, which his intended's family, back in the village, insisted on? Or what to do about tribal traditions of mutual support? For example:

> I am well-known, with a big family to feed. My house is by the bus-stop and every day I receive visitors from the home village. It is my duty to give my tribesfolk food and money for their journey needs. But my family suffer from hunger and I go without the decent clothes my position calls for. Though I have a good job I am kept poor by home-people. I do not dislike them, but what can I do to be saved from them?

Women's role also began to shift. The impact of larger changes—social, economic, and political—on African women provoked important debate. On the one hand, women gained new functions as men's ties with families loosened. On the other hand, women typically concentrated in more traditional economic sectors, including agriculture, in order to protect their economic status. As governments became more effective, first under colonial rule and then with independence, informal local power of women often declined. Some observers argued that women were net losers in this process, despite certain new freedoms. In addition in some areas, such as the Muslim northeast, traditional limitations on women persisted, including practices of circumcision that were designed to limit a woman's sexual pleasure and consequently to promote fidelity. Yet new educational opportunities and even some of the disruptions promoted new ideas among some women, including a growing belief that women should stick together; here too, old ideas of family unity could combine with a desire for schooling and birth control to create a novel outlook. Upper-class urban women also managed to put pressure on some governments to improve legal rights for women.

CONCLUSION: DEFINING THE NEW AFRICA

Disruptive transformation was no African monopoly in the 20th century. Most civilizations faced challenges to established institutions and values. And Africans in various ways remained able to rely on traditions; their accustomed life styles were not totally overwhelmed by novelty. Yet the upheaval brought by colonial impositions, population growth, and new urban and commercial institutions was considerable, particularly when it was unrelieved by significant improvements in standard of living. At the same time, change brought new hopes to many Africans. Intellectuals proud of their culture, politicians enthusiastic about national independence, were joined by more humble people, like the young woman in Kenya who noted the opportunities available for the alert. Describing her mother's large family and hard physical labor on a subsistence farm, she discussed how her own views had been shaped by the experience of school:

> My life is very different from my mother's. . . . Women have to get an education. Then if you get a large family and don't know how to feed it, you can find work and get some cash. That's what I will teach my children: "Get an education first."

Africa remained the poorest of the world's civilizations by the late 1980s, as its vulnerability to famine starkly attested. Modernization, including political independence, had not brought all the benefits that many had hoped for, and may have jeopardized some sources of cultural strength. Yet change continued to generate aspirations for the future, in a culture still defining its relationship to the contemporary world.

SUGGESTED READINGS

Various source materials have contributed to research in recent African history. W. E. B. Du Bois, *The World and Africa* (1974), presents an American black nationalist perspective. Work by nationalist leaders include J. Kenyatta, *Facing Mount Kenya* (1953), and, from South Africa, A. Luthuli, *Let My People Go* (1962). F. Fanon, *Wretched of the Earth*

(1965), is a stinging indictment of Western colonialism. Novels by C. Achebe, particularly *Things Fall Apart* (1978), deal with changes in African society and culture. See also B. Fetter, *Colonial Rule in Africa: Readings from Primary Sources* (1979). The colonial period is covered by R. O. Collins, *Problems in the History of Colonial Africa, 1860–1960* (1970). See also Ali Mazrui and Michael Tidy, *Nationalism and New States in Africa* (1984); Martin Meredith, *The First Dance of Freedom: Black Africa in the Post-War Era* (1984); and S. A. Akintoye, *Emergent African States* (1976). On more recent developments, consult: P. C. Lloyd, *Africa and Social Change* (1972); A. Hopkins, *An Economic History of West Africa* (1973); and C. Legum, *Congo Disaster* (1961). Competent works on South Africa include R. W. Johnson, *How Long Will South Africa Survive?* (1977), and Gail Gerhart, *Black Power in South Africa* (1978). On an important social topic, see N. H. Afkin and E. Bay, eds., *Women in Africa* (1977).

Toward the Future:
World History Yet to Come

Focal Points

What are the connections between past, present and future? How does world history help us understand the world we are in and the world that is likely to emerge in the future? This chapter focuses on several different orientations, toward using world history for on-going understanding. Issues of continuity and change provide one orientation. The historical basis for prediction provides another, along with an assessment of leading 20th-century trends. Finally, the implications of the 20th century as a new period, and some specific questions about civilizations and global forces, connect to analytical themes that have long been part of world-historical study.

CHANGE AND CONTINUITY

At any stage in world history, some balance between change and continuity has described the world as a whole and major civilizations within it. This remains true. Recent developments remind us of the importance of substantial continuity. Various Asian leaders urge values of collective loyalty and obedience against what they see as excessive Western individualism, using adaptations of the Confucian heritage. Islam changes, but its ongoing vitality is obvious. In the cultural arena, particularly, legacies from deep in the past often continue or reassert their sway. The collapse of communism in Russia has led to a reassertion of beliefs in Orthodox Christianity and Russian spirituality; decades of repression had not crushed cultural commitments that go back to the postclassical period and that were redefined by conservative nationalsm in the 19th century. A whole set of questions about the present and future involves asking about what will happen to beliefs and institutions that are at least partly traditional, whose force can be understood only through the perspective of a long world-historical span.

But key questions also emerge from change. We know that the 20th century introduced novel technologies, a redefined world economy, and important new cultural values. We know also that developments in the late 20th century, including the spread of democracy and new levels of economic interactions between industrial leaders and societies like Mexico, South Korea, China, or Turkey raise additional issues. Over the past decade, industrial giants like Western Europe, Japan, and the United States have faced new competiton from other areas: how will they adjust? Will powerful multinational companies, developing for at least a hundred years, make nation-states increasingly irrelevant? Have some of the important political responses tossed up earlier in the century, like fascism and communism, run their course, or might they reemerge? Change leaves its mark in two ways: we know what some of the shifts have been and we wonder if they will continue, and if they will further erode some of the persistent earlier legacies; we know that some changes are still open-ended—the world future of democracy, for example—and we wonder when and how they will clarify.

World history does not provide definitive answers, so much as shaping the questions to ask. Yet a historical perspective is inescapable: we can only interrogate the future by juxtaposing it with what we know of the past.

FORECASTS AND PERSPECTIVES

Since the formation of civilizations, the history of the world has involved relatively rapid change—sometimes in directions already set, but sometimes in new trajectories. People in various civilizations have attempted to devise schemes to look beyond the present. From the ancient river valley civilizations to the 20th century, some have used astrology or other divinations to predict the future. More systematically, some scholars have assumed that time moves in cycles, so that one could count on repetition of basic patterns. Others, as in Christian belief or in more secular faiths such as Marxism, have looked toward some great change in the future: the Last Judgment, the classless society, toward which history is steadily working. The idea of some master plan guiding history, so that it moves in some steady direction and toward some purpose, runs deep in the thought of several cultures, including our own. Whatever the approach, the human impulse to know what we cannot definitely know seems inescapable.

Yet all the evidence suggests that our vision of the future remains cloudy at best. It has been calculated that well over 60 percent of all predictions or forecasts offered by serious social scientists in the United States since 1945—called upon to sketch future business cycles, for instance, or family trends, or political currents—have been wrong. How many observers, just 50 years ago, could have predicted such basic recent transformations as the end of the Cold War, the invention of computer and genetic engineering technologies, the industrial breakthroughs of many Pacific coast regions of Asia? How many observers just 25 years ago could have foreseen the Iranian Revolution or the collapse of the Soviet Empire? A few of these events could be discerned in advance, to be sure, but many were great surprises. And other developments, confidently predicted, have not come to pass: Americans are not riding about in helicopters rather than automobiles (an anticipation in the 1940s), nor have families been replaced by promiscuous communes (a forecast of the 1960s).

But if we cannot know the future, we can use history to develop a framework for evaluating it, even partially anticipating it as it unfolds: we know what factors to monitor.

Recent patterns, and their relationship to older themes in world history, allow an orientation toward what is to come. There are several possible relationships from past to present to future, but no assessment or prediction can avoid a commitment to history.

THE WORLD'S FUTURE AS PROMISE OR THREAT

One tempting way to end historical surveys is to offer glowing words of hope about the achievements and bright prospects of humankind. Contemporary Western culture continues to value optimism and to believe that students especially should be inspired to think well of the society around them, not discouraged as they face their own future. Yet the message of history, including contemporary history, is decidedly ambiguous on the question of hopefulness.

World history is without question a record of impressive, even inspiring, human achievement. The 20th century has contributed at least its share to the record of progress. Advances in industry and agriculture have permitted the birth and survival of more people in our century than in all previous centuries combined. Life expectancy has risen notably in almost all societies, and not just in those with a sophisticated industrial apparatus. Scientific discoveries add greatly to our knowledge as well as to our technology, though some civilizations continue to prefer alternate ways of viewing the world. Our capacity to organize large groups of people has also improved, at least in certain respects. Most societies today can operate larger businesses or school systems or census-taking operations than ever before. The spread of education, another general development in the 20th century, also provides a basis for claiming a genuine increase in human knowledge, not just at the level of advanced research but also among ordinary peasants and workers. Many of these developments provide additional hope for the future as well.

Yet history is also, unquestionably, the record of humankind's inhumanity toward its own. The 20th century has generated particularly troubling questions about human impulses wedded to awesome technologies and wider contacts among peoples. The century has produced the bloodiest wars on record; 60 million people were killed in World War II alone. The introduction of sophisticated weaponry, combined with ongoing political tensions, has resulted in massive slaughter even aside from formal wars: the deaths of hundreds of thousands as part of revolution in Russia and China; Hitler's insane efforts to exterminate the Jews; the execution of additional hundreds of thousands stemming from racial or religious conflict in Uganda, Cambodia, and on the Indian subcontinent. The 20th century has been a violent period, taking its rank among centuries marked by nomadic invasions and surpassing these in the sheer volume of slaughter, if only because of the availability of technologies for mass killing.

There is more. The technologies that allow more people to survive in our world have also generated frightening levels of pollution and have created potential imbalances in the natural environment. The daily elimination of acres of natural vegetation, in expanding societies like those of Latin America and Africa, hinders the natural production of oxygen through photosynthesis, while in other regions industrial plants lower air and water quality—the United States and China are now world leaders in emission of pollution,

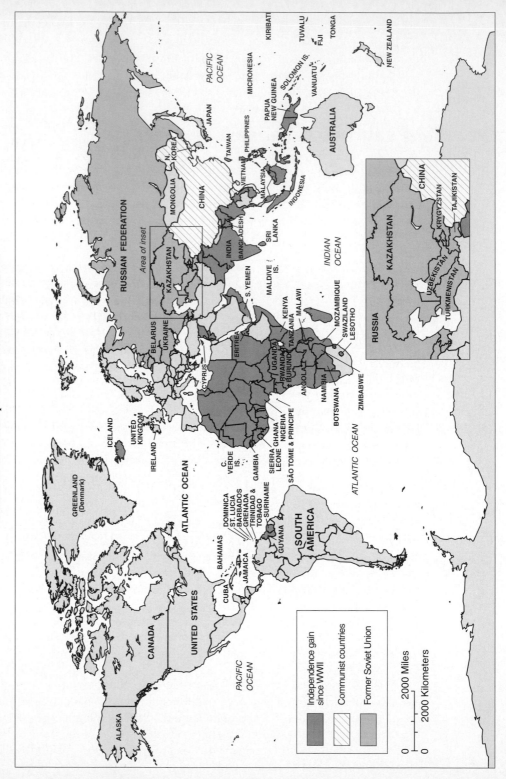

Global Relationships at the End of the 1990s

but other centers, new and old, add to the problem. Our ability to sustain growing populations, though unquestionable in recent history despite warfare, may be jeopardized in the future, or at least the amenities to which many people have become accustomed may be reduced.

The 20th century also stands open to some attack for its relative neglect of spiritual and aesthetic expressions, though here, of course, evaluation is more subjective. Crowding, war, and the sheer concentration on economic development may have tended to shunt artistic and religious creativity to the side, reducing the beauty available in many human lives. Critics who worry about the undermining of African cultural traditions and those who bemoan the mindless mass entertainments of the contemporary West may be identifying an important common problem in our own time and in our future.

The point here is not to argue that the world's prospects are glorious or that they are unrelievedly dismal, though a review of both optimistic and pessimistic cases provides useful ways of summing up historical patterns and deciding what one's own standards of evaluation are. Some of humankind's most hopeful recent endeavors have not worked out particularly well: the United Nations organization, for example, founded after World War II to provide a forum for the preservation of world peace, has not produced serious mechanisms for conflict resolution, though its facilitation of discussion is not useless. Some of humankind's direst recent fears have not come to pass either: population has not yet overwhelmed available food supply, the United States and the Soviet Union did not yield to some inevitable dynamic that forces world diplomatic rivals to resort to all-out war.

HANDLES ON THE FUTURE

ANALOGY

Besides philosophizing about the human prospect on the basis of history, several kinds of forecasts attempt to use history to make educated guesses about what is yet to come—to speculate intelligently about what is inherently unknowable. One technique involves using historical analogies. Many people who predict that new technologies like computers will revolutionize education or the economy compare the future with the known example of the industrial revolution. "The computer will do for education what the steam engine did for manufacturing," is an example of analogy. The result does not provide details about the future, and of course the whole example may be wrong; but many people use analogies routinely, always drawing on history to provide guidelines for the future.

Western thinkers in the 20th century have recurrently used analogies drawn from the fall of the Roman Empire, contending that the West is about to decline the way Rome did 1500 years ago, and for similar reasons of moral decay and inept leadership. Some analysts similarly compare prospects for the United States to the decline of Britain at the end of the 19th century: here, say the analogists, are two cases of societies that overextended themselves in military commitments, lost the internal drive that had made their economies powerful, and inevitably fell back in world power. Of course, what actually happened to Britain has not yet fully happened to the United States; even beguiling analogies may be wrong.

Some Latin Americans like to compare their civilization to that of the West at the end of the Middle Ages—still behind in world affairs but gaining new vigor and about to surge ahead. Similar analogies, we have seen, apply to contemporary Africa. Again, the analogy game can be spun out endlessly, and the results may both firm up a knowledge of history and provide at least some intelligent questions about the shape of the world in the future.

PROJECTION

The second most common form of forecasting on the basis of history involves using current trends and projecting them into the future. We "know," for example, that populations in the United States and Japan will increasingly include more aged, for the birth rate is already low and life expectancy is gaining; so average age in both countries, already unusually high by historical standards, will go up further by the year 2010, bringing new problems of pensions and medical care. This forecast assumes, of course, that present trends will not be disrupted by some new birth rate surge, or a higher death rate among adults in late middle age, or new immigration patterns that alter the demographic structure. Trend projections are always vulnerable to new, unforeseen factors.

The beginnings of the new warfare: U.S. atomic testing; Nevada, 1952.

By the late 1990s, trend projections are also beclouded by the sheer novelty of developments in many parts of the world. Questions, rather than projections, seem to be the order of the day. What kind of durable political and diplomatic structures will emerge in central Asia or Eastern Europe, now that the Soviet Union has collapsed? Will China manage to continue its combination of economic liberalization and authoritarian politics? Will Western Europe make good on its halting march toward greater unity? Events since the late 1980s have been unusually significant, producing all sorts of interesting news but a very murky future.

Nevertheless, even amid more than usual pattern changes, several trends have developed in the 20th century, or in recent decades, that pose more precise questions about the future than simply "What do you think will happen next?" One trend is demographic. Although huge population gains continued in the 1990s, the world growth rate is slowing down. China and many parts of Latin America, though in quite different ways, have converted to lower birth rates; other parts of the world followed more gradually. Will this trend continue? Will it stabilize population in time to prevent catastrophic pressures on resources and the environment? Will most of the world, in the 21st century, become similar in demographic structure to the model established earlier by the West, Russia, and Japan?

Political trends provided another set of coherent questions. Except for China and the Middle East, democratic forms were spreading widely by the 1990s. One of the key 20th-century themes—what political forms will work best, given the decline of traditional arrangements like monarchy?—seemed to be receiving a clear answer. Other 20th-century options, such as communism and authoritarianism, persist, but with decreasing vitality in most regions. Will the democratic surge continue? What caused it, and were the causes solid? Can fledgling democracies in Eastern Europe and Latin America survive almost certain problems of economic adjustment and growth? The democratic current resulted in part from a belief that political change would generate economic vitality. Was this assumption correct? And if democracy fails, what would replace it?

Two kinds of questions are used to explore world economic trends. The first, standard since World War II, involves the ongoing gaps between industrialized and "underdeveloped" areas. Can new areas make the turn to full industrialization, as South Korea and Taiwan seem to have done since the 1960s, and begin to catch up with the industrial giants? Or will a have–have not division continue to bedevil world politics and the living standards of the majority of people around the globe? Actual 20th-century history reminds us that the two-fold division around industrialization has become vastly oversimple, which is where a second set of questions comes into play. A number of societies have expanded their modern manufacturing sector without undergoing a full industrial revolution process. Mexico, Turkey, Brazil, China, and, to an extent, India have all established significant economic dynamism, along with countries like Malaysia and Indonesia on the fringe of the Pacific Rim. A few African countries may be joining in. Where will this evolution lead? How will the advanced industrial economies adjust to ongoing competition in goods in metallurgy and textiles produced successfully outside their borders? Significant economic malaise in the industrial regions in the 1990s, including Japan, involves considerable unemployment among lesser-skilled workers; countries like Mexico and Indonesia, with higher growth rates, seem to preempt certain manufacturing sectors. How will the world economy, and the several kinds of participants in it, continue to develop, and how will its growing complexity be managed?

Cultural issues also loom large. Many regions worry about their cultural identity in an age of growing international contact and standardized mass offerings in sports, television, and films. Most attempts at cultural isolation had failed by the 1990s. A growing division emerged between groups and societies whose cultural definitions remain strongly religious, and those that have moved to a more secular orientation. New militance and intolerance among some religious groups within regions like the Middle East and India, directed both against foreign influences and against secular elements in their own societies, highlight this division. Where will the future balance lie?

A variety of social issues also cut across civilization boundaries. Most societies face new questions about the roles of women. Feminism influences international bodies like the United Nations, and the power of Western public opinion in this area is considerable. But feminism is not a uniform international force. Some regions resist it in the name of tradition; furthermore, in India, the Middle East, and Africa, some women's voices seek a different kind of feminism, less influenced by the individualism of the West. Concrete questions vary: Western women focus strongly on their new economic roles, but in some parts of the world women worry more about the erosion of their traditional production functions because of new commercial forms. Are there some common issues and probable trends for women worldwide, or do regional differences in traditions and current economic and political status predominate? Trend projection—including current patterns of declining birth rates—suggests flux in gender relations, but it does not necessarily suggest clear trajectories for an international future.

Disruptive Forecasts

Predicting future trends, or at least asking questions about them, on the basis of major recent developments risks neglect of major changes in direction. By definition, forces that might introduce vital new themes cannot be easily anticipated; yet these can readily change the shape of the relationship between future and past. The ending of the cold war left a considerable vacuum in the world's diplomatic framework. Many observers predict that regional tensions will increasingly define the horizons of international relations. Certainly, potential trouble spots are numerous. The Middle East is an obvious ongoing candidate; so potentially is divided Korea, the divided Indian subcontinent, divided central Asia, and the disputed states of east-central Europe—and all contain nations capable of nuclear development. But will some larger diplomatic alignment, currently unforeseen, supersede these troubled regional contests, as the cold war once had done?

Forecasters frequently project other dramatic factors that might change the face of world history to come. In the 1960s, "population bomb" predictions argued that the current rate of global population growth promised increasing misery, environmental strain, and have–have not warfare. This gloom was less fashionable by the 1990s, as population growth had not led to a global worsening of living standards. But predictions of environmental catastrophe, as a result of growing industrialization, wastefulness, and population growth, sent a somewhat similar message. Many of the current issues in world history might be replaced by radical deterioration of the environment.

Or, said some of the pundits of a postindustrial age, new technologies, headed by the computer, might create unprecedented vistas for information exchange and economic growth. Societies might be able to bypass the industrial revolution and head directly into postindustrial, computer-driven production. Cities will change from being manufacturing centers to service as meeting places and concentrations of entertainment. Social structures will be based not on property but on educational levels and control of information.

Forecasts for a radical break about to occur—and they are quite varied—assume the importance of a single major factor: diplomacy, population, or war. They argue that other facets of world history will come to reflect this basic determinant. Other world historians argue not only that many dramatic forecasts have not come to pass, but also that world history has more commonly been shaped by a mixture of factors rather than a sole dominant cause. But by definition predictions of a major change in direction cannot be disproved—or proved. They can only be discussed on the basis of prior analogies and an understanding of other significant trends.

REVISITING A NEW WORLD HISTORY PERIOD

Forecasts that modern people encounter reflect both major types. Pundits bombard with projections of current trends—about aging, for example, or about the movement toward democracy. Others grab attention with the dramatic argument about some major new factor that will move society away from its recent past—toward a technology-dominated postindustrial future, for example. What the actual mixture will be, in moving the world from past to future, cannot be determined until we get there.

One forecasting complexity seems obvious when the past century is interpreted in world history terms. Insofar as a major new period has opened, we can assume that many past patterns will progressively weaken, but because the period is still emerging we cannot possibly say what patterns will durably take their place. Political structure offers an obvious example: it would be startling if monarchy revived, for it has been declining worldwide for at least a hundred years. But confidence that democracy will become the international norm is harder to come by. Assessing the 20th century as a new world history period fairly readily demonstrates that the relative power of the West has diminished (though some Westerners dispute even this). But will a new world-dominant civilization come into view (as the West did, after a period of transition following Arab decline), or will world power be more evenly distributed (as it was in the classical period)? Growing international contacts suggest an increasingly common international culture, but the growing strength of key regions may support reassertions of more particular identities: is increasing homogeneity or diversity, and possibly friction, the most likely future path? It is just as hard to define the full dimensions of the emerging new world history period as it would have been in the 15th century, beyond considerable assurance that most trends of the previous period—in our case, the 19th century—have either declined in importance or, as in the case of Western power, shifted direction.

THE ROLE OF CIVILIZATIONS

A final prediction question requires comment in the perspective of world history: will civilizations continue to be as important as they have been during the past 3000 years? Will major international contacts and trends continue to be mediated by the distinctive traditions and institutions of the world's key regions? Or will one of the features of the new world history period see the gradual decline of this staple framework, thanks to accelerating global contacts?

Not surprisingly, there are voices on both sides. Regions continue to differ greatly. While all areas have participated in expanding education in the 20th century, literacy rates in the 1990s range from 30 to 40 percent of the adult population, in Africa and India, to 80 percent in Latin America, to 95 percent in Western Europe, Japan, and Russia. Annual population growth is well under 1 percent in the West and Russia, almost 3 percent in sub-Saharan Africa. There are 700 television sets per 1000 people in North America, 50 in Asia. Some of these distinctions may decline with more general economic development, but they add up to very different lives at the opening of the 21st century.

Different cultures matter too. One forecaster in 1993 argued that, given the end of the cold war, the next set of conflicts in the world will follow civilizational lines, as zones of Muslim, Confucian, and Western tradition compete on the basis of their widely different inherited values. Eastern Europe, following this pattern, also remains distinct because of different beliefs, experiences, and industrial levels, and the roles of Africa and Latin America are not spelled out. The forecast is uncertain, partly because several key regions are not clearly aligned, but it called attention to the continued relevance of often longstanding cultural boundaries. Persistent tensions between people of Christian background and the new Muslim minorities in Europe or the pressures of Islamic fundamentalism, and the obvious reluctance of the Common Market to admit Muslim Turkey despite the latter's urgent application, bring home the force of traditional identities. So do recurrent disputes about individual rights and social authority between Western commentators and their counterparts in China and Singapore.

Yet the world is drawing closer together. This trite generalization draws meaning from the increasing cultural as well as commercial contacts around the globe, and from the operations of giant multinational corporations that spread specialized manufacturing and distribution activities literally worldwide. By the 1990s, many international groupings exist that defy civilization boundaries. Scientists and social scientists accept many assumptions that allow them to do common work whether they are in China or Chile, Boston or Bombay. International sports figures make the same easy transition from one competition to another regardless of locale. Businessmen share key values across national lines, particularly with the increased popularity of capitalism in the final decades of the century. One of the leading questions for the future, in fact, involves the still unpredictable balance between homogenizing and differentiating characteristics.

World history has long consisted of new contacts and parallels, juxtaposed with the ongoing divisions among cultural and institutional traditions. The eve of the 21st century in one sense merely repeated this old tension. Yet the force of contacts has attained new levels during the 20th century, based on new communications and exchange. Many of the

Change and Diversity in the Contemporary World

1975–1980 Annual rates of population growth

World	1.7%
Africa (entire)	2.9%
North America (includes Mexico)	1.0%
Latin America	2.5%
East Asia	1.4%
Southeast Asia	2.1%
Indian subcontinent	2.2%
Western Europe	0.3%
USSR	0.9%

TV sets per 1000 people

	1975	1982
World	98	121
Africa	6	17
North America	564	618
South America	84	111
Asia	25	38
Europe	232	309
USSR	Data not available	

Commercial energy consumption per capita, 1982 (equivalent kilograms of coal)

World	1900
Africa	300
North America	6700
South America	900
Asia	400
Europe	4200
USSR	6000

Percent of GNP (gross national product) devoted to research and development, 1980

Africa	0.4
North America	2.1
South America	0.5
Asia	1.2
Europe	1.8
USSR	4.7

Percent literacy over 15 years of age, early 1970s

Africa	30
United States	99
Latin America	79
India	34
USSR	100
Middle East	50

Source: United Nations statistics.

leading issues in predicting the future—how much democracy, how much industrialization—really ask whether the world is likely to follow some roughly common political and economic patterns. No sensible observer claims that homogeneity is right around the corner. The example of Japan's success reminds any Westerner of how different a fully industrial society can be from the Western model of modernization. Yet the sharp edges of individual civilizations might blur further, making world history in the future more a matter of shared developments and less a catalogue of separate dynamics than had been true for the 5000 years since distinct civilizations began to be defined.

Yet even on the edge of a new millennium, the hand of tradition does not rest lightly on the contemporary world. The key task of the historian is to convey how this force plays against the pressure to change. Revolutions never prove to be fully revolutionary, as they build within certain traditions while attacking others. Even the undermining of agricultural society—a fundamental drama of 20th-century world history—does not destroy all traces of the past. Traditions, themselves evolving, give identity to key civilizations and shape responses to international markets and technological exchange, world diplomacy, and international fads and styles. Changes within specific civilizations alter traditions and, often, add new ingredients to worldwide patterns—as witness Japan's industrial surge. The revival of religion at the end of the 20th century demonstrates a need for traditional beliefs and particular identities—in part because homogenizing forces generate their own resistance. We can assume that the interplay between tradition and change will continue, but our uncertainty about the future lies in the inability to know precisely what balance will result.

So we cannot assume the directions of world history's further unfolding, but, informed by knowledge of trends and examples from the past, we must instead examine them as they occur. Here is a source of understanding and also of pleasure, for world history has never lacked for drama, or analytical challenge, or even humor. The human species, along with its capacities to destroy, to create, and to master, also has the precious power of contemplation, and the traditions of many cultures would argue that this remains one of the surest sources of satisfaction. We can count on the emerging future to challenge our understanding, even as we learn to use our grasp of the past as a partial guide.

SUGGESTED READINGS

Several serious books (as well as many more dubious popularized efforts) attempt to sketch the world's or the West's future. On the postindustrial society concept, see Daniel Bell, *The Coming of Post-Industrial Society* (1974). For other projections, consult R. L. Heilbroner, *An Inquiry into the Human Prospect* (1974), and L. Stavrianos, *The Promise of the Coming Dark Age* (1976). See also Ronald Inglehart, *Modernization and Post-modernization: Cultural, Economic, and Political Change in 43 Societies* (1997), and Harold Perkin, *The Third Revolution: Professional Elites in the Modern World* (1996). On environment and resource issues, D. H. Meadows and D. L. Meadows, *The Limits of Growth* (1974), and L. Herbert, *Our Synthetic Environment* (1962), are worthwhile. M. ul Haq, *The Poverty Curtain: Choices for the Third World* (1976), and L. Solomon, *Multinational Corporations and the Emerging World Order* (1978), cover economic issues, in part from a non-Western perspective. On military and diplomatic issues, A. Sakharov, *Progress, Coexistence and Intellectual Freedom*, rev. ed. (1970), is an important statement by a Russian dissident; other useful texts include S. Hoffmann, *Primacy or World Order: American Foreign Policy Since the Cold War* (1978), and W. Epstein, *The Last Chance: Nuclear Proliferation and Arms Control* (1976). On women, see P. Hudson, *Third World Women Speak Out* (1979). A major interpretation of the 20th century is T. von Laue, *The World Revolution of Westernization* (1989). For a recent forecast based on the cold war's demise, see F. Fukizawa, *The End of History* (1991).

Index

Note: Italicized letters *i*, *m*, and *t* following page numbers indicate illustrations, maps, and tables, respectively.

Credits